Impression de Voyage

The sea was sapphire coloured, and the sky
Burned like a heated opal through the air;
We hoisted sail; the wind was blowing fair
For the blue lands that to the eastward lie.
From the steep prow I marked with quickening eye
Zakynthos, every olive grove and creek,
Ithaka's cliff, Lycaon's snowy peak,
And all the flower-strewn hills of Arcady.
The flapping of the sail against the mast,
The ripple of the water on the side,
The ripple of girls' laughter at the stern
The only sounds: - when 'gan the West to burn,
And a red sun upon the seas to ride.
I stood upon the soil of Greece at last!

Oscar Wilde

IT'S ALL GREECE TO ME

Impressions Of Contemporary Greek Life

John F.L. Ross

ISBN 960–86395–0–6

Cover photos: © Athens News, Eurokinisi

Printed and bound in Athens, Greece by Lambrakis Press S.A.
Pre-press by Multimedia S.A.

CONTENTS

AUTHOR'S PREFACE

This volume brings together a collection of brief essays written during 1997-98, their common if rather loose theme being aspects of contemporary Greece. They were written originally for my *Athens News* column 'On Second Thought', and appear here with relatively minor changes, corrections, and consolidations. But selection (along with its flip-side, elimination) is a difficult process, and those included here tend to be less time-specific and to give variety to their subject, not just to meet some subjective notion (mine or anybody else's) of 'best' or 'favourite' pieces. Generally I have given more space to the broadly social, rather than narrowly political, aspects of Greek life.

Though I started writing this column partly as a diversion from the routine of university lecturing and academic writing, it quickly took on a life of its own. As a foreigner in Greece, I began it as an odyssey of exploration: to deepen my own, and secondarily readers', understanding of modern Greek society in all its remarkable variety and complexity. A second factor, as much hope as aim, was the possibility of stimulating some wider discussion in a society where the public debate is not always characterised by nuance or restraint.

Lingering in Athens's numerous bookshops (for many Greeks are voracious readers), I have often been struck by how comparatively little has been written - in any language - about the nature of contemporary Greek society. Browse any selection of literature on Greece and you will be overwhelmed with scholarship on Byzantium, tomes on the ancient legacy, poetry, contemporary fiction, and of course reams of tourist guides. Yet few, it seems, have attempted to dissect modern Greece itself: how it draws on (or diverges from) its own myths and history, how the society functions, what makes it, and its resourceful people, tick. Having tackled this task on a weekly basis, I now know why: because it is such a complex undertaking, fraught with possibilities for misunderstandings to occur, especially whenever a non-native makes the effort. Yet there is so much to tell, so much that is implicit that needs to be made explicit. 'Wintertime' Greece is also an utterly different place from the dreamy, sun-drenched tourist mecca familiar to most visitors, and has changed profoundly in recent years. Ironically, a much-visited country remains a little-understood one.

All along, I have had three guiding aims in writing these pieces: to inform, to enlighten, and to entertain, with the intention of providing a critique - as opposed to a criticism - of aspects of Greek society. Sometimes this effort has involved walking a fine line: to be fair without being equivocal, general without stereotyping, analytical without being pedantic, and occasionally lighthearted without being flippant. Surely Greece, and those trying to understand the country and its people, are ultimately far better served by an earnest attempt to provide a realistic portrayal (perhaps the literary equivalent of 'tough love' in family psychology) rather than through blind praise or gratuitous flattery designed to massage egos but lacking any deeper purpose. To the extent that reader responses tell anything, I am cautiously confident that this approach has struck a wider chord. Thus I would hope that not only resident foreigners and temporary visitors, but also the growing legions of Greek expatriates returning from abroad, and not least, native Greeks themselves can find elements of interest here.

Any book of collected vignettes - what someone once uncharitably described as a 'writer's yard sale' - is perhaps best read in the spirit in which it was written, that is as short, more or less self-standing individual pieces. The result is a mosaic, rather than a seamless cloth. Readers might better enjoy dipping here and there as opposed to reading cover-to-cover, and thus not be limited by the order of appearance. For those new to Greece, however, I have tended to group more 'generalist' pieces in the first section.

Thus qualified, I hope that readers can come away with a better understanding and appreciation of this complicated, ever-changing, sometimes infuriating, and endlessly fascinating country that is modern Greece. And I hope that you derive half the pleasure from reading these pieces that I had in writing them.

JFLR
Athens, January 1999

ACKNOWLEDGEMENTS

My first expression of gratitude goes to Romolo Gandolfo, the *Athens News* editor, who provided the forum for expressing these views, thoughts and musings on a regular basis. His belief in what I was trying to do was unflagging, and he helped secure this publication despite a horrendously busy schedule. More broadly, the newspaper's staff is a hard-working, spirited and supportive bunch that has made my too-infrequent visits to their premises such a pleasure; my thanks to them are general. I should also like to thank certain individuals who have offered encouragement and feedback. Nikos Konstandaras provided welcome support early on, and Philip Pangalos later on; the effervescent Derek Gatopoulos, the steady Dinos Mitsis, the cultured Manolis Polentas, the courteous Allan Wilson, and the multitalented George Gilson were friendly constants; Angelika Timms was as full of ideas as she was generous with sharing them; and Brian Church helped push this project along in typically energetic fashion. My wife has combined the roles of supporter, ideas-generator, and occasionally stern critic. Constanza Miliou and Vassia Theriou were very helpful with the layout and typesetting. Finally, I am grateful to all those readers, some known to me but many unknown, whose responses - quiet or vocal, written or oral, direct or indirect - have all been deeply appreciated. The many suggestions I have received for compiling such a selection have been largely responsible for the product now in your hands.

CHAPTER ONE

The Modern Greek Cosmos

Greece: Impressions

Claude Monet's sublime masterpiece, *Impression: Sunrise,* gave birth to an eponymous school of art aimed at capturing fleeting visual sensation, which quickly flowered and transmuted with the mad, post-Impressionist genius of Van Gogh before fracturing into Expressionism, Abstractionism, Cubism and other early 20th century art forms. Look closely and you will see that the painting's brilliance stems not only from the pure beauty of that red orb playing on the water, but also from the sun's profound contrast with its decidedly unbeautiful industrial surroundings.

What could the master's brush have done with Greece! This country of ten million people aching for self-expression is, equally, one that offers up its own impression of contrasts, and contrasting impressions. The brilliance of cubist whitewashed villages set against stark brown Aegean landscapes; ancient pillars soaring skyward amongst the rubble; the play of light and shadow; a capital such as Athens in a region of . unparalleled beauty. Any weekend outing provides a precious few days to renew acquaintance with these contrasts, to escape from workaday routine into a countryside of fresh breezes and wildflowers, providing a chance not only to change gears but to shift into an entirely new frame of mind and spirit.

The numerous, life-affirming Greek contrasts are, however, equally capable of creating a sense of disharmony, in distinct opposition to the dictum of another artist, Finnish architect Alvar Aalto, whose philosophy, 'form follows substance', emphasised the need for every structure to achieve a balance and harmony with its surroundings. In Greece, the Monet-like contrasts frequently outdistance the Aalto-like balances, in two different directions.

On one hand, we find the majesty of the Classical legacy and its evident contrast with its urban surroundings. The flowering of ancient Athens and the enduring power of the Periclean building boom had much to do with the powerful physical impression it made, indeed still makes, on the onlooker. The temples of the Acropolis remain so stunning partly because they are uniquely unlike anything else around them; timeless, unearthly beauty surrounded by a sea of grey concrete. More recently, the 19th century neoclassical tradition of Schiller and others again stands out because its soaring façades contrasted so sharply with the city around. Yet unfortunately, this grand legacy crumbles around the edges; the sheer cost of maintaining such intricate work is too great for many building owners or even for the state itself. Such deterioration is more marked in other cities with neoclassical traditions like Bucharest, but it saddens to see such painstakingly detailed construction fall into disarray.

The contrast is equally vivid when comparing exterior with interior. Athens University's grand, imposing buildings, especially its law faculty, disguise insides showing years of wear and tear and insufficient upkeep, producing a rather depressing counterpoint. This goes double for the National Library on Panepistimiou St., whose beautiful winding staircase I long admired before it beckoned me inside once, a misadventure that may not be repeated. Given the library's importance as a repository of Greece's national archives and its symbolism as a fount of learning in the birthplace of modern political thought, the poor organisation came as a distinct letdown.

Exit Athens into the world of the village and the countryside, and we often find the opposite phenomenon; exquisite beauty within humble surroundings. So often the simplest abodes hide the most richly appointed decorative touches. The island of Skyros comes to mind, but it is not alone in its carefully tended house-interiors. The wealth of the poor was long found in works produced by hand; the painstaking handiwork, needlepoint, and crafts that took years to complete and formed traditional dowries for young women - now, sadly if inevitably, passing into the hands of antique dealers making a comfortable living selling such priceless works to middle class suburbanites seeking to recapture some of the lost flavour of a bygone era.

Impressions are by definition diverse and fragmented, and these, no doubt imperfectly expressed, are but a few by one set of eyes. If sheer variety and contrast are the spices of life, then Greece is life itself.

The Churchill Connection

Its title notwithstanding, this piece has little to do with foreign affairs, international diplomacy, or 20th century British politics. All are subjects of considerable interest to yours truly, but not necessarily today. The case of Sir Winston arises in a completely separate connection: one involving matters of presentation, decorum, and the old distinction between style and substance. Once, when asked to describe the Prime Minister, a Churchill family friend gave an answer along the lines of "When you first meet Winston, you immediately see all his faults. Then you spend the rest of your life finding out all the good things about him".

Extrapolating very slightly from one individual (foreign, long deceased) to an entire nation (domestic, still very much alive), it would seem that herein lies a pretty apt description of Greece itself, and its inhabitants. Many Greeks certainly have their own individual style, but Style is a rarer commodity, and particularly that element of Style that provides a sense of pleasing proportion, something with a certain harmony between outer appearance and inner reality, involving subtle gradations and nuances.

Put another way, Greece is not a delicate sort of place. There is something elemental and essential about it, chock-full of life, with an energy and a vitality that is unshielded, unfiltered and unadulterated. No one here, native or visitor, can be unaware of the sheer, almost urgent physical force with which Greek reality intrudes. Seasonal changes are abrupt; the summer heat is intense; the reflected sunlight from whitewashed walls blinding; the traffic stifling; the political opinions unyielding; the music loud; the raki and ouzo harsh; the desserts extra sweet; the feta cheese...well, just don't leave it unrefrigerated for long.

Pursuing the theme of Greek impressions, the crucial first impact Greece makes on the visitor or the returnee from abroad is immediately vivid. Flying in from the north, one is struck by the stark-ness of the landscape, the sharp divisions between very dry land and very wet water, the abrupt mountain ranges, the little villages clinging precariously to hillsides, reached painstakingly by serpentine dirt roads. Then you are over the vast Attic basin, remote hinterland suddenly replaced by endless urban agglomeration. Stepping off the plane, the intense light and heat off the tarmac comes as a hammer-blow, rendering coat and cardigan, earlier a part of basic attire, not only useless but a ridiculous burden. Sweat glands go into overdrive. Then the lurching bus ride delivers you to the airport terminal, with the chaos of baggage claim, the gruff manners and dour faces, the jostling in the taxi-ranks, and the screeching ride into town along the unbeautiful and functionally challenged Vouliagmenis Avenue, all present an unholy procession of sensory assault on the unwary.

It is almost as though Greece has reserved its worst side for the very beginning (whether for the purposes of instant, forced acclimatisation or simply out of benign neglect I have never been able to figure), after which you are at leisure to be enchanted and bewitched by all the positive things for the rest of your stay. How utterly different from the principle applied in the old Eastern bloc, where visitors were presented with spotless airports and gleaming, dirt-cheap metro systems designed in part to hide woeful societal inadequacies elsewhere. But the message here - delivered with a characteristic combination of honesty and bluntness - seems to be: Pay no attention to the presentation; this is what we are.

With Greece or with the Greek, file away the rougher exterior edges that sometimes appear - the touristic tackiness, the occasional blustering and tough-guy posturing - and you will find a richly substantive and sensitive essence, a hard piece of Pendelic marble revealed like a statue by Praxiteles. But it remains a difficult truth, in this high-speed world where appearance and image are increasingly important, that patient, careful presentation is not a dispensable luxury but an increasingly irreducible necessity: whether appealing for international support on national issues, competing for a larger share of the tourist market, or merely interacting on a personal level.

The Foreign, The Foreigner, and Greece

Greece, a country with no shortage of national identity and nationalist impulses, has had a long and complicated relationship with what, and whom, lies outside its frequently unsettled borders. The very notion of 'foreign' is a complex one, reflecting contradictions so abundant in Greek society. The term o ξένος, according to the Oxford dictionary by D.N. Stavropoulos, refers simultaneously to 'stranger... foreigner, alien', yet also to 'guest, visitor', the former's vaguely sinister implications counteracted by the latter's positive and open tone. There is also a linkage of sorts involved, beyond the fact of foreign origins from non-Greek parentage. Similarly, o κόσμος simultaneously refers to 'people...society' and 'the world', that is to the sociological as well as the physical. Both terms thus sub-divide even while uniting disparate concepts.

Considering the rather offhand treatment Greece historically has received (and according to many, still receives) from foreign powers, it is hardly surprising that there is a great ambivalence in the Greek relationship with the outer world: at once embraced, respected, feared, awed, and envied. Language again provides a faithful mirror: the land that gave birth to *filoxenia* (hospitality, transliterated 'friend to the foreigner') also brought forth *xenophobia* and labelled outsiders barbarians. Even the net movement of people has reversed course in modern times; from a country of emigration, creating one of the world's most productive diasporas, Greece is now a net importer of humanity, not least as a result of the ongoing travails of neighbouring Albania.

These crosscutting impulses are equally evident to the foreign resident here, enjoying privileges while facing challenges. Passage into Greek society involves several stages à la Elizabeth Kübler-Ross (no relation), Sociologist and author of *On Death and Dying*, though the effort to cope with life here - a decidedly more positive undertaking than her five stages of accepting death - simplifies it to three: initial delight followed by the inevitable disillusion and, if one hangs around long enough, a kind of fatalistic yet animated acceptance of life's obstacles, with the occasional fit of undirected rage thrown in for good measure.

All outsiders, from whatever origin, face similar expectations of representing their home culture. Apart from the diplomatic community, few represent governments directly; yet all who come here act, consciously or not, as a sort of roving ambassador for their native societies, helping their Greek hosts paint their mosaic of foreign impressions partly by what they see in us. The traditional, and so highly valued, western distinctions between individual and society become blurred when one steps beyond the border. With freedom comes responsibility, or something similar.

The task of fitting in may be somewhat easier for Americans abroad, ironically due to our long and rich national tradition of philistinism and amiable ignorance of the outside world. An ability to utter complexities like *yia sou*, and to distinguish Parthenon from Pantheon (that's in Rome), goes far here. Pity the poor European, faced with living up to expectations of solemnity, linguistic fluency and intimate knowledge of the latest archaeological discoveries in Mycenae; the pressure must be unbearable. Both, however, enjoy a remarkably open reception, to the great credit of Greeks themselves, who love nothing more than love of their country, yet remain acutely sensitive to uppity outsiders pointing out the same societal shortcomings they themselves parody nightly on television. This is a trait they share with most other countries, surely, although while here it does seem striking.

The relationship between foreign resident and Greek host is complicated, however, by expectations that the mutual relationship is temporary. While the non-Greek who assimilates is truly admirable, the foreigner here is generally thought, to borrow a phrase made infamous by British journalist Sir Robin Day, 'here today, gone tomorrow' - just as the Greek abroad awaits the Grand Return Home. If the prevailing Greek attitude - welcoming the outsider into his home, yet wary of his ultimate intentions - seems occasionally contradictory, it is no more so than that of the foreigner, semi-literate in Greece's culture, comfortably ensconced in a foreign ghetto and serenely indulgent of local mores and customs. As no one has a monopoly on self-deception, the responsibility lies with both sides to make the experiment, however fleeting, work.

Greece's Simple Complexities

Are Greeks - as if they were all cloned - a simple or a complex people? The question is a simple one - unless, perhaps, it is complicated? Even this secondary question poses a riddle.

Inevitably, the answer is: they are both. Contemplation of Greek reality is a source of endless amazement, and occasional amusement, in terms of how the simplest things, like paying bills, can get so complicated, where seemingly routine matters become half-day adventures, indeed where the constantly unexpected makes it difficult to keep any sense of routine at all. The Greek genius at introducing complications enables the likes of Austin Kark to write entertaining books (his being *Attic in Greece*, on buying a house here) based on singular transactions run amok.

Yet Greece is, equally, a place where the complications of life - the meshing of emotions and the intellect, the multiple challenges and the constant balancing act they require - can be marvellously simplified and clarified in a bit of cryptic, Delphic erudition. 'Know thyself'; 'all things in moderation'; if only we could follow them. True gems of insight can come from the most unlikely sources; people with only a rudimentary education can quote ancient proverbs at will. The very rocks seem to breathe timeless wisdom.

But then, Greek reality - reality itself - is not always what it seems. There is the blunt, literal side of the Greek character, which somehow coexists with the mysticism of Orthodoxy, the evil eye and the unexplained occurrence. Even the multitude of deities on Olympus seemed to reflect the complications of life for the ancients - a god for every mood, whim, and need. Reality, modern Greek style, is also complicated by the lack of any one prevailing perspective here. Each person has his own viewpoint and world-view; after all it is, gloriously, a land of proud, if occasionally strong-headed, individuals, which complicates things a bit when more than two people get together to decide anything. Perhaps you have heard the old saying "un grec, l'excellence; deux grecs, la combine; trois grecs, la révolution"!

Many come to Greece to experience life in undiluted form, devoid of pretense, the foggy north European skies stripped clean by the dazzling Greek light. As an Aussie might say, coming here helps one 'cut through the bullshit' and experience life (metaphorically if not literally) in the raw. During a recent two-day escape from Athens, the elegant simplicities of rural life struck me with special force. Intensely vivid, momentary images linger: mountain silhouetted against setting sun, a fisherman rowing his humble boat across the waves, an artisan harmoniously at work in his little shop. Coming to Greece is, for some, like a return to the basics, before civilisation got in the way.

Yet there are those who misread a Durrell or a Miller, and mistake a humble station for a simple mind. Simplicity is, after all, neither light-hearted nor shallow; in a way, it is depth itself. To think of Greece, and Greeks, merely in terms of elements and bluntness is to do a grave disservice to the country. Greece is not a land of peasants baking bread. It is not merely a living museum, nor is its present reducible to 'sun, sand,...' well, you know the rest. The noble savage died with Byron. Greece is no longer even cheap to visit. To risk stating the obvious, it is a modern, thriving, European country, whose glorious past is, partly, a burden on the present.

I might further suggest that it is an even more complex place than most - whose mystery merely deepens the more we look, like investigating the Byzantine era which arguably has influenced modern Greek attitudes, lifestyles and practices much more profoundly than has its more celebrated Classical legacy. And this is to say nothing of Greece's political relations internationally, and its labyrinthine national and even local politics.

Exposure to Greece enables the mind to focus and then to open up to new possibilities previously undreamt of. But the opposite is equally true - its apparent simplicity masks an often ferocious, richly layered complexity. As usual, Oscar Wilde put it best when he said "life is rarely pure, and never simple". And Wilde was not even Greek.

The Politics of 'Centredness'

If any single notion can define Greek self-views and world-view alike, it is the conviction that Greece's national circumstances are truly different. History and myth have lent an ample hand in sustaining such beliefs. To the ancient Greeks, Delphi represented not only an oracle and holy site but the navel of the earth; the place from which all things sprang. Go there today, of course, and you will be forgiven for thinking that the river of life has reversed course, and that all the world gravitates to Delphi, in air-conditioned coaches.

Ancient Cycladic (= circular) culture revolved, almost literally, around the Aegean and centred on ancient Delos, with its holy sites and treasury. Then there is the mythological birth of Athens, and the contest between Poseidon, who summoned a stream of water from the parched earth, and Athena, who did him one better by producing an olive tree. Again, notions of birth, Greece, and civilisation become interwoven; and the historical thread linking the Minoan, Classical, and Byzantine eras sustained for millennia a belief in the uniquely powerful elements of Greek culture.

Such themes, while enriching the classical literature and sustaining notions of geographical determinism, are kept alive faithfully, but perhaps too literally, in today's Greece. Despite - perhaps even because of - history's twists, many Greeks are convinced their country is totally unlike any other, or as in Orwell's *Animal Farm*, 'more equal than others'. Belief in a country's traditions, values and norms is the very essence of nationalism and forms a basis for interacting with the outer world. Nationalism, of course, can be a negative force, as Yugoslavia's breakup painfully showed. Greece's sense of nation is less blatant, yet more wide-ranging.

Greece's media, for example, delight in the accomplishments of individual Greeks abroad (and those of foreign nationals with Greek blood, which is not quite the same thing), thereby subconsciously sustaining beliefs that Greeks are an exceptional people. Even Greek graduate students abroad, who almost invariably bend their dissertations to Greek themes, contribute to these perceptions.

Yet in the realm of international relations, the premise here is that

Greece's problems are sometimes different, rather than always unique. While far from easy, Greece's situation nonetheless finds rough parallels elsewhere in Europe. It is small and relatively poor, but so are Ireland and Portugal. It suffers bureaucratic inefficiency, but so does Italy. Greece's democracy has suffered instability, but Spain and Portugal faced more entrenched postwar dictatorships. Greece certainly has the Cyprus problem to worry about, but Cyprus is an independent country, tragically divided, not a Greek province. Greece is geographically scattered, but so is Denmark. Greece faces a large and sometimes menacing neighbour, but so does Finland. Greeks are culturally distinct, but so are Swedes and Scots. Greece cares about indigenous Greeks in Albania and Cyprus, but so does Hungary for ethnic Hungarians in Romania, and Russia for Russians throughout the former Soviet Union. True, Greece faces all these together; but it is the highest per capita recipient of EU funds in compensation.

Excessive dwelling on Greece's own special concerns, verging sometimes on political navel-gazing, has been more successful as a past negotiating tactic than a long-term strategy for promoting Greek national interests, however defined. Having long claimed that its individual circumstances required tailored solutions, it is going to take a sustained, concerted effort at national self-examination to come to terms with the fact that the world is moving on, and that a policy built around demands for special treatment are losing - or have lost - their moral force.

Thus the urgent need for a genuine societal dialogue on Europe, concerning not only what Greece can gain from its evolution, but about the overall nature of the European enterprise itself. Such a rational debate could help transcend the split thinking about Greece as Europe's ancient birthplace but its modern appendage. The country can ill-afford to sustain the impression that long obtained: that it cares about Europe only insofar as it reaps material rewards from it.

A genuine realisation that Greece's position is not fundamentally different should be cause for hope, not despair, as it lessens the burden of convincing the world of the uniqueness of Greek circumstances - a tall order even in the best of times. The more Greece's interests are, and are seen to be, in line with international principles, the more genuinely secure the country will be.

Greece's Modernisation,
With Lots of Holes

Visitors to Greece - and this goes triple for residents here - might be surprised by then Culture Minister Venizelos's comment to the *International Herald Tribune*, that industrialisation may have passed Greece by, but that its ever-active citizens are ideal candidates for 'post-industrial' life. How, you might well ask, can a society hope, much less claim, to be postmodern without first being fully modern?

Greece's headlong thrust into the future - fast-forwarding, you could say, through the 20th century for the 21st - has become almost holy writ, something to be accepted without question. Outsiders have provided both the target dates (the 2004 Olympics) and the means to do so (the EU with its development aid), and now, led by a relentlessly modern-minded government, most here have picked up the gauntlet with the zeal of the newly converted. But the process inevitably produces uneven and unintended side-effects, like some miracle drug that becomes harmful in large doses. Rarely has Mother Nature herself provided a more fitting example of what happens when things are pushed too far, too fast than the holes recently and mysteriously appearing in (on? under?) Panepistemiou St., swallowing kiosks whole, as Attiko Metro plows ahead, pushed by officials despite engineers' warnings, to complete the first metro line to service the city's main square.

Superfast modernisation has a price, and archaeologists (and unsuspecting kiosk-owners) aren't the only ones paying for it. I have no intention of promoting a misty-eyed version of a might-have-been past, but nonetheless values are clearly being lost without being replaced with anything comparable. The glare of the new also stands in stark contrast with the old and established. Wander through a contemporary suburb, and you are greeted by fantastic new houses with exquisitely terraced gardens, while in the kitchen an ageless *yiayia* (grandmother) cooks traditional dishes in huge pots fit for an army, while chickens run around the backyard. Paradoxically, it is precisely the 'old' - in this case, ties to the land, especially fields once used for grazing or olive-growing - that has fueled the 'new', as skyrocketing urban land prices made millionaires out of goat-farmers suddenly able to shower sports cars and computers on a new generation of materialist-minded offspring now on display (and displaying themselves) in the likes of Kifissia and Glyfada.

Societal modernisation has jolted Greece from a largely traditionalist to a consumerist society as fast as any country in Europe. But consumerism feeds on itself, via a troubling belief that the most expensive goods are also the most desirable, and that having the 'best' (read 'imported') products give one an inside track to a fulfilled, happy life. The trouble is, like Goethe's Faust, those following this path seem fated never to be satisfied - which, of course, is precisely the intention of the advertising industry.

While many seem to think that getting rich quick will enable them to catch up with an idealised version of Euro-American lifestyles, that destination will remain elusive. One sad symptom of the effects of copycat (hence inferior) imitation is the recent suburban craze to build gleaming shopping centres, which soon start flaking concrete, remain half-empty, and deteriorate before their time - arguably because there is nothing 'Greek' in them. Chasing after imported, second-hand materialism may go hand-in-hand with quick modernisation, but it is a fool's paradise: getting there is expensive, and what do you find on arrival? When the mind knows the price of everything, it knows the true value of nothing.

Unquestionably, making a living is a necessity not a luxury, and who would deny anyone the right to strive after life's comforts? Still, the effort is unnecessarily complicated by the societal message to buy, buy and pay more, more, and thus to conform to a falsely idealised version of the good. People here might do well to consider what societal postmodernism truly implies: toning down excessive material ambition, adopting simple or classical tastes rather than showy ones, and seeking an existence more meaningful than anything that can be bought if you just work yourself, and your mobile phone, 18 hours a day.

Modernisation is a slow historical process speeded up only at cost. And post-modernism is a state of mind, not a gaudy outfit or the latest electronic gadget.

Greece's World, in a Fishbowl

When I was in graduate school, a professor of mine had a cartoon on his door. It showed an exhausted man slumped behind piles of papers, saying, "You know, for a minute there, I almost had it!" 'It' meant what psychologists, borrowing a Greek term, call a *'keros moment'* - one where everything comes together and suddenly makes sense.

Many claim that Greece is on the verge of a national *keros*, its long-awaited moment in the sun. The perennial underachiever and exporter of ideas and people is now seeing the birds, happily, coming home to roost. The world is pushing a Cyprus solution; the Olympics are returning to their birthplace; migrants and even long expatriated Greeks flock here. Do we now have, as Paul McCartney once sang, 'hands across the water'? Has the mutual suspicion of past years been replaced by harmony, transparency, and free ice-cream for all, just in time for the new millennium?

My own response to such ideas is very mixed. While attitudes all around have clearly improved, the 'revolution' is fragmented, unfinished, and accompanied by lots of empty rhetoric. If you remove the pretensions about international goodwill, openness and the endless *irini* (peace) mantra, Greek society remains remarkably bottom-heavy, even closed. Those whose glass is half-full will regard this as strength and tenacity. Those who see it as half-empty might call it provincial.

In itself, Greek culture's staying power is marvellous; turn the radio dial, and station after station gives you real Greek music, not some warmed-over version of Europop. How good it is that there are traditions left to preserve. Yet optimist or pessimist, it is hard to escape seeing Greek life as basically insular, whatever the visible cosmopolitan trappings: the dozen brands of salmon in the supermarkets, the flashy new cars, the international hotels. But shopping is no sign of openness; even being a major tourist destination can reinforce a 'don't worry, they're temporary' attitude about foreign visitors.

Geography certainly plays a role. Greece doesn't lack for excursion

possibilities, but if you want to go somewhere truly different there is
nowhere obvious; it is the travel equivalent of the pre-party 'I have
nothing to wear!' syndrome. A trip to Cyprus? Too much like Greece.
Turkey? Too politically fraught. Albania, FYROM (the Former
Yugoslav Republic of Macedonia), Bulgaria? Think I'll pass. Mt. Athos?
Intriguing, but problematic if you're female. Psychologically, Greece
really is an island; it 'feels' separate, different, remote. Make no mistake: you come for Greece, not Europe; Ευρώπη is somewhere else.

Domestically Athens remains, as ever, the dominant centre, with
endless smaller microcosms. Foreign communities are comfortably
self-contained. The civil service operates according to its own rules,
the political culture remains clique-ridden, decision-making opaque.
Few countries anywhere have their national life so dominated by a
single city, and few capital cities are so dominated by an overcrowd-
ed city centre. Thus a remarkable juxtaposition: a truly open, international culture, yet centred on a semi-closed political system about
one square kilometre in size. Greece's world is a strange fishbowl:
small, enclosed and surrounded by water, yet as difficult to penetrate
as a Red Sea coral reef. Describing it is worlds easier than functioning within it effectively.

Insular attitudes are hardly unique to Greece. Often, societies that
export ideas and culture - France the Enlightenment and an expressive
language, Britain notions of pragmatic utilitarianism, America those of
individual enterprise and popular democracy - have provincial elements, precisely because others have adapted to them, rather than vice
versa. Indeed it can be a sign of cultural strength as much as weakness.
But excessive talk about openness and international bridge-building
can resemble hot air, liable to blow away at the next setback; it sometimes lacks measure and can verge on a double-standard.

Reality without ideals is pretty bleak. But ideals and rhetoric lacking
a realistic basis - in Greece's case, a relatively closed society extolling
openness and internationalism - can mislead, and disappoint. Greece's
moment may indeed be arriving; but keep it in perspective.

Athens, Restless City

On any given midsummer morning, I am jolted awake by the usual seasonal combination: of early rising sun, rendering useless my door's darkening shield; stifling heat, circulated vainly by a rickety fan; and worst of all, an ungodly chorus of jackhammers, tractors and electric saws echoing from all the building sites nearby. Lovely summer; lovely city.

With the neighbourhood looking increasingly like a war zone, my contempt is growing for land-developers who will not rest until every available inch of spare land in Attica is swallowed up. From one spot I can watch workers at no less than five different building sites; number six seems certain to follow, if a giant cubic hole that until recently was a nearby field is any indication. I have begun fantasising about sneaking out one night and dynamiting them all to smithereens, like Howard Roark in Ayn Rand's novel *The Fountainhead*, though other developers would simply return, like ants at a picnic, to start again.

The construction trade is a useful measure of the Greek pace of life and change. In Greece, things rarely happen at a deliberate or even speed or direction. They either happen quickly and abruptly, or not at all. It is no accident that the old fable about the tortoise and the hare was created by Aesop, an ancient Greek. But these are archetypes in modern Greece as well. Take construction again, where two extremes operate. Private houses often go up at a snail's pace; one level completed for the basic family dwelling, with rusting metal rods sticking from the roof in defiance of every aesthetic consideration, forlornly awaiting completion. Half-finished apartment blocks are even worse, hideous concrete hulks that sit idle for years.

At the other end are apartment buildings thrown up at breathtaking speed that makes you wonder how safe they are. To complete a building in Greece takes either three months, or twenty years, seemingly with nothing in between. But when happening, the pace of construction is ceaseless. Workers toil from dawn until midafternoon; sometimes they even appear on Sundays. Who says people here don't work?

One of the oldest clichés about Mediterranean life is that the pace of life is slow, and that the people are calm, measured and easygoing. Tee shirts in Plaka proclaim profundities like 'no job, no money, no problem', which on closer inspection is advice rather than any statement of local reality. In fact, Greeks very often want things to happen yesterday, and can be remarkably impatient if thwarted; why else would people lean on their car-horns so much, when it is so obviously futile in clogged traffic? There is no apparent Greek equivalent of Spain's storied *mañana* ('tomorrow') mentality.

In my experience, the same holds true for eating out. As often as not you will have your entire meal in front of you within minutes, without even waiting for the *mezedes* first, served up by a hyperactive, moonlighting waiter with a photographic memory. A perceptive friend points out the contradictions embodied even in the simple phrase σιγά - σιγά ('slowly, slowly') - which, naturally, is said at great speed, and usually with impatience.

We could even say that eternal restlessness is a defining cultural characteristic of Athenian life, along with (and related to) an entrepreneurial penchant for tinkering and change. Maybe it is just as well that systematic planning hardly ever occurs here, because of this neverending desire to experiment, all in the name, if not the service, of progress. I used to think that the laws here continually changed because the two main parties disagree on everything. I now think that they change simply because it is the acceptable norm and mutually desired course; the same undoubtedly would happen even if Greece were a one-party state.

You might think that such an ancient place could rest on its laurels, or simply rest. But no; Athenians, from the developer-class and lawmakers on down, continue to heed Pericles's admonishment to 'build, build, build'. Recently, after a very brief time away, I returned to a bewildering host of changes; a nearby road newly paved; new electronic traffic signs posted on main access roads; a thriving neighbourhood store suddenly vacated; new neighbours moved in; and that ugly dirt hole that appeared. What must people think who return after years away?

Athens remains true to its character: a bee-hive of frenetic activity, restless change and constant experimentation. A lazy place? Don't believe a word of it.

CHAPTER TWO

A Different Way of Life

Aliki's Illusion

Q: Why was Aliki Vouyouklaki, the much-loved actress who sadly and prematurely died several years ago, so strikingly popular among Greeks?

A: (1) She was blonde; (2) she was a great actress; (3) she was attractive; (4) she smiled a lot.

Though her legions of admirers would opt for some or even all the above, only one was a mark of uniqueness. Hefty peroxide sales have created more blonde heads here than in Norway, a rich thespian tradition and animated society have produced an entire nation of actors, and any walk down the street will prove that beauty is not in short supply here. Aliki was truly different because she dared to smile. In public. Unprompted.

A common observation among visitors here, verging on astonishment, is that Greeks, who inhabit a wondrously beautiful land (forgetting about the capital) and have managed to carve a reasonably workable society out of a rather unpleasant corner of the world, frequently seem so downcast or dour. Watch any televised news conference or political gathering - hard to miss, since they happen eight days a week - and the participants glare and growl behind the microphone. Pity the front-row journalist in fear of his safety.

Though they could sometimes be more serious about their work, most Greeks are even deadly serious about their leisure time. That frowning man over there, nervously fingering his *komboloi* (worry-beads) on the hotel veranda, is bound to be a native; anybody else would be smiling contentedly. I am reliably informed that this trait is fully exportable; go abroad, find the person looking particularly ill at ease, and he is more likely than not Greek. Even so, the art of seriousness strikes American eyes as a general European trait (in contrast to the patented American happy-face Europeans enjoy ridiculing, though only half-accurately, as a sign of shallowness or naïveté).

Facial expressions are a question of societal conditioning, not genetics; though not born to frown, Greeks quickly learn the habit. But saying so merely begs the question of why. An interpretive dissection of the socio-pathology of an entire country requires somewhat more than 800 words, and I have no easy answer. Many have pointed to the ancient tradition as an explanation, since of the four commonly known playwrights (Euripides, Sophocles, Aeschylus and Aristophanes) three wrote tragedies, and the absurdities marking the last-mentioned have tragic undertones as well. Some have speculated that Greeks have been trying, ever since, to live up (down?) to them, a seeming example of life imitating art. In reality, probably the opposite was true: the great plays were reflecting a societal trait as prevalent then as now.

Nonetheless a modern national history littered with setbacks is partly to blame (if that is the word), seconded by its reflection at individual level. Life is hard, especially for Athenians for reasons too obvious to need elaborating here. Much goes back to that void at the centre, where a particularism that puts a premium on the family unit, the neighborhood, the region, is both cause and effect of the lack of trust in public life: a suspicion of what goes on in the chaos (yet another Greek word) outside the small, trusted circle.

Faced with the daily demands of an often hostile world, the Greek is not naturally inclined to smile about it. Indeed the very idea would strike most as illogical or even absurd. There is a tragic sense about life in Greece that gives weight, depth, pathos - but also meaning - to everyday existence here. Valéry Giscard d'Estaing, a former French president, once noted the distinction between the pensive, thoughtful, philosophical Greek, and the uninhibited, joyful, Zorba-like exhibitionist. He was only half-right: read Zorba closely and you will find a highly refined tragic sense as well. Alexis Zorba did not dance because he had a light-hearted attitude: he did it in order to stay alive, as a means of escaping from the disasters - indeed in many ways the disaster - of life itself.

The joyful and uninhibited celebration of small things is meaningful by its very rarity and its contrast with the drudgery, setbacks and petty humiliations marking everyday existence. Such was the essence of the German philosopher, Schopenhauer, who argued that pessimism is the only logical attitude because the good times are so rare. Perhaps so, but such an outlook also makes Aliki's smile all the more precious, and immortal.

Proud of Insomnia?

I must have reached my limit over the weekend, when I unfairly snapped at a woman for allegedly cutting me off at a kiosk. Normal behaviour in Athens, of course, but I don't usually react so - especially to someone British, the one nationality guaranteed never to queue-jump. Call it vacation overdose, post-holiday fatigue, January blues or whatever; it's a natural reaction to two harassed holiday weeks of jostling by shoppers, endless greetings, standing in postal lines, eating and drinking, and staying up too late.

Apologies if I sound like the resident curmudgeon, but from the looks of pouchy eyes and grouchy tempers around, I'm not the only one tired before the year is a week old. My continuing search for decent shut-eye has also led to some inadvertent research into Greek sleeping habits: when, or if, they sleep. Some famous individuals - Napoleon, Churchill, Alexander the Great - needed just four or five hours nightly. I'm not so fortunate; if you know the old saying 'six hours for a man, seven for a woman, eight for a fool', then you can guess where that puts me.

It is common here to get up early, work two jobs, then stay out to all hours; most decent televised movies don't even begin until after midnight. If the Big Apple (occasionally known as New York) is 'the city that never sleeps', where on earth does that put Athens, a city of 25-hour days which would shut down without nonstop ingestion of coffee and cigarettes? Some call it 'being active'; I call it defying gravity. It's hard to adapt to this aspect of Greek society, whose people take a justifiable pride in their inbred stamina.

The old Mediterranean cliché - that daily life begins and ends late - is, in Greece, only half right. True, vestiges do remain. Most newspapers come out closer to noon, and 'καλημέρα' (good morning) can be heard until midafternoon. But life here also starts frightfully early. Commuters from the north assure me that they must get going by 7am or are hopelessly traffic-bound. Many civil servants are at work, or at least at the desk, by 7:30am, in offices that close at noon. Most postal services and banks close at 2pm - the latter even earlier on Fridays, contrary to everywhere else - allowing entertainment service industries to crank up. Two seemingly complete days are thus crammed into one.

Traditionally, there was only one answer to the relentless pace of life here. 'Siesta' may be a Spanish word, but the legitimacy of the afternoon nap is one of Greece's greatest contributions to mankind, far outweighing piddling things like classical architecture and the rule of law. The West has all but banished the afternoon sleep from polite society; you are distinctly odd, old, or uselessly lazy if you indulge, not to mention losing half a working day in the process. Ironically, the siesta - a perfectly natural response to midafternoon slowing of biorhythms - is under threat here too, due to the gradual introduction of continuous working hours. Midafternoon in Athens now seems little different from other hours (except in summer, when only mad Englishmen and dogs - or is it the other way around? - venture out); traffic is as bad as ever, offices still hum with activity, cafés overflow. Indeed I am struck not by how many Greeks take afternoon naps, but how few. Yet a nap is one of life's unheralded pleasures and, sometimes, necessities; it can make a bad day better, or at least shorter. Here is an interesting cultural commentary on the effects of modernisation and westernisation: needed rest gets squeezed at both ends, since the sanctity of nighttime activity remains undiminished. If Greek culture spans the globe, its daily lifestyle now spans the clock.

For a people who make no secret about their enjoyment of the good life, however humble their circumstances, there is a curious general denial of any interest in its necessary (and equally enjoyable) corollary, sleep. Most seem genuinely embarrassed when they are literally caught napping - something Henry Miller noticed about George Katsimbalis in *The Colossus of Maroussi*. One delicate problem this raises is when to call people at home, since there are few things worse than being woken by a jangling telephone (why people don't just pull the plug for an hour is beyond me). Even in recent weeks, I seem to have woken people by phone at these hours: 10pm; 11:30am; 5:45pm; 8:15pm; and 7pm (though the last one was ill). Aside from having irritated five friends, all I can conclude from this is that, in the modern Greek lifestyle, irregular sleeping patterns are the norm, not the exception. 'Did I wake you?' I ask. 'Oh no, I was just resting/out/listening to music/reading' they will say, politely, untruthfully, and groggily.

Of course, nature sometimes needs a boost, and another reality here is heavy use of pharmaceuticals. Pharmacies are pervasive, yet I have never passed one without customers inside, day or night. Many people are regularly helped along by a *xapi* (a 'happy', a little sleeping pill). I have read that Greeks rely on these more than other Europeans, to combat life's stress; but then, I've read the same about the French and British, not to mention the Americans; nowadays a powerful antidepressant, Prozac, is doled out in the U.S. freely as a supposed cure for unhappiness.

Seriously, inadequate rest is one of the unspoken maladies of our time - contributing to domestic arguments, work problems, and traffic accident rates. What a pity that, in modernising, Greece may be losing one of its notable characteristics - a conveniently, humanly broken day. Personally, though, I'll be happy to uphold the virtues of the humble siesta - whenever I can find it.

Life on Greece's Grapevine

The people of Greece sometimes present a contradictory face, but this is a subject - Greek drinking habits - in which information is, itself, strangely contradictory. Ever seeking out truths, I reluctantly but bravely decided to investigate this phenomenon further; not for any personal reasons of course, but purely in the interests of providing you, the discerning public, with some unbiased, factual information about an important subject. Then again, if this brief sketch seems as clouded as a glass of diluted ouzo, just blame the hazards of the job.

Along with the olive tree, the grapevine - the real item - is a quintessential Greek symbol. Accordingly, many guidebooks tend to gush about the land of Dionysos, God of wine, the beauty of the vineyards and the wine festivals everywhere, as if the country did nothing but carry on in inebriated exultation amidst permanent sun-drenched summer. Newcomers here are thoroughly disabused of this notion around mid-November, which brings rain and cold and 1000 drachmas-a-kilo grapes in the markets.

Another, more informative approach holds that Greeks are marvellously relaxed, even permissive, about their approach to alcohol. This one reflects the wider Mediterranean culture in which the local stuff, whether rough *retsina* from the barrel or the recent vintage, is as much a part of the dinner table as are olives and bread. Here, a ten-year-old can walk into the neighborhood cava, and walk out with a bottle of Johnnie Walker (red or black label, it makes no difference), no questions asked and with a friendly pinch on the cheek.

Even within the Western world, attitudes to drinking are sharp definers of national or regional cultures. In Britain, the off-licence, the pub and (until Mrs Thatcher relaxed closing hours) last calls for drinks at 10:50pm long featured in everyday life. In Scandinavia (and Canada), high taxes and restricted access via sterile, government-controlled shops - along with frequently severe alcohol abuse - are pervasive elements of life there, and maintenance of the public alcohol monopoly remains a sticking-point with the EU. I was reared in the southern U.S., where misguided morality and befuddled fundamentalism long conspired to produce some breathtakingly convoluted practices - since, mercifully, abandoned - like 'brown-bagging', where restaurant-goers had to bring their own bottle in, yes, a brown bag, if they wanted to drink, and where entire state legislative sessions were given to fighting over whether establishments should be permitted to serve 'liquor by the drink'. There were even (perhaps still are, unless everybody moved away) totally dry counties, with absolute prohibitions on alcohol sales, including beer. Even today, supermarkets sell only beer and wine; and you can't buy anything stronger than coca-cola on Sundays. Little wonder visitors to Greece think they're in heaven.

Not only are drinking practices an indication of societal tolerance, they are becoming a useful measurement of societal change. Until recently, Greece has enjoyed a positive correlation between free access and relaxed attitudes to alcohol, and a lack of apparent problems with it. Why create a hassle where none exists? Public drunks are still a rare sight. Recent years, however, have brought a spate of traffic accidents which led to a severe if temporary crackdown on drink-driving and raised a public stink (no pun intended) about random breathalyzer tests. Then in early 1998 came an incident involving an apparently drunken Greek MP who wrecked his car coming home from a nightclub, killing a young passenger.

Here we have an emerging two-level approach to alcohol, the traditional/domestic and the modern/imported. The traditional approach enjoys drink in moderation, and rarely by itself. Drinking primarily accompanies a meal with a doubly benign effect, enhancing the food's flavour while tempering the alcohol's impact. Food and drink (wine in winter, cold beer in summer) remain a substantial, delightful and mutually beneficial pairing. Yet even among younger people, the evening aperitif of choice is still as likely to be an ice coffee as Campari on ice, showing an admirable tendency to imbibe primarily with meals.

Against this traditional approach have come newer, imported, fashion-driven drinking habits. Hard-liquor consumption has skyrocketed over the past decade, as Greeks became among the world's highest consumers of whiskey. Around Christmas, sales boom. Perhaps because it is non-domestic in origin, this side of the ledger is associated with some less desirable developments: adulterated bottles found in police raids, outrageously priced and usually watered-down mixed drinks, consumption alone rather than with meals, and an association with an entire nightlife culture that only gets going after midnight. This is not the alcohol of soothing enjoyment, but that of hard living and potential abuse. Perhaps its sometime-linkage with the growing drugs problem is a useful reminder that alcohol itself is a drug, not just a refreshment.

Ever since the ancient Greeks discovered that wine mixed with water enhanced a pleasant evening, their successors have carried forth a tolerant tradition of wide availability and moderate use. But imported modernity has brought a newer, and potentially more dangerous, drink-tradition, existing almost in an alternative universe. But then, humble vineyards and fancy nightclubs always did make for strange neighbours.

Too Many (Greek) Notes?

There is a memorable scene in the film version of Peter Shaffer's excellent if historically dubious play, *Amadeus*, when Mozart, having just conducted the royal premiere of *The Magic Flute*, eagerly asks Emperor Franz Joseph for his opinion. The latter, fumbling as always for words, finally takes a cue from an underling by pronouncing to the maestro that it was wonderful, "but... but...too many notes. Yes, just cut a few out and it will be perfect"!

This was, of course, an interchange between Austrians, not Greeks, although as Mozart's controversy stemmed partly from introducing German-language operas rather than the safe Italian versions traditionally preferred, perhaps some cross-national licence will be permitted here. Fact is, truer words have rarely been spoken with relevance to Greek society.

Perhaps it is the caffeine, perhaps the nicotine, or likely both, but individual Greek life operates at a prodigious energy level. People rise early, tend to the kids, rush off to work along with the masses, attack last week's pile of papers, sew contacts, run errands and stand in queues during coffee breaks, work the mobile phone incessantly, fight the traffic back home, tend to the house, fix meals, and go out until late with friends before falling into bed after midnight - then do it all over again the next day. For someone who gets exhausted just pushing words around a computer screen, it remains a never-ending source of amazement.

The endlessly restless spirit that pervades the Athenian atmosphere produces more ideas, notions, and flights of fancy than one would think possible. The super-quick Greek mind, 'hyper' in the American vernacular, prowls ceaselessly in search of that new angle, darts about to spot openings, keenly eyes possibilities, sensing trends and conceiving of ways to maximise any advantages. Obstacles are not so much avoided as actively sought out as challenges to be overcome on a daily, even hourly basis. In few places is life lived to the fullest each day, in terms of giving all one has.

Yet go to any gathering - social, political, cultural or whatever - and a curiously similar pattern tends to recur. Initial reticence (that unspoken but ever-prevalent Greek trait) tinged with wariness, and politeness all around, opens up gradually to a bit of humour and the occasional penetrating insight, as the group dances around the subject at hand, poking at the beast little by little.

Then the group comes to the inevitable fork in the road, where it can either trend toward a resolution of the problem and a quick wrap-up (this option, by the way, is primarily theoretical, as it has rarely been recorded, in practice, in modern Greece), or else it can take the well-trod path: fragmentation into mini-conversations and own-initiative opinions, rising voices, flashes of temper, multiplication of tangents and new, increasingly divergent sub-topics.

At some late point, endless discussion becomes empty discussion; process triumphs over result; diminishing returns become vanished ones; *ad infinitum* merges into *ad absurdum*. A cacophany of words, ideas, and opinions repeats itself over and over again, yet becomes, oddly, like something that never happened. At the end of the day, people are happy they had their say, furious at the fool across the table, and go home worn out. Results? Who needs them? Let us hope that governmental cabinet meetings manage to avoid some of these tendencies.

There comes a time, though, when ideas need to be focused, plans to be laid, courses of action to be plotted, a viable way found for implementing them, timetables established, and a means of measuring progress agreed upon. It also requires a realisation that, yes, perhaps yesterday's idea was good enough after all, that the hairs have all been split finely enough already, and that it is time to get on with it.

There is also room for those other qualities like brevity, succinctness, closure, and listening. More of that extraordinary energy spent on conceiving ideas and making plans could be channeled into executing them. Long after the initial burst of enthusiasm has burnt itself out, the application becomes the difficult part. Difficult, but oh so necessary if getting somewhere is, in fact, the aim.

A Very Greek Afternoon

Awhile back, I was invited for lunch at the home of an older Greek couple whom I had not seen for ages. Not getting such invitations every day, I accepted but without much enthusiasm, since I was pretty sure not to know anybody else there. When the day rolled around, sunny and almost hot, I wished I could back out and do something out-of-doors, instead of sitting inside with people I didn't know, eating triple the usual amount and exhausting myself trying to follow chattering conversations in colloquial Greek while trying to avoid saying stupid things in response. Anyway, I went.

After circling half the city to find, in a strange neighbourhood, a street with the same name as 25 others in Athens, I arrived at the appointed hour. At least two dozen people were already there (it had been advertised as a 'small get-together'), sitting in a circle, holding little glasses of liqueur and eyeing each other pensively; unacquainted Greeks can be extraordinarily shy, although they don't like to admit it. After some desultory conversation, everyone transferred across the room to a table groaning with food, as the hostess and two helpers shuttled back and forth, fussing over everything from the temperature of the sauces to the plate arrangements. I was wedged in the corner, between an old lady and a piano, but never mind.

Slowly, the chatter became more persistent as an endless parade of dishes was passed around. As the lone foreign visitor, I had five people all over me in self-assigned roles as waiters and waitresses, making it useless to try to serve myself. I lacked a fork, and three people rushed into the kitchen to fetch one. As the wine decanter was passed around, the slightest hesitation on my part produced a minor crisis, as the keen eye of Greek hospitality spotted my desire for a drink more attuned to the weather, and in a flash warm wine turned to cold beer. The host, gleam in his eye and whiskey bottle at the ready, offered colourful toasts to everybody and everything in great spirits (κέφι), as I leaned back almost painfully, three plates (and way too many roquefort cheese balls) under my belt.

Suddenly an old guitar was produced, dusted off and tuned by a deft ear, then a second, then the piano was opened up, and pretty soon the whole place was ringing to music. God knows what the neighbours must have thought. The singing host with a silky voice and his sidekick, a Monday-to-Friday accountant with a lousy one, played and sang Greek songs ranging far and wide with a mighty gusto, all the more impressive because it was so unpretentious and unexpected. People sang along with the folk ballads, the words long memorised. Soon many were up dancing; not the younger people - they sat worn out on the couch - but the elderly. Greece is one of the few places where, like some reversed version of *Dorian Gray*, the spark of life never seems to fade away.

Elsewhere, people would use such occasions to talk, and complain, about their professional lives. Here, working life and worldly problems were a million miles away as the room echoed with laughter, tearful reminisces and outrageous tall tales, as photo albums were passed around, showing long-forgotten uncles with handlebar moustaches in pre-war poses at Loutraki and Gytheio. The music subsided, then picked up again for a lively encore before the party gradually broke up to great protests from the hosts, as the sun began to set across the southern horizon.

I relate this little tale not because it is unusual, but because it is usual; not because those present were rich or famous, but because they were ordinary folk; not because it was a holiday or a special event but because it was just a normal Sunday afternoon; not because there was any reason for me to be there, but because it was the result of generosity of spirit. I had nothing in particular to offer, yet was treated as an honoured guest. With such unbridled friendliness, and the care and anxiety expended to ensure my enjoyment and to feel welcome, the only problem was in saying 'όχι άλλο, ευχαριστώ' ('no more, please') at least fifteen times - all in vain, of course. And it all happened for no special reason, in an anonymous little corner of Athens. That, to me, represented the very essence of the best of Greece.

Driving in Greece: Some Survival Tips

Now we get down to the nitty-gritty in order to investigate the one area in which Greeks are truly different and, in their own unique way, excel: driving.

First, the good news. In Greece, you are statistically less likely to be shot in a road-rage incident than in Los Angeles, less likely than in New York to have parking spaces stolen from under your nose (since there aren't any free ones anyway), and less apt to die of inhaling diesel fumes than in London. But Greece operates under a completely different set of driving principles, which are as much a part of Greek reality as mountains are to Austria. So forget everything you know about road etiquette; such manners merely confuse drivers here, and set you up for problems later.

Following these practices, however, will acclimatise you better:

1. Use your horn liberally. It is not only a warning device but a common flash-alternative and mainly, an instrument for driver self-expression in a country that respects noise and noisemakers.

2. Remember that a green traffic light does not mean 'go'. Here it means 'honk, repeatedly and loudly'.

3. Take maximum advantage of the 'lag-time' rule: the practice of following the stream of cars that continue turning left on a green arrow long after it has turned red. A fun diversion is to see how many cars make it with you through the red, and how much confusion this causes in the other turn lanes, which then develop their own lag-times.

4. Never wait meekly in the turn-lane queue. This is the height of stupidity, since you will wait several light cycles to get through. Instead, drive to the queue's head and wait there, if possible beyond the light itself so you can't see it change, bringing a chorus of angry honks when it turns green.

5. Never keep proper space between you and the car in front. Though normally a good way to prevent accidents, here it is a particularly dangerous manoeuvre. A small opening is all most drivers need to cut right in front of you, so think twice about admiring

that sunset across the way while driving along.

6. When approaching a yellow light in heavy traffic, never stop at the line, but continue into the intersection. With luck, you and the other drivers will get stuck, and caught between the cross-street traffic. Total gridlock, with drivers getting out to look, chat, scream, and check their tires, is of course the ultimate aim.

7. Never signal when changing lanes or turning. This is considered wimpish and frankly unnecessary. If you insist on using your flash, at least wait until you are already halfway through the change or turn, rendering the effort token and thus effectively meaningless.

8. When stopping at a kiosk, do so directly in front, preferably double- or even triple-parked, with yellow blinkers on and door ajar. This gives the necessary impression of urgency and total disregard for other drivers, and seems a particularly effective means of impressing a new girlfriend.

9. If you ride a motorcycle, disregard petty nuisances like helmets, cars, lane-dividers, and traffic lights. Cars are only for weaving in-between, and for hurling curses at. When in doubt, just imitate what motorcycle cops do; they never follow the rules, either.

10. When driving a large truck, e.g. one overfilled with construction materials or with long metal rods sticking perilously out the back, do so only at peak traffic hours, on the most crowded streets. If you want to stall, do so only at busy intersections.

11. When stopped for petrol, make sure the attendant is smoking. He usually is anyway, though occasionally he forgets. This simple act turns a dull chore into a potential thrill, as you contemplate the entire city block, you included, going up in flames.

12. If you have a collision, make sure that, when you both get out to inspect the damage, you berate the other driver for his general stupidity and ignorance about driving in Greece. There is one overriding principle: 'it is always the other guy's fault'.

Finally, back home watching the news a few hours and grey hairs later, and you hear officials bragging about how Athens's traffic woes will be solved with the new ring-roads and metro, give a good, hearty laugh. It is a wonderful tension-releaser and, under the circumstances, a singularly appropriate response.

The Joys of August

One of the truly predictable, almost official, annual Athenian events is signalled on the last day of July, the arrival of which has the effect of a starter's pistol in a 100-metre dash. If you happen to live outside the capital, the month of August may not mean that much. But if you are one of the city's four million or so residents, then you are keenly aware of the sanctity of the August exodus: desperate souls fleeing the crowded city to partake in the annual joys of over-booked ferries, sunburn, and tavernas all but out of decent food by 9pm because early-dining foreign tourists have eaten all the good dishes. Don't even bother calling people; they're not home, or if they are, they're just back for a day to water the plants.

With even the government scattered to the four winds, this annual dis-appearing act gives weight to the prevailing assumption that Athens simply rolls over and plays dead, or envelops itself in a cocoon for the month. In fact, much the opposite is true. A different city emerges as the old one sheds, ever so briefly, some of its rough, often hostile exterior and assumes a much more benign existence - revealing the butterfly rather than covering it up. The shutters are down, the roads half-empty, life's pace a bit slower. Minus the excess of humanity, the city puts on a more human face; one of the many paradoxes of Athenian life.

For those left behind, this exile-in-reverse comes as a secret blessing, for Athens has a seductive charm that appears only in August, like the shy Alpine chamois that hides away for most of the year and puts in only a rare appearance. The effect is equally great in psychological terms; the worries seem slightly less intense, even for those perennial-ly caught up in existential angst; the deadlines more bendable; and you can read fiction without feeling guilty about wasting time. The world seems to languish in a month of mid-afternoon doldrums.

Of course, being caught here with unfinished work, or stuck with doing the job of ten colleagues off lounging beside the pool somewhere, may not be everyone's idea of a good time. Noise levels can even rise as human activity moves outside and stays up even later. On the other hand, the work - any work - now seems slightly less burdensome: you can progress more at your own speed, without a boss in your face. Shaving becomes even more optional than it is in Greece already; ties disappear altogether, unless you're unlucky enough to be a diplomat on duty. We should also make exception for the heroic handful who continue to staff the *Athens News* offices without thought of happiness or personal comfort, facing the daily challenge of finding some serious news while desperately hoping a war doesn't break out an hour before final copy is due.

Then comes the 15th of August, the deadest of the dead periods, when a secondary exodus occurs, leaving a virtual ghost-town in its wake. For a precious few days, strolling down the middle of Panepistimiou St. becomes a viable recreational proposition, even for those not bent on self-destruction. On the 15th the icons are paraded solemnly from churches along deserted streets; you feel slightly odd being here to see it, but also rather privileged.

Granted, many don't have a choice; offices often simply close up and send people away. Still, there is something slightly perverse about leaving just when things are improving. It also makes you wonder about the power of the herd mentality. In Greece, ostensibly a place of individualism run rampant, you find an equally great propensity for following others; it is definitely not a society for, or of, loners or eccentric individualists. Sit in a forlorn corner of a taverna, and soon others will gravitate in your direction. Find your favorite spot in an outdoor cinema, and wait for a couple (chain-smokers and nonstop talkers, naturally) to plunk themselves in front of you. It is as if they, even while believing themselves to be exceedingly clever, somehow don't entirely trust their own judgement, and suspect you know something they don't. And when it comes to holidays, the recreation people seek becomes more like re-creation - of the very conditions (noise, crowds) from which they have just fled.

One need not be a permanent contrarian or a misanthropist to avoid the worst excesses of the herd. It isn't necessary to celebrate Christmas in September or to take your island holiday in February. But it is good, even a source of strength for the human spirit, to resist, just a little, what society may expect of you. How else are we to leave our own individual mark? Next year, consider taking your August break - right here in Athens.

-

Summary Holidaying: Theory and Practice

You leave in a surge of excitement and exhilarated anticipation; you return tired, disoriented, looking older (too much sun) and heftier (too much food), feeling poorer, and depressed at the prospect of eleven months of work before the next one. Why then do we celebrate summer holidays so? I ask this in a rhetorical rather than curmudgeonly sense; and following a recent such break, I have a few random thoughts on the subject before other demands push summertime into the recesses of distant memory, where positive images linger and negative ones conveniently are forgotten.

Once, entire families decamped to 'summer' at the seaside, be it Newport, Brighton, or Loutraki. Now, the incredible shrinking holiday is measured in weeks or even days, not months, though Greece's hardworking prime minister, reassuringly, manages a good 20 days away. In turn, less time puts more pressure on us to relax while we can; work compresses the free period from both ends like a vise; and we have to work harder than ever to enjoy ourselves. Never have vacations been so exhausting. Before leaving you dash around completing errands that, left undone, will surely cause the world to collapse. Then almost before you adjust to noisy hotel neighbours, a strange pillow and weird-tasting tapwater, you face a return-trip ordeal, readjustment at home, and a pile of new demands while your defenses are down.

'What we need', says one of Jerome K. Jerome's immortal characters, 'is a change'. Despite their nuisances, holidays appeal because they are modern man's nearest equivalent to a complete break from the routine. The change must also involve a different location and environment; and must bring an altered, preferably relaxing, physical sensation. To be beneficial, it must open the pores and senses, figuratively and actually, to the 'state of nature' so easily forgotten in a crowded city.

I used to take piles of work along on holiday, less actually to do than to assuage any lingering Protestant-guilt about being away. Now, I don't even bother. I listened with astonishment to a friend's ambitious holiday reading list that included Umberto Eco, Gabriel Garcia Marquez, and

The Dead Sea Scrolls. I took *Three Men in a Boat* - and didn't even finish that. Indeed, I have given up all pretenses to mind-expansion and cultural enrichment on holiday. Last time around, my only investigative work consisted of scouting out the ever-original uses to which the English language is put. Where I went, diners could choose between such mouth-watering starters as 'craw', 'wild greens balls', 'various salty' (?), 'piquant cabbage', and 'vinegar octopus'. Main meals could centre around such delicacies as 'stufed burger', 'cempap', 'Greek Specialty Name Spetsofai', 'dog-fish with garlic', and 'Lamp cooked in Tom' (poor Tom!). Sweet-tooths could be satisfied with 'yoghort frese fruits', 'parfe wiped cream', or 'sweets of pan'. Thank goodness that Greek authenticity still reigns in tavernas, as it does in churches; I personally witnessed a kissing Swedish couple kicked physically out of one.

While away, I want my brain to shrink like a prune, its cluttering thoughts to slip away like an ebbing tide, while I float around a shimmering sea, idly watch olive trees sway in the breeze, eat and sleep. Speaking for myself - although seeing so many Greek adults unself-consciously reading comic books on the beach and noting the ever-dwindling subtlety of tee-shirt messages, I believe I reflect the vast majority here - holidays are for avoiding things normally called constructive. This is very different, however, from being hedonistic; it is more like a search for mellowness, for a Zen-like state of being for a short while without wants, needs, or desires. The aim is to slow down the runaway train and to rekindle a fascination for the small and elemental - noticing flowers, searching for the perfect seashell, savouring a grilled fish, enjoying rather than gulping a morning coffee. For a thinking type, holidays are surely about rediscovering senses heightened by sun, wind and (still thankfully clear) sea.

But it is an error to think that such idle activities equal doing nothing. While disengaged, we are in fact doing a great deal: restoring, healing, preparing. Only with an emptied mind can we see our own cluttered lives with any clarity, to see what needs to be changed, just as the mountain is only clearly visible from the plain. The distractions will return; but that clarity of vision which only time away can offer is priceless. Thus does idling become constructive, and the superficial become meaningful; thus, indeed, does so little become so much. And Greece is the best place on earth, hands down, to discover these things anew.

CHAPTER THREE

A World of Culture

An Embarrassment of Riches

Ancient Greece bequeathed to modern man an unparalleled understanding of the human condition, expressed both via its political philosophies and its socio-cultural emphasis on the theatrical arts. Of the two strands - the intellectual and the artistic or expressive - there is little question as to which has had the more profound impact on today's Greece. On one hand, trying to analyse political affairs here occasionally gives the feeling of being the odd man out. It is like being in love with Renaissance painting and living in Canada, or studying Moorish architecture in Belgium; the fit just isn't right. On the other, Greece's true greatness - not its ancient legacy, but its modern existence - lies in the arts. Greece is both an inspiration for artists and an artistic inspiration, creating an astonishing range and variety of applied talent that would flatter a country five times its size.

I would be hard-pressed merely to list the more famous modern Greek artistic personalities worldwide, both among the deceased (Constantine Cavafy, Nikos Kazantzakis, Odysseus Elytis, George Seferis, Maria Callas, Dimitris Mitropoulos) and the living (Vangelis Papathanasiou, Agnes Baltsa, Costa Gavras, Irene Pappas). Indeed such a list would be both incomplete and beside the point, because here culture in all its manifestations is not merely the sum total of individual artists, but something much greater still, and extends far beyond the capital itself.

There are numerous reasons why: the unique light, inspiring painters and filmmakers; the rich ancient tradition and living, breathing venues from the Herod Atticus Odeon to Epidavros; a culture that values matters of soul and heart no less than the intellect; a society of enterprising individuals. Less often appreciated, however, are the inherent limitations that Greek artists face. These include a lack of national resources to expose Greek talent abroad, and a rich language with few foreign speakers, meaning that any art with words requires careful translation. Further, the above would explain why inspired art is often produced here, but not the phenomenal success of many Greek artists who have worked abroad - from El Greco right up to Nana Mouskouri and Yanni.

Other elements include:

- The remarkable range of Greece's artistic offerings, from film to the letters to painting, music, and theatre. In each field, the abundance of talent is such that most individuals will never be well known, but no less fulfilled because of it. Greece thus escapes the frequent small-state problem of creative giants who overshadow other worthy figures (Finland's Jean Sibelius; Norway's Edvard Grieg and Edvard Munch). Perhaps even the competition stimulates; just think how well the composers Mikis Theodorakis, Manos Hadzidakis, Ioannis Markopoulos, and Stavros Xarhakos have complemented each other musically.

- Culture as a two-way street. Greece itself is a channel for constant circulation of new blood. Though traditionally a stepping-stone for artistic talent going abroad, Greece is increasingly a magnet as well, in the footsteps of Jules Dassin and attracting the likes of Sir Peter Hall and Montserrat Caballe year after year. The recent expansion of Austria's International Belvedere operatic competition to include Greece in its qualifying rounds further exemplifies the mutual value of such interactions.

- Culture both high and low. Greece's year-round involvement in the European classical music scene via the Megaron Mousikis and the underrated National Opera, with recent productions of Mozart and Richard Strauss, is especially visible. Yet obvious in any walk downtown is the astonishing number of local theatres offering up delicious farce as well as drama nightly. Most are run on a shoestring, with minimal public financial support and necessarily low ticket prices; the physical deterioration of many premises is saddening. And what Greek audiences sometimes lack in understanding (please, don't clap between symphonic movements), they often compensate for in enthusiasm.

- Culture as high politics. The Nobel Prize-winning poet, Seferis, combined the two exquisitely; few even realise that he was also a prominent diplomat. The Greek Culture Ministry has long been a crucial cabinet appointment, not the political backwater it can be in other countries, if one exists at all. The incomparable Melina Mercouri popularised the post, but her successors have been equally aware of the potential value of cultural diplomacy - whether in clamouring for the Parthenon marbles or establishing European Cultural Capitals (Thessaloniki enjoying the limelight during 1997, as did Athens, inaugurating the annual custom, in 1985, and as will Patras in 2006). Related here is the passionate belief in culture as a civilising and peaceable force; have you ever noticed the absence of violent undertones of musical videos here, compared with those of, e.g., Michael Jackson?

- Sacrifice. Lots of cultural activity in a small country of modest means strictly limits support for individual ventures. Romantics have long associated the arts with material want, but the truth is that many here are willing to sacrifice plenty for the sheer love of creation. Even established acting stars, like Katia Dandoulaki, frequently must combine daytime television work with nightly theatre performances to make a decent living. From where does the energy come?

The main danger of such an embarrassment of riches is that it can lead to viewer paralysis. Deciding what to choose may be difficult, but personally, I can think of worse dilemmas.

The Olympics Are Coming Home

In the end it was a matter of perspective. Even the context of the International Olympic Committee's vote, in September 1997, to award the 2004 Summer Games to Athens - awkwardly sandwiched between worldwide mourning for the deaths of Princess Diana and Mother Teresa - symbolically demythologised Greece's Olympic bid from the life-and-death connotations it long had. The result vindicates some healthy principles: the value of hard work and perseverence, and a newfound pragmatism refreshingly devoid of the pretensions formerly driving Greece's Olympic dreams.

Few issues touch Greek national sensitivities like the Olympics. This quadrennial sporting and cultural festival was, after all, born here (776 BC, Olympia and all that), and was celebrated for a millennium until being disbanded by Roman Emperor Theodosius I for supposed paganism. Moreover, they reflected a broader appreciation of such festivals; the Pythian and Isthmian Games were also notable events in the ancient calendar. Above Delphi, there is (or was) an athletics stadium, situated higher even than the holy site itself. Olympics imply achievements at the very pinnacle; the country's own geographical summit was the eponymous home of the gods themselves. Such is the stuff of powerful myths and mythologies; and Baron de Coubertin stirred these waters further by awarding Athens the first revival Games back in 1896.

Understandably, the initial euphoria at being selected by the IOC above the four competing cities (Rome, Buenos Aires, Stockholm, and Cape Town) was peppered with promises of delivering a 'dream Games'. However, it was tempered by an immense, quieter satisfaction at having taken a huge step toward recognition and respect by the international community. Although the omens were cautiously positive, Athens's success was hardly inevitable, less serendipity than proof of an old religious admonition: the gods help those who help themselves. In this case, the Athens campaign benefited enormously from its striking contrast with its previous bid, for the 1996 Games.

In that failed effort ending in 1990, arrogance and ineptitude bat-
tled vainly for supremacy in the Greek camp. Woeful unpreparedness
was followed by an equally overdone reaction of recriminations, and
even threats to boycott the Atlanta Games, and it took years for tempers to settle. But what a difference seven years makes. This bid was
in a different league, marked by low-key, fact-wielding (if occasionally slick) professionalism, quiet confidence, and arguments emphasis-
ing modern infrastructure rather than ancient temples. Relative as
well as absolute competence was evident, even if the charm offensive
sometimes tended uncomfortably toward sugary platitude and unver-
ifiable claims of total nationwide support.

The dramatic transformation of Athens's bid file seemed to reflect
the maturing of Greece itself in the 1990s: less prone to bombast and
dubious claims to uniqueness, and more cognizant of the virtues of
quiet diplomacy, preparedness, and the relationship of its own efforts
with the wider world. While the Olympics are coming home to their
ancient roots, it was not those roots themselves, but rather Greece's
emergence as a more confident and competent modern society, that
spelled the difference.

Realistically, there are some clear advantages to hosting the Games.
It will put Greece back (temporarily) on the world map; it will
undoubtedly boost tourism revenues; it will create a sense of positive
national purpose. Most important of all, perhaps, is that winning the
Olympics, though a victory in its own right, is also a significant means
to achieve other ends. Principally, it will light a fire under ongoing
urban infrastructure projects, long in the planning stage, speeding
completion of the new airport at Spata, the Athens metro extensions,
and new ring-roads around the capital. Such would further under-
score the refreshingly pragmatic spirit of this entire bid.

Even so, care must now be taken that winning the Games does not
become a Pyrrhic victory. The potential downsides are all too evident.
It will increase the already frenetic pace of construction in the capital,
if that is possible. Athens can scarcely afford to lose more natural
space, which it will, permanently, with the proposed construction of
new rowing facilities on the east coast at Skinias, a new baseball arena
destined for instant obsolescence, and a huge new Olympic village at

the base of Mt Parnitha. The village will inevitably be converted to low-cost, possibly refugee, housing afterwards. The overall effort will unduly concentrate national resources on the capital, at the direct expense of Greece's needful regions. Environmental advocates, in making similar points, have been airily dismissed as crackpots and spoilsports. Further, the desired sense of national purpose could easily revert to endless infighting and backbiting; there is already evidence to this effect in the troubled Olympics preparatory committee established in the wake of the bid committee. The devil, as always, lies in the detail; and then there is always the potential for major disruption once the Games begin, in which much of the international goodwill toward Greece could well evaporate like the morning dew.

The key issue, cost, has been so downgraded as to seem almost nonexistent. It is bound to loom larger in years to come. In Montreal, 1976 host, huge Olympic-related cost overruns created a political climate of bitterness lasting for two decades. The Greek taxpayer needs to be told that s/he will be footing a bill that could run over $2 billion. Having long ridiculed the excessive commercialism of the Atlanta and Los Angeles Games, the Greek promoters have painted themselves into a corner of having to rely on public funding, even though a huge new financial undertaking, at a time of severe, EMU-related budgetary cutbacks, is about the last thing Greece needs. Donations from the wealthy are mere drops in buckets; EU structural funds are not available for sporting events. On these issues, the Greek public deserves more than glittering generalities.

Hosting the Games will require a country-wide, years-long effort for a weeks-long festival in 2004. The question now is whether it can succeed without tears; this will be a much sterner test of Greece's international emergence.

Christmas Seasons, of Change

If you, like me, have gorged on enough *melomakarona* to raise your blood-sugar to dangerous levels, hacked and coughed your way through endless *kourambiedes* (whose powdered-sugar coating always seems to go down the wrong way), and been woken up at insane hours on Christmas Eve by triangle-toting kids singing woefully off key, then you are well aware of Greece's unique Christmas customs.

Christmas is a season of nostalgia: for reliving customs that are accepted, indeed embraced, in December precisely because they have repeat, thus ritual, value. It is a contextual holiday, best observed only in its time and place, which is why finding one's personal sense of Christmas spirit, originating in childhood, is so difficult in other places. Nonetheless Greece, a country that rightly reveres its traditions, is changing the way it celebrates Christmas; the holiday is even emerging as a vanguard of change itself. The bad news is that attempts are being made here to imitate the more Western, and commercial, celebrations; the good news is that the effort is not, yet, entirely successful.

There are times when the proliferation of holidays can water down their meaning. Here is an example of holiday-stretching. The Western Christmas has become, in business jargon, a saturated market; in Greece, it is on a substantial upward growth curve. Any guidebook will tell you, in this case accurately, that Christmas plays a poor second fiddle to Easter in the Orthodox calendar, with few churchgoers or candles in sight. According to tradition, the old-style Greek Christmas merely opened a two-week holiday season (hence the Twelve Days of Christmas), ending at Epiphany (January 6th) and peaking at New Year's: the day of present-giving, of card-playing, and of cutting the *vassilopitta* (New Year's cake) in search of that elusive lucky gold coin. If you're the sociable type, you might get many opportunities in January to find the coin on your plate, or in your mouth. And hope it works; the last time I got it, I vaguely recall having a really miserable year afterwards.

But by an odd twist, Christmas nowadays is moving backwards, cal-endar-wise, supposedly showing the country the way forward. Increasingly, Christmas Day competes with New Year's for attention. Awkward matters of protocol arise: when do you give presents and say 'Χρόνια Πολλά' (many years)? Pre-Christmas Sunday shop-open-ing, common in December throughout the West, was only recently (and partially) introduced here. And the once post-Christmas, post-Boxing Day shopping rush now increasingly precedes December 25th itself. You can even buy live trees.

Grand-scale lighting is another indication of change. Mayor Avramopoulos's efforts have certainly made nighttime Athens more visible. It all seems slightly over the top (literally so, in the case of Lykavitos hill) but it does have undeniable charm. Privately too, homes and apartment blocks increasingly deck themselves out in red and green, another would-be innovation. And technology, ingenuity and dubious taste are being combined in some amazing mini-light shows on balconies. One enterprising family near me strung up lights shaped like huge bells, which don't just blink but actually fade in and out gradually, like theatre lights going down before a performance. And in competitive urban zeal, Athens erected Europe's tallest Christmas tree, though in stringing so many lights, they forgot the tree itself.

I'm not a closet Scrooge; I like Christmas as much as anyone, but these changes seem slightly contrived, imported, second-hand. They don't exactly fall flat, and all the lights around do have a certain allure, even those in Kolonaki with the strange blue hue (somehow, the one colour I never associated with Christmas). But upstarts and copycat imitations inevitably give the impression of having been parachuted in, like Santa himself on his sleigh, to a country that always seems to have warm sunshine at Christmas. And as Greece looks ever westward, despite its eastern roots, perhaps it is only fit-ting that such a major holiday can itself have an identity crisis, caught in this strange amalgam of encroaching Western commercial-ism and traditional Eastern sanctity.

Long ago, Greece figured out a delightful, well-paced way of cele-brating the holiday, with a beginning (Christmas), a peak (New

Year's) and an ending (Epiphany). That is why these changes speak volumes about the powers of globalisation, but are also just a touch sad. They are also ironic, considering that Greece, the land of families and rich emotional lives, long has celebrated a more measured and 'rational' Christmas holiday, in contrast to the compacted, stressed-out holiday increasingly found further west. Here, two weeks' preparation leads to a two-week season; elsewhere, two months' preparation precedes a two-day mini-holiday, centred narrowly around Christmas Day and terminating, abruptly (in the U.S., anyway) with post-Christmas sales that often begin, incredibly, at 8 am on December 26th. The stress can be reinforced as scattered, often dysfunctional families are thrown together once yearly to carry on last year's arguments while opening their presents. The anticipation, and the memory, are so often greater than the experience itself; past and future are, after all, appealing alternatives to a more prosaic present. Stressed-out, overemotional West, meet measured, rationalist Greece; now, there's a new twist.

Greece has its own customs that will never be matched, and might be diluted, by Santa Clauses imported too freely; if we're not careful, the new Christmas could become an event without meaning. It would be a pity to see Greece, tinkering with a successful formula, succumb too readily to foreign versions of the holiday. I'm all for modernising economies and bureaucracies; but with holidays - by definition non-transplantable - it's a different story.

Easter's Rites

Easter in Greece is less an event or holiday than an all-encompassing experience; it unfolds over an entire season and throughout Η Μεγάλη Εβδομάδα (Holy Week), not just on the Sunday. Its coming, like the early morning tolling of the church bells presaging it, is slow, methodical, measured. Repetitive bell-tolling opens up numerous other, complex rites marking the season and distinguishing the Orthodox world.

The gradual westernisation of the Greek Christmas is lamentable. The Orthodox Easter is however too powerful a celebration to suffer a similar fate. Indeed in Greece it is the western (Catholic) Church, though not the stubborn Protestants who raised me, which has coordinated its celebrations with the Orthodox ones in a tangible nod toward bridging the religious divide so long separating Eastern from Western Christian churches. The Western world has both shortened and partly secularised its Easter; even Good Friday is sometimes a working day, and the weekend is marked by earthly pleasures like chocolate rabbits and the Masters golf tournament in blooming Augusta. Both Easters may be rites of spring, but the similarities pretty much end there.

Two things strike me about Easter, apart from the usual, well-known elements like the smells and tastes of the Easter feast, the candles and the flower-strewn επιτάφιος (funerary procession) carried around the streets on Friday evening, escorted by a mournful band. One is that it involves both ritual and miracle. Miracles, by definition, are one-offs, yet Easter is treasured so because its annual celebration involves a series of rituals every schoolchild knows by heart. Theologically, of course, the resurrection and ascendance of Christ is the miracle, but also, in secular terms, its coincidence with spring - seemingly dead earth springing magically to life - offers an earthly equivalent even for the jaded or non-believer. We know it will happen, yet its qualities seem miraculous. The 'rebirth' is both temporal and spiritual, and their overlap reinforces each other.

Secondly, Easter offers up a host of seemingly sharp contrasts between pre- and post-resurrection celebrations. The notion of a 'season of contrasts in a land of contrasts' may be a cliché-lover's dream, but even clichés contain a modicum of truth. The season captures numerous distinctive pairings, apparent opposites that nonetheless derive meaning from each other. Fasting is followed by feasting; austerity by plenty; frequently, rain by sunshine; solemnity by noisy celebration; avoidance of animal products by indulgence in them (rather awkward for committed vegetarians); mysticism by earthly delights; candlelit ceremonies by firecracker displays; solitary pensiveness and penitence by joyful camaraderie; sombre church choruses by lively folk music. It is all quite special, and soon we recognise that these contrasts are all part of the broader scheme of things. It was not a theologian but a philosopher, Heraclitus of Ephesus, who stressed that opposites are also matching halves; the idea of a 'unity of opposites' is a seeming paradox but, perhaps, an actual truth.

Here too we can find significance in the symbolism of Lent's forty days, which reflects a common numerical tradition passing down through many cultures; from the forty thieves of Ali Baba to Moses's forty years of wandering in the desert with the Israelites; even we today look for forty winks of sleep. Such symbolic representations indicate the many threads between eras, cultures, and religions so often overlooked within, and by, individual cultural milieus. Though a distinctly Christian celebration, Easter is not without its interlinkages across time and across seeming divides between religions.

But Easter's true significance remains its juxtaposition of life and death, between the crucifixion of Christ and His subsequent resurrection. In 1998, the funeral of Greece's late Archbishop Serapheim on Η Μεγάλη Δευτέρα, the first day of Holy Week, and the grave condition of elder statesman Constantine Karamanlis, who died shortly thereafter, were timely reminders of this that not all would regard as mere coincidence. Easter is often taken as a victory of life over death, and perhaps, of optimism over pessimism for true believers. But an alternative reading, borrowing a page from Heraclitus, is that the holiday does not contrast death and life, but rather insists on their pairing; it shows their linkage as inexorable partners moving hand-in-hand through the stream of existence. The notion of life triumphing over death is a powerful theological message; yet its equally profound mirror-image is that even the son of God can die. Christ's suffering and death made possible the resurrection, but the resurrection is impossible without first the death.

Yet even this message is life-affirming. Life is remarkable not because it might be eternal, but because, as we now know it, it is so fleeting and temporary. To think that we are not permanent residents here (and I don't mean in Greece) but merely passengers in transit can be a source of comfort, even inspiration rather than one of melancholy. We are privileged to be here, not just condemned to live it out.

Throughout the country, Greece beckons us to partake in, as well as watch and witness, its Easter celebration. It involves us mind, body and spirit; and those privileged to be here are drawn to the essential spirit of the country - making us all, during Easter week, honorary Greeks.

Monasteries on the Rocks

Two weekend trips in a month surely establishes a new personal travelling record. Recently I drove solo up to Meteora, toward northern Greece without quite being there: west of Metsovo and the Pindus mountains, east of Olympus and Pelion, south of Macedonia. And while these articles were intended as neither confessionals nor 'what I did last weekend' enterprises, I have thought of nothing else since being awestruck by the place.

After Easter, and the election of a remarkably jolly and worldly new Greek Archbishop (Christodoulos), seemed a fitting time for journeying to Meteora, both a home of Orthodoxy and an escape for those practicing it. The drive was unremarkable, apart from competing Labour Day demons tearing northwards at the ungodly hour of 6:45am, and my wasting fifteen frustrating minutes yanking at a stuck seat-belt. The national road is undergoing heavy construction, caught between the original road network initiated by Constantine Karamanlis in the 1950s, among his many achievements, and the EU's current effort to upgrade them to motorway standard. Once in Kalambaka, a nearby town, I found an unpretentious place to stay (who could resist a charmingly devious sign for 'clen rooms with separately bathroom'?), then set off on my pilgrimage.

At Meteora, religion was very much in the air, as hundreds of devout Greeks, many clearly moved at being there, descended on the place for the holiday weekend. Rather, they ascended to it, for religion is physically in the air too. Six inhabited monasteries, and eighteen others in ruins, dot the peaks of huge, fantastically misshapen rock pillars reaching skyward from the Thessalian valley floor. The region would be a huge draw on the physical force of geology alone. And when you crown these pillars with exquisite, functioning monasteries perched like clifftop sentries in defiance of gravity and in celebration of vertigo, you have a truly otherworldly combination. I have never seen anything comparable.

Meteora first attracted monks and hermits escaping persecution a millennium ago, though any hopes of escaping modern worldly influences are nowadays dampened by tourist coaches and hordes tramping up and down steps. Saturday morning dawned spectacularly clear, and I went up (there's an accessible, circular road looping through the area) very early. For a precious short while - standing alone at sunrise, high up on rocky outcroppings, breeze in face, surrounded by majestic scenery transplanted from another era if not planet - there came a remarkable sensation of being at one with...I don't know, the fantastic powers of creation of some kind. The very best moments can neither be captured on film nor expressed in words; they reside within. At such times, time itself doesn't just stand still; it seems not to exist at all.

My rather dated guidebook noted the monasteries were in danger of being abandoned, but I had the opposite impression. All seem well kept (including new loos); several are adding new wings, as if expecting guests; many monks are young and friendly, contrary to the wild-eyed ascetics I had half-expected. Remarking on the minor building boom, a jaded photographer said 'wherever there's religion there's good business', but I was relieved at the absence of the decay so poignantly described in Patrick Leigh Fermor's *Roumeli*. The gift shops do a thriving trade in icons, incense burners and gold-plated crosses, but they also have little alternative. And the 'air' of devoutness is palpable, the atmosphere hushed. An ageless monk presided in a corner of the church of the Grand Meteoron (the largest and historically most influential of the monasteries), blessing children proferred by their equally wide-eyed parents; holy relics were kissed by old and young alike; bottles were filled with holy water on site. The clanging of evening bells echoing off the granite pillars, and the banging of monastery doors by hooded nuns and robed monks at day's end, indicated that tourists remain tolerated visitors in an otherwise holy place.

The well-preserved monastery churches are mini-masterpieces of religious art and alone worth the trip. Alongside exquisite beauty and colour, several depict gruesome scenes of Christian martyrdom, an indication (and justification) of why they were originally built; most are 400 years old or more; and all the interiors are totally covered with frescoes from floor to the Pantocrator high on the cupola above. I have no photographic record of the church interiors; for good reason, pictures are not allowed.

Seeing this late Byzantine legacy was a powerful indicator of Greece's separate identity from the rest of Europe. On the evening news that night, Messrs. Simitis, Papantoniou, and Papandreou sat glumly as Greece was the only country excluded (not by choice) from the euro group, a temporal reminder of past economic excesses. But the separation is also ecclesiastical; a country that remains actively Orthodox has fundamental differences from the other EU14. Surveys consistently show Greece remains among the 'most religious' of European countries. I believe it, although visitors to such a place as Meteora cannot be considered a cross-section of the society as a whole, which itself is secularising along with the West in general.

Turning off for Athens after my 300-odd kilometres' return journey, in quick succession I (a) heard my first car-horn that entire day, (b) saw my first traffic argument full of gesticulating arms, and (c) was cut off rudely while waiting at a phone booth. They couldn't have said 'welcome back to the real world' any better.

A Night at the Opera

If you ever decide to attend the opera in Athens - the Greek National Opera, on Academias Street - remember to go to the right one. Not that there are too many opera houses (this is one problem the city definitely does not have), but that it's easy to confuse it with the better lit and advertised Opera cinema next door. I nearly stumbled into *The Full Monty* (a movie about unemployed Englishmen-turned-strippers, by which I don't mean they stopped being Englishmen as a result), instead of my actual destination, *The Magic Flute* by Mozart, which has a slightly different theme.

I am one of those types who like classical performances yet who rarely actually get out to them. But this time I was lured by (a) the year's last performance of a renowned Greek production, (b) Sunday boredom, (c) a desire to indulge my liking of Mozart, and primarily, (d) a desperate search for something, anything, to write about to fill my weekly column. Remarkably I managed to knock off all four birds with one stone. Papageno, the Queen of the Night's birdcatcher-extraordinaire, would have been proud.

I arrived at 6pm sharp, after being advised by phone (first attempt, no recording, helpful lady) to get there an hour early for returns. As one who has trouble planning for tomorrow, I naturally had no ticket. I was fourth in line, with little to do except people-watch; I swear a well-dressed elderly gentleman came in wearing medals on his lapel, like a First World War veteran, if any are left. Yet I only secured a seat after 55 nail-biting minutes. The reason (surprise) was an absence of any identifiable system, apart from Darwin's, to manage the elementary task of ticket exchange. Though the line was right by the box-office window, the people there showed little regard for our legitimate interests in securing returned tickets. The 'queue' disintegrated, forcing the growing legions of seat-seekers into a bad-tempered scramble whenever someone came in waving a ticket around - even if they had negotiated the black-market maze outside. There is something humiliating (not to mention utterly unnecessary) about well-dressed people scrounging for tickets to an event like an opera, which seems, by definition, to demand some courtesy, decorum and civility - especially by an institution that surely faces this problem on a nightly basis. Have I made my point?

Finally I accosted a teenage girl with an extra ticket for a seat amongst the rafters, stifling with limited view and bad acoustics. Cheap-seat conditions are wearily similar everywhere and, anyway, beggars can't be choosers. But it was surprising to find I couldn't fit my legs between my seat and the one in front, so I had to dangle them in the aisle for three hours. Transatlantic economy class seems comparatively palatial; and I don't exactly have a weight problem.

But if infrastructure and procedure were wanting, the good news was the art itself: the performance was delightful, polished and well performed. The Queen of the Night handled the toughest aria with great aplomb; Tamino and Pamina sang exquisite duets; Papageno brought the house down. *The Magic Flute* was Mozart's final operatic work, and along with his other late compositions (the last piano concerto; the Jupiter symphony in C; and of course the *Requiem*) showed a profound maturity. Here, his lighthearted exterior, embodied in a story of optimism and faith, also conveyed a deeply serious search for wisdom and truth, incorporating much of the symbolism he revered as a Freemason in 18th century Austria. The audience seemed genuinely appreciative.

It came off remarkably well considering the cramped quarters; the place really is small, and no place to put on *Aida*. The solid wood-finishing interior gives it a rather austere look, in contrast to the plush velvet generally found in opera-houses. Every performance was sold out, reflecting the popularity of quality cultural events in Greece, despite people's busy lives, strict economies and traffic tie-ups getting to them. A recent book presentation at the Gennadius Library, replete with 2 hours' worth of speeches and on a bitterly cold night, was packed to standing-room-only. At the Megaron Mousikis, a recent organ recital - one man playing one instrument - was jammed; every seat taken.

With such extraordinary collective cultural appetite, and with the Megaron presenting an exquisite orchestral counterbalance, it seems a no-brainer to argue that a new opera house - one less prone to upstaging by a cinema - should be high up the national agenda in the land of Callas and Baltsa. Even if trying circumstances aid the creative process (the 'poor artist' syndrome and all that), they are a shaky assumption for a national cultural policy, and merely allow that policy to be driven endlessly and needlessly by petty politics. The present opera, though far from a national shame, still needs a better home - which it will have if and when plans to expand the Megaron Mousikis are realised. The result would be essentially Greek, in two senses: by its usage of private rather than state capital in ambitiously promoting the arts, and by Greece's potentially dramatic leap from being Europe's operatic laggard to being the continental showcase.

Quite a Show

For a few brief moments one night in summer 1997, past and future became fused in an electrifying present. The opening ceremonies of the world athletics championships in Athens may seem like a distant memory now - as modern life imitates the sprinters in moving ever faster - but this was one of those rare events up to the challenge of a written postscript even though, almost by definition, it defies description. If a picture can tell a thousand words, can less than that possibly do justice to such a singular event?

There is something fresh about any opening, carrying promise and anticipation even if you know, like sitting down with the morning newspaper, that a comedown likely will follow. And I search in vain to find any real downsides to the magnificent display choreographed by Vangelis Papathanasiou, despite unpromising omens beforehand. The original tickets were printed for designated seating in the 'real' stadium at Irini, but apparently, printing new tickets for the changed venue was too much trouble. One had to walk miles to get there, only to find waves of sweating bodies pushing and shoving to get up the stairways (of which a grand total of 2 exists; what happens in a panic?) to the cheap seats, which, alas, have not softened with time. And did anyone think that huge plastic colonnade fronting the marble stadium, which looked like a poor excuse for a Tower of Babel when being built, would ever look impressive once finished?

But the show itself hit the right note in every sense: a thoroughly modern spectacle which duly highlighted the wealth of tradition. As a blend of Greek culture with a celebration of athletics and the human spirit, the show was grand without resorting to grandiosities; uplifting without being pompous; respectful of the past without wallowing in it; a celebration of the national spirit without being overtly nationalistic; and universalist without being too dreamy or cloying about it. Even the political speeches were kept to a minimum, which alone made the event a great success. Thanks to a worldwide audience, it even started and finished on time.

I always thought I was immune to the charms of green laser lights, but even these were put to great effect, fanning out across the stadium, occasionally looping around and passing directly by, as if you yourself had been singled out for a split second in the spotlight. Sometimes the lights arched skyward, meeting high above in the night sky like the apex of a huge, open-air Gothic cathedral. Vangelis himself, waiting in the wings, briefly took centre stage with Montserrat Caballe, presiding like a benevolent patriarch beaming with pleasure at his own creation. And after the physical fireworks followed the metaphorical ones, it seemed fitting that the politicians slinked out in the dark, almost unnoticed. There was even artistic justice in that the *hoi polloi*, in the upper decks, had by far the better view of the moving spectacle projected onto the stadium floor. In all, it demonstrated that a creative spirit, touched by inspiration, can produce something quite extraordinary indeed - especially if he has artistic control without a thousand meddling hands.

I admit to wondering, however, if Vangelis's production was not *too* grand - especially in light of two other noticeable, and seemingly contradictory, elements about the Games that followed. On one hand, is it possible that we have gone too far in celebrating those who run faster and jump higher? Undoubtedly, there is something poetically simple, or simply poetic, about seeing great athletes at their very best. Participant sports are surely beneficial; my own experiences have left many good memories, if also a permanent aversion to chlorinated swimming-pools. And if this event gives a boost to Greek athletics, it is surely for the good. But when we devote huge sums and time and energy to stage such professional events, other things get short-changed, like creating more permanent green spaces in Athens. Who among us has ever attended a laser show for a book publication, or seen a stadium full of people cheering on scientists in search of a vaccine? Perhaps it is in the nature of truly great accomplishments to be out of sight, just as our greatest revelations often come at our quietest moments.

The second, reverse thought is that the athletics championships were, for a time, curiously short-changed. The IOC president, Mr Samaranch, paired them with the Olympics and World Cup football as the world's premier sporting events (though who could possibly omit Wimbledon?), but low attendance at events where Greeks were not likely to win medals gained Greece few kudos. Furthermore, official Greece, and much of the media, often did the entire event a great injustice by speaking of it as if it were some sort of warm-up or dress rehearsal for the 2004 Olympics, and a means by which to get them. Such an attitude is both presumptuous and illogical. To say that these Games, with 2000 athletes staying in local hotels and performing in a single stadium, were a pre-Olympics is like running the 1500 metres and pronouncing yourself fit for a marathon. The Olympics, requiring venues for dozens of sports, are ten times as large and are on a completely different level. It reminds me of the old saying about life itself - 'something that happens to you when you are planning for something else'. This was Greece's biggest sporting event in a century, not a side-show; fortunately, this reality eventually did dawn on the local scene.

Lawrence Durrell and
Greece's 'Spirit of Place'

A long with summer comes the search for a good beach and a pleasant after-swim read. Might I recommend something from Lawrence Durrell, one of modern Greece's greatest literary publicists and door-opener to Greek life for myself and many others in the Anglo-Saxon world? Apart from his works themselves, Gordon Bowker's recent biography (*Through The Dark Labyrinth*, St. Martin's Press, 1997) has provided a life history to complement the poetic prose.

Durrell (1912-1990) was a one-of-a-kind character and an evocative purveyor of what he called 'spirit of place', the idea that culture closely reflects geography and location. Born in imperial India of British-Irish parentage, he was immediately cast into the unsettled role of foreign resident which he was to repeat in numerous locales throughout his life. He seems to us almost stateless, footloose even if not fancy-free, more closely associated with Greece and France than with the England he often despised and sporadically visited.

A master of the written word (novel cycles down to prolific letter-writing), he was truly an all-round artist: an accomplished abstract painter (under a pseudonym), jazz pianist, and not least, raconteur. Bowker's nonstop recounting indeed suggests more like nine lives lived rather than merely one - appropriately for a subject who, in his youth, bore a faint feline resemblance.

To call Durrell a Philhelline would do scant justice to his near life-long association with this country. He did as much as any single foreigner to promote Greece abroad through his writings and actions (e.g., promoting the return of the Elgin, or Parthenon, Marbles before it became fashionable), even if his attitude sometimes betrayed an element of paternalism. His appreciation of the people - both everyday and the literary elite - the landscape, and the mythologies shine through his triumvirate of single-island Greek travel books. *Prospero's Cell*, set in 1930s Corfu, was his most untroubled and lyrical rendition of an island idyll. *Reflections on a Marine Venus* was a paean to beautiful Rhodes in its difficult postwar recovery. And the celebrated *Bitter Lemons* documented the political strife in 1950s Cyprus that eventually drove him from his own home, just as he was forced by war from his Corfiot house in 1939. Indeed, for Durrell, Greece's tragic modern history and its beauty were closely interwoven, which lent his island studies increasing depth and pathos. Yet he kept returning, as late as the 1980s, as the perambulatory eccentric around Corfu in his camper-van.

His travel writings alone - which include the delightful *Spirit of Place* and *The Greek Islands* - merit a fair literary reputation; but Durrell's voluminous oeuvre attests to a Vesuvian mind's lava flow of ideas and imagery. He regarded himself primarily as a poet (13 collections published), though his main impact was via the novel, starting with *The Black Book* in the 1930s, endorsed by T.S. Eliot but long banned in Britain. His reputation was sealed with *The Alexandria Quartet*, set in the murky wartime atmosphere of Cavafy's city, and later, *The Avignon Quintet*. To be sure, he is not universally hailed as a classic fiction writer. His circuitous plot lines, dreamy characterisations and linguistic somersaults have been called deceptive or worse; and they can make for difficult and abstract reading. His frustrations over being denied the Nobel Prize for literature were evident in his voluminous correspondence with a close friend, American writer Henry Miller.

With Durrell, there is a tight connection between art and artist. By all accounts, his outsized personality (accentuated further by his diminutive stature), his magisterial command of English, and an effervescent physical presence captivated those around him, including literary comrades-in-arms like Miller and Patrick Leigh Fermor. The downside of living the artist's life, however, was the need to 'get inside' his novels, sometimes to the brink of madness, often provoking his multiple wives, countless lovers and, not least, his daughter Sappho, who eventually committed suicide. Durrell's exuberant exterior apparently masked a deep melancholy and a never-ceasing internal struggle with his own demons; indeed he purposefully harnessed this struggle to drive himself to greater creative heights, or depths.

The description 'troubled genius' obviously lends itself to such an overflowing talent; and his later dabblings into yoga and Buddhism indicate continuing efforts to achieve some measure of peace.

Though opinion is divided about his ultimate literary merits, Durrell's travel works are always engaging, while his fiction challenges the reader's thoughts, values, and moral certitudes. And his vivid sense of living what he saw as the liberating Greek spirit makes this a particularly apt place in which to explore the fruits of this uniquely fertile literary mind.

In summer 1996, on a personal pilgrimage to his cherished Rhodian home, the Villa Cleobolus, I was saddened to find a shuttered and neglected little house and environs. For such a *homo universalis* as Durrell, it is a rich irony that matters of nationalism (the house is set in a picturesque old Turkish graveyard) stand in the way of providing a more fitting shrine to such a vivid exponent of Greek life, and such an effective channel between Greece and the wider world. Let us hope that someone soon wakes up to the need.

Patrick Leigh Fermor, Philhellene Extraordinaire

Here is a human subject who has left such an indelible mark on modern Greece and its literary scene that I almost cower at the prospect of tackling it in such a limited space. Juxtaposed next to a sketch of Lawrence Durrell, this piece on Patrick Leigh Fermor might otherwise seem as the second summery, if not summary, book-end. Born just three years apart (Durrell 1912, Fermor 1915), both came to Greece in the 1930s in youthful idealism as expatriot British writers (both also mixed Irish). Each was caught up in great political struggles, Fermor in wartime Crete, Durrell in tumultuous late-1950s Cyprus; both have been peerless documenters of the unusual and remote. But there the similarities end.

Fermor remains a standard bearer of 20th century Philhellenism and amongst the most knowledgeable foreigners of Greek and Balkan customs. Through him we meet local peoples on their own terms, without cultural blinders or haughty preconceptions. Unlike Durrell, who left in some bitterness for Provence and returned sporadically, Fermor settled here to write, in a house he designed in Mani, and is still at it in his early 80s. Whereas Durrell chronicled far-flung island idylls, Fermor has covered the mainland in his inimitable style. His Greek companion volumes *Mani* and *Roumeli* together unearth countless customs, dialects and local histories of, respectively, the southern Peloponnese and northern Greece way off the beaten track, almost before there was a beaten track. Durrell's *Bitter Lemons* describes Greek-Cypriots' astonishment one evening at hearing Fermor, an accomplished linguist, break into obscure Greek folk-songs long committed to memory. Yet his brief volume *A Time to Keep Silence* also betrays a quieter side, evoking the curious monastic life.

Arguably his real masterwork is found in a still-ongoing trilogy. *A Time of Gifts* (Penguin: 1977) chronicles the first, exuberant stage of his foot-journey as an eighteen-year-old in 1933, the year of Hitler, from Rotterdam to Constantinople, the narrative ending, symbolically, mid-stream in the Danube between Slovakia and Hungary. The book almost breathes with the exhilaration of the footloose youth craving adventure, yet enriched by an elapsed half-century of learning. His description reflects my own giddiness upon first setting foot in Europe as a postcollegiate backpacker - the only two nights running I have ever spent totally without sleep for sheer excitement - "I wandered about the silent lanes in exultation...I could scarcely believe that I was really there...with a thousand wonders waiting" (pp. 34-5). It takes a special writer to say things we normally only feel or think.

The second volume, *Between the Woods and the Water* (Penguin: 1986), takes us through Hungary and Rumania, from the Austro-Hungarian to the Balkan/Ottoman world. Its rich tapestry of local colours, clannish feuds and histories exceeds even the first, perhaps because his stays were longer, which more than compensates for the slight loss of the 'edge' of the journey's newness. Surely few books (questionably) categorised under the 'travel' genre have been so eagerly awaited as his concluding volume and entry into Constantinople (Istanbul) itself.

Fermor's style is exceptionally authoritative, dense, rich; you feel in the presence of someone for whom the English language is a powerful yet pliable tool, like a master potter with wet clay. It avoids the poetic, quixotic flights of fancy Durrell sometimes indulged in; nor is it easy reading. It exudes other, stoical qualities of careful craftsmanship - deliberate, terse, unyielding, disciplined, scholarly. Scarcely a word is wasted or misplaced. To me his rendering of the past reads almost like an alternative history, an immensely more interesting version of ostensibly the same world (especially its obscure medieval times) than anything we studied formally. But while his books document personal journeys, they refuse to slide into autobiographical sentimentality. Sometimes you find yourself wanting more of the person - the spirit and doubts along with the exuberance - even as you respect his authorial detachment and, perhaps, modesty. Possibly this combined participant/observer style reflects a stability in his personal life that Durrell's lacked (less need to explore the psyche in print); his commitment to the stabilising force of longterm friendship (the European books are prefaced by letters to a deceased friend, Xan Fielding) is evident too.

Fermor seems bequeathed from another, more heroic era: a true scholar-adventurer who put his life on the line in - and for - Greece. During the war he lived among the *andartes* in the forbidding Cretan mountains, disguised as a shepherd (!), plotting the abduction of the local German commander, Karl Kreipe, thrillingly described in *Ill Met by Moonlight* by his fellow commando, Stanley Moss. We can only imagine the excruciating dilemmas and dangers involved for Britons posing as both Greeks and German officers, and for the Greek Resistance they were seconded to. Twenty years ago Kreipe and Fermor were reunited in a Greek television documentary, in a remarkable display of postwar reconciliation. In 1998 Penguin has published a new edition of George Psychoundakis's *The Cretan Runner* (original edition by John Murray, 1955), a uniquely first-person, ground-level account by a member of the Greek Resistance - translated (back in 1952) and introduced by Fermor.

Painstakingly, Patrick Leigh Fermor has created an unsurpassed oeuvre of Balkan and Greek history and personal adventure through an unconventional approach suitably reflecting a unique talent and extraordinary life. And there's more to come.

CHAPTER FOUR

Public Greek, Private Greek

The Colours of Grey

For the everyday Greek - stereotyping wildly yet again - the contrast between private and public life is razor-sharp. A nation of individuals, of colourful personalities that exude a zest for life until remarkably advanced years, somehow loses its shine and becomes dull in the workaday world of public life. Where else could there be such an astonishing contrast between a countryside of brilliant colours, of atmospheric clarity and timeless beauty, and an urban public façade that seems determined to define itself, above all, by its lack of colour?

The vivacity of the individual Greek seems to evaporate when it comes to public existence. The (in)famously grey walls of public office buildings, with their external shutters painted in grey, trying to keep out the grey-tinged *nefos* (pollution cloud), lined inside with endless metallic grey bookshelves and oversized grey desks where grey people dressed (yes) in grey, poring over stacks of grey folders - obviously utilising a huge oversupply of paint from the Greek navy - creates, from 8 until 2 weekdays, nameless, faceless bureaucrats. Often the very same person doubles as the voluble fellow at the corner taverna who dishes out souvlaki with such relish until well past midnight.

The irony is compounded when considering that these civil service positions - boring routines though many must surely be - traditionally have been so sought after by clever citizens seeking regular, predictable work for themselves or their offspring. Political party loyalty may be partly a question of ideological affiliation, but here it is no less a matter of jobs for the boys and girls.

Much of this official, public greyness is traceable (apart from a lack of motivation to make these ever-present public offices spicier and more pleasant places to be in) to a much broader fear, shared by many, of being demonstrative in front of strangers. In private, of course, Greeks can be as warm and generous as any people in the world, but displays of personality in public are often interpreted as a sign of vulnerability and even weakness, a damaging assessment indeed for a society in which power is so revered. One dare not let his guard down in public, lest someone else try to take advantage. Perhaps there is a touch of superstition lurking somewhere; relax now, and disaster is sure to follow.

A similar pattern seems to hold true for fashion. With the notable exception of aspiring female models under 25, daytime wear tends toward the unexpressive or, more rarely, excessively fashionable - usually in black. Greece looks like a nation of perpetual mourners, to judge from the prevailing choice of colour. This goes double for the poor foot: scan any shoestore window and your eyes will be deluged with a riot of colours, ranging all the way from black to dark brown. Walk around downtown Athens in blazing mid-summer, and still you will almost never see a native caught out in a pair of shorts (never mind a hat), both considered hopelessly frivolous in a city centre; you can see more shorts in Los Angeles in January than here in July. Hence the startling contrast to evening wear; in the protective environs of a friend's home, the nightclub, the restaurant, few put more care into their dress, into being presentable, than Greeks.

Yet another element here is a need for control, of oneself. Perhaps due to an innate volatility bubbling below the surface, and to a society at large conspicuously lacking any sense of order, decorum must be maintained as a sort of body armour against unwarranted attacks from what lies outside, but perhaps also to protect oneself from losing control in front of others. A society that has produced a tradition of often withering cynicism has also created a body of citizens that fears such cynicism, or any criticism, directed against themselves. Zorba notwithstanding, Greeks can be acutely self-conscious and fearful of making a mis-step, thus opening themselves up unnecessarily to possible ridicule.

Even if it were possible, it would be a shame to iron out the differences - to trade away the delightfully uninhibited, off-hours individual behaviour for more user-friendly, relaxed, trusting attitudes in public services. There are times, however, when that elusive happy medium - a pleasing shade of grey rather than an odd mixture of black-and-white - would be a welcome trade-off.

A Question of Trust

Once, standing in one of those endless bank queues, I found myself in front of a matronly, middle-aged woman who kept nudging me forward with ample breasts, muttering πω-πω-πω (a common expression of impatience or anxiety) as we shuffled along. She became increasingly anxious and short of breath; eventually she had to sit down while I held her place. This woman seemed genuinely afraid of being prevented from making her transaction (a simple withdrawal, as it happened) - despite only being there to collect some of her own money. Afterwards she walked off quite relieved, the morning's operation completed without any major calamities.

Sheer boredom during this wait led my thoughts, of all places, to J.J. Rousseau, who published *The Social Contract* in 1762. His idea of a civil society involved an unwritten contract, creating a positive bond of public trust between individual and society, via freely chosen social obligations. Regarding the woman, her reaction seemed reflective of a less focused, floating anxiety about dealing successfully with Official Greece. Rousseau's all-important public bond - involving some faith in the system at large, based on elements like regularity, routine, and fulfilled expectations - was, here, somehow fractured.

Though public trust is an increasingly problematic issue in societies everywhere (as underlined recently in a thoughtful book, *Trust*, by Francis Fukuyama), established with difficulty yet easily broken, it is an especially complex matter in the Greek context. For such an open-hearted people, trust comes naturally; but unfortunately, so do hurt and feelings of betrayal. Outsiders often point to Mediterranean family bonds providing the rock of stability on which such trust is built. However, its antithesis is the eruption of stubborn and sometimes bitter family feuds - years-long, intra-family splits, not merely the clannish rivalries traditionally marking places like Crete and Mani. A nation that so values pride does not easily make for ready apologies, or even for concessions that another's argument may, in fact, have some merit.

At societal level, this trusting instinct is suppressed or even reversed, to the point where the individual's response to external stimuli is frequently one of active distrust and narrow-eyed wariness. What do they think of me? What did he mean by that? How can I protect myself? It can result in a tendency to read a great deal into mere opinions or statements, leading to fanciful reinterpretations of such statements as full of innuendo and hidden meaning, no matter how far such interpretations may be from what was intended. It can also produce some pretty creative arguments concerning the machinations of others - be they plotting foreign governments or scheming neighbours.

Another element, damaging if understandable, is a tendency for official pronouncements to be actively doubted, discounted, or even dismissed. All this reflects a chronic mistrust of what is said in the public discourse; that discourse itself combines, oddly, dead-seriousness (news broadcasts at all hours, endless talk-shows, agitated café-chat), which the public thrives on, yet leaving a sense that it is all a sort of ongoing public game. But while expressed scepticism about what public officials say is undoubtedly a sign of a healthy, functioning democracy, it can easily be carried too far into the realm of pervasive cynicism.

Much of this implies under-reaction by people to what governments may say - assuming that whatever the rules may be, they likely will be changed soon anyway - though it can also lead to overreaction. A decade ago, when Chernobyl blew its top in the Ukraine, there was an immediate run on the supermarkets here. Why did this occur in Greece but not in northern Europe, where prevailing winds created a much more urgent problem of nuclear fallout? Was it merely the reaction of an emotional people, or did a socialised sense of unease about what people were being told also play a part? When reasoned scepticism becomes knee-jerk doubt, it is not that much further to a conviction, Orwell-like, that the truth is precisely the opposite.

Trust, credibility, and the truth itself are precious commodities, too valuable to dissolve away in chronically suspended belief. Their establishment, or re-establishment, requires a painstaking, all-round, continual effort - here in the cradle of democracy no less than anywhere else.

The Void in the (Greek) Middle

Recently I had occasion to spend two pleasant hours with a Greek businessman, a manager, amongst delightful outdoor, late-December surroundings that one finds only in Greece. What transpired was most remarkable.

For the first hour he was, well, businesslike: cagey, practical, taciturn, even stern. Once, though, he discovered my professional standing as a (struggling) writer and (once and future) university lecturer, this model of corporate rectitude opened up like the skies after a summer storm: the hands quickened and eyes sparkled; the talk became more voluble and animated; even his physical countenance seemed to expand. Right before my eyes, an accountant metamorphosed into a scholar and philosopher. The moth had become a butterfly.

I gradually realised that what I was seeing, against that extraordinary sunset, was two Greeks in one, or rather, two sides of the single, complex Greek character. Here was a man, unveiling the duality of the Greek persona; here indeed was Greece itself. Here also perhaps lay an answer to the riddle that has long puzzled outsiders: why is the Greek so capable, yet modern Greek society so wanting?

This sharp duality juxtaposes the two extremes of particularism and universality. Part of the Greek genius lies in championing both, often simultaneously. At one (individual) end lies the ultimate pragmatist. Greeks often make superb businessmen because of an extraordinary adaptability to changing circumstances, an ability to maximise opportunities and even turn liabilities to their advantage. This goes double for risky, entrepreneurial enterprises, like restaurants and (on a grander scale) shipping, in markets that can turn at the drop of a hat or a spike in the world oil price - concerns that put a premium on nimble-footed ability to shift with the winds.

At the other end, or rather extreme, lies the Greek of Η μεγάλη ιδέα (the Big Idea), with a periodic tendency to generate national issues and push them skyward in a crescendo of unity and abstract idealism. This tendency has produced notable national reference-points - the war of independence, the Asia Minor campaign, the Resistance, the anti-junta reaction, Cyprus, the 'Macedonia is Greek' issue, the Parthenon Marbles, the Olympic bids of the 1980s and 1990s. Each case, however resolved, has seemed less a cause than a crusade, trending into a firm moral certitude that can seem to outsiders like an exasperating combination of over-emotionalism and stubbornness. Consequently, few countries have known such national highs, and lows.

But what of my mock-sociological analysis? This quirky divergence between individual pragmatism and national idealism, between practice and theory, has innumerable and profoundly far-reaching effects on Greece's public life. Over-emphasis on the one leads to chronic underperformance of Greece's capabilities; over-emphasis on the other leads to overreaching and, ultimately, disappointment. Arguably the essential problem of Greece today is neglect of what lies between, the malfunctioning centre, the void of the title: which could be realigned by fruitful societal discourse that draws the two extremes closer together.

One result is a curious responsibility gap. Individually, many Greeks tend toward a certainty (sometimes well-founded) in their own opinions as solutions for others as well, whether from the intruding relative, the back-seat direction-giver, or the coach-driver who forces his awful music down his riders' throats, or rather ears. Yet at public level, especially in the civil service, one sometimes encounters an avoidance of responsibility; hence the endless paper-shuffling, futile recycling of issues and cases, and faulty natural disaster-relief efforts.

This unresolved gap has a corrosive effect in Greek public affairs, and hinders efforts to lay the building blocks of modern Western society - a healthy, realistic sense of nationalism, civic pride, a pragmatic publicspiritedness. The country will lag so long as 'Greece' remains an abstract ideal, lauded in theory yet often, as a semi-functioning state, loathed in practice. The task of bringing about a happier medium must be approached from both ends: in governmental overhaul of public institutions making them honest, decent, and accountable, and an equally earnest change in attitude from below. Harder than a stroll in the countryside, but cynicism and lassitude will get you nowhere.

The Power Game

Could it be that Niccolo Machiavelli, the Renaissance-era diplomat and writer who advised political leaders to use ambiguities to their own political advantage, was actually Greek rather than Florentine? The question may be only hypothetical, but surely there are few societies in which the question of where one stands in the personal and professional pecking-order - power being strictly a relative term - is a matter of such intense interest as here. This is neither praise nor criticism; simply observation.

Greek interest in power issues is not limited to the political world; we could even say that power relationships and struggles are key determinants of how Greek society operates at every level. Further, there are apparent parallels between societal relations and Greece's unusual international position. In both cases, like many of life's riddles, two apparent opposites - empowerment (real or merely imagined) and powerlessness - go hand-in-hand.

Take the second issue first. Imagine, if you can, the strange political legacy of being the dominant power in three major historical periods (Minoan/Classical/Byzantine), only to be subsequently trampled underfoot by a foreign power (the Ottomans) until liberation came your way. Then add in all the modernist impulses that passed Greece by (Renaissance, Enlightenment, Industrial Revolution), and you have the makings of a country that combines a legacy of unrivalled historical influence with a modern reality of being internationally marginalised.

Another complication is that Greece combines regional weakness, as a lagging EU economy, with a sub-regional (Balkan) position of great influence. Balkan gunslinger thus merges with Europe's 98-pound weakling. If elements of an inferiority complex arose, it would not be surprising; indeed, given the harsh hand of history, one might expect more of a split personality than is the case already. Thus any criticism of Greece's foreign policymakers should be prefaced by some appreciation of the inherent difficulties of continually trying to balance these opposites.

Just as foreign policy positions are meant to reflect national values, so too does this international paradox find parallels in domestic society. Within Greece, there is a striking imbalance of power at all levels. Despite major and needed strides toward gender equality, many families still favour the male offspring over the female, and the first child over the others. Greek boys are often shamelessly pampered, doubly so if they are single children, which can lead to a certain feeling of innate privilege, a sense of male arrogance and exaggerated sense of belief in one's cleverness, ingenuity, and prowess.

Outside the family, institutional power is rarely distributed evenly. While organisations everywhere are top-heavy in terms of decision-making authority yet bottom-heavy in terms of personnel, in Greece the imbalance seems greater. Despite a tradition of proud individualism, there is a marked tendency toward fatalistic acceptance of a sort of invisible, organisational caste system that can make a mockery of myths of participatory democracy. Greece may no longer have formal titles and nobilities, but this absence merely reinforces the importance of other status signs, such as visible displays of wealth and education.

The translation of these elements into influence over others can become almost an end in itself. One frequent result is a marked inversion of talent, notably in officialdom, which sometimes verges on a sort of arrogance of mediocrity, an unofficial 'mediocracy' sustained by clientelistic traditions as impermeable as they are increasingly indefensible in modern society. Faced with such chronic organisational constipation, industrous and bright individuals are forced into a familiar game: cultivate your contacts, don't share information, promote yourself to those who matter. 'Looking out for number one' too often becomes 'don't let the other guy get ahead'. Paralysis of initiative and a tendency to pass the buck naturally also follow, along with a fear of committing one's own name in writing. Needless to say, upward mobility, meritocratic advancement and collective morale all suffer in such an environment.

One familiar, unsavoury and sometimes petty way of perpetuating power positions, from which those here on foreign payrolls are blissfully protected, is delayed payment for services rendered, even by employees, and sometimes for many months. Aside from creating useless uncertainty and anxiety in working relationships, such practices perpetuate a power imbalance between payer and payee; control over the account-books becomes control over people. In the universities, exploitation of graduate student talent is at least as rampant as in other countries. Even in the private sector, notions of middle management are still poorly developed here. Top-down organizational pyramids are still the norm.

The system does have its uses. With authority concentrated in so few hands, conducting business becomes much simpler - provided, crucially, that you are similarly well situated. Someone with sufficient access can simply go to the top for an answer, without being put off by self-important underlings or busybody secretaries.

Getting ahead in this environment requires vocal, sometimes obnoxious, assertion of one's rights, because more subtle methods go unappreciated and even unnoticed. Personal qualities like modesty and flexibility are often derided and considered undeserving of respect. But until there is broader recognition that there is nothing wrong in being occasionally less than strong, that vulnerability is a natural human trait rather than a shameful weakness, then something will remain out of balance.

The World of the Greek Student

Not long ago, several students prevailed upon me to describe the experience of college-level teaching here. Maybe they were motivated by seeing their names in print; but it's better to avoid showing favoritism or exposing my appalling inability to remember names. First names are hard enough; last names (especially 14-syllable Greek ones) you can forget about, as I usually do. But when you teach four Marias, all talented, this poses a slight problem.

Though similar in age, students here differ widely in background, interests and abilities; this makes it difficult, sometimes touchy, and often plain wrong to generalise. Yet they do emerge from the same basic educational system and thus reveal its characteristics. In this respect they are a microcosm - and a rather special one - of Greek society itself.

Greece's schooling system is a hybrid of public and private. Contrary to popular belief, public schools are not always on strike. Even so, shortage of funds to fix decaying classrooms, along with vaulting parental ambitions, create a thriving market in private schools and *frontisteria* ('cramming schools') on every street corner. Parents pay small fortunes to educate their offspring, or at least to maximise the number of those diplomas from odd-sounding institutions that decorate every office wall here. Greek families with barely literate grandparents and grade school-educated parents produce Harvard, Sorbonne, and Oxford graduates with amazing frequency. Despite the seemingly perennial crisis in higher education (and not only here; remember the 1998 German student demonstrations), something is quite obviously going right. Greece indeed takes education policy seriously, which means, of course, constant tinkering; what other country could transfer a Defense minister (Gerasimos Arsenis) to Education, and call it a promotion without evoking general laughter?

The students I am privileged to teach (and frequently taught by) come with plenty of depth; reasonable background in basic subjects; variable and sometimes amusing grasp of English; a refreshing way of cutting through nonsense; a diplomatic tendency to laugh at my feeble jokes;

and an impetuous inability to sit still and listen for an hour. If these aspects make them both more and less mature than, say, British or American students, this merely reflects the Greek character's contradictory nature - without its occasional cynicism - in younger faces. They do come with preconceptions about Greek and world affairs, but are less politically predisposed either way than you might expect. They (at least those generous, or bored, enough to read my newspaper column) are also among its best critics; a few even agree with me.

They take a wide range of courses - marketing, literature, psychology - proof that not everyone is browbeaten by overambitious parents into becoming doctors or lawyers. The challenge is to motivate those not, initially, interested in your subject. The mental light-bulb can click on slowly or suddenly, or never; but the sight (however rare) of widening student eyes - giving the term 'dilated pupils' new meaning - makes even professional setbacks and puny pay levels seem worthwhile. Many have a suppressed hunger to learn, because of (or despite) the same experiences most of us suffered; pompous schoolteachers demanding fact-memorisation rather than independent thinking or originality. The only, if difficult, remedy is to come not just as answer-provider but as question-poser, especially since few of us, as the state of the world readily indicates, have cornered the market on Truth. Admittedly the available role-models, both ancient (Socrates) and modern (G.B. Shaw's *Pygmalion*; Robin Williams's splendid *Dead Poets Society* character) are tough acts to follow.

Naturally, there are downsides. The worst is a tendency toward acceptance of cheating. Is this opportunism? Lack of scruples? Intense pressures (societal, parental, peer) to succeed? Few things are so depressing as being told 'it's the Greek way'. Must it be? Cracking down requires a hard-fist approach that feels alien; we're supposed to stretch minds, not bash heads. I try telling myself a different set of cultural values is at work (and in an age when entire PhDs can be plagiarised over the Internet, maybe it's not worth the worry); but it still disturbs.

Education is universal, yet the individual case - single lives in the making, like unfinished works of art, if only they could believe it - is paramount. There are inevitable cross-cutting interests: me in getting them to think and learn, them to pass with good grades and minimal hassle. Wherever these paths cross, sparks can fly, and minds can open.

'Thinkers of the Hellenic World, Unite!'

The provocative thinker and writer, Ayn Rand, once published a gargantuan novel called *Atlas Shrugged*, in which society's cultural and intellectual elite downed tools, as it were, in order to make a statement, with huge societal consequences. The late Ms Rand was not everybody's cup of tea (she also wrote a book called *The Virtue of Selfishness*), but her mid-century philosophical movement, Objectivism, did gain quite a following in the West, especially the U.S. And her premise that individual thinkers form the basis of all that is crucial for society's functioning was certainly different.

What would happen if Greece's most educated people decided to quit work for awhile: downing pens, shutting off computers and boycotting Internet servers? After all, everybody else strikes here: pensioners, students, teachers, farmers, administrators, you name it, they have all clogged their full share of Syntagma traffic. All are out to protect vested interests, and their impact reflects how strong those interests are. But just imagine the spectacle of black-robed, mortarboard-wearing, diploma-wielding folk marching on Parliament, shouting lines from Aristotle and toting copies of Plato's *Republic*. Academic ceremonies can be pretentious non-events at the best of times, and one conducted in Athenian streets would add a note of sublime comedy as well. It's imaginable only in Greece, yet utterly impossible here. Even if it did happen, the result would be: nothing at all. Life would go on as before, because they have few interests to protect.

Greece as a society may revere education, but it is sometimes less than charitable toward its educated own. Here I am not speaking of the intellectual pantheon of the august Athens Academy, but the professional class. Those at the top frequently do have advanced degrees: strikingly, today's two main politicians, Costas Simitis and New Democracy leader Constantine Karamanlis, both hold earned PhDs, as did Simitis's predecessor as Prime Minister, Andreas Papandreou, a distinguished economist. But they are exceptions who made their way through political party hierarchies. Several conversations with multiple-degreed Greeks, returning after time abroad, have reinforced my belief that theirs is an unfortunate lot. One friend estimates about 50,000 people with advanced (primarily foreign) degrees floating around Athens, feeling isolated, searching for something useful to do, scratching a living somehow or other.

The problem is that collective Greece cannot absorb and utilise so many talented individuals. These underemployed thousands have much to offer: not only degrees but contacts, language skills, exposure to other cultures and ways of doing things, and a rounded perspective on Greece in relation to the outer world. Yet Greek society is structured in ways that not only fail to incorporate this incoming talent but can actively deny it a proper role.

This situation has partly, but not wholly, to do with the fact that Greece is not a meritocracy, though it is also true that degrees alone do not create merit. Sometimes education even brings certain less desirable traits: inapplicable skills, overqualified people with an attitude, that sort of thing. A PhD means little in itself (please believe me on that one). Nonetheless this huge pool of semi-employed, struggling, educated people is a fabulous national asset that is being overlooked by a system that either cannot or (worse) often will not accommodate them. The universities are too few, and advancement within them is too loosely based on teaching and publications, while think tanks and institutes are often closed-shops serving purposes other than research or public policy needs.

So rather than Greece opening up to this, its own great national asset, the asset has to break itself down like a conglomerate business being sold off, its individual components offering up its services on an individual basis, hat in hand. People returning from abroad have to adjust to the Byzantine ways of organisations here, reestablish lost contacts, and try to break into a system they temporarily left to test other pastures. They must wonder sometimes about the effort and sacrifices they have made. It is, of course, a great testament to the ultimate lure of Greece for its own people that they would return. But equally, it is to the country's own detriment that more is not being done to incorporate its returnees and maximise their offerings.

At present, there seems to be no collective agency, public or private, for helping returnees get reestablished and reconnected. Family

ties, or anodyne social networks like associations of university graduates, simply cannot fill this vital function. There are few job-finding
agencies or other registries that can match qualified, skilled people
with available work, although the demand side is equally opaque.
Establishing them, of course, needs thought, foresight, and organisation, and no, it is not impossible here. It might even make someone
an interesting new profession. But almost anything seems preferable
to a situation where people with master's degrees and doctorates
work as glorified part-time secretaries. For Greece to realise more of
its great potential, it really must collectively learn to learn from its
learned.

Gearing Towards EMU

The Simitis government's decision, in March 1998, to seize the day and enter the drachma into the EU's Exchange Rate Mechanism (ERM) was arguably Greece's most tangible step toward European integration to date and has boosted its overall European standing. Despite expressions of surprise all around, the move itself, if not its precise timing, was surely one of the worst-kept secrets of recent times. The government long has indicated its aim of joining the single currency (euro) as soon as is practicable. Thus ERM entry, while fulfilling a longstanding policy goal, remains but a stepping-stone to EMU membership by 2001, for which two years of managed currency stability is a prerequisite.

Momentous as the move itself was, its significance derives largely from what it indicates in terms of both past performance and likely future policy direction. That it happened at all speaks to the Simitis government's substantial recent progress in inflation and deficit reduction, and to outside (EU) recognition that the direction remains positive. As late as 1997 such a move would have been unthinkable, not just improbable. Nonetheless, it is but a preview of much sterner, deeper-reaching measures to reform the public sector which, if realised, will reshape the entire face of the Greek economy and even partly its political life. That prospect is the government's unique opportunity, its challenge and its danger.

The decision generated predictable howls of domestic protest. The main opposition leader, New Democracy's leader Costas Karamanlis, criticised the government for not issuing a prior warning, even though that would have caused vastly greater market turmoil - at Greece's direct expense - than actually occurred. And the small leftist parties, traditionally in favour of a weaker currency, immediately lambasted the government for bringing it about. Consistency: ever the elusive virtue. A fairer criticism (apart from troubling reports of leak-related, windfall bank profits just prior to the 13.8% devaluation) is that the government's claims to be pursuing a hard-currency policy while clearly angling for a devaluation were duplicitous. Even so, it is hard to see any viable alternative, especially as the aim was to engineer, and thus control, an inevitable drop, rather than watch the drachma being pummelled yet again in the global marketplace.

The EMU drive has underscored the growing linkages between Greece's domestic economic health and its international standing. But linkages often betray vulnerability, and the very fact that Greece has been an occasional speculative target - even as it develops more sophisticated capital markets - indicates its continuing exposure to doubting Thomases running international hedge funds. Impressive though it was, the Greek market's record-setting advance during 1998 did not fundamentally change this reality.

In the broader EU context, Greece's decision neatly turned some tables. Entering the ERM ahead of Britain (which exited in 1992) and Sweden (which has never joined) signalled the government's intention to throw off Greece's old reputation as Europe's laggard; and it may be that Greece could slip into Euroland ahead of Britain, Sweden, and Denmark. By the same token, the simultaneous decision in Brussels to revalue the Irish punt by 3% - a second currency among the group (including, besides Greece, Spain and Portugal) long denoted the 'poor four' - tells of Ireland's successful liberalisation efforts that Greece has yet to take.

Attention now turns to the ultimately far more significant structural reforms to follow: partial or wholesale selloffs of inefficient state-owned industries and banks, and changes in the social security system. The short- and medium-term costs will be high even if the long-term benefits are great. Thousands of jobs will be threatened, including many now held by people believing themselves unsackable, and the government would do well to begin - now - to consider measures to counteract the higher levels of structural unemployment almost certain to follow. A vivid indication of the Simitis-Papantoniou success in guiding the terms of the debate is the continuing focus on reducing inflation down to 2.5%. But the more difficult, longer-term task will be dealing with the social complications of lost jobs, restive unions and a changing national economic, not just monetary, climate. Monetary and labour market policies have traditionally been separated, both here and in Europe; but one wonders for how long.

Despite the recent progress, Greece remains hampered by a reputation, dating back to the 1980s, as a taker not a giver, a problem-creator not a problem-solver. The country urgently needs to overcome such lingering doubts if it hopes to be taken as a serious, reliable European partner for the long haul. Time is crucial, for the EU has now entered into what is a third major phase since Greece's 1981 entry. After the rapid increases in agricultural supports in the 1980s, and the infrastructure aid for mega-projects in the 1990s, the foreseeable future will bring a much less welcome combination: more member states with equal if not greater claim to structural aid, and a stagnant if not shrinking budgetary pie. A sober realisation that the free ride is over should provide impetus for deeper reforms on the home and diplomatic fronts that can only help Greece's case in the future. Replacing the old vicious circle with a virtuous one would also help prevent, in a future crisis, an EU response along the lines of 'there go the Greeks again'.

Make no mistake: the effort to clean up the public sector mess at home will not be painless. Plenty of Greek beneficiaries of the cosy clientelistic system will have to be dragged kicking and screaming toward more equitable prosperity. If you thought the political blast over ERM was loud, I'd suggest purchasing a good pair of earplugs for the next round. And consider buying Greek; imported ones may have risen a bit in price recently.

Inner Landscapes

After watching the most recent film version of Leo Tolstoy's *Anna Karenina* - a great novel reduced to 104 celluloid minutes - I began reading up on the author, arguably Russia's greatest writer. In his later life, he was described as a gnostic: one who believed that the world operates according to underlying, fundamental principles, unknown except to an enlightened few. Rightly convinced of his deep insight into human nature, Count Tolstoy felt that he, on his vast estate, was one of the chosen few with the wisdom to see, and that his vision was equally relevant to others.

Whether you know your Levin from Lenin, perhaps you might see a Greek connection here too, gnostic-like. Gnosticism, in fact, has Greek roots, deriving from a fusion of early Christian and neo-Platonic thought. Many in Greece today subscribe to a modern gnosticism: a belief that what happens in the world, and in (or to) Greece, is not chance but part of a much larger plan which they cannot control but at least have got all figured out, as a sort of consolation prize. Some of these people, for whom opinion and reality tend to merge, drive Athenian taxis; others write for the tabloid press; still others spout their world-view on talk-shows.

The common thread is a conviction that hidden explanations lie behind, and link, every event, and that a sort of parallel reality separates surface developments from what 'really' is happening, below. This implies that the randomness all around us is merely apparent, a semi-façade obscuring a reality that is both tidier and more underhanded. In foreign policy this 'reality' is often expressed in two parts, first, that 'outside forces' effectively control Greece's destiny, and second, that these forces are frequently or even inherently hostile to Greek interests, however defined.

This phenomenon is too frequently observed by visitors to dismiss as opinionated individualism. Thus it is important for outsiders and Greeks alike to comprehend its origins and implications; only then might more mutual understanding, free of the usual two-way biases, begin to emerge. It is perfectly understandable that many in Greece think this way, for several reasons. One is the country's limited size and influence, and the natural tendency for small states to feel more exposed than larger or less sensitively located countries. A second factor is a history of outright domination (the Ottomans) followed by decades of being pushed around the geopolitical chessboard. Many Greeks felt led on, and let down, in the 1922 Asia Minor catastrophe, intruded on by the West in the civil war (1946-49), and manipulated during the junta years (1967-74) and over Cyprus ever since. Layered history gets interpreted as layered tragedy, largely at others' hands.

A third influence could stem from the ancient mythology. The Olympian deities orchestrated events down below, but the gods themselves were fallible - prone to mistakes, pettiness, greed, and vindictiveness as well as great deeds of magnanimity. Perhaps the attributed modern equivalent - grand-plotting but petty-minded, intrusive foreign interests - sustains the belief that Greek affairs are similarly outer-directed, and the country's fate largely out of the hands of its own titular leadership.

But here is a flawed transposition of logic. Whereas the gods constantly fought amongst themselves, there is a tenacious belief here that the West - implying some combination of British, German, American, French and possibly Israeli governments, in cahoots with the EU and NATO, coupled with impersonal demons like global capital - aims to undermine Greece or its region; in its crudest form, this is expressed as a plan to 'carve up' Greece amongst themselves or their friends. Such views are reinforced when they see Greece's main source of concern, Turkey, constantly taking liberties with little rebuke, often interpreted as free licence, from the West.

Even so, when confronted with such opinions I am tempted to say: 'Relax!' It is questionable whether 19th century geopolitical land-grabbing remains a guiding state principle in a 21st-century world of global technology, while 'the West' encompasses a whole range of different, often contradictory interests. And even if Greece has been treated in offhand fashion, without due respect - i.e. a victim of neglect - this is very different from a deliberate, systematic effort to thwart its interests. Interestingly, few of these same people believe

Greece itself - a single country with a focused sense of national destiny - to be capable of pursuing one line of interest for a lengthy time. Foreigners are united, while we at home are divided; it is a refrain common in Greece but familiar the world over. Furthermore, thanks to its own national virtues and rich legacy, the country benefits from a widespread phenomenon - Philhellenism - which has provided a steady, timeless cultural and intellectual bridge over the often turbulent waters of politics and foreign policy, and gives Greece many friends in high places elsewhere.

Human nature pushes us to seek out the causes of things, and to believe that things do, in fact, have causes, which make sense and can be grasped; this is no less than the basis of all learning. But even an earnest search for causation does not necessarily mean they can be found, or even exist at all. Life itself is a mystery, the root of which we must look for yet, equally, seem destined never to find. Tolstoy's character Levin (modelled on himself) put it exquisitely when mourning his brother's death: 'all my life I have sought the meaning of existence, yet I know I shall never find it. Therefore, what purpose is there in existence itself?' A puzzle indeed.

Human need, along with the modern world's growing complexities, provide ample fuel for 'universalist' theories, of which conspiracy theories are a subset. Universalist theories appeal to the intellect and command our interest; they also provide a cohesive belief-system linking random elements into patterns, helping counteract the frightening prospect of exposure to forces beyond our control or even comprehension. As fact and fiction increasingly intermingle (a recent James Bond villain is a world media-mogul creating incidents between big powers to generate headlines), we naturally seek out alternative explanations. But problems arise when facts are dropped, added or twisted to match the ideas, rather than the reverse. This also leaves little room for complications, extenuating circumstances, cross-pressures or other nuances that can shape overall circumstances that are frequently, maddeningly, resistant to generalisation.

Conspiracy theories are more problematic, because they are not subject to needed rigorous analysis, and can never really be proved or disproved. They can be both vague and all-encompassing, with the detail being extraneous rather than central. They abound in environments where all is not as it seems, where the entire truth will likely never be known, and where rich imaginations encumbered by only a modicum of actual knowledge are filling in the puzzle's missing pieces. Less often recognised is the indirect self-flattery of their adherents, assuming an elevated, but possibly false, sense of superior insight: as Tolstoy-like repositories of valuable knowledge elusive to others, and as seers of patterns where others merely see chaos. Again, Greece is hardly unique here; just listen to Hillary Clinton blame 'right-wing conspirators' for her husband's problems, watch any Oliver Stone film, read Marx or Hitler, see Peter Shaffer suggest that Salieri killed Mozart, or watch Anna Karenina rail against Count Vronsky in her drug-laden final days. The often terrifying randomness of life and death, and the sometimes indeterminate official versions of major events, naturally give rise to alternative explanations. Whether they are correct or not is beside the point; sometimes they might be, but either way, the complexities of the modern world, and modern Greece, provide fertile feeding ground for their proliferation and acceptance. The obvious danger, in drawing on our innate need to clarify the murky, is letting our imaginations get the upper hand against our interpretive faculties: our ears, eyes and minds.

Such thinking has a curious double reflection on Greece itself, which emerges, paradoxically, as both stronger and weaker than circumstances warrant. It indirectly puts Greece on a pedestal - believing that the country is crucial enough to be a target of supposedly coordinated Western efforts to manoeuvre or manipulate events. Yet equally it unfairly diminishes Greece, by implying that the Greek government cannot really act alone, and that Greece is forever at the mercy of powerful forces outside. Either way, Greece emerges as a righteous victim, forever aggrieved, forever on the defensive, usually in the right but incapable of acting upon it because others won't let it. The problem is that Greece may be righteous but, like any country, it has not always been right, or virtuous, or even a victim. Its own political establishment has, at times, let it down in the past - thankfully not the case presently, as patient, rational explanation of Greece's justified interests is finally paying some dividends in the court of world opinion. Indeed there is much solace in the thought that Greece is far from friendless in the problems it currently faces.

Countries, like individuals, frequently have little control over their own destinies, regardless of what proponents of 'empowerment' might say. But there is equal peril in the opposite development, victimisation and its rough corollary, defeatism. Some greater recognition that we all face similar twists and turns from life, rather than artificially dividing the world between perpetrators and victims, might lift the collective thinking out of the mists and toward clearer light.

CHAPTER FIVE

Variations

The Depths of Language

The other day, I kicked myself. Not literally - that's rather difficult while sitting in a hairdresser's chair (getting my hair 'dressed'?) - but figuratively. Getting a haircut brings an unspoken assumption of conversation, and 'doing it' in Greek (I mean conversing) is of course more challenging for non-natives whose command of the language is less than pristine. At one point I reached that inevitable stage where I could not say exactly, or even approximately, what I wanted to, so I simply closed the subject off with something tangentially related and which probably made me sound like an illiterate fool. Talk about descending into second childhood.

To many, language is the defining characteristic of nationality, and the master-key for unlocking the mysteries of that nation. Unless you learn Greek, we are told, you'll never fit in, you'll be hopelessly at the mercy of a voracious bureaucracy or greedy hoteliers or whatever, you'll stick out like a sore thumb, you'll forever be an outsider. Even so, I have several problems with the often-propagated, well-meaning dictum to non-Greeks: you'll never fit in unless and until you learn the language, along with its presumed corollary: you will once you do.

There is no disputing the relative merits of learning some of the language of your host country, and laziness is its own punishment. And as my little embarrassment shows, insufficient knowledge in a situation can produce frustration, even anger, when you don't measure up to your own standards - especially when your working hours are devoted to communication. Still, the commandment 'learn Greek!' merely begs the question: what is it to 'know' a language? Knowledge, in any field, is a continuum, not a hurdle. You can know relatively more or less, but knowledge, like maturity, is not always measurable. Advancement comes fitfully, and is subject to backsliding. Command of something is not achieved via a gold-embossed certificate to wave around or display on the wall.

Intangibly, it is equally difficult to say when you know enough.

Enough for what? Ordering a meal? Watching the news? Conversing with in-laws? Translating professionally? It all depends on the need. In certain ways I am still learning the language, and here I mean English: better ways of expression, the odd word, making the phrases come to life. This quest will continue as long as I sit hunched over a computer (or until I throw it out the window on a bad day). Total fluency, like total knowledge, is a fool's paradise. And if depth is a problem, breadth is equally so. For those who say English is becoming the universal language, I say that we are reaching a semiliterate, lowest-common-denominator world. Many may know it, yet few Know it.

I am reminded of this verity whenever grading essays by Greek students who supposedly 'know' English. They, or some of them, unfortunately do not, at least by my standards, however much I sympathise with their task. But even those nearing fluency are hardly close to being Anglicised, Canadianised or Americanised. The problem for many, me included, is equally great, in reverse: even if/when we achieve some designated level of expertise, we will, at most, understand more of what goes on; but we will never blend into the scenery.

Even within a common language structure, variations in syntax, inflexion and word choice can all highlight, rather than diminish, the differences - as any transatlantic verbal exchange will illustrate. And if Brits and Americans remain divided by their common language, so are Belgian Walloons from the French, Austrians from Germans, and even Sicilians from other Italians. Such differences frequently also carry social or economic class implications.

Borrowing a page from logic textbooks, linguistic facility is - perhaps - a necessary, but not sufficient, condition for what we could call 'getting into' a country's life and culture. Taken alone it isn't enough, and even the question of necessity is a dependent variable. I have several friends, academics, who are scholars of ancient Greece, extremely fond of the modern version, and well travelled in the country. Yet, their knowledge of modern Greek is relatively scant, and in one case, non-existent. Does this make them ignorant of matters Greek, or less profound Philhellenes? I think not. And their case is frequent, not freakish. The opposite is equally true. Once, sitting in a taverna, I overheard a young British woman, chatting with the other waiters, rattling on in colloquial Greek at astonishing speed. At first it was impressive, but then merely tiresome as I realised that what she was saying was profoundly superficial. Though able to converse, that knowledge alone did not make her Greek, and it certainly didn't improve the content behind the words.

A practiced ability to string words together in Greek does not, alone, make a Hellene in spirit or even a communicator. Linguistic knowledge helps, of course, in getting through the practicalities of day-to-day life. On balance, knowing more is better than less, but that is very different from saying that it is the essence - any more than knowing how to surf the Internet guarantees that you can write a good research paper, or that eating bread and drinking water is sufficient for a good diet. Language is a tool, a medium, a channel, with an ever-elusive end-goal. It is a means of advancement, sometimes a vital one, but not the advance itself.

Buddy, Can You Spare a Drachma?

No, this item is not about street-begging - more common than ever in these hard times - but about Greek attitudes toward money, specifically the hard stuff clinking around your pocket or purse. Actually the two are closely related. I occasionally help beggers, including barefoot Gypsy girls taking turns carrying around the communal baby, but generally I abstain from giving. The reason is not hardheartedness, but rather sheer terror at the very thought of running out of change in Athens.

The chronic drachma shortage - more complicated than it first appears - may well explain the government's drive to join European Monetary Union; somebody else will mint the coins. Recently, out doing errands, I went to a kiosk, then to pay bills at the post office. The first charge came to 450 drachmas, the second to 9,950; both just below nice, round numbers. But presented with 500 and 10,000 notes respectively, both clerks dared ask me for 50 drachmas more, so they could return a 100-drachma note instead of a precious coin.

Most places, the paper money is the valuable thing. Of course, people here like, need, and worry about it as much as anybody else. But in this traditionally cash-based society, even wads of notes seem to be handled effortlessly; it is the small change that creates big problems. Judging from shop-clerks' pained expressions whenever you whip out a note, coin-related anxiety seems universal. One of my worst fears - can you believe this? - is having urgently to buy something inexpensive with a 10,000 note. Recently, I tried to buy a bar of chocolate with 5,000 drachmas, and the man nearly had a heart attack on the spot.

Life in Greece can be problematic even with spare change, but it is truly disastrous without it. You can't park, buy a bus ticket, or leave a taxi without a fight. But where do you get it? Standing in a 45-minute bank queue is no answer; change-machines are non-existent; and forget about asking kiosk-owners for some. One of my most prized possessions is not a book or music collection, but a little dish of coins for emergency use. Yet carrying them around all day is no better, as the Greek treasury, in its great wisdom, managed to produce the world's heaviest standard-issue (100-drachma) coin.

Guide books tell you that the Greek economy is based on the drachma. Now, guides often stretch the truth, but here is a barefaced lie. A drachma hasn't been seen here for years. Apparently they did once exist, as did even a 1/2 drachma coin, the latter slightly heavier than a sheet of paper and about as thin. The magical drachma-disappearing act is now complete; even the 5-drachma coin is becoming a relic, with the 10-drachma coin destined to follow. So much for official 3% inflation claims.

To compensate for the coinage problem, Greece has developed undoubtedly the world's finest schooling in advanced mathematics. Ample evidence is provided in every shop, where clerks dance mental circles around me, an arithmetical imbecile, in phenomenally complex calculations. If you owe 7,770 drachmas, you might normally expect back 230 on 8,000; but that is too simple. Instead, be prepared to give another 20, 70, or (better yet) 270, so that, by returning 250, 300 or a 500-note to you, the cashier will save coins. In the process, they also save themselves and their customers trouble, as a conditioned response to the public's dislike of coins. Thus does an apparent problem - undersupply - transform into a collective oversupply, held not by individuals or shops but by retail banks.

Another complicating factor is duplication. By some stroke of inspiration, the financial powers-that-be managed to produce two basic coins - 50 and 100 drachmas - that look, feel, weigh, and no doubt smell and taste, almost identical. The problem is less acute for the 100- and the slightly smaller 200-drachma notes. Powerful unions, led by kiosk owners and taxis, must have lobbied intensively for these designs, given the opportunities of short-changing unaware or harassed customers. None of this, however, is as bad as the U.S. treasury, which has long printed paper money in the same size, shape, design, and colour; only the presidential portrait varies. As usual, the Dutch have the last laugh, with their green, blue, and red notes. At least you can tell one from the other.

As European officials struggle to finalise the new euro coin designs, might I suggest they worry about a more prosaic concern, like how to tell them apart - without a magnifying glass.

My Local Wailing Wall

Each day one of the stark realities of life, and of life in Greece, is brought home to me in heart-rending, sometimes gut-wrenching force. One of my neighbours has an old man, presumably a relation, who apparently has fallen into senility. His occasional wails and moans echo upwards and outwards, carrying through the walls and floors of the *polikatoikia*, until they reach my pained ears at any and all hours.

To my knowledge I have never seen this man, only heard his anguish. He seems to live in his own private world: perhaps in pain or confused, unable to communicate his needs, fears, desires. Maybe he has Parkinson's disease and is unable to move around physically; maybe he is a stroke victim having lost the ability to speak coherently; or maybe he has advancing Alzheimer's and not always able even to recognise those closest to him - a condition that reportedly characterised the last years of Greek actor Dimitris Horn, and now afflicts former U.S. president Ronald Reagan, sharing a fate with millions of others everywhere.

Old age is a basic, often brutal, fact of life. The challenge of dealing with its fact and consequences - in others first, in ourselves eventually - is surely one of the great personal and collective dilemmas of contemporary society. And its significance is increasing, for two major reasons. One is longer lifespans due to healthier lifestyles and better medical facilities and expertise. The other is the growing problem of societies, ever pressed for public funds, to provide adequate communal care for the growing legions of elderly people. And then there are the obvious consequences of a speeded-up world for those slowing down. How can you feel anything but sympathy for an elderly person trying to board a packed bus, or manoeuvring around cars parked halfway up the sidewalk?

Like other Mediterranean countries, Greece traditionally has dealt with this issue humanely, via in-home care. I know Greeks who have been active caretakers of infirm and even bedridden parents for a decade or more, with a stoicism and self-sacrifice that is something to behold. And here, modern youth culture has not yet managed to drown out the perceived value of experience. In the politically confused late 1980s, Greek parties turned to an octogenarian, Xenophon Zolotas, as caretaker prime minister; and respect for elders sustained two old legends, Andreas Papandreou and Constantine Karamanlis, in office well after either one was able to function as a vigorous statesman. The elderly remain part of society rather than being relegated to retirement centres on its fringes. The elderly widow in black, doubling as still-dominant matriarch, is no cultural cliché.

These family-level sacrifices however are partly negated by the nonstop, almost Darwinian pace of Athenian life. Irritating practices, like cars not stopping at marked road crossings, make street life for the elderly, not to mention everybody else, both hazardous and antisocial. I have often thought of Greece, or at least Athens, as a place for the young and vigorous, but not for the old or sick. The system functions well for those with families able and willing to provide; but what of the rest? The lamentable state of old-age homes may even be a consequence of continued assumptions that the burden will be private rather than public.

The problem of caring for aging or sick parents is one of the most difficult and complicated tasks that life asks of anyone. By nature we cannot know, and thus empathise with, their concerns; we were all younger once and can remember something of childhood, but none of us was older than we are now. Those pushing midlife already face the busiest time of their lives: career challenges and heavy workloads, often with children to rear and houses to pay for. For those (like myself) living abroad and far from aging parents, a different toll comes from creeping guilt due to physical absence. And those already involved in the process of institutionalising a parent must deal with the situation from afar and often without adequate information, help or support. This factor alone is surely responsible for many thousands of Greeks returning from abroad, often abandoning good careers because of ties that truly bind.

Whether caring for aging parents or arranging for it by others, the situation is doubly complex because of the psychological and emotional aspect of reversing lifelong roles, as the traditional caregivers become the - frequently unwilling - recipients of care. A thousand uncertainties are involved in deciding how and when to step in and take decisions with, for, and sometimes over those long used to deciding things for themselves, and for you. And how hard it must be to be told that you can no longer safely drive, or even make basic judgments about your own life. The role-reversal is hard for everyone involved. Pablo Picasso once claimed that 'age only matters when one is aging'. Not so; it matters greatly to others with a conscience and a notion of responsibility as well.

And sometimes sympathetic decisions are required for people who may not always have acted sympathetically themselves, even - perhaps especially - toward their own offspring. 'Forgive and forget' is easier said than done, even when we recognise just how difficult their job was. Few things are harder than making rational decisions for emotionally-charged relationships. Misunderstandings can lead to resentment and sometimes anger; after all, even if people choose to be parents, they do not choose to have them. This often lifelong problem was laid bare in the portrayal of Ingmar Bergman in the Swedish film *Sondags Barn (Sunday's Children),* chronicling his still-unresolved relationship, even in late middle age, with his dying father. And then there is the melancholic conclusion: even the best caretaker can only hope to ease the difficulty of those in their last years. Yet their condition puts us face-to-face with our own eventual mortality, ready or not.

These are difficult problems that defy clear answers. And those who are called upon by circumstances to grapple with them, and do so with firmness and sensitivity, are the true heroes of our time.

Nature's Bounty, in Athens

As a city, Athens frequently gets a bum rap. The place everyone loves to scapegoat does have its shortcomings; comparatively it sometimes seems doubly cursed, being one of Europe's least beautiful and most crowded capitals, and also contrasting unfavourably with the rest of Greece. Yet listening recently to Joni Mitchell's appealingly melancholic song *Both Sides Now*, sung with rare feeling by Judy Collins (why does my inspiration always come from the radio?), it struck me how often our view of life - here as everywhere - is a matter of interpretation and perspective. "I've looked at clouds from both sides now, from up and down, and still somehow, it's life's illusions I recall, I really don't know life at all". Whereas in one's youth the clouds have silver linings and offer secret possibilities, as time marches on, as sadnesses and setbacks impinge on our adult lives, we realise that clouds' darker side is what often prevails.

Yet if we substitute 'Athens' for 'clouds' and reverse the Mitchell/Collins thematic direction, it is possible to turn the tables and convert negatives into positives. Perhaps the secret of Athens, as with life, is not in what is obvious but in what is submerged, partially hidden, hard to distinguish: things we must search for, but which, if we are willing to look more closely, will reveal their beauty in a quiet, unobtrusive way. I live in a neighbourhood that is far from the city's most appealing (unless you enjoy being woken up by jackhammers and concrete-mixers every morning), yet recently, out for an evening stroll to clear my muddled head, I was enchanted by so much small-scale vivid beauty.

The late-afternoon sun, rimmed with a reddish hue, was setting in a sky marked by that early spring, razor-sharp blue. The air had a mellow softness about it. The street was lined with the most exquisite almond trees, bursting with delicate pink flowers giving off a soft fragrance and which, when plucked, disintegrated into a dozen petals that scattered with the light breeze. And this, mind you, was the end of February! Spring, the miracle season, comes remarkably early to

Greece, the days lengthening almost imperceptibly from the winter solstice. Call me a desperate straw-grasper, or merely a romantic badly in need of a break. Whatever, if I cannot go to nature, then I'll let nature come to me. And it can, even here.

Athens is unplanned and disorganised, yet even this aspect offers up endless delightful contrasts. Even the most horrid building site, if left idle for a week, will start to be overtaken by grass and wildflowers. It must take less talent to grow plants in Greece than anywhere else on earth; all you need is a patch of dirt to throw water on, then wait for green shoots to appear out of nowhere. Go past any vacant lot in spring, and notice the profusion of wildflowers, red and white and yellow; I don't know their species, but who cares? Even in midwinter, Athens offers up isolated green patches that are all the more striking because of their sheer contrast with what lies all around: mini-pine forests, noble cypresses, streetside bitter orange trees bursting with fruit in defiance of the car exhaust thrown at them from a few feet away. Even in an urban jungle you find spots of beauty. But the point here is different: it is that those spots of beauty are more enticing, noticeable and striking precisely because of their rarity, and their vivid contrast with their surroundings. The beautiful things in life are not the common, but the uncommon.

We, or at least I, often think of nature as a thing of permanence and politics as ever-changing. Yet if you survey the ongoing regional news - another parking ticket scandal in Athens, major political parties in turmoil, failed diplomacy in Cyprus - there is an irritating sameness to it all. Perhaps the reverse is true: that the political world sustains itself in world-weary fashion, while it is nature that is ever changing and renewing itself. That springtime brings its newness to this ancient city, its ephemeral beauty in the midst of concrete, and its delicacy in the midst of a human community seemingly bent on despoiling it, strikes quite a blow for old Mother Earth.

A Powerless City

In case you slept through it, Greece in late March 1998 was battered by high winds, torrential rains, metre-deep mountain snows and temperatures more appropriate to midwinter than the first week of spring. And in an inspired moment of national coordination, the country's capital had its entire power supply knocked out, leaving 40% of Greece's population dark and cold and rendering essential infrastructure useless for hours. Needless to say, I loved it.

Naturally, I would feel differently had I suffered the fate of some other area residents: had I been stranded on an island, my car been smashed by a falling eucalyptus tree, my basement flooded in Ano Liosia, my freezer factory's contents been thawed out, my dark cinema unable to show *Titanic* for the thousandth time, or my home dialysis machine been shut down, the threat to my livelihood or well-being would have been real enough. I still don't know how newspapers appeared the next day; I had visions of journalists setting type by hand, Gutenberg-style, all night long, working by candlelight and sustained by (cold) coffee, then slogging on foot through torrents to deliver the news to grateful, information-starved locals.

Bad weather just happens sometimes, but rarely does it leave an entire city on the blink. I found it to be a remarkable phenomenon, even apart from slightly unreal headlines like 'Athens Plunged Into Chaos', suggesting a major divergence from the usual state of affairs. Indeed if anything, road traffic seemed to move more smoothly without traffic lights. For me it laid bare a usually latent truth, that modern society is linked by a single thread of infrastructure, the electrical grid, which gives us the sensation of being 'wired' and having access to everywhere and everything (they don't call it 'power' for nothing), yet which is still so vulnerable to disruption. Society is - we are - at the mercy of a single strange commodity, electricity, which we cannot see, can kill us instantly, travels at speeds over 300,000 km/second along thin lines strung across overhead poles, extending from somewhere in northern Greece, produced by burning some fuel or other, imported from somewhere else. We are all utterly dependent on something we know nothing about and take totally for granted.

In an information society, the disruption is worse still. Systems integration means that many telephones ceased to work because they are plugged into computers and faxes; e-mail messages, now the main source of communication for many, were lost in cyberspace because servers were down; the news couldn't even be heard because nobody owns transistor radios any more. In other words, the contrast between being able to do everything, and to do nothing, is not endless but becomes razor-thin. One minute the Internet gives us the world at our fingertips; the next minute we are digging through bottom drawers to find half-burned candles, groping our way downstairs, looking out at a darkened city, and in bed by 10pm because there's nothing else to do. It returned us, briefly, to human lifestyles prevailing up until barely a century ago yet which, by modern arrogance, we presume ourselves to have transcended. I doubt if Hobbes or Rousseau had the Athens blackout in mind when describing the 'state of nature', but the parallel does seem appropriate.

In this temporary New Dark Age, all the anger unleashed at official Greece for its alleged lack of storm preparedness simply passed me by like so much hot air (or cold wind). Blaming the government - presumably meaning the cabinet, though in politics it helps to be vague - for the results of lousy weather is like blaming the media for bad news. True, roads often flood because of bad planning (e.g. poor drainage), but they reflect yesterday's shortcomings, attributable to an entire range of factors; opposition critics unwittingly may even be blaming themselves. And these problems occasionally happen everywhere. The same month, eastern Canada was without power for a full week because of ice. A decade ago, Manhattan island lost power one hot summer evening, which was problematic for a friend of mine, then living on the 33rd floor of a (very) high rise. And once, my childhood family home lost power during an ice storm for two days. It was an adventure as well as a nuisance.

Personally, I found the inability to do anything normally considered useful to be refreshing and liberating, at least until cabin fever set in. It was a nice excuse to sit and watch the candlelight flicker on the walls in mysterious patterns, to forget about the world's problems for a night, and to be denied the option of turning on the word processor or shuffling papers. Funny thing was, when the power returned mid-evening, my immediate reaction was one of resentment at the glare of intrusive reality. So I turned the lights back off, and merely contemplated in the semi-dark. Nothing at all got accomplished.

For a short while, I rather liked the idea of Neanderthal Man sitting in his cave. Maybe we are more like him than we think.

The Promised Land

After a summer of crises, violence and scandal, perhaps you'll appreciate something to lighten up the worldly gloom. Here's a tale from an August past that sheds light on Greece's paradoxical land development situation, families, the remarkable powers of human self-deception, and the sometimes painful process of growing up in a world of false pretenses. It happened here but might have happened anywhere.

Some years ago, a friend of mine who shall remain nameless (not to himself, of course, just to you) inherited, out of the blue, a little parcel of land deep in the Peloponnese. No one in his family had actually seen it, except an elderly uncle at the time of original purchase back in the 1960s. But knowledge, or lack of it, is not always a deterrent to human aspirations, and they all insisted that the place was a gold mine, by now surely full of lovely homes surrounded by a riot of bougainvillea. To prove it, the entire clan gathered one evening and got out a dusty old rolled-up land-development plan, looking like a parchment from the ancient library at Alexandria.

But as we surveyed the plan, it was clear that they were right. Every last square metre was carefully marked, each street and public space laid out painstakingly, the community sloping gently down a mountainside, obviously affording each lot an unobstructed sea-view. His particular parcel was small, only a half-stremma or so, but wonderfully situated - adjacent to a park and a pedestrian-only street! The very names breathed with the intoxicating scents of summer: Jasmine Street, Rose Avenue, Hyacinth Place. There and then we decided to ride down the next day and see this new Eldorado in person. Slapping palms, we toasted his good fortune and our upcoming trip. We were headed for paradise.

Next morning dawned clear but very hot and windless, a genuine *kafsonas* (heat wave). Off early, we wound our way across Corinth, down into the Peloponnesian heartland, where it grew hotter still. But our anticipation and good humour carried us through the elements, and our spirits soared further as we got tantalisingly close to our destination. Something was odd, however, because contrary to expectation, the landscape seemed to grow increasingly barren and wild. Even the paved road deteriorated until the asphalt disappeared, with no road-signs either. We backtracked till we discovered that this must be the right road after all - it was the only one around - and rattled ever further up a precarious dirt track. Still no sign of civilisation.

Finally we rolled atop a ridge, and caught view of the shining sea. This seemed to be it. But as we surveyed the vast plain below, it was clear that development had not progressed quite as far as we had been led to believe. As far as the eye could see, there was a total of two houses - more like corrugated-tin shacks - along with a grand total (if memory serves) of four trees. The rest was a vast plain of rock. Rocks and stones everywhere, more than it seemed possible for earth itself to create. But where was this Peloponnesian Oz, this thriving community of grassy squares, splashing fountains and seaside walks? Where was Jasmine Street? Where was the human race?

We were, in fact, there. Reality was slow to sink in, given our own curious readiness to believe enthusiastic but ignorant relatives back home rather than our own eyes, but finally it hit us like the waves of heat on our heads. This was not a thriving seaside village, it was not in the process of becoming one, and even in a hundred years it will likely remain exactly as it is now: a vast, forlorn plain of parched rock and stone, denied even a breath of fresh wind or drop of water, baking in the pitiless sun, a place less worth fighting over than T.E. Lawrence's Arabian desert. 'Jasmine Street' was a gutted, dusty path which not even a self-respecting mule would bother with; my friend's plot, insofar as we could see, was a slippery slope of sliding pebbles. All hopes now crushed, we wound our way down a dirt track for a soul-saving swim, and discovered - a seaful of jellyfish. Suffice it to say that, on the long drive back to Athens, my friend didn't have much to say. The poor fellow was crushed, along with any dreams of a seaside villa in which to write inspired novels.

Naturally, there is a fitting epilogue to this dismal trip. I am told that the family self-deception continues to this day. Though none of those stubborn believers has ever bothered to retrace our steps, most remain utterly convinced that it is only a matter of time before the place develops into the promised land - our detailed, first-hand descriptions of that wasteland maddeningly brushed aside in favour of blind faith in wild promises made years before by some fast-talking land-developer, long since disappeared. Apparently, one of those relatives has now bought (sight unseen) a second, small parcel near the first one, obviously gearing up to bequeath to some young nephew a new piece of seaside fortune. The purchaser was beside himself at the great bargain he had secured, at an especially low price. He can hardly believe his luck. My friend and I, casting memory's glance back, think otherwise. Sometimes he wants to discourse on the nature of gullibility to them all, but then familial propriety, and respect for elders, usually win out. Barely.

(Near-) Death in the Afternoon

In Oscar Wilde's great play *The Importance of Being Earnest*, the character Lady Bracknell, with a touch of irony and gallons of understatement, refers to the French Revolution as a 'regrettable incident'. I too have been through such an 'incident' - delivering my first speech entirely in Greek - which at the time seemed most regrettable for all concerned, yet which, oddly enough, I don't regret. Time is indeed a great healer. And - see? - I even lived to tell the tale, bloodied and bowed, but no longer broken.

The 'incident' occurred at a symposium held by the Hellenic-Italian Chamber of Commerce. I'm not of the business world, my only commodities for sale being words, some knowledge of world affairs, and a certain tragi-comic view of that world. I agreed to speak as a favour to a friend; you know, scratch my back and I'll scratch yours, someday. As the date loomed closer, the task multiplied. 'Some remarks' became a 'presentation', then a 'ten-minute speech'. Then over the weekend, another footnote: it became 'a speech in Greek'. 'But I can't really speak in Greek!' I objected, without the slightest exaggeration. 'No problem, you can bring somebody to help if you want'. Setting aside wild thoughts of disappearing to Meteora for a week, I wrote out my comments with (for me) unusual ease, figuring I'd worry about the language part later. That's when the fun really began.

Some of my students kindly volunteered to translate, and slaved away overnight to render (unto Caesar, as it were) my English text into the native tongue. However, a divided workload meant that the first half was written by hand (but not my hand) and double-spaced, while the second half was typed, single-spaced, and reached me just 3 hours before the thing began; little time to practise. And it is a funny thing about Greek. Every non-native knows it's hard: the grammar, verb declensions and range of vocabulary all make what embassies call an 'exotic language'. I too laughed when Brian Church brought out 'Learn Greek in 25 Years', though now I think he is being wildly optimistic. I also missed a crucial lesson, 'Everything you ever wanted to know about Greek speechmaking...but were afraid to ask'.

But Greek is also long, and unease crept in when my modest few pages lengthened alarmingly. Even within single words you need a breath in the middle before reaching the accent. And when you pepper your talk with 'enterprise' (επικοινωνίες), 'globalisation' (παγκοσμιοποίηση) and similar clever-sounding words of indeterminate and sometimes non-existent meaning, their Greek equivalents stretch intimidatingly across the page. Truly, there is a difference between reading a speech and reading a taverna menu - especially on a podium, under time pressure, and in front of a hundred serious-looking professionals. I told myself just to relax and do my best. I did not listen to myself.

I tend to believe the message to be more important than the messenger, but public speaking is far less enjoyable than writing in the first-person; even in English it's nerve-wracking hard work. (Teaching is something else altogether.) So sitting there trying, unsuccessfully, to look cool, the panel soon hopelessly behind a schedule that had me down as the seventh (!) speaker, I put pen to paper. Not to add, but to cut. Phrases, sentences, entire paragraphs disappeared in a flash. Journalists talk of 'killing' a story, though I rather regarded this as a mercy killing, both for the audience and myself. Hope flickered when some people departed after the first speakers; perhaps nobody would be left by my time. No such luck; the place was packed.

After endless waiting and watching my respective neighbours doodling and rolling cigarettes, High Noon arrived. They say that people having an intense experience enter a 'zone', after which they don't remember what happened. Unfortunately, I do remember, all too clearly. I took the microphone, promptly forgot my carefully-prepared joke, and launched into it. Actually, I started fairly well, 'start' meaning the first two words (το έτος [the year]). Then came '1998', which looks so innocent as numbers, but trying to say Χίλια Εννιακόσα Ενενήντα Οκτώ (from memory), the words tend to get tangled. Off to the races, on the wrong foot. Heart sinking fast.

Pushing through the pain, I got to my dreaded middle section, with

all the fancy words. Even my scribbled-in transliterations now merely added to the confusion. I can't truthfully say I 'lost it', though I
was definitely hovering on the edge. The audience - presumably still
there, though I dared not look up - must have wondered whether I
had not temporarily switched to another, unknown or not yet invent-
ed language. Then near the end, I congratulated myself (non-verbal-
ly, I hope) for having had the foresight to delete a long, late para-
graph. Thus was my speech executed - in both senses.

Afterwards, me soaked in sweat and everyone else merely baffled,
the moderator graciously thanked my efforts. Think of it: it took
3,000 years for Greek poets, orators, philosophers and playwrights to
refine and bequeath to humanity a noble language; it took me 20
minutes to tear it down. And I was applauded for doing so, having
just followed in the footsteps of Lord Elgin, Sulla and Attila the Hun
as a plunderer of civilisation. Only one speaker was left, my Greek-
American partner-in-crime who claimed not to know Greek well.
After my damage, her talk was as a heaven-sent model of exquisite
oratory. There is nothing quite to match the sensation of making a
public nuisance of yourself. Then again, what's left to fear?

Well Vicky, I promised great literature to commemorate our battle-
scars. Even if it's not Hemingway, at least it makes sense to borrow
his title on Spain's blood-sport, after we've been gored by the linguistic bull. Or perhaps I was the bull, tearing helter-skelter through
the china shop. Either way, like Dean Martin sang, 'memories are
made of this'.

ABOUT THE AUTHOR

John F.L. Ross has pursued a varied career as a writer, lecturer, analyst and editor since taking his doctorate at the London School of Economics. He has written widely in the fields of international relations and European affairs, and is author of two other books, most recently *Linking Europe: Transport Policies and Politics in the European Union* (Praeger: 1998). He has also taught at a number of universities in both the U.S. and Europe, including a year as a Fulbright Fellow.

After numerous prior visits to Greece, and spurred by a deep enchantment with the country's landscape and culture, he and his Athens-born wife have lived in Greece for the past several years, where he has combined lecturing at the American College of Greece with various writing pursuits.

Athens News
Your Daily Guide to Greece

CONCISE, UNBIASED GREEK AND WORLD NEWS
PLUS IN-DEPTH ARTS & ENTERTAINMENT
AND BUSINESS SECTIONS.
WEEKEND supplement every Friday.

Check out our Internet edition on
http://athensnews.dolnet.gr

Subscriptions: (30-1) 368-6544 Fax 363-4772
Classifieds: (30-1) 333-3404, 333-3170 Fax 322-3746
Display Adverts: (30-1) 368-6837 Fax 362-6963

**Editorial: 3 Christou Lada, 102 37 Athens, Greece
(30-1) 333-3161 Fax 323-1384**

STEPHEN J. SPIGNESI

THE OFFICIAL GONE WITH THE WIND COMPANION

THE AUTHORIZED COLLECTION OF QUIZZES, TRIVIA, PHOTOS— AND MORE

A PLUME BOOK

PLUME

Published by the Penguin Group Penguin Books USA Inc., 375 Hudson Street, New York, New York 10014, U.S.A.
Penguin Books Ltd, 27 Wrights Lane, London W8 5TZ, England
Penguin Books Australia Ltd, Ringwood, Victoria, Australia
Penguin Books Canada Ltd, 10 Alcorn Avenue, Toronto, Ontario, Canada M4V 3B2
Penguin Books (N.Z.) Ltd, 182-190 Wairau Road, Auckland 10, New Zealand

Penguin Books Ltd, Registered Offices:
Harmondsworth, Middlesex, England

First published by Plume, an imprint of New American
Library, a division of Penguin Books USA Inc.

First Printing, July, 1993
1 3 5 7 9 10 8 6 4 2

LIBRARY OF CONGRESS CATALOGING-IN-PUBLICATION DATA
Spignesi, Stephen J.
The official Gone with the wind companion : the
authorized collection of quizzes, trivia, photos—and more /
Stephen Spignesi.
p.   cm.
Filmography: p.
Includes bibliographical references and index.
ISBN 0-452-27069-3
1. Gone with the wind (Motion picture)—Miscellanea.   I. Title.
PN1997.G59S65   1993
791.43'72—dc20   92-44842
CIP

Printed in the United States of America
Set in Century old style, Futura Book and Rockwell Condensed

Designed by Steven N. Stathakis

BOOKS ARE AVAILABLE AT QUANTITY DISCOUNTS WHEN USED TO PROMOTE PRODUCTS OR SERVICES. FOR INFORMATION PLEASE WRITE TO PREMIUM MARKETING DIVISION, PENGUIN BOOKS USA INC., 375 HUDSON STREET, NEW YORK, NEW YORK 10014.

You Must Remember This *Sixteenth-century poet Philip Sidney could very well have been writing about this classic Rhett and Scarlett moment when he wrote, "Oh heav'nly fool, thy most kiss-worthy face / Anger invests with such a lovely grace." (Clark Gable as Rhett Butler; Vivien Leigh as Scarlett O'Hara)*

Do you know what color Melanie's eyes were? Which scene from the film was shot first? Whether Mammy approved of Scarlett's marriage to Rhett? If you think you know everything about *Gone With the Wind,* from Ashley to Tara and back, then try your hand at these quizzes—guaranteed to stump true fans . . . as God is our witness!

1. How did Scarlett learn she was pregnant with her second daughter?
2. In the novel, Rhett's last words are "my dear, I don't give a damn." What are his last words in the film? (Trick question!)
3. What was the one subject Scarlett firmly believed should never be spoken of?
4. What physical illness tormented Vivien Leigh after the making of *Gone With the Wind* and eventually killed her?
5. What childhood accident did Margaret Mitchell recreate in her famous novel?
6. What was the inscription on the Twelve Oaks sundial?
7. Which American president quipped, "My favorite scene was the burning of Schenectady, New York, and Grant surrendering to Robert E. Lee?"

STEPHEN J. SPIGNESI is the author of many books on popular culture, including two Stephen King Quiz Books (Signet). He lives in East Haven, Connecticut.

PREFACE

The only living life is in the past and future . . . the past is an
interlude . . . strange interlude in which we call on past and future
to bear witness we are living.
—EUGENE O'NEILL, *Strange Interlude*, Part 2, Act 8

Flung roses . . .
    *As she was writing her "story of the Old South," Margaret
Mitchell probably never dreamt how far her petals would fly; how
scattered to the wind would be the roses . . .*

"A DREAM REMEMBERED"

The Official "Gone with the Wind" Companion is meant to be more than
just a collection of trivia: To *Gone with the Wind* fans, there is nothing
trivial about Tara, Twelve Oaks, or the life and times of some of our
favorite people: the O'Haras, the Wilkeses, Mammy, Rhett Butler, Aunt
Pittypat, Prissy, and of course, that firebrand herself, Scarlett.
    The Companion is intended to be a companion to the entire *Gone with*

the Wind experience: the original novel, the film, the novel's sequel, *Scarlett,* and the life of the tale's progenitor, Margaret Mitchell.

You will find close to 1,900 very specific questions here covering every facet of the *Gone with the Wind* phenomenon, and frankly, my dears, many of them are no piece of cake. (Or corn bread, for that matter.)

The answers are definitely *there* in the original sources, though they may require some literary and cinematic archaeological work to unearth—but that's part of the fun. And to help you get started, each quiz on the texts offers a unique "Question/Chapter Key," which directs you to the chapter in both *Gone with the Wind* and *Scarlett* in which the answer can be found. If all fails, the answer section provides not only the correct answers, but also the page number in the Avon paperback edition of *Gone with the Wind* and the Warner Books hardcover edition of *Scarlett* where the "answer" information can be found. Thus, *The Companion* can also be used as both an exhaustive reference to the entire *Gone with the Wind* experience and a "jumping-off" point for further study, reading, and enjoyment.

For the *serious* collectors and fans (and you know who you are), there are a handful of quizzes and questions drawn from material outside the original novel, film, and sequel. These quizzes—the "Presenting" quiz, the "Southern Cooking" quiz, and the "Margaret Mitchell" quiz—offer you an opportunity to dig out your *other* books about *Gone with the Wind* and about movies in general and have some fun looking up the ancillary information needed to complete these quizzes.

"THE GONE WITH THE WIND EXPERIENCE"

The cover of the Avon paperback edition of *Gone with the Wind* describes the book as "The Epic Novel of Our Time," and inside, the novel is called "The Immortal Love Epic of Scarlett O'Hara and Rhett Butler."

Over the years since its publication in 1936, the book's reputation has focused on the love story.

And, yes, *Gone with the Wind* is a love story. A *classic* love story.

But it is much, much more than that, and fans of the film who have never bothered to read the novel are missing a great deal.

Margaret Mitchell has taught me a lot. Like many others, I never paid attention in school when we were taught about the Civil War. It was *history,* you know? And history meant facts, and dates, and other boring details that I believed I would never, ever have use for. But Margaret

Mitchell achieved something that all my long-forgotten teachers couldn't: She made history *come alive*. (And I know Mrs. Mitchell would forgive me the use of such a cliché, but when a phrase is right, it's right.)

I have mixed feelings regarding the much-loved film version of this brilliant novel. Yes, it is a masterpiece. But, it is still an *adaptation* of a *more* masterful work, and thus, what we have is the story as though it were passed through a funnel. Such are the vagaries of novel-to-film adaptations. I can only offer this suggestion: If your entire perception of the *Gone with the Wind* experience is limited to having seen the film several times, *you don't know what you're missing*. The book is richer, has more depth, more subtext, and more texture. But most important, it has more *story*. Yes, in the novel, you will meet more characters, witness more events in the lives of these people we've all grown to know and love, and see the whole broad canvas Margaret Mitchell painted on, rather than a snapshot of a painting that has been reduced and reproduced in miniature.

Fans of the film, do not misunderstand me. Every time I watch the movie again, I am caught up in the whirl of events; I am captivated by its cinematic brilliance. But the novel is an even more overwhelming experience. The writing is superb; the back story rich and detailed, and I wholeheartedly suggest that those of you who have never read the book, do so. (You'll have to read through it if you want to answer the questions I drew from it, and I envy you the experience of your first encounter.)

THANK YOU . . .

Gone with the Wind is a special novel—a special *experience*—and I am especially grateful to have been able to live and work in timeless Tara (both in the Deep South and in Ireland) and environs for the past year or so while writing *The Official "Gone with the Wind" Companion.*

A lot of people were helpful along the way, and I'll just take a moment to acknowledge their assistance.

· My wife Pam has my Tara-sized affection for her continuing belief and support;

· My mother, the amazing Lee, has my love and thanks for help above and beyond and in more ways than can be enumerated;

· My editor Ed Stackler was always there with the perfect piece of advice or answer exactly when I needed it. He has my sincerest thanks for helping make the book better than I could have hoped;

· Editorial assistant Charles Gibbs handled a lot of my phone calls and messages to Ed with aplomb and unbelievable efficiency, and made my work a lot easier by always being ready to do whatever it took to find something out for me. My thanks and appreciation;

· Assistant editor and *Gone with the Wind* authority Rena Korb was the first reader of this book in manuscript. Rena is passionate about the *Gone with the Wind* experience and is one of the few genuine "experts" on the subject I've had the pleasure of working with. Her suggestions and comments made the book tighter and more entertaining, and if you enjoy taking the quizzes in this tome, you owe Rena a round of applause. *I,* on the other hand, owe her a standing ovation. Words fail to express how grateful I am for her priceless contribution;

· My agent John White has my sincerest thanks for his dedication and intensity, and for always knowing the right steps to make in this peculiar ballet;

· Angelyn Spignesi, who finds the oddest things in the oddest places, has my heartfelt affection and grateful appreciation for her gift of a first edition of Evelyn Keyes's autobiography, and for her continued interest in this Rube Goldbergian career of mine;

· Toni Capelli has my warmest affection and thanks for acting as a second mother to me, and for teaching me what "Now, Thorndyke! Now!" means;

· Harry and Cindy Friel at Cindy's Hallmark in Branford, Connecticut, have my fond wishes and thanks for their interest, friendship, support, and photo help;

· Ron and Howard Mandelbaum at PHOTOFEST in New York have my deepest thanks for their terrific assistance in my photo search—both on my previous book, *The Woody Allen Companion,* and with this book also;

· Steve and Marge Rapuano came through again, as always, with healthy and boundless doses of love and support and they have my sincerest thanks;

· George Beahm and Dave Hinchberger have my friendship and my thanks: Two finer guys you ain't gonna find, and that's the truth, Ruth.

Tara awaits. May the road rise to meet you.

Time present and time past
Are both perhaps present in time future,
And time future contained in time past.
                                     —T. S. ELIOT, "Burnt Norton"

Stephen Spignesi
December 1992

THE OFFICIAL
GONE WITH
THE WIND
COMPANION

WORDS ON THE WIND:

A COMPENDIUM OF QUOTATIONS

⟨❦⟩

INTERESTING, ENTERTAINING, PECULIAR, AND INFURIATING
GONE WITH THE WIND QUOTATIONS AND EPHEMERA

"Words on the Wind" looks at quotations, statistics, lists, and other material of interest to the *Gone with the Wind* fan.

You will find here blurbs about the *Gone with the Wind* novel, its sequel, *Scarlett*, the *Gone With the Wind* film, and Margaret Mitchell, as well as interesting bits of trivia and lore about the entire *Gone with the Wind* legend.

The quotations are in two main parts, "The Novels" and "The Film," and there is also a "Last Word" section, which exquisitely encapsulates the impact Margaret Mitchell's "Story of the Old South" has had on popular culture over the past six decades.

"The Players" feature offers biographical mini-blurbs about the people who said what they said, and the "Footnotes" section offers some fascinating statistics. "Footnotes" ends with a menu. By the time you get to that point, you should be hungry anyway.

All the quotations are in chronological order and, together with the original *New York Times* reviews of the book and film reprinted elsewhere

1

in this volume, these "Words on the Wind" should provide some insightful perspective on the entire *Gone with the Wind* phenomenon.

THE PLAYERS

Alexander, Holmes: American essayist.

Arling, Art: *Gone With the Wind* camera operator.

Benét, Stephen Vincent: Renowned American writer and poet.

Bishop, John Peale: American poet.

Brickell, Herschel: Book reviewer, New York *Post;* Margaret Mitchell correspondent.

Bridges, Herb: Atlanta, Georgia, *Gone with the Wind* expert and author of *The Filming of Gone With the Wind; Frankly, My Dear . . . ; Scarlett Fever;* and *Gone With the Wind: The Definitive Illustrated History of the Book, the Movie, and the Legend.*

Brown, Katharine: The head of David Selznick's New York office.

Camden, Thomas E.: Curator of the Hargrett Rare Book and Manuscript Library at the University of Georgia, repository of the largest Margaret Mitchell collection in the world.

Carter, Jimmy: Former American President.

Colquitt, Harriet Ross: Margaret Mitchell correspondent.

Corbett, Edward P. J.: American literary critic.

Cowley, Malcolm: Renowned literary critic.

Culyer, Colonel Telamon: Margaret Mitchell correspondent.

De Voto, Bernard: Editor of *The Saturday Review of Literature.*

Dick, Jackson, Jr.: Margaret Mitchell correspondent.

Dietz, Howard: The editor of the souvenir *Gone With the Wind* program handed out at the Atlanta premiere of the film.

Dooley, Robert: Author of *From Scarface to Scarlett: American Films in the 1930s.*

Drake, Robert Y., Jr.: American essayist and critic.

Ebert, Roger: Renowned film critic and writer.

Edwards, Anne: Author of *Road to Tara.*

Faulkner, William: Legendary American writer.

Gable, Clark: American actor; played Rhett Butler.

Govan, Gilbert: Margaret Mitchell correspondent.

Granberry, Edwin: Book reviewer, New York *Sun.*

Hamilton, James Shelley: National Board of Review of Motion Pictures film critic.

Hart, James D.: American essayist.

Hecht, Ben: Renowned screenwriter who worked on the script for the first nine reels of *Gone With the Wind.*

Hinckley, David: Renowned film critic and popular culture commentator for the *New York Daily News.*

Hoellering, Franz: Film critic and writer for *The Nation* in the 1930s.

Howard, Leslie: British actor; played Ashley Wilkes.

Keyes, Evelyn: American actress; played Suellen O'Hara.

Kirstein, Lincoln: Film critic for *Films* magazine in 1939 and 1940.

Leigh, Vivien: British actress; played Scarlett O'Hara.

Life: American news and entertainment magazine.

McDaniel, Hattie: American actress; played Mammy.

Mayer, Louis B.: MGM vice president in charge of production.

Mayo, Charles: Margaret Mitchell correspondent.

Mitchell, Margaret: Author of *Gone with the Wind.*

Movie Mirror: Movie fan magazine of the 1930s.

Myrick, Susan: *Gone With the Wind* "Southern" technical adviser; Margaret Mitchell correspondent.

Newsweek: American weekly news magazine.

Patton, Mark: Margaret Mitchell correspondent.

People: American weekly entertainment magazine.

Plunkett, Walter: *Gone With the Wind*'s costume designer.

Reiman, Joey: Chairman and chief creative officer of the Atlanta advertising agency, Babbit & Reiman.

Ripley, Alexandra: Author of *Scarlett,* the official sequel to *Gone with the Wind.*

Rosenbaum, Belle: American essayist and writer.

San Francisco Chronicle, The: American daily newspaper.

Selznick, David O.: Producer of *Gone With the Wind.*

Selznick, Myron: David's brother.

Shearer, Norma: American actress.

Sheppard, R. Z.: *Time* magazine book reviewer.

Spears, Jack: Author of *The Civil War on the Screen.*

Thalberg, Irving: MGM production chief.

Time: American weekly news magazine.

Wagenknecht, Edward: American biographer and critic.

THE NOVELS: GONE WITH THE WIND AND SCARLETT

I beg, urge, coax, and plead with you to read [Gone with the Wind] *at once . . . I know that after you do you will drop everything and buy it.*
—KATHARINE BROWN, in a cable to David O. Selznick, 1936

[*The novel* Gone with the Wind *is an*] *entertainment that will carry* [*women*] *through the idle moments of a fortnight.*
—MALCOLM COWLEY, 1936

[Gone with the Wind *possesses*] *a simple-minded courage that suggests the great novelists of the past.*
—MALCOLM COWLEY, 1936

[Margaret Mitchell] tosses out of the window all the thousands of technical tricks our novelists have been playing with for the past twenty years.

—HERSCHEL BRICKELL, New York *Post*, 1936

[Gone with the Wind is] an alternative to the pessimism, obscurity and fatal complexity of most contemporary novelists.

EDWIN GRANBERRY, New York *Sun*, 1936

Could it be possible that Gone with the Wind *might make it difficult hereafter for the pinched, strangulated novel which pays more attention to manner than matter?*

—EDWIN GRANBERRY, New York *Sun*, 1936

I seem to be so out of touch with the Kotex Age here.

—WILLIAM FAULKNER, 1936

No story takes a thousand pages to tell.

—WILLIAM FAULKNER, after admitting he had never read the novel, 1936

Being a product of the Jazz Age, being one of those short-haired, short-skirted, hard-boiled young women who preachers said would go to hell or be hanged before they were thirty, I am naturally a little embarrassed at finding myself the incarnate spirit of the Old South!

—MARGARET MITCHELL, to Gilbert Govan, July 8, 1936

I have always loved old people, and from childhood listened eagerly to their stories—tucking away in my mind details of rickrack braid, shows made of carpet, and bonnets trimmed with roosters' tails.

—MARGARET MITCHELL, to Harriet Ross Colquitt, August 7, 1936

Nothing could have pleased me more than to have a psychiatrist praise the pattern of Scarlett O'Hara's emotional life.

—MARGARET MITCHELL, to Charles Mayo, August 22, 1936

[Gone with the Wind] is a long book and a copious one, crowded with character and incident, and bound together with one consistent thread, the strong greediness of Scarlett O'Hara who was bound to get her way, in spite of the hampering ideal of the perfect Southern Gentlewomen and the ruin that follows men's wars.
                        —STEPHEN VINCENT BENÉT, 1936

Scarlett . . . [is m]ean, superstitious and unsurpassably selfish, [and] only in girlhood does she even superficially wear the manners of her apparent class; their emotions she never shares.
                        —JOHN PEALE BISHOP, 1936

Gone with the Wind *is an encyclopedia of the plantation legend.*
                        —MALCOLM COWLEY, 1936

You asked if Tara and the characters really existed. No, they all came out of my head with the exception of the little black maid, "Prissy."
                —MARGARET MITCHELL, to Mark Patton, July 11, 1936

If you wonder why Gone with the Wind *is so popular, think what a Dickens, a Thackeray, or a Fielding could do for America—for the greatest single chunk of people ever made simultaneously literate—a chunk of people yearning for a tale well told, for the sake of its telling, by a teller who loves the tale and the art of telling it. There has never been any other secret to popular literature. Once in a while a writer stumbles on it.*
                        —BELLE ROSENBAUM, 1937

I don't see how [the book] could possibly be made into a movie unless the entire book was scrapped and Shirley Temple cast as "Bonnie," Mae West as "Belle," and Stepin Fetchit as "Uncle Peter."
                        —MARGARET MITCHELL, 1937

I always considered [Ashley] the greatest realist in the book because his eyes, like those of Rhett, were always open. He saw things with a cruel clarity but, unlike Rhett, he was not able to do anything about them.
—MARGARET MITCHELL, to Jackson Dick, Jr., February 16, 1937

The Negro characters were people of worth, dignity and rectitude—certainly Mammy and Peter and even the ignorant Sam knew more of decorous behavior and honor than Scarlett did.
    —MARGARET MITCHELL, to Herschel Brickell, April 8, 1937

Margaret Mitchell is a gifted story teller. . . . She is twice as important as the clever back-biters who review because they cannot write. . . . I do not know Miss Mitchell. But I think, and I am not alone, that whoever discourages her from writing more and more novels has committed a literary murder.
                                            —HOLMES ALEXANDER, 1938

Gone with the Wind *. . . is basically wish-fulfillment literature. . . . The old crack about back-biters who review because they cannot write does not impress us.* Consumer's Research *cannot make automobiles but it is qualified to report on their use.*
                                            —BERNARD DE VOTO, 1938

The letters I have received and personal comments I have heard indicate that your selection for the part of Melanie has met with general approval.
    —MARGARET MITCHELL, to Olivia de Havilland, January 30, 1939

With the success of Gone with the Wind *the historical novel was even more firmly established as a popular genre. The year after its publication, four of the five best-selling works of fiction were historical novels.*
                                            —JAMES D. HART, 1950

It was exhilarating to watch Scarlett fight and win; even if she did not always employ the most genteel means, at least she did not lie down and die.
                                            —EDWARD WAGENKNECHT, 1952

The stature of GWTW unquestionably dwindles when it is set up against Tolstoy's War and Peace. *GWTW pales, too, when it is compared with such great American novels as* Moby Dick, Huckleberry Finn, The Scarlet Letter, *even* The Red Badge of Courage.

Maybe this touchstone method of assessment is our truest index that GWTW is not a great novel. But great or not, Gone with the Wind *may very well be one of the few books from the 20th century that the great mass of readers will assure of survival into the next age. It would not be the first time that the people had made a "classic" in despite of the critics and the academicians.*
—EDWARD P. J. CORBETT, 1957

I know of no other Civil War novel with as much "breadth" in conception as Gone with the Wind. *What it lacks in "depth" and in "art" it compensates for in the clarity and vitality of its presentation of the diverse and yet unified issues involved, in sustained narrative interest, and in the powerful simplicity of its structure.*
—ROBERT Y. DRAKE, JR., 1958

This one will never be mine. It's a foster mother kind of thing.
—ALEXANDRA RIPLEY, 1988

I am trying to prepare myself for a universal hatred of what I'm going to do.
—ALEXANDRA RIPLEY, 1988

It's a challenge, a triple dare. I might be able to pass up a double dare, but a triple—never.
—ALEXANDRA RIPLEY, 1988

Scarlett is going to buy us a new front porch.
—ALEXANDRA RIPLEY, 1988

My hand just won't write "fiddle-dee-dee." But I figure in my 1,000 page book I'll have to give them at least three and throw in "God's nightgown!" "Great balls of fire!" and "As God is my witness!"
—ALEXANDRA RIPLEY, 1988

Well, they could live unhappily *ever after. Or they could become Zen Buddhists and meditate for 400 pages. Heck, if I had the time, I could write* ten *versions of the sequel to* Gone with the Wind.
—ALEXANDRA RIPLEY, 1988

The first half of [Scarlett] finds America's original Material Girl, now 30, shopping and socializing in Atlanta, Savannah and Charleston, where she bumps into Rhett Butler, a wealthy scalawag. She still wants what she cannot have: him.
—R. Z. SHEPPARD, in *Time* magazine, October 7, 1991

While Scarlett *errs on the side of political correctness,* Gone with the Wind—*its minstrel-show dialogue intact—still sells like buttermilk biscuits. . . . Ripley, a seasoned professional, apparently understood what she was getting paid so well to do: write the book that was doomed from conception to be endlessly compared to the original.* Scarlett *is the South's new Lost Cause.*
—R. Z. SHEPPARD, in *Time* magazine, October 7, 1991

Frankly, I don't think the [ad] *industry gives a damn* [about Scarlett].
—JOEY REIMAN, 1991

[Scarlett] *adds new zest to a much-loved classic . . . Ripley keeps the pace racing.*
—*The San Francisco Chronicle,* 1991

Well fiddle-dee-dee! Damned if Alexandra Ripley hasn't gone and written a sequel to Gone with the Wind *that is surprisingly readable and absorbing . . . fun and entertaining.*
—*People* magazine, 1991

THE FILM

Forget it, Louis, no Civil War picture ever made a nickel.
—IRVING THALBERG, to Louis B. Mayer, 1936

[Prissy] *is the only part I myself would like to play. For this reason whoever plays Prissy will be up against a dreadful handicap as far as I am concerned.*
—MARGARET MITCHELL, to Katharine Brown, August 13, 1937

Scarlett is going to be a difficult and thankless role. The one I'd like to play is Rhett Butler.

—NORMA SHEARER, 1938

To have filmed every page of the book with the actual conversation and action would have required nearly a million feet of film, which would take a solid week to show with the projector running 24 hours a day.

—HOWARD DIETZ, 1939

I haven't the slightest intention of playing another weak, watery character. I've played enough ineffectual characters already.

—LESLIE HOWARD, 1939

David, I want you to meet Scarlett O'Hara.

—MYRON SELZNICK, to his brother David, 1939

Miss Leigh was selected to play Scarlett O'Hara because she has the dark hair and green eyes of Miss Mitchell's description and because her intelligence, determination and talent foretokened success in the most difficult assignment a Hollywood actress ever faced, the longest sustained part ever played on the screen by a man or woman . . . Miss Leigh is shown in more than nine-tenths of the 680 master scenes outlined in the script.

—MGM studio blurb announcing the casting of Vivien Leigh, 1939

I hope I've one thing that Scarlett never had. A sense of humor. I want some joy out of life . . . And she had one thing I hope I never have. Selfish egotism . . . Scarlett was a fascinating person whatever she did, but she was never a good person. She was too petty, too self-centered . . . But one thing about her was admirable. Her courage. She had more than I'll ever have.

—VIVIEN LEIGH, 1939

Why not cast Chiang Kai-shek and change the part to Gerald O'Hara?

—A *Movie Mirror* magazine correspondent, upon hearing of the casting of Vivien Leigh as Scarlett, 1939

[Vivien Leigh's] casting as Scarlett O'Hara happened fortuitously. After all efforts and tests had been made with the issue still in doubt, David O. Selznick actually started filming his picture without his heroine. Miss Leigh was a guest witness at the opening scene when the producer was struck by her resemblance to the Scarlett as described by Miss Mitchell.

—HOWARD DIETZ, 1939

There were months when I went to the studio directly from my home at 6:30 o'clock in the morning; breakfasted while making-up and having my hair done, then reported to the stage for the first "shot" at 8:45 A.M. And it was the rule, rather than the exception, to leave the studio at 9 or 10 o'clock that night. Needless to say, I saw none of Hollywood's night life!

—VIVIEN LEIGH, 1939

Rhett was too big an order. I didn't want any part of him . . . Rhett was too much for any actor to tackle in his right mind.

—CLARK GABLE, 1939

My reaction to playing Rhett Butler is both frank and simple. "The condemned man ate a hearty meal." Now don't get me wrong. As an actor, I loved it. As a character, he was terrific. As material for the screen, he was that "once in a lifetime" opportunity. But as Clark Gable, who likes to pick his spots and found himself trapped by a series of circumstances over which he had no control, I was scared stiff.

—CLARK GABLE, 1939

I arrived at the house and rang the doorbell, and there was a kind of scurrying around on the inside of the house, and I kept waiting and waiting, and finally she came out to the door and she said, "Oh! Mr. Plunkett, I'm so sorry! When I looked out and saw you here, you were wearing a blue suit, and Mama's loose, and to Mama, any man in a blue suit is a damned Yankee, so I had to put her away!"

—WALTER PLUNKETT, on his visit to a woman who had a trunk of period garment underpinnings, 1939

I wish Mr. Selznick could be put into a corset and laced down to 16 inches and be laid upon a bed with the request that he get some beauty sleep. I think he might then understand the reason for loosened stays.
　　—MARGARET MITCHELL, to Susan Myrick, upon hearing that David Selznick refused to let the actresses loosen their stays for the Twelve Oaks "nap" scene because he didn't want their busts to visibly droop, 1939

Victor Fleming . . . in my personal opinion has forever established himself as one of the great motion picture directors of all time.
　　　　　　　　　　　　　　—DAVID O. SELZNICK, 1939

At noon I think it's divine; at midnight I think it's lousy. Sometimes I think it's the greatest picture ever made. But if it's only a great picture, I'll still be satisfied.
　　　　　　　　　　　　　　—DAVID O. SELZNICK, 1939

Vivien, I know it's tough on you right now, particularly being away from Olivier, but when you win the Academy Award you'll forget it all.
　　—ART ARLING, *Gone With the Wind* camera operator, 1939

Yesterday I put on my Confederate uniform for the first time and looked like a fairy doorman at the Beverly Wiltshire—a fine thing at my age.
　　　　　　　　　　　　　—LESLIE HOWARD, January 1939

[Leslie] Howard has always been the almost unanimous choice of Southerners for the role of Ashley.
—MARGARET MITCHELL, to David O. Selznick, January 14, 1939

If I can judge from the reactions of the newspaper men last night and that of the men on the afternoon papers who have called me this morning, they are well pleased with the choice of Miss Leigh. Everyone thought it was a fine thing to have a girl who was comparatively unknown in this country because her rendition of

Scarlett would not be mixed up by past performances of roles of a different type.
—MARGARET MITCHELL, to David O. Selznick, January 14, 1939

I have been living in the pockets of the newspapers for days and they telephone at all hours about all subjects; requests for minor parts in the picture come in every minute; people who wish to sell me their grandparents' furnishings to be used in the picture have swamped me; anxious folks who want to know if you are going to do right by the South must be soothed; and, on top of it all, an incredible number of people who want personal letters of introduction to you so they can get on the lot and watch the entire proceedings.
—MARGARET MITCHELL, to David O. Selznick, January 30, 1939

Since the announcement [of the film's cast] was in the papers my life has been a bedlam.
—MARGARET MITCHELL, to David O. Selznick, January 30, 1939

I had feared, of course, that [Twelve Oaks] would end up looking like the Grand Central Station, and your description confirms my worst apprehensions. I did not know whether to laugh or to throw up at the two staircases . . . When I think of the healthy, hardy, country and somewhat crude civilization I depicted and then of the elegance that is to be presented, I cannot help yelping with laughter.
—MARGARET MITCHELL, to Susan Myrick, February 10, 1939

Far from "okaying" the pictures, I cried "Godalmighty" in horror before I caught myself. My eye had lighted on Scarlett's widow's bonnet and long veil in the midst of the décolleté gowns of the Atlanta belles. I cannot imagine even Scarlett having such bad taste as to wear a hat at an evening party and my heart sank at the sight of it. . . . A quick view of the uniforms showed not a one that looked as if it had seen active service. Nor was there a wounded man to be found even with a microscope. The Armory

looked vaguely like Versailles and not like the rough room in which drills were held. . . . I have an idea that Mr. Kurtz and Susan were overridden on these points.
   —MARGARET MITCHELL, to Colonel Telamon Culyer, February
      17, 1939

I am impressed by the remarkable number of different faces [Vivien Leigh] has. . . . [S]he looks like a different person every time she is shown in a different mood.
   —MARGARET MITCHELL, to David O. Selznick, March 24, 1939

The last stills . . . sent me showed the exteriors of Tara and, so help me God! there were white-painted, barred fences. Not a split-rail fence was to be seen. Everyone who saw the pictures spotted that immediately and yelled bloody murder. Couldn't Mr. Selznick have rented the elegant split-rail fences from the "Jesse James" company?
   —MARGARET MITCHELL, to Susan Myrick, April 17, 1939

[Laura Hope Crews] . . . looks too cute to be true. She sounds as if she'd be so much fun.
   —MARGARET MITCHELL, to Susan Myrick, April 17, 1939

Artistically as well as sentimentally, Gone With the Wind *was a smash hit in Atlanta. At the end, Margaret Mitchell quavered: "It was a great thing for Georgia to see the Confederates come back."*
   —*Life* magazine, December 25, 1939

One admires an excellent cast and a hundred technical details, but one's heart seldom beats faster. While one waits to be carried away, critical thoughts have time to develop. The feeling grows that one is sitting in a Hollywood Duesenberg with nowhere to go.
   —FRANZ HOELLERING, from *The Nation,* December 30, 1939

This is one of the happiest moments of my life and I want to thank each one of you who had a part in selecting me for one of the awards. For your kindness, it has made me feel very, very humble. And I shall always hold it as a beacon for anything that I may be able to do in the future. I sincerely hope I shall always be a credit to my race, and to the motion picture industry. My heart is too full to tell you just how I feel. And may I say thank you and God bless you.

   —HATTIE MCDANIEL, accepting her Best Supporting Actress
      Oscar, 1940

The word about Gone With the Wind—*if you haven't heard it already—is that it is about on the same level as the novel from which it was derived. It is exceptionally long, as the book was, and it isn't likely to disappoint those who liked the book, who number so many that no one else counts very much.*

                    —JAMES SHELLEY HAMILTON, 1940

Perhaps Sidney Howard and Selznick assumed that everyone who saw the picture must already have read the book. Hence, they accelerated toward the end to batter down the tired audience with a series of violent personal incidents isolated from a social background, which, if only one took the testimony of what is seen on the screen as opposed to what may have been remembered from reading, are arbitrary, unmotivated, and largely unexplained.

          —LINCOLN KIRSTEIN, from *Films* magazine, 1940

David [O. Selznick] was outraged to learn I had not read Gone with the Wind, *but decided there was no time for me to read the long novel. . . . For the next hour I listened to David recite its story. I had seldom heard a more involved plot. My verdict was that nobody could make a remotely sensible movie out of it.*

                             —BEN HECHT, 1954

The only real indicator of Gone With the Wind's *age is the reflection on what has happened to its principals. Its author, Margaret Mitchell, is dead, killed by an auto in Atlanta in 1949; so are Miss McDaniel and Leslie Howard. Gable, of course, is still going strong. So are Olivia de Havilland (Melanie) and Thomas Mitchell. Cammie King, who was Scarlett and Rhett's 4-year-old daughter, is now a 19-year-old student at the University of Southern California. Vivien Leigh is in semiretirement in Europe. (Her waistline has expanded 3 inches from her 22½ as Scarlett.) Summing up: Durable, isn't it?*

                         —*Newsweek,* June 14, 1954

*My favorite scene was the burning of Schenectady, New York, and
President Grant surrendering to Robert E. Lee.*
                                            —PRESIDENT JIMMY CARTER, 1977

To say that I knew Gone With the Wind *would become the lasting
classic it has would be a lie. It was certainly a super-production. But
I wasn't impressed by Selznick's attention to each stitch, design,
color, show buckle, down to using thorns for fastening clothing
during the Civil War period (when buttons would have disappeared) and importing Georgia red dust to stain our shoes and
skirts.*
                                            —EVELYN KEYES, 1977

*Working under the most difficult of circumstances, Victor Flem-
ing did an admirable job on the construction of* Gone With the
Wind. *He has had a bad shake, and deserves far more recognition
than he is likely to ever receive. In lesser hands unable to bring a
leveling influence to Selznick's dictums,* Gone With the Wind *could
have been an incredible disaster.*
                                            —JACK SPEARS, in *The Civil War on the Screen,* 1977

As it did with so many other movie trends and tastes of the '30s,
Gone With the Wind, *set nearly eighty years in the past, wrapped
up at least one phase of the "scarlet woman" image—not in
Scarlett O'Hara, who remains technically pure after her offer to
Rhett Butler in the Atlanta jail is rejected, but in the important
secondary character of Belle Watling (Ona Munson), who plays
much the same role in Rhett's life as Dixie Lee did in Yancey
Cravatt's in* Cimarron *(1931). Though she is warmly thanked by
the good Melanie for saving Ashley's life, Scarlett continues to
scorn her. Belle is the classic madam with a heart of gold, by
implication more decent than many a so-called good woman, especially Scarlett herself.*
                                            —ROBERT DOOLEY, in *From Scarface to Scarlett: American
                                              Films in the 1930s,* 1979

For the entire state of Georgia, having the premiere of Gone With
the Wind *on home ground was like winning the Battle of Atlanta
75 years late.*
                                            —ANNE EDWARDS, 1983

How does Gone With the Wind *play after fifty years? It is still a great film, above all because it tells a great story. Scarlett O'Hara, willful, spoiled, scarred by poverty, remains an unforgettable screen heroine, and I was struck again this time by how strong Vivien Leigh's performance is—by how stubbornly she maintains her petulance in the face of common sense, and by how even her heroism is undermined by her character flaws.*

—ROGER EBERT, 1989

[David] Selznick and [Victor] Fleming acted out the entire story, scene by scene, burly David playing the parts of Scarlett and Ashley, and Fleming doing Rhett and Melanie. [Ben] Hecht sat on the sofa, banging out the words on a typewriter. This went on for five endless days and nights, at the close of which a blood vessel dramatically, and rather gorily, burst in Fleming's right eye and Selznick collapsed on the sofa in a sleep so deep, the other two feared it was a coma.

—HERB BRIDGES, in *Gone With the Wind: The Definitive Illustrated History of the Book, the Movie, and the Legend,* 1989

Maybe you enjoy the movie so much because you love the state it puts you in.

—The Georgia Department of Industry, Trade & Tourism, in a print advertising campaign featuring a Vivien Leigh look-alike, 1990

Gone With the Wind, *book and movie, may be as close to a perpetual-motion machine as the entertainment business is likely to get.*

—R. Z. SHEPPARD, in *Time* magazine, October 7, 1991

I think Gone With the Wind *is the greatest B movie ever made.*

—DAVID HINCKLEY, 1992

THE LAST WORD

If the circumstances were right, we could be the Graceland of Georgia. We don't want that.

—THOMAS E. CAMDEN, 1991

FOOTNOTES

STATS

Date David O. Selznick bought the rights to *Gone with the Wind:* July 30, 1936

The price he paid: $50,000 (the highest price ever paid for a first novel)

Total pages in the novel: 1,037

Copies sold the first day of publication: In excess of 50,000

Number of candidates interviewed for the role of Scarlett O'Hara: 1,400

Number of actresses screen-tested for the role: 90

Number of feet of film used for the Scarlett screen tests: 13,000

Cost of the search for the actress to play Scarlett: $92,000

Percentage of this cost represented by the actual screen tests: Two-thirds

The cost of casting *all* the other characters: $10,000

Date David O. Selznick met Vivien Leigh: December 15, 1938

Date David O. Selznick signed her for the role of Scarlett: January 16, 1939

Number of preliminary sketches drawn by the film's art department: More than 3,000

Number of separate items of wardrobe designed by Walter Plunkett: More than 5,500

Number of wardrobe sketches drawn by Walter Plunkett: More than 400

Date production of the film began: January 26, 1939

Date of the film's final shot: November 11, 1939

Feet of film shot: 449,512

Feet of film printed: 160,000

Feet of edited film: 20,300

Number of set sketches drawn: 1,500

Number of sets designed: 200

Number of sets constructed: 90

Number of buildings in the "City of Atlanta" set: 53

Number of feet of streets in the Atlanta set: 7,000

Length of the "Peachtree Street" set in feet: 3,000

Amount in feet of lumber used to build the 90 sets: 1,000,000

Number of horses used during filming: 1,100

Number of other animals used: 375

Number of vehicles used during filming: 450

Number of days of employment given to extras and bit players: More than 12,000

Number of extras and bit players: 2,400

Number of feet of film run through the cameras: 1,350,000

Number of days Vivien Leigh worked on the film: 150

Number of Vivien Leigh's costume changes: Over 40

Number of articles offered for sale at the Charity Bazaar: 10,000

Number of rare cameos used on Scarlett's dresses: 25

Number of cameras used to film the "Burning of Atlanta" scene: 7

Size in acres of the burning Atlanta set: 40

Number of Los Angeles police officers on hand during the fire: 25

Number of pieces of fire department equipment on hand during the fire: 10

Number of studio firemen on hand during the fire: 50

Number of studio helpers on hand during the fire: 200

Gallons of water used to douse the fire after shooting: 15,000

Number of man-hours devoted to pre-shooting preparation: 250,000

Number of man-hours used in actual production: 750,000

Number of costumes worn by the film's female characters: 2,500

Number of bales of cotton used for the female characters' costumes: 7

Amount of the cleaning bill for the film's costumes: More than $10,000

Number of carpet designs used in the film: 34

Number of wallpaper designs hand-painted for the picture: 36

Number of people estimated to be waiting to see the film in 1939: 56,500,000

Price of the souvenir program booklet given out at the Atlanta premiere: Free

Price for additional copies of the program: 25 cents

Typical 1992 price for one of the original programs: $50

THE MENU

for the Academy of Motion Picture Arts & Sciences Party
Held on February 29, 1940
in the Cocoanut Grove Room
of the Los Angeles Ambassador Hotel
in Los Angeles, California

Canape of Fresh Lobster, Georgette
Hearts of Celery   Ripe Jumbo Olives
Essence of Tomato Madrilene en Tasse
Grilled Filet Mignon, maitre d'Hotel
or
Breast of Capon Saute with Fresh Mushrooms and Virginia Ham, Colbert
Parisian Potatoes   Fresh String Beans, Julienne
Endive and Grapefruit, Lemon Dressing
Individual Bombe Glace, Melba   Petits Fours
Demi Tasse

Exeqi monumentum aere perennius.
I have executed a memorial longer lasting than bronze.
—HORACE, Odes, III, iii.1

SAGA SCRUTINY

AN ELUCIDATORY INTRODUCTION
TO THE INTERROGATORIES

The *Gone with the Wind* and *Scarlett* questions in *The Official "Gone with the Wind" Companion* are broken into three major sections, "People," "Places," and "Things," and then within those categories, the quizzes are organized thematically, by either character, locale, or item. For each text quiz, I have provided a "Question/Chapter Key" (which can be found *before* the "Answers" section [we don't want your eyes to wander now, do we?] in the back of the book) which tells you the chapter of the respective books the question was drawn from, and thus, where the answer can be found.

Also provided are "Chapter/Page Concordances" for both *Gone with the Wind* and *Scarlett.* These will allow you to easily find the specific chapters in either novel referred to in the "Question/Chapter Key" provided for each quiz.

For instance, if the Key for a *Gone with the Wind* quiz refers you to Chapter XLIV for a certain question, this concordance will easily tell you that that is Chapter 44 in *Gone with the Wind,* and that the chapter runs from page 769 through page 781 in the Avon paperback edition of the novel. Thus, the concordances will save you a lot of page flipping and will allow you to concentrate on the fun part of quiz-taking: finding the right answers! (As an added convenience, the concordances also provide the page length for each chapter.)

As indicated, all page references are to the Avon paperback edition of *Gone with the Wind;* ISBN 0-380-00109-8, and the Warner Books hardcover edition of *Scarlett: The Sequel to Margaret Mitchell's "Gone with the Wind";* ISBN 0-446-51507-8.

PART ONE

GONE WITH THE WIND

THE NOVEL

THE MACMILLAN COMPANY'S ORIGINAL ANNOUNCEMENT OF THE PUBLICATION OF MARGARET MITCHELL'S *GONE WITH THE WIND* (FROM MACMILLAN'S 1936 CATALOG)*

GONE WITH THE WIND

BY MARGARET MITCHELL

The stirring drama of the Civil War and Reconstruction is brought vividly to life in this really magnificent novel.

Scarlett O'Hara, born of a gently bred mother from the feudal aristocracy of the Georgia coast and an Irish peasant father, inherited charm from the one, and from the other determination and drive.

As the belle of the county, spoiled, selfish, Scarlett arrives at young womanhood just in time to see the Civil War sweep away the life for which her upbringing has prepared her. After the fall of Atlanta she returns to the plantation and by stubborn shrewdness saves her home. But in the process she hardens. She has neared starvation and she vows never to be hungry again. In the turmoil of the Reconstruction she battles her way to affluence.

Scarlett's friend, Melanie Wilkes, of finer fiber, meets the same hardships with equal courage and better grace. Scarlett uses any available weapon; Melanie refuses to break with her ideals. Side by side with Scarlett and Melanie are the two men who love them: Ashley Wilkes, for whom the world died when Appomattox "fell"; and Rhett Butler, blockade runner and charming scoundrel.

The story epitomizes the whole drama of the South under

the impact of the War and its aftermath. The ruggedness and strength of north Georgia's red hills are in the characters—bluff, blustering Gerald O'Hara; Ellen, his wife; Mammy, who both loved and chastened Ellen's daughters; the rollicking Tarleton twins; the quick-tempered and murderous Fontaines; stately John Wilkes, and a host of others, white and black, forming a rich picture of Southern life.

The author is descended from people who have loved and fought for Georgia since the Revolutionary War. She was born and raised in Atlanta and was for several years feature writer on the Atlanta *Journal*.

Cloth, 12 mo. $2.50. To be published April 21.

20/20 HINDSIGHT
DEPARTMENT

THE ORIGINAL <u>NEW YORK TIMES</u> REVIEW OF THE GONE WITH THE WIND NOVEL

INTRODUCTION

This book contains five original and important *Gone with the Wind*–related pieces from that venerable "newspaper of record," *The New York Times*. Included are the original *New York Times Book Review* of the *Gone with the Wind* novel; a discussion of the reasons behind the book's success; the original review of the film following its New York opening; a brief interview with Margaret Mitchell's husband, John R. Marsh; and a piece that looks at "Peggy" Mitchell's reaction to the then-new *Gone with the Wind* phenomenon.

Regarding the book review: It is quite sobering for any writer (and any ardent reader, for that matter) to read the names of currently popular (in 1936, that is) books and authors and realize that they have been completely and utterly forgotten by our current culture. But ironically, such a title recitative also intrigues that same inveterate reader and makes us want to seek out these warmly spoken-of books.

29

This critique also illustrates the purpose of a good book review. It is not only to evaluate the book's "quality" for potential readers, but also to place the tome in a cultural, social, and literary perspective.

We tend to take for granted today a creative property's "place" relative to its "colleagues" because we are all *so* aware of all the cultural and artistic products published and produced contemporaneously with the work being reviewed. (Blame TV, if you consider this lamentable.) But by reading this old (and, until now, forgotten) "current" book review (when "current" means almost sixty years past) one can get a clear sense of just how important (and helpful) such a summary is for the review reader.

The second piece is an essay called "What Makes a Book a Best Seller?" (p. 120) which astutely examines that titular question and, for further enlightenment (and entertainment, it must be acknowledged), offers the reader the critic's tongue-in-cheek "chemical analysis" of *Gone with the Wind*.

The third piece is the original "Yankee" review of the *Gone With the Wind* film (p. 179). (New York, after all, was part of the North, right?) This review is so discerning and perceptive it reads as though it were written today. It has that kind of "big picture" (pun intended) perspective. But it *was* written in 1939, after all, and there are a couple of comments that make that all too clear, one of which is the remark that the critic considers Mammy's first scene (the window scene) "unfittin' " and wrong. Why? He doesn't say. And moreover, it is absolutely hilarious to read in the 1990s that in 1939 a film critic believed that color was too hard on the eyes for so long a picture!

The fourth piece is a rare interview with Margaret Mitchell's husband, John R. Marsh, (p. 231) in which it is again acknowledged that if it hadn't been for his prodding, *Gone with the Wind* may never have seen print.

Finally, "Success Amazes Peggy Mitchell," (p. 235) offers a fascinating peek at the real-life Margaret Mitchell and is the kind of "human interest" story that back then seemed to be the exception but which today all too often substitutes for real reporting.

This selection of literary memorabilia goes a long way toward helping us recognize the significance of the *Gone with the Wind* phenomena. As preponderant and loved as the *Gone with the Wind* world is now, it is clear from reading these articles that all we big-shot "next-generation" fans certainly do not have the monopoly on popular culture mania. And I guess that is probably the most telling assessment of the impact of Peggy Mitchell's "Story of the Old South" as can be made.

[Special thanks to Phyllis Collazzo and *The New York Times* Rights and Royalties Department and Penguin USA for their assistance with the reproduction of this material.]

A FINE NOVEL OF THE CIVIL WAR*
MISS MITCHELL'S *GONE WITH THE WIND*
IS AN ABSORBING NARRATIVE
BY J. DONALD ADAMS

GONE WITH THE WIND. BY MARGARET
MITCHELL. 1,037 PP. NEW YORK:
THE MACMILLAN COMPANY. $3.

This is beyond a doubt one of the most remarkable first novels produced by an American writer. It is also one of the best. I would go so far as to say that although it is not the equal in style or in artistic conception of such a first novel as Miss Roberts's *The Time of Man,* it is, in narrative power, in sheer readability, surpassed by nothing in American fiction. *Gone with the Wind* is by no means a great novel, in the sense that *War and Peace* is, or even *Henry Esmond,* to name only novels which dealt, like this one, with past periods of time. But it is a long while since the American reading public has been offered such a bounteous feast of excellent story telling. If this tale of the Civil War and the Reconstruction days which followed does not attract to itself more readers than even *Anthony Adverse* I shall be more than mildly surprised.

Miss Mitchell's performance is remarkable on several counts. She spent, we are told, seven years in writing this book. One can readily believe that, and as heartily wish that more young novelists would follow her example. Even so, that a first book should display a narrative sense so sure, so unwaveringly sustained through more than a thousand pages is little short of amazing. But Miss Mitchell can do more than tell a story. She can

*From *The New York Times Book Review,* Sunday, July 5, 1936. Copyright © 1936 by The New York Times Company. Reprinted by permission.

people it with characters who are not merely described, but who live, grow older and change under our eyes, as do our friends. At least four of the people in this book achieve a quality of life as vivid as may be caught on the printed page.

Gone with the Wind seems to me the best Civil War novel that has yet been written. It is an extraordinary blending of romantic and realistic treatment, as any worthwhile re-creation in fiction of those years should be. I am not forgetting Mary Johnston's *The Long Roll* and *Cease Firing,* nor Miss Glasgow's *The Battleground,* of which the first two contained the most vivid battle scenes of the Civil War that have been done in fiction, and the last, though by no means on the level of Miss Glasgow's maturer work, a vivid picture of what the war meant to non-combatants in the South. Nor am I forgetting a more recent book, Stark Young's *So Red the Rose.* But that novel, looked at now in retrospect, was more a personal statement, a memorial wreath laid before a cherished tradition and way of life, than it was a work of the creative imagination.

Miss Mitchell's book is more objective to its approach, more in the mood, let us say, of McKinlay Kantor's *Long Remember*. It is, however, much wider in scope and filled with a greater vitality. Miss Mitchell, like Mr. Kantor, paints no battle scenes; like him, she chooses a focal point about which swirls the war itself. Many things happen in her book; it is full of movement, but the guns are off-stage. So too are the great figures which the war produced; they are only spoken names, and the things which happened to Scarlett O'Hara and to Ashley Wilkes, to his wife Melanie and to Rhett Butler, are the things which happened to many other lives in that time and place.

The story opens in the plantation country of Northern Georgia, immediately before the war. Most of the action takes place in and about Atlanta, the sprawling new city of the South, a crossroads planted in the red mud and soon a hustling town, rising as the railroads come and cross it east and west and north and south. That choice of Atlanta (Miss Mitchell's native city) as the focal point of her novel was a happy one. It has not been done before in the fiction of the period, and it brings her book a freshness and vitality of background.

Atlanta, once the war was begun, was much more the nerve center of the lower South than Charleston, where it was born, or the other older cities, like Savannah and Augusta, which looked pridefully askance at the blustering and arrogant newcomer. There were army headquarters and feverishly busy hospitals, and much of what industrial activity the South could then muster. There too, when the war was over, the brutal and crushing force of Reconstruction closed in most ominously. Miss Mitchell has brought those scenes vigorously before us; the anxious and bedeviled city leaps to life before our eyes. This is background done with a skill more practiced hands might envy.

But Miss Mitchell's real triumph is Scarlett O'Hara, a heroine lacking in many virtues—in nearly all, one might say, but courage. She is a vital creature, this Scarlett, alive in every inch of her, selfish, unprincipled, ruthless, greedy and dominating, but with a backbone of supple, springing steel. Daughter of an immigrant Irishman who by force of character and personal charm fought his way into the ranks of the plantation nabobs and married a belle of an aristocratic family, she was earthily Irish, with but little trace of her mother's gentle strain, and a complete rebel against the standards and taboos of the society in which she was reared. She is a memorable figure in American fiction, a compound of Becky Sharp and of a much better woman, Dorinda of Miss Glasgow's *Barren Ground*. But she lives in her own right, completely, and will, I suspect, for a long time to come.

An almost equally vital figure is Rhett Butler, scapegrace son of a Charleston family, cynical and hard-bitten realist (but no more realist than Scarlett herself), who saw the hopelessness of the South's position from the first, and who, as a daring blockade runner, lined his pockets during the war. The remarkable thing about Miss Mitchell's portrait of him is that she has taken a stock figure of melodrama and romance, even to the black mustache, the piercing eyes and the irresistible way with women, and made him credible and alive.

The battle of wills between these two, set against the crosscurrent of Scarlett's self-deceiving love for Ashley Wilkes, makes an uncommonly absorbing love story, and one that Miss Mitchell manages to tell with rarely a false note, and which she carries to a logical and unforced conclusion. It is an ending entirely in key with Scarlett's character; if there is any weakness, any lingering doubt in one's mind as to the validity of the final scene between Rhett and Scarlett, it must lie in the motivation of Rhett. One wonders whether a man as deeply in love with a woman as we are told he was with Scarlett could have made her believe that he wanted only her body.

Melanie, whom Ashley Wilkes married, and Ashley himself, are foils for these two. Ashley was the man of honor and the romantic idealist, swept from his bearings and left purposeless when the life he loved and into which he was fitted was swept away; he cannot adjust himself to the new time and to the made-over world, as Rhett could, and Scarlett, with her fighting salvage of her father's plantation and her shrewdly managed but unprincipled handling of her lumber business in Atlanta. And Melanie—she is all that Scarlett is not, outwardly Amelia of *Vanity Fair* to Scarlett's Becky, but underneath the shyness, the sweetness, the generous loving heart, a core of courage and determined will which save her from flatness and the milk and water of negative goodness.

These are only Miss Mitchell's most fully drawn characters, the central figures of her story. She has a host of others, excellently if sketchily done. She draws on the whole social fabric of the ante-bellum war time and Reconstruction South for her people. They are all there, from the field hand and the Georgia Cracker to the Yankee carpetbagger, and she interests us in them all. Her dialogue is good (though I doubt the authenticity of her rendering of Negro speech—it would not, I think, meet with Joel Chandler's approval) and her telling of such events as Scarlett's flight from Atlanta to Tara (her plantation) with Melanie and her new-born child, through the war-swept countryside, is excellent narration. Her style is not distinguished, but if it seldom touches beauty it is a good instrument and serves her purpose well.

Let me end by saying that although this is not a great novel, not one with any profound reading of life, it is nevertheless a book of uncommon quality, a superb piece of story-telling which nobody who finds pleasure in the art of fiction can afford to neglect. He would be a rash critic who would make any prophecies as to Miss Mitchell's future. She has set herself a hard mark to match with a second book, and I hope only that she will not set too soon about it.

PEOPLE

QUIZ 1

SCARLETT O'HARA HAMILTON KENNEDY BUTLER

. . . caught by her charm . . .

The character of Scarlett O'Hara is one of the most memorable women ever created by a writer. It is evidence of Margaret Mitchell's genius that we are literally (and literarily) taken inside the sensibility of this tempestuous, spoiled Southern belle, and we get to see the sea-changes that take place in her as she tries to cope with the Civil War, her unrequited love for Ashley, her hollow marriage to Rhett, and her obsessive fear of poverty.

The following questions concern the life and times of Scarlett, and the answers can be found in *Gone with the Wind*. (See Quiz 33 for questions about Scarlett drawn from *Scarlett: The Sequel to Margaret Mitchell's "Gone with the Wind."*)

1. How old was Scarlett when the war began?
2. What color were Scarlett's eyes?
3. What preparatory school did Scarlett graduate from?
4. What was Scarlett O'Hara's given name?
5. What was the size of Scarlett O'Hara's waist in 1861?
6. Who told Scarlett that she was going to marry a man with jet-black hair and a long black moustache?
7. What was Scarlett's best subject in school?
8. What "musical" expletive was one of Scarlett's favorite exclamations?
9. While visiting Aunt Pittypat after Charles's death, what "bedroom window behavior" of Scarlett's shocked Miss Pitty?
10. How old was Scarlett when she first fell in love with Ashley Wilkes?
11. Scarlett O'Hara was "Irish enough" to believe in what precognitive psychic ability?
12. What was the one subject Scarlett firmly believed should never be spoken of?
13. What classic language did Scarlett manage to "evade" at preparatory school?

Stairway to Heaven? *Scarlett O'Hara on the elaborate staircase of her ostentatiously decorated Atlanta mansion.*

14. What were little Wade's duties at Tara in early 1865?
15. After the war, what was the only thing left that could frighten Scarlett?
16. What mathematical skills was Frank Kennedy "thunderstruck" (he felt them unbecoming in a woman) to learn that Scarlett possessed?
17. Why did Will Benteen hurry Scarlett away from the gravesite at her father's funeral?
18. What building did Scarlett consider "quite the ugliest dwelling she had ever seen"?
19. What was the name of Scarlett's first daughter?

Accustomed to Her Face *We wonder if Margaret Mitchell would have begun Gone with the Wind with, "Scarlett O'Hara was not beautiful" if she had seen this lovely portrait of Vivien Leigh as Scarlett. This photo was one of the publicity stills used to promote the release of the film.*

20. For whom was Scarlett's first daughter named?
21. How long after the birth of her first daughter was Scarlett out of bed and declaring she had to get to her mills?
22. According to Rhett, what kind of taste did Scarlett have?
23. What did Pa and the girls keep saying over and over to Scarlett in her "gray mist" nightmare?
24. Where did Scarlett and Rhett honeymoon?
25. Where in her Atlanta bedroom did Scarlett hide Aunt Pitty's "swoon bottle" of brandy?
26. What was the given name of Scarlett and Rhett's daughter, and by what name was she actually known?
27. What was the first card game Scarlett ever learned to play?
    A. Gin rummy
    B. Poker
    C. Pinochle
    D. Whist
28. What was Scarlett's usual hair-brushing regimen?
    A. 200 brush strokes every night
    B. 100 brush strokes every night
    C. 50 brush strokes every other night
    D. 10 brush strokes twice a day
29. What was the size of Scarlett's waist after she gave birth to Bonnie?
    A. 22 inches
    B. 18 inches
    C. 20 inches
    D. 28 inches
30. How old was Scarlett at the time of Melanie's death?
    A. 28
    B. 29
    C. 30
    D. 31

BONUS QUESTION 1. Who was "Lady Bountiful"?
BONUS QUESTION 2. What were the "intricate and complicated problems" Scarlett had had to deal with in the old days before the war?

Home Alone *A lovely portrait of Mr. and Mrs. Rhett Butler at home in the bedroom suite in their Atlanta mansion.*

QUIZ 2

RHETT BUTLER

. . . . who is that nasty man downstairs?

Rogue. Rascal. Scoundrel. Cad. Cheat. Knave. Scalawag. Rake. These are the colors with which Margaret Mitchell painted the portrait known as Rhett Butler. Yes, Rhett may have swaggeringly flaunted these traits, but he was also trustworthy, caring, kind, and capable of great warmth and generosity. Rhett Butler was a complex man; and after Bonnie's death, he became for a time a besodden, mournful, and lost man. Margaret Mitchell evinced astonishing insight into the nature of men in the creation of Rhett Butler. Answer the following questions about this stalwart South Carolinian.

1. What military academy expelled Rhett?
2. What was Rhett's hometown?
3. Who brought Rhett to the Wilkes's 1861 barbecue and ball?
4. What color was Rhett's hair?
5. What did Rhett donate to the Atlanta fund-raising bazaar gold collection?
6. What did Rhett feel was as barbarous as a Hindu suttee?
7. What is the Hindu suttee?
8. What was Rhett's "occupation" during the war?
9. How old was Rhett when he was disowned by his father?
10. In the mid-1800s, what did Rhett sell to the revolutionists in Central America?
11. What type of crops did Rhett's brother grow?
12. What was monogrammed on Rhett's handkerchiefs?
13. Where did Rhett live when he was in Atlanta?
14. After volunteering for Hood's army, where did Rhett fight barefoot and contract dysentery?
15. In what two European countries did Rhett spend time during the months following the Confederacy's surrender?

16. What was Rhett's motto?
17. When Rhett insisted on being allowed to bathe while being held prisoner by the Yankees in Atlanta after the war, what did the Yankees offer him as a bathing facility?
18. How did Rhett get out of jail when he was imprisoned in Atlanta after the war for the murder of a Negro?
19. What was the only thing Rhett absolutely could not stand—and would not tolerate—from Scarlett?
20. During Reconstruction in Atlanta, how did Rhett spend most of his time?
21. According to Rhett, what was the only "training" his father gave him before throwing him out into the world?
22. What was the name of Rhett's sister?
23. Where did Rhett's "legal ward" attend school?
24. Where was the house located that Rhett bought for his mother and sister after the death of his father?
25. How did Rhett get into Belle Watling's house on the night the Klan raided Shantytown?
26. According to Rhett, in what less-than-reputable way did he spend his early youth?
27. What hated postbellum Republican candidate (later governor) was a friend of Rhett's?
28. What nocturnal fear did Bonnie Butler have that troubled Rhett?
29. What type of behavior was on Rhett's agenda as part of his plan to "cultivate every female dragon" of Atlanta's Old Guard and secure societal acceptance for Bonnie?
30. Where did Rhett live after Scarlett told him that she wanted separate bedrooms?
    A. At Tara
    B. In Liverpool
    C. At Belle Watling's house
    D. In Savannah
31. Where did Rhett work during his campaign to have Bonnie accepted into Atlanta society?
    A. At Belle Watling's house
    B. At the Atlanta Bank
    C. At Scarlett's lumber mill
    D. At a pharmacy

Foreplay *The "I'll smash your skull" scene: A quite drunken Rhett confronts Scarlett about her foolish love for Ashley and then carries her upstairs for a night of passionate lovemaking.*

32. How old was Rhett at the time of Melanie's death?
   A. 48
   B. 47
   C. 46
   D. 45

BONUS QUESTION 1. Rhett once boasted to Scarlett that he was such an excellent shooter that he could "drill a dime" at what distance?

BONUS QUESTION 2. How did Rhett annoy Scarlett when he took her to plays?

My Heart Belongs to Daddy *Mr. Rhett Butler of Atlanta and his charming daughter, Bonnie Blue. This was one of the film's publicity stills. (Cammie King as Bonnie Butler)*

QUIZ 3

ASHLEY WILKES

> *Who reads*
> *Incessantly, and to his reading brings not*
> *A spirit and judgment equal or superior*
> *(And what he brings, what needs he elsewhere seek?)*
> *Uncertain and unsettled still remains,*
> *Deep versed in books and shallow in himself.*
>   —MILTON, *Paradise Regained*

Ashley Wilkes was the epitome of the refined Southern gentleman. The only problem was that at times he was *too* refined. Ashley was a self-described coward who appeared to be torn apart by his emotions, and yet, when called upon to summon the inner strength needed to fight in a war in which he did not believe, he was able to do so. Answer the following questions about this Georgian bibliophile.

1. How long did Ashley once spend in Europe?
2. What color were Ashley's eyes?
3. Why was Ashley elected captain of the Troop?
4. What was Ashley's rank when he came home on furlough in 1863?
5. What was the promise Ashley exacted from Scarlett as he went back to the battlefield after his 1863 furlough?
6. For which holiday did Ashley come home on furlough in 1863?
7. Who mended Ashley's uniform before he came home on furlough in 1863?
8. What was the name of Ashley's body servant?
9. What was the name of the prison camp in Illinois where Ashley was taken in early 1864?
10. What was Ashley's real first name?
11. Where did Ashley first see action during the war?
12. What religion's burial service did Ashley usually read over slaves buried at Twelve Oaks?

Stolen Moments *Ashley gives in. Beset by guilt over his perceived failure as a man and inadequacy as a breadwinner, Ashley finds illicit solace in the arms of Scarlett.*

13. Why did Ashley want to go work in a bank in New York after the war and leave Tara?
14. After Archie came to work for Scarlett, what were Ashley's excuses to Melanie for being out so late at night in postbellum Atlanta?
15. What story did Rhett and Melanie tell Ashley regarding the money Rhett secretly lent Melanie?
16. TRUE OR FALSE: Ashley once won $200 from Gerald O'Hara playing poker in Jonesboro.
17. TRUE OR FALSE: During the War, Ashley first went into action at Bull Run.
18. TRUE OR FALSE: Ashley first killed another man during combat at Gettysburg.
19. TRUE OR FALSE: Ashley caught cold easily.
20. TRUE OR FALSE: Ashley was a practical kind of guy.

BONUS QUESTION 1. At Gerald O'Hara's funeral, how did Grandma Fontaine describe Ashley Wilkes to Scarlett?

BONUS QUESTION 2. What was Ashley's criteria regarding granting credit to customers at Scarlett's lumber mill?

QUIZ 4

MELANIE HAMILTON WILKES

She is the only dream I ever had that . . . did not die in the face of reality.

—ASHLEY WILKES

Upon her death, Rhett Butler described Melanie Wilkes as "the only completely kind person I ever knew." Melanie was loving, kind, generous, and unceasingly trusting—even after rumors flew that her husband Ashley was caught in Scarlett's arms. Answer the following questions about this spectacular woman.

1. Who once described Melanie as "a sweet quiet thing . . . with never a word to say for herself . . ."?
2. What color were Melanie's eyes?
3. What did Melanie once do in a linen closet after she assisted Dr. Meade in an operation in which he cut out a soldier's gangrenous flesh?
4. What was the nature of Melanie's pelvic structure?
5. What did Melanie grip in her hands like a "life line" during her labor to help her deal with the pain?
6. What did Melanie insist that Scarlett take with them when they fled Aunt Pittypat's house in September 1864?
7. When Melanie was having her baby in besieged Atlanta in September 1864, what did she say to Scarlett after each excruciating labor pain?
8. What did Wade Hamilton call Melanie?

9. What particular trait of Melanie's aggravated Scarlett as the two of them tried to deal with a dead Yankee in their dining room?

10. What happened to Melanie when she worked in the cotton fields at Tara after she had her son?

11. What was the name of Melanie and Ashley's son?

12. According to René Picard, what was the only "bettaire" name for a boy than what Melanie named her son?

13. How did Melanie "name" Scarlett and Rhett's daughter?

14. What type of child did Scarlett grudgingly admit Melanie had a way with?

15. What did Melanie, on her deathbed, make Scarlett promise her?

16. How did Melanie behave toward her elders?

17. What special reason did Melanie have for choosing the house she and Ashley bought when they moved back to Atlanta after the war?

18. What were the last words Scarlett ever heard Melanie speak?
    A. "Scarlett, I forgive you."
    B. "Captain Butler—be kind to him. He—loves you so."
    C. "Ashley isn't—practical."
    D. "It isn't all so bad."

19. TRUE OR FALSE: Melanie never once invited Belle Watling into her house.

20. TRUE OR FALSE: Half of Atlanta was kin to or claimed kin to Melanie.

21. TRUE OR FALSE: In the novel, India Wilkes was the first person to call Melanie "Melly."

22. TRUE OR FALSE: Uncle Peter once scolded Melly for crying on Peachtree Street.

23. TRUE OR FALSE: The largest party Melly ever gave was a surprise birthday party for John Wilkes.

24. TRUE OR FALSE: Melanie was the first person to bathe her son Beau Wilkes.

25. TRUE OR FALSE: Melanie and Ashley were cousins.

BONUS QUESTION. What Atlanta civic organizations did Melanie Wilkes assume the secretarial posts for in the summer of 1866?

QUIZ 5

MAMMY

. . . an' affer Miss Ellen an' me done labored wid you.

—MAMMY

Rhett Butler was sagely perceptive when he told Scarlett that "Mammy's a smart old soul and one of the few people I know whose respect and good will I'd like to have." (This was right after Mammy had called Scarlett "a mule in hawse harness.") Mammy's sense of pride and honor was higher than many of the white people she was called upon to serve, and her strength was a resource to Ellen, Scarlett, and almost everyone who came to know and love her. Answer the following questions about this extraordinary African matriarch.

1. Where was Mammy raised?
2. Why was Mammy's subservient role as a slave who was "owned" by the O'Haras actually a facade and a contradiction?
3. After the Yankee occupation of Tara, what was Mammy's "diagnosis" of Wade Hamilton's "ailment"?
4. How did Mammy react to the death of Miss Ellen?
5. What did Mammy do with Tara's silver during the Yankee occupation of the plantation?
6. When asked by Scarlett to work in the fields, what did Mammy "vehemently" cite as her right to refuse?
7. What was Mammy's hard-and-fast rule regarding the postbellum returning soldiers who visited Tara?
8. Until she saw Belle Watling in Atlanta during Scarlett's "Borrow-Money-from-Rhett-to-Save-Tara" trip, when was the last time Mammy had seen a "professional bad woman"?
9. What did Mammy weigh?

Southern Comfort *Mammy, the real power behind the throne at Tara. Mammy kept a close watch over the doings of the Tara slaves and the entire O'Hara clan. (Hattie McDaniel as Mammy)*

10. What political persuasion did Mammy insist she could smell, "same as a horse could smell a rattlesnake"?
11. What specific monetary gift from Rhett did Mammy once refuse on the grounds that she was a "free issue nigger" and didn't need his money?
12. Until the birth of Rhett and Scarlett's daughter, what was the only title by which Mammy would address Rhett?
13. What physical ailment was slowing Mammy down by the time of the birth of Scarlett's second daughter?
14. How did Mammy make Bonnie afraid of the dark?
15. What did Mammy call Bonnie?
16. TRUE OR FALSE: Mammy was part Jamaican.
17. TRUE OR FALSE: Mammy was born in Africa.
18. TRUE OR FALSE: Mammy greatly approved of Scarlett's marriage to Rhett.
19. TRUE OR FALSE: Mammy was married to Pork.
20. TRUE OR FALSE: Mammy died when Bonnie Butler's horse kicked her in the head.

QUIZ 6

GERALD O'HARA

Hoc erat in votis: modus agri non ita magnus,
Hortus ubi et tecto vicinus iuqis aquae fons
Et paulum silvae super his foret.
This was one of my prayers: for a parcel of land not so very large, which should have a garden and a spring of ever-flowing water near the house, and bit of woodland as well.

—HORACE, *Satires*

Even though he was actually born in Ireland, Gerald O'Hara was a born Southerner. He loved the land, the customs, the people, and he enjoyed life with a vengeance. He lost his way after his wife died, and when the riding accident killed him, he was but a lifeless shell of his former self. He nonetheless left a legacy for his daughters and grandchildren: Love of the land, and a birthright that included the pride, strength, and a sense of honor that made Gerald one of the most loved and respected men in Clayton County. Answer the following questions about this Irish gentleman.

1. How many years in age separated Ellen and Gerald O'Hara?
2. How old was Gerald O'Hara when he came to America from Ireland?
3. How old was Gerald when the war began?
4. How tall was Gerald O'Hara?
5. What did Gerald consider "the most useful of Southern customs"?
6. What did Gerald consider the only thing "worth working for, worth fighting for—worth dying for"?
7. What was Gerald's father's parting admonition to Gerald?
8. What were the names of Gerald O'Hara's three sons?
9. Where did Gerald's brogue come from?
10. Aside from Mrs. O'Hara, who was Gerald O'Hara's favorite lady in the county?
11. What was Gerald O'Hara's nickname for Scarlett?
12. What month and year did Gerald O'Hara die?
13. After Ellen's death, what oath did Suellen want her father to sign?
14. What phrase did Gerald O'Hara always use to describe a woman's pregnancy?
15. Who dug Gerald's grave?
16. Which of Gerald's physical and emotional characteristics were blatantly evident in Bonnie Butler?
17. What color were Gerald O'Hara's eyes?
18. What were Gerald O'Hara's last words?
19. TRUE OR FALSE: Gerald O'Hara died in battle during the Civil War.
20. TRUE OR FALSE: Gerald O'Hara died in a gunfight with Rhett Butler.

BONUS QUESTION. By February 1864, how much cotton did Gerald O'Hara have stored away under the shed near the gin house at Tara, unable to sell?

QUIZ 7

ELLEN ROBILLARD O'HARA

A Lady with a Lamp shall stand
In the great history of the land,
A noble type of good,
Heroic womanhood.
      —HENRY WADSWORTH LONGFELLOW, from *Santa Filomena*

Ellen O'Hara was grace, charity, and womanhood personified. She was worshipped by her husband, emulated by her daughters, and held in high regard and esteem by everyone who knew her. She was a daughter to Mammy, a doctor to the slaves, and a paragon of decorum and virtue. Scarlett felt Ellen's influence every day of her life. Answer the following questions about this icon of kindness.

1. How old was Ellen O'Hara when the war began?
2. How old was Ellen when she married Gerald O'Hara?
3. What happened to Ellen's first three children?
4. What nationality was Ellen O'Hara?
5. What was the name of Ellen's mother?
6. Where was Ellen Robillard born?
7. Who was Ellen in love with prior to marrying Gerald O'Hara?
8. What did Ellen teach her daughters to say if they were proposed to by a gentleman, and they wanted to keep him "on the string," but didn't want to hurt the man's feelings or commit to anything at the moment?
9. What did Ellen teach Scarlett were the only appropriate gifts a lady may accept from a gentleman?
10. During the last hours before her death, what did Ellen hallucinate?
11. What type of bed did Ellen die in?
12. What did Ellen receive as a wedding present from Gerald?
13. How long did Ellen nurse Big Sam when he once got pneumonia?
14. TRUE OR FALSE: Ellen O'Hara was a blonde.

Oh, My Papa *Gerald O'Hara, Scarlett's father and one of her spiritual role models. (Thomas Mitchell as Gerald O'Hara)*

15. **TRUE OR FALSE:** Ellen O'Hara required the services of two maids and Mammy when dressing for a ball or guests.
16. **TRUE OR FALSE:** Ellen O'Hara grew up in Jonesboro.
17. Which of the following duties did Ellen O'Hara *not* perform at Tara?
    A. Bookkeeping
    B. Sewing and embroidery
    C. Cooking
    D. Medical care
18. Which of the following killed Ellen O'Hara?
    A. Pneumonia
    B. Cancer
    C. Typhoid
    D. Heart attack
19. What age was Ellen when she first arrived at Tara?
    A. 15
    B. 20
    C. 18
    D. 9
20. When Scarlett was a young girl, she confused Ellen with which of the following religious figures?
    A. St. Theresa
    B. The Virgin Mary
    C. Joan of Arc
    D. Mary Magdalene

BONUS QUESTION. What were the names of Ellen's two sisters?

Speaking Words of Wisdom *Ellen O'Hara, Scarlett's mother and another of her spiritual role models. (Barbara O'Neil as Ellen O'Hara)*

QUIZ 8

INDIA WILKES AND HONEY WILKES

Honey and India are sweet but—

—MELANIE WILKES

Honey and India Wilkes. Two young Southern women who never had the looks, the beaus, or the popularity that came naturally to someone like Scarlett. Their life was spent taking care of their widowed father, John, and their idolized brother, Ashley. Answer the following questions about these two sisters.

1. Which Tarleton twin briefly courted India?
2. Who was India Wilkes's maid before Dilcey was sold?
3. Scarlett felt that India Wilkes could only be described by what word?
4. Why was Honey Wilkes called "Honey"?
5. How long did India work to prepare for the Wilkes's 1861 barbecue and ball?
6. Where did Honey and India Wilkes spend Christmas, 1863?
7. Where did Mr. Wilkes send India and Honey when Atlanta was on the verge of being occupied in 1864?
8. What responsibility did Melanie at one time consider giving to Honey and India, but eventually changed her mind and chose Scarlett instead?
9. How did India feel about anyone who was not from the eastern seaboard?
10. How did India Wilkes feel about Honey's husband?
11. How old was India in 1866?
12. What state did Honey Wilkes's husband come from?
13. Where did India Wilkes live upon her return to Atlanta from Macon in 1866?
14. After Rhett and Scarlett's marriage, what role did India play by moving in with Aunt Pitty?
15. According to Melanie, why did India hate Scarlett?

BONUS QUESTION. At Gerald O'Hara's funeral, how did Grandma Fontaine describe India and Honey Wilkes to Scarlett?

QUIZ 9

CHARLES HAMILTON

Love's like the measles—all the worse when it comes late in life.
—DOUGLAS JERROLD, from "A Philanthropist" in *Wit and Opinions of Douglas Jerrold* (1859)

Charles Hamilton really wanted only two things out of life: to serve the Confederacy and love Scarlett O'Hara. He did end up doing both, but his devotion to the Cause killed him, and his love for Scarlett was unrequited and thrown to the wind. Answer the following questions about this blameless bystander.

1. Who was Charles dating before he "accidentally" married Scarlett?
2. What color was Charles's hair?
3. What was the name of Charles's father?
4. Who was Charles Hamilton's father's best friend?
5. How old was Charles Hamilton in 1861?
6. What sleeping arrangements did Charles acquiesce to on his wedding night, and why?
7. How did Charles Hamilton die?
8. What was the name of Charles Hamilton's son?
   A. Charles Hampton Hamilton
   B. Wade Charles Hamilton
   C. Wade Hampton Hamilton
   D. Charles Hamilton, Jr.
9. Where was Charles Hamilton buried?
   A. In Atlanta's Oakland Cemetery
   B. In an unmarked grave in Pennsylvania
   C. In Savannah
   D. In Washington, D.C.
10. What did Charles give Scarlett as an engagement ring?
    A. An emerald and diamond ring
    B. A large sapphire solitaire ring
    C. A ruby and diamond ring
    D. A pearl and opal ring

It's My Party *A quintessential Scarlett moment: In a retaliatory response against Ashley's devastating "engagement to Melanie" first strike, Scarlett coyly manipulates each of the eligible bachelors (especially Charles Hamilton) at the Wilkes barbecue into believing that she would be eating only with him. It didn't work: Ashley didn't even notice that she was surrounded by fawning, adoring men.*

QUIZ 10

FRANK KENNEDY

The cynosure of neighbouring eyes.

—MILTON, *L'Allegro*

Frank Kennedy was yet another spider caught in Scarlett's web; one more helpless male emasculated by Katie Scarlett O'Hara. Answer the following questions about this principled storekeeper.

1. Who was Frank Kennedy's beau before his marriage to Scarlett?
2. How old was Frank Kennedy in 1861?
3. What color was Frank Kennedy's beard?
4. What were Scarlett O'Hara's nicknames for Frank?
5. What did Frank Kennedy own more of than anyone else in Clayton County?
6. What type of handkerchief was Frank Kennedy carrying when he came across Scarlett in Atlanta after she had been to see Rhett in jail?
7. What was the nature of Frank Kennedy's war injury?
8. How long was Frank Kennedy's "whirlwind courtship" of Scarlett?
9. What digestive organ of the chicken was a particular gustatory favorite of Frank's?
10. What "phrase" had dominated Frank Kennedy all his life?
11. What was Frank Kennedy's affectionate nickname for Scarlett?
12. Who were the witnesses at Scarlett and Frank Kennedy's wedding?
13. How did Frank always refer to Scarlett's pregnancy?
14. What month and year did Frank die?
    A. April 1866
    B. March 1866
    C. March 1867
    D. June 1869
15. TRUE OR FALSE: The only thing Scarlett ever did that gave Frank Kennedy "any real happiness" was to bear him his daughter, Ella.

BONUS QUESTION. When Scarlett was coolly evaluating the prospects of marrying Frank Kennedy for his money, how did she "appraise" him personally?

QUIZ 11

AUNT "PITTYPAT" HAMILTON AND HER FRIENDS

> *Anything like the sound of a rat*
> *Makes my heart go pit-a-pat!*
> —ROBERT BROWNING, *The Pied Piper of Hamelin*

One can sympathize with Henry Hamilton's refusal to have anything to do with Pitty: After a while, a frail, fainting, trembling, fluttering, quivering, unremitting whiner of a woman would get on anyone's nerves! Answer the following questions about this anxious Atlantan and her friends.

1. What was Aunt Pittypat's real name?
2. What was the name of Aunt Pittypat's coachman and houseboy?

High Anxiety *Aunt Pittypat, everyone's favorite nervous wreck. (Laura Hope Crews as Aunt Pittypat)*

3. Who were Aunt Pittypat's best friends?
4. What was the name of Maybelle Merriwether's "especial beau"?
5. What did Mrs. Merriwether think should be done with any man who didn't think the Cause was "just and holy"?
6. When was the first time Mrs. Merriwether kissed her husband?
7. What did Aunt Pittypat donate to the Atlanta hospital in 1864 "in a burst of patriotism which she immediately regretted"?
8. After they returned to Atlanta after Sherman's departure, what did Maybelle and Mrs. Merriwether go out and collect in a wheelbarrow?
9. Why wasn't Aunt Pitty's house burned when Sherman's troops left Atlanta?
10. After the war, why did Aunt Pitty lose her money, farms, and town property?
11. Before the war, where did René Picard's family live?
12. What preparatory school did Aunt Pittypat attend?
13. What did Mrs. Bonnell do to earn extra money?
14. What was Mrs. Meade's occupation?
15. What was the one term that Uncle Peter had never been called by a white person in his entire life?
16. According to Melanie, why did Mrs. Elsing always hate Scarlett?
17. How did Aunt Pitty survive financially after Scarlett stopped contributing to her household in the wake of the "Ashley-Scarlett" Atlanta scandal?
18. What was the name of Uncle Peter's nephew who taught Mr. Butler to jump?
19. Which of the following did Aunt Pitty like "better than anything else in the world"?
   A. Food
   B. Bridge
   C. Sex
   D. Gossip
20. TRUE OR FALSE: Aunt Pitty was delighted when she heard that Scarlett and Ashley had been seen embracing at the lumber mill.

BONUS QUESTION. What size shoes did Aunt Pittypat wear?

QUIZ 12

THE TARLETON FAMILY

Four things greater than all things are,—
Women and Horses and Power and War.
          —RUDYARD KIPLING, "Ballad of the King's Jest"

The Tarleton family was noted for two things: loads of horses and loads of kids. The Tarletons, along with the Wilkeses, were probably the O'Haras' best friends in Georgia. Answer the following questions about this spirited family.

1. How did the Tarleton twins acquire ownership of Jeems?
2. How many children were in the Tarleton family?
3. How many Negroes did the Tarleton family own?
4. What did the Tarleton family have more of than any other family in the county?
5. What were the names of the Tarleton twins' two older brothers?
6. What color was Camilla Tarleton's hair?
7. What was Beatrice Tarleton's motto when it came to raising children?
8. Who was the "carrot top" Tarleton daughter?
9. After Fairhill was burned by the Yankees, where did Mrs. Tarleton and her four daughters live?
10. What was inscribed on the Tarleton twins' tombstone?
11. Where did Mrs. Tarleton buy the Tarleton twins' tombstone?
12. What caused Beatrice Tarleton's first miscarriage?
13. What physical characteristics distinguished Betsy Tarleton's postbellum Lovejoy husband?
14. Which of the following is the Tarleton twins' correct height?
    A. 5'10"
    B. 6'2"
    C. 6'6"
    D. 5'4"
15. **TRUE OR FALSE:** Randa and Camilla Tarleton became teachers after the war.

BONUS QUESTION 1. What was the fourth university to expel the Tarleton twins?

BONUS QUESTION 2. What were the other three universities from which the Tarleton twins were expelled?

QUIZ 13

THE O'HARA SISTERS: SUELLEN AND CARREEN

For there is no friend like a sister
In calm or stormy weather . . .
—CHRISTINA ROSSETTI, "Goblin Market"

It would be safe to say that Scarlett and her two sisters did not get along, although Scarlett and Carreen seemed to be on better terms than Scarlett and Suellen. Answer the following questions about Scarlett's two adversarial siblings.

1. What was the smallest Mammy could pull Suellen's stays before she fainted?
2. What was Carreen's real name?
3. What was Suellen's real name?
4. Which O'Hara sister "prided herself on her elegance and ladylike deportment"?
5. Which O'Hara sister was "delicate and dreamy"?
6. Which of Scarlett's sisters had spied on their father jumping his horse the week prior to Scarlett finding out about Ashley's engagement?
7. At what age did Ellen allow Carreen to go to balls?
8. How old was Scarlett when her sister Suellen was born?
9. What illness did Carreen contract in July 1864?
10. What was Carreen's nickname?
11. Why was Suellen *especially* happy at Christmas, 1864?
12. After the war, what did Suellen say "once too often" that prompted Scarlett to give her a "long-promised" slap?

13. After the war, what was Suellen's greatest joy?
14. What was the lie Scarlett told Suellen's beau, Frank Kennedy, regarding Suellen's marriage plans?
15. What calling did Carreen O'Hara choose for herself after the war?
16. Who married Suellen O'Hara?
17. Who was the cause of Gerald's death?
18. What was the name of Suellen's oldest daughter?
19. TRUE OR FALSE: Immediately after the war ended, a feud developed between Scarlett and Suellen over Suellen's use of Tara's only mule.

BONUS QUESTION. What items of their own clothing did Carreen and Suellen allow Scarlett to wear on Scarlett's "Borrow-Money-from-Rhett-to-Save-Tara" trip to Atlanta?

QUIZ 14

THE SERVANTS AT TARA

The moment the slave resolves that he will no longer be a slave, his fetters fall. He frees himself and shows the way to others. Freedom and slavery are mental states.
— MOHANDAS KARAMCHAND GANDHI, *Non-Violence in Peace and War*

The slaves at Tara were, for the most part, part of the O'Hara extended family. They were cared for and treated with fairness and dignity. And even though many fled the plantation after the Yankees came, there were still a few to whom the O'Haras meant more than freedom. Answer the following questions about the servants at Tara.

1. How did Gerald acquire Pork?
2. What was the name of Dilcey's wench?

3. What was the name of Pork's wife?
4. What was the name of Tara's upstairs maid?
5. What was the name of the Tara slave who handled Gerald O'Hara's horses?
6. What was the sole function in life of the small Negro slave girl who always accompanied Ellen O'Hara about the mansion?
7. Who did Gerald O'Hara consider the "best damn valet on the Coast"?
8. Who was the valet-butler at Tara?
9. What was the name of the female Tara slave who was part Indian?
10. How old was Prissy when she first came to Tara?
11. What was the first position of responsibility given to a male slave at Tara?
12. What was the lowest ranked slave position at Tara?
13. How tall was Big Sam?
14. How many slaves did Tara have before most of them either fled or ran away with the Yankees?
15. What type of work did Pork feel was beneath his dignity?
16. Who looked after Gerald O'Hara when he was "sick and feeble"?
17. After the war, what did the wife of the Yankee colonel who "hired" Big Sam to tend his horses call Sam that almost made the former slave drop in his tracks?
18. In March 1867, what specific event took place that made Big Sam feel "bigitty"?
19. In March 1867, why did Big Sam want to return to Tara instead of staying in Atlanta?
20. A BONUS MATCHING QUIZ. Match the Tara position from the left column with the slave who performed the duty from the right column. (As a helpful hint and a starting point, all of the answers to this matching quiz can be found in Chapter 3 of *Gone with the Wind*.)

20-1.	Cobbler	A.	Cookie
20-2.	Cow man	B.	Old Daddy
20-3.	Mule boy	C.	Cuffee
20-4.	Fly-swisher	D.	Amos
20-5.	Wheelwright	E.	Jack
20-6.	Cook	F.	Big Sam
20-7.	Maid	G.	Phillip
20-8.	Foreman	H.	Teena

QUIZ 15

DAMN YANKEES!

O tell her, Swallow, thou that knowest each,
That bright and fierce and fickle is the South,
And dark and true and tender is the North.

. . .

O tell her, Swallow, that thy brood is flown:
Say to her, I do but wanton in the South,
But in the North long since my nest is made.
—Alfred, Lord Tennyson, *The Princess*

Union means union, and the North was not going to sit by and watch state after state secede in the name of slavery. The Yankees became the most-feared people in the South and the damage inflicted by the Bluecoats during the war was enormous. Answer the following questions about the Damn Yankees.

1. Which Clayton County plantation owner married a Yankee?
2. Why was Jonas Wilkerson barred from any social contact with the Clayton County natives?
3. Where were the Yankee firms located that Rhett Butler bought from while working as a blockade runner during the war?
4. How did the Yankees replace fallen soldiers?
5. Who was in command of the Yankee assault on Vicksburg in May 1863?

Young at Heart *The innocent Prissy, who swore she knew everything about "birthin' babies," but who really knew nothing at all about childbirth. (She did know a folk remedy or two, though.) Prissy also did not like cows or dead folks. (Butterfly McQueen as Prissy)*

6. During the war, why did the Yankees recruit Confederate prisoners for frontier service?

7. Who was the Yankee general thought of by the South as "a butcher"?

8. Who was the Yankee general whose name brought dread to Southern hearts?

9. What did Carey Ashburn find in the tobacco pouch of a captured Yankee in the spring of 1864?

10. What was the name of the Yankee commander who brought his troops into Georgia, above Dalton, in May 1864?

11. What were some of the rumored atrocities attributed to the Yankees that terrified Scarlett in July 1864?

12. What did the Yankees promise the black wenches in order to persuade them to run away from the plantations with them?

13. What Southern vegetable did the Yankees think was "jes' roots" during their occupation of Tara?

14. Where did Scarlett bury the Yankee that she shot in Tara's dining room?

15. Where was the first place the Yankees went when they occupied Tara?

16. How wide a swath did the Yankees cut through Georgia with their looting and burning during the war?

17. What specific element of Jonas Wilkerson's "nigger-equality business" bought him a death sentence?

18. Who killed Jonas Wilkerson?

19. What book did Yankee women accept as "revelation second only to the Bible"?

20. What "nasty and ill-bred interest" fascinated the postbellum Atlanta Yankee women?

21. Why were Scarlett and Frank Kennedy in the "Yankees' black books" in postbellum Atlanta?

22. How did Rhett Butler find out about the planned Yankee Shantytown ambush of the Atlanta Ku Klux Klan?

23. What was the name of the Yankee captain who came to Melly's house the night of the Klan raid on Shantytown?

Armed and Dangerous *Another staircase scene, only this one ended violently when Scarlett pulled a gun out from behind her back and shot the "Damn Yankee" deserter plumb dead in the face. (Paul Hurst as the Yankee deserter)*

24. **TRUE OR FALSE:** The Yankees fully supported the Ku Klux Klan in the postbellum Reconstruction South.

BONUS QUESTION. According to Rhett, what was "the trouble" with Yankee girls?

PLACES

QUIZ 16

THE ANTEBELLUM TARA AND LIFE
BEFORE THE WAR

Here in this pretty world . . .

Answer the following questions about life in and about Tara before the start of the Civil War.

1. What did Gerald O'Hara plan to do with Tara if Scarlett married one of the Tarleton twins?
2. Whose was the only voice obeyed on the Tara plantation?
3. What type of trees were planted in Tara's backyard to disguise some of the ungainly architectural characteristics of the house?
4. Who was the overseer at Tara?
5. How far from Tara was Jonesboro?
6. How long was Tara built to last?
7. Which room at Tara was Scarlett's favorite?

BONUS QUESTION. What were the two "hands" that gave Gerald O'Hara the Tara plantation?

QUIZ 17

THE POSTBELLUM SOUTH AND TARA, AFTER THE YANKEES

Sed haec prius fuere.
All this is over now.

—CATULLUS, *Carmina*

The rebuilding was long and hard. The obstacles were sometimes insurmountable; the pain, sometimes unbearable. But the South rose again, didn't it? Answer the following questions about life in the South and in and about Tara after the war.

1. How much cotton was left at Tara after the Yankees' occupation?
2. After the Yankees twice plundered Tara, what was the strictest rule on the plantation, rigidly enforced by Scarlett?
3. After the war, who was in charge of the local Freedmen's Bureau in northern Georgia?
4. In the months following the war, who were the hungry and homeless "visitors" that came to Tara on a regular basis?
5. What was the name of the organization established after the war to help freed slaves?
6. Where did Scarlett house the postbellum returning soldiers who visited Tara?
7. Who brought the news of the Confederacy's surrender to Tara?
8. Who were the Scallawags?
9. After the war ended, what Southern town became the invading Carpetbaggers' headquarters?
10. After the war, what was "the surest way for a white person to get himself into trouble"?

Runaway *Scarlett fleeing Tara and the scolding voice of Mammy after the Tarleton brothers tell her about Ashley's engagement to Melanie. Before the war, what to wear and who to romance were the most crucial issues on Scarlett's mind. After the war, this changed. (Fred Crane and George Reeves as the Tarleton twins; the peacocks were uncredited)*

11. During Reconstruction, what members of Atlanta society were considered the worst "traitors" to the old ways?

12. What were two of the most popular names for black children in the South after the war?

13. How did the Georgia legislature vote on the postbellum amendment that would have allowed "darkies" to vote?

14. Where did the 1867 Atlanta chapter of the Ku Klux Klan hide their robes?

15. Where did the 1867 Atlanta chapter of the Ku Klux Klan hold their meetings?

16. What were the specific incidents that caused the Ku Klux Klan to "spring up overnight" in the South after the war?

17. What was the best *farm* in postbellum Clayton County?

BONUS QUESTION 1. What two mint julep ingredients weren't available at Tara after the Yankees' occupation?

BONUS QUESTION 2. In the postbellum South, what was the "biblical" reason the Negroes joined the Republican party?

SUPER BONUS QUESTION. Name the postbellum "If" topics of conversation that dominated in Atlanta whenever two (or more) former Confederates got together and conversationally "refought" the war.

QUIZ 18

THE NORTH GEORGIA PLANTATIONS AND THE FAMILIES OF CLAYTON COUNTY

I have a dream that one day on the red hills of Georgia the sons of former slaves and the sons of former slave owners will be able to sit down together at the table of brotherhood.
——MARTIN LUTHER KING, Speech at Civil Rights March in Washington, D.C., on August 28, 1963

Ben Hecht wasn't kidding when he called the Old South "a land of Cavaliers and Cotton Fields" in the metaphorical Foreword to the film version of *Gone With the Wind.* Answer the following questions about the families and plantations of the north Georgia counties in the 1860s.

1. What did the O'Haras grow on their plantation?
2. What did the Tarletons grow on their plantation?
3. What family lived on three acres of land that bordered Tara on the right?
4. What plantation bordered Tara on the left?
5. What was the name of the Tarleton family plantation?
6. After fleeing Atlanta, Scarlett and company spent the night on the front lawn of what dead plantation?
7. What was the name of the Calvert plantation?
8. What were the "two enemies of Georgia planters"?
9. TRUE OR FALSE: The Yankees didn't burn the Calvert mansion during their second foray into northern Georgia because the Calverts' overseer was a Yankee, who interceded with the army to spare the house.
10. TRUE OR FALSE: The Slatterys owned fifty-seven slaves.

BONUS QUESTION. What was the Fontaines' notorious "claim to fame" in Clayton County?

SUPER BONUS QUESTION. At Gerald O'Hara's funeral, how did Scarlett feel that Cathleen Calvert Hilton looked?

QUIZ 19

ATLANTA

. . . The town was a mixture of the old and the new . . . in which the old often came off second best in its conflicts with the self-willed and vigorous new.

—*Gone with the Wind*

Atlanta always held a special place in Scarlett's heart for one exquisitely self-centered reason: Scarlett and Atlanta were christened in the same year.

Much of *Gone with the Wind* takes place in Atlanta, and many of its characters and locations have become cherished parts of America's shared Southern culture. Answer the following questions about this dynamic Southern town.

1. What name was given to Atlanta immediately prior to it being christened "Atlanta"?
2. What three ladies were the "pillars of Atlanta"?
3. What was the first name given to Atlanta?
4. What was the name of the high ridge of land in Atlanta that had been blazed by Indians?
5. What was the population of Atlanta at the beginning of the war?
6. Where did Henry Hamilton live?
7. Who was Atlanta's doctor?
8. Why weren't the young ladies of Atlanta permitted to work as nurses during the war?
9. Aside from the men in the army, who was the most talked-about man in Atlanta during the war?
10. What was the name of the street in Atlanta where Mrs. Merriwether lived?
11. Where in Atlanta was the Confederate military headquarters located?
12. What was Atlanta's population by early 1864?
13. During their occupation of Atlanta, what did the Yankees do to the cemetery?
14. What municipal building did Sherman blow up when he left Atlanta?
15. What two-story, red-brick Atlanta city building survived the burning of the city?
16. What were "Sherman's Sentinels"?
17. Where did the Meades live in Atlanta after the war?
18. Who was the most notorious madam in postbellum Atlanta?
19. How many rooms did Ashley and Melanie's first house have?
20. After the 1867 "Klan affair," what fact aroused the "hottest hate" of Atlanta ladies against Rhett Butler?

Part-time Lover *Belle Watling, the leading madam of Atlanta and Rhett Butler's confidante and occasional lover. Belle was the archetypal "whore with a heart of gold" and was probably the mother of Rhett's son. (Ona Munson as Belle Watling)*

21. After the 1867 "Klan affair," who were Atlanta's "most unpopular citizens" (excluding Yankees and Carpetbaggers)?
22. After their honeymoon, where did Rhett and Scarlett live in Atlanta until their house was built?
23. Which of the following Atlanta social organizations got involved in varieties of ways in the "Ashley-Scarlett" scandal?
    A. The Thalians
    B. The Sewing Circle for the Widows and Orphans of the Confederacy
    C. The Association for the Beautification of the Graves of Our Glorious Dead
    D. The Saturday Night Musical Circle
    E. The Ladies Evening Cotillion Society
    F. The Young Men's Library
    G. The Ku Klux Klan
    H. All of the above
     I. None of the above
    J. A, B, C, D, E, F
    K. B, E, G

BONUS QUESTION. Who was the best behaved and most lovable child in postbellum Atlanta?
SUPER BONUS QUESTION. During the war, why was Atlanta known as the "heart of the Confederacy"?

QUIZ 20

SOUTHERN PLACES AND SOUTHERN CUSTOMS

He is a barbarian, and thinks that the customs of his tribe and island are the laws of nature.
—GEORGE BERNARD SHAW, *Caesar and Cleopatra*, Act II

The antebellum nineteenth-century South was a structured, rigidly provincial place, and its culture reflected an obsession with generations-old customs and rules. Margaret Mitchell's impeccable research showed us what it was like to live in an age of "gentlemen" and "ladies," two terms that transcended their ordinary definitions in the prewar South and transmuted into archetypes. Answer the following questions about the places and customs of Georgia and environs.

1. Where did the Troop meet twice a week?
2. Where were Scarlett and Ashley riding home from when Scarlett felt that Ashley was going to confide to her the news of his engagement to Melanie?
3. According to Ellen O'Hara, where could most of America's "gentle blood" be found?
4. How many times must a lady refuse a gentleman's proposal of marriage before she could correctly accept?
5. What did Southern women do to their clothes when there was a death in the family?
6. What did Mrs. Meade's cook, Cookie, tell Prissy would cut Melanie's labor pains in half?
7. What did the old Southern custom of hospitality require of Southerners?
8. According to Rhett Butler, how did Southerners feel about a losing cause?
9. What was often used in the South to warm up a cold bed (and a cold person)?
10. What was the Southern convention (complied with to the letter by Mammy) regarding women and hired conveyances?
11. What was the chauvinistic Southern tradition in which Scarlett (and all the other women in the South) were reared?
12. In deference to public opinion, what symbolic Catholic after-death "destination" did Ashley omit from his prayers at Gerald O'Hara's funeral?
13. What did Ashley Wilkes realize had caused half of the quarrels and some of the shootings in the South during the years he had lived there?
14. What did Southern chivalry say about a woman lying about a man, and vice versa?
15. What phrase did Southern ladies genteelly use to describe pregnancy?
16. Why was Suellen O'Hara held in contempt by her family, friends, and neighbors after Gerald O'Hara's death?

17. What was the rule of Southern life regarding indigent or unmarried female relatives?
18. What was the postbellum "unwritten code" that Atlanta ladies were passionately devoted to?
19. Which of the following cities became the South's chief blockade port after Charleston's port was sealed by Yankee gunboats?
    A. Savannah
    B. Wilmington
    C. New Orleans
    D. Raleigh
20. What was Ellen and Gerald O'Hara's religion?
    A. Roman Catholic
    B. Episcopalian
    C. Baptist
    D. Orthodox Jewish

BONUS QUESTION 1. What type of "professions" did Southerners consider proper and suited to their station in life?
BONUS QUESTION 2. According to Rhett Butler, what characteristics marked "a fine old gentleman of the old school"?

THINGS

QUIZ 21

WEAPONS, UNIFORMS, AND MATTERS OF WAR

The Minstrel Boy to the war is gone,
  In the ranks of death you'll find him;
His father's sword he has girded on,
  And his wild harp slung behind him.
                    —THOMAS MOORE, "The Minstrel Boy"

The following questions concern the weapons, militia, and battles of the Civil War, especially those that involved or concerned the people of Georgia and environs.

1. What mandated Gerald O'Hara's older brothers' flight to America?
2. Who was the first man Scarlett ever heard do the Rebel Yell?
3. How old was Willie Guinan when he joined the militia?
4. What did Louisiana Zouaves wear as uniforms?
5. What was the "stay-at-home" Atlanta military unit called?
6. After Charles Hamilton's death, what happened to the pistol belt and revolver that he had worn into battle?
7. On July 4, 1863, Atlanta learned of what terrible battle?
8. What did Confederate soldiers use on the battlefield to patch their uniforms?
9. Where did Ashley Wilkes get the boots he wore home on his furlough in 1863?
10. Who gave Melanie Wilkes the material with which she made a coat for Ashley?
11. In what state was much of the powder and arms used during the war by the Confederate army manufactured?
12. What depleted and weakened the Confederate army, but was not looked upon in the same light as desertion?
13. What weapons did Uncle Henry Hamilton take with him to war when he left Atlanta with the Home Guard in 1864?

83

14. What were "Joe Brown pikes"?
15. Before the Yankees got to Atlanta, what did the Confederate army do with the commissary warehouses?
16. What was Rhett Butler armed with when he arrived at Aunt Pittypat's house in September 1864 to ferry Scarlett and company out of Atlanta?
17. The first time Scarlett met Archie, what weapons was he carrying?
18. After Archie refused to drive her to her mills, how did Scarlett protect herself when she drove there alone?
19. TRUE OR FALSE: There were eleven cannon factories south of the Mason-Dixon line.

BONUS QUESTION. What was engraved on the hilt of the sword bequeathed to Charles Hamilton from his father?

QUIZ 22

CLOTHING, JEWELRY, AND OTHER FINERY

—"You left us in tatters, without shoes or socks,
Tired of digging potatoes, and spudding up docks;
And now you've gay bracelets and bright feathers three!"—
"Yes: that's how we dress when we're ruined," said she.
                    —THOMAS HARDY, "The Ruined Maid"

The South is hot, right? In fact, it's *damn* hot, right? Yet men and women of the ante- and postbellum South routinely wore layers and layers of long-sleeved, high-necked clothing during heat waves that today would demand shorts and T-shirts—or even less. Answer the following questions about the sartorial and cosmetic wonts and mores of the Southern beaus and belles.

1. What did Gerald O'Hara once buy for Scarlett in Atlanta to match her green flowered-muslin dress?

2. What was Ashley Wilkes wearing the day he visited Scarlett after returning home from Europe?

3. What was depicted in the cravat pin Ashley was wearing on the day he visited Scarlett after his return from Europe?

4. What color gown did Ellen feel was suitable to Suellen's complexion?

5. What color shawl did Ellen O'Hara wear when she went to assist at the birth of Emmie Slattery's child?

6. What piece of jewelry did Ellen allow Suellen to wear to the Wilkes's ball?

7. What type of skirt was Dilcey wearing when she first arrived at Tara?

8. What color was Scarlett's watered-silk ball dress with the ecru lace?

9. What gown did Scarlett wear to the Twelve Oaks ball that took place in the summer of 1861?

10. What suit did Gerald O'Hara wear to the 1861 Twelve Oaks ball?

11. Which of Scarlett's ball gowns set off her white skin nicely, but made her look a little elderly?

12. After Rhett Butler overheard Scarlett's blatantly phony flirtatious conversation with Charles Hamilton, Rhett looked at her in a way in which Scarlett felt as though he knew what she looked like without what article of clothing?

13. What did Charles Hamilton wear to the Wilkes's 1861 barbecue?

14. What outfit did Melanie Hamilton wear to the Wilkes's 1861 barbecue?

15. What type of handkerchiefs did Rhett Butler carry?

16. What was the customary garb for Southern widows?

17. Whose wedding dress did Scarlett wear for her marriage to Charles Hamilton?

18. What color shawl was Belle Watling wearing the first time Scarlett saw her in Atlanta?

19. What did Maybelle Merriwether wear to the Atlanta fund-raising bazaar?

20. What did Rhett Butler wear to the Atlanta wartime fund-raising bazaar?

21. What piece of jewelry did Fanny Elsing donate to the Atlanta fund-raising bazaar gold collection?

22. What piece of jewelry did Melanie donate to the Cause after Rhett Butler returned her wedding band?

23. What piece of jewelry did Scarlett donate to the Atlanta fund-raising bazaar gold collection?

24. Who was the main source of fashion information for Atlanta's young ladies during the war?

25. What was the name of the new hairdo—the "rage at the Capital"—that Maybelle Merriwether taught Scarlett?

26. By February 1864, how much did shoes cost in the South?

27. What was Rhett Butler wearing when he arrived at Aunt Pittypat's house in September 1964 to ferry Scarlett and company out of Atlanta?

28. What article of clothing did Scarlett use to tie up the animal she came across on her flight to Tara from Atlanta?

29. After the war, what did Scarlett use to reinforce her threadbare slippers?

30. On the day Cathleen Calvert rode to Tara to announce her marriage, what held her bonnet on her head?

31. What did Cathleen Calvert wear to the Wilkes's 1861 barbecue?

32. For Fanny Elsing's wedding in Atlanta, what cosmetic accoutrement did Scarlett send Mammy out to buy, much to Mammy's horror?

33. What did Emmie Slattery wear to Tara the first time she visited the plantation after her marriage to Jonas Wilkerson?

34. What did Scarlett use to make her hair lie down flat for Fanny Elsing's wedding?

35. What did Scarlett wash her hair with for Fanny Elsing's wedding?

36. What jewelry did Scarlett bring to Atlanta on her "Borrow-Money-from-Rhett-to-Save-Tara" trip?

37. What type of handwear did Scarlett wear when she visited Rhett in jail in Atlanta?

38. What type of outer garment did Scarlett wear over her green velvet "curtains" dress when she visited Rhett in Atlanta?

39. What articles of clothing did Aunt Pitty make for Scarlett to wear on business calls during her second pregnancy?

40. Who loaned Scarlett Kennedy a black mourning dress when Gerald O'Hara died?

41. What was Scarlett wearing when Rhett visited her on Aunt Pitty's porch in December 1866?

42. Describe the engagement ring Rhett gave Scarlett.

So Fine Rhett and Scarlett in some of their sartorial finery. Who but the bold and brassy Scarlett O'Hara could wear such a bright and bodacious dress, eh? (One can't help but wonder how many posings it took to get a shot where her sleeve fans out so perfectly.)

43. Where did Rhett buy Scarlett's engagement ring?
44. What dress did Rhett insist Scarlett wear to Ashley's surprise birthday party?
45. What hairstyle did Scarlett want to try but was prevented by Rhett's promise that he'd shave her head if she did?
46. What was Scarlett wearing the day she was caught embracing Ashley at the lumberyard?
47. What type of dresses did Rhett allow Bonnie to wear, much to Mammy's dismay?
48. Describe Bonnie Butler's riding outfit.
49. How many yards of material did it take to make Scarlett's green flowered-muslin dress?
    A. Ten yards
    B. Fifteen yards
    C. Twenty yards
    D. Twelve yards
50. What trick did Cathleen Calvert use to make her lips look redder?
    A. She bit them
    B. She repeatedly kissed the back of her hand
    C. She rubbed them with a combination of rouge and lard
    D. She scraped them with calico

BONUS QUESTION. Where was Scarlett's postbellum underwear made?

QUIZ 23

SOUTHERN DATELINE

Dost thou love life? Then do not squander time, for that's the stuff life is made of.

—BENJAMIN FRANKLIN, June 1746

This quiz focuses on specific dates from the period in which *Gone with the Wind* takes place.

1. What year did Ellen Robillard O'Hara leave Savannah for Tara?
2. In what month and year did the Wilkes's barbecue and ball at which Scarlett first met Rhett take place?
3. How long did a Southern widow have to wear the black crêpe veil on her mourning bonnet at knee-length?
4. How long was Scarlett married to Charles Hamilton before she became a widow?
5. What was the date of Ashley Wilkes's marriage to Melanie Hamilton?
6. What was the date of Charles Hamilton's marriage to Scarlett O'Hara?
7. What year did the state of Georgia authorize the building of the first railroad in the state?
8. On what date did Ashley Wilkes arrive in Atlanta on his first furlough since the war had begun?
9. What month and year did the Confederacy win a "great victory" at Chancellorsville?
10. When did Atlanta learn of the fall of Vicksburg?
11. What was the weather like in Atlanta in January and February 1864?
12. According to Rhett Butler, when was the siege at Drogheda?
13. When did the Confederate army evacuate from Atlanta?
14. What month and year did the Yankees make their second "visit" to Tara?
15. By 1865, how long had the Yankee Mrs. Calvert lived in Georgia?
16. How soon after General Johnston's war-ending surrender did the news reach Tara?
17. What month and year did Scarlett write her tenth letter to Aunt Pitty explaining why she couldn't return to Atlanta from Tara?
18. What month and year did the war end?
19. What month and year did Uncle Peter visit Tara with a letter for Melanie from Ashley?
20. What month and year did Scarlett think she'd be forced to retire to the confines of Aunt Pitty's house because of the undeniable visible evidence of her imminent second child?
21. How many years was Archie in prison?
22. Where was Archie in 1864?
23. After the "Ashley-Scarlett" Atlanta scandal broke, how long was Rhett away from Atlanta?

24. When did Charles Hamilton come into his property?
   A. Summer 1861
   B. Fall 1862
   C. Winter 1864
   D. Spring 1865

BONUS QUESTION. On what date was the north Georgia Troop established? [WARNING: TRICK QUESTION!]

QUIZ 24

MONEY MATTERS

> *The universal regard for money is the one hopeful fact in our civilization, the one sound spot in our social conscience. Money is the most important thing in the world. It represents health, strength, honour, generosity, and beauty as conspicuously as the want of it represents illness, weakness, disgrace, meanness, and ugliness.*
>
> —GEORGE BERNARD SHAW, *Major Barbara*

Money was important to Scarlett O'Hara—especially after having had it and losing it. This created in her an obsessive fear of poverty, which resulted in a rather intense interest in the accumulation—and protection—of wealth. Answer the following questions about the financial doings of Scarlett and the other inhabitants of the *Gone with the Wind* world.

High Stakes *Rhett playing poker in jail with the Yankee soldiers. Since Rhett was quite shrewd about "money matters" and was also quite a good gambler, his losing so graciously to the Yankees illustrates that he was also a shrewd diplomat as well.*

1. How much did Gerald O'Hara pay John Wilkes for Dilcey and Prissy?
2. When Scarlett went to visit Aunt Pittypat after Charles's death, how much money did Gerald give her for the trip?
3. Who was trustee of Miss Pittypat's and Melanie Wilkes's estates?
4. During the Atlanta fund-raising bazaar's "lady auction," how much did Rhett Butler bid for Scarlett O'Hara?
5. What was the amount of the donation Belle Watling made to the Cause, in care of Melanie Hamilton?
6. How much money did Miss Ellen give to Big Sam when he went off to dig rifle pits?
7. How much money did Gerald O'Hara have left after the Yankee occupation of Tara?
8. What did Frank Kennedy do with his money when he enlisted in the Confederate army?
9. Where did Scarlett hide the wallet she took off the dead Yankee when the Yankees "visited" Tara for the second time?
10. What did Jonas Wilkerson promise freed slaves they would be given if they joined the Republican party?
11. What was the amount of the extra tax levied on Tara after the war?
12. After the war, what did Mrs. Elsing do to make ends meet when her sewing, Fanny's china painting, and Hugh's firewood peddling was not enough to survive on?
13. How did Scarlett plan on paying back Rhett if he lent her the $300 she needed for Tara's tax?
14. What were the two *legitimate* collateral offers Scarlett made to Rhett (before she offered herself) in exchange for the $300 she needed for Tara's tax?
15. What lie did Rhett Butler's mother and sister tell regarding the new house they bought after the death of Rhett's father?
16. How much did Scarlett spend on flour and pork each month to feed the five leased convicts at her Gallegher-run lumber mill?
17. Match the commodities from the left column with their February 1864 selling prices from the right column.

17-1.	Beef, pork, and butter	A.	$150,000
17-2.	Flour	B.	$500 a pound
17-3.	Tea	C.	$35 a pound
17-4.	Gerald O'Hara's stored cotton	D.	$1,400 a barrel

BONUS QUESTION 1. What was the primary factor that contributed to the prewar South's burgeoning tide of prosperity?

BONUS QUESTION 2. What was the size of Tara's cotton crop in the fall of 1865?

BONUS QUESTION 3. How much was salt selling for in 1861 and in 1863?

QUIZ 25

VEHICLES, TRANSPORTATION, AND MATTERS OF TRAVEL

The road goes ever on.

—J. R. R. Tolkien, *The Hobbit*

Metaphorically, there were many roads to Tara, and to Atlanta, and to England, and beyond in *Gone with the Wind*, and Margaret Mitchell sensitively chronicled the many and varied journeys undertaken by her characters. This quiz tests your knowledge on the many and varied means of transport detailed in *Gone with the Wind*.

1. How long was the minimum visit a Southerner made if he or she took the trouble "to pack a trunk and travel twenty miles"?
2. What was the distance from Tara to Atlanta?
3. During the war, how many railroad lines were there from Wilmington, North Carolina, to Richmond, Virginia?
4. What types of vehicles were used to cart wounded soldiers from the battlefield to the Atlanta Hospital in the summer of 1864?
5. How did the Yankees hinder the rebuilding of any railroad lines they tore up?
6. After the old horse that Rhett stole for Scarlett's flight from Atlanta died, what other mode of conveyance did Scarlett and the others at Tara have for traveling?
7. On what day of the week did the prostitutes in postbellum Atlanta ride through the city in covered carriages?

On the Road *Rhett and Scarlett in one of the South's most ubiquitous modes of travel, the horse-drawn carriage. In the South, getting around was simple: You either rode a horse, rode in a carriage, or walked.*

8. When Scarlett told Rhett that she wanted to borrow money from him to buy a sawmill, what animals and vehicles did she tell him she would need if she bought the mill?
9. Who accompanied Scarlett on her daily trips out to her sawmill?
10. After the war, what happened to the wagon in which Scarlett, Melanie, Prissy, and Beau fled Atlanta?
11. Why did Archie stop driving Scarlett in late 1866?
12. How did Big Sam get back to Tara in the spring of 1867?
13. During the second year of the war, how many blockade-running boats did Rhett Butler own?
    A. 4
    B. 12
    C. 1
    D. None

14. **TRUE OR FALSE:** It's likely that Charles and Scarlett Hamilton would have traveled to London or Paris for their honeymoon if the war hadn't started.

BONUS QUESTION. In the postbellum South, what did the Republicans pay to ride the state-owned railroad?

QUIZ 26

BUSINESSES AND BUSINESS MATTERS

Every one lives by selling something.
  —ROBERT LOUIS STEVENSON, "Beggars," in *Across the Plains* (1892)

Business in the postbellum South was markedly different from the antebellum South. The war changed the *way* people made money, and it changed *who* made money. Answer the following questions about the business of business in the South as depicted in *Gone with the Wind*.

1. Who handled the bookkeeping for the Tara plantation?
2. Rhett Butler reminded the warmongers at the Wilkes's 1861 barbecue and ball that the South was sorely deficient in what critical war-related industries?
3. Where in the South did the majority of blockaders land their cargoes during the war?
4. What speculative purchase did Rhett Butler make right after Fort Sumter fell?
5. What was the name of the French store where Rhett bought Scarlett a new green bonnet?
6. After the war, what did Scarlett consider building on the Atlanta site of her "Sherman-burned" warehouse?
7. What three "vice-related" businesses sprang up quickly and thrived in Atlanta during Reconstruction?

8. Where was the sawmill located that Scarlett bought after the war?
9. Who did Scarlett hire to run her first lumber mill after she fired Mr. Johnson?
10. In the postbellum South, how did the states solve the dual problem of not having a civilian labor force large enough to handle the demands of Reconstruction, and also not being able to support all the incarcerated convicts?
11. What "payroll" problem did Hugh Elsing have with the Negroes he hired to work at Scarlett's mill?
12. In late 1866, how many convicts did Scarlett Kennedy lease to work in her lumber mills?
13. Who replaced High Elsing as foreman at one of Scarlett's lumber mills in late 1866?
14. What name did Rhett suggest when Scarlett wanted to rename the general store left to her by Frank Kennedy?
15. After the war, what was the amount of the loan Mrs. Merriwether wanted in order to expand her bakery business?
    A. $5,000
    B. $2,000
    C. $1,000
    D. $10,000

BONUS QUESTION. In postbellum Atlanta, what type of "blackguarding" comments did Scarlett make about competitors' wood to her own prospective lumber customers?

QUIZ 27

ANIMALS

Animals are such agreeable friends—they ask no questions, they pass no criticism.
                                        —GEORGE ELIOT, *Mr. Gilfil's Love Story*

Animals were extremely important to the people of Tara and environs: They served as transportation and food, and offered recreation and friendship. Answer the following questions about these Confederate companions.

1. According to Mammy, how should proper young ladies eat?
2. According to Mammy, how would Scarlett eat at Twelve Oaks if she didn't eat at home first?
3. According to Mammy, the sight of what animals should make proper ladies faint?
4. Scarlett felt that her two sisters didn't have any more spirit than what animal?
5. What Clayton County woman loved horses and talked about them constantly?
6. Scarlett felt that Honey Wilkes had the "odd lashless look" of what animal?
7. How did Gerald O'Hara's pet hunting dog die?
8. What horse did Mr. Wilkes ride into battle in the spring of 1864?
9. In what kind of shape was the horse that Rhett stole to take Scarlett and company out of Atlanta in September 1864?
10. During their flight to Tara from burning Atlanta, what animal did Scarlett and company come upon in the woods outside the MacIntosh house?
11. How did the Yankees feed their horses during their occupation of Tara?
12. What animals were left on the Tara plantation after the Yankees left?
13. What happened to the dogs and cats of Atlanta after Sherman invaded the town?
14. What happened to the only sow left at Tara when the Yankees "visited" the plantation a second time?
15. What type of animal did shy Frank Kennedy remind Scarlett of?
16. According to Harriet Beecher Stowe in *Uncle Tom's Cabin,* what type of dogs did every slaveowner keep to hunt down runaway slaves?
17. What was the name of Scarlett and Rhett's cat?
18. What was the name of Bonnie's pony?
19. TRUE OR FALSE: The Tarleton twins' horses were red.

BONUS QUESTION. In November 1864, why did Scarlett order the only calf left at Tara killed?

QUIZ 28

FURNITURE, SILVERWARE, AND OTHER "PRECIOUS" THINGS

Der ewige Friede ist ein Traum, und nicht einmal ein schöner und der Krieg ein Glied in Gottes Weltordnung. . . . Ohne den Krieg wurde die Welt in Materialismus versumpfen.
Everlasting peace is a dream, and not even a pleasant one; and war [is] a necessary part of God's arrangement of the world. . . . Without war, the world would slide dissolutely into materialism.
　　—HELMUTH VON MOLTKE, in a letter to Dr. J. K. Bluntschli,
　　December 11, 1890

The loss of many of their cherished and "precious" possessions during the war seemed to bother some Southerners more than the loss of life. Answer the following questions about the material possessions of the Champions of the Cause.

1. After being rejected by Ashley in the library at Twelve Oaks, what did Scarlett hurl across the room and smash against the mantelpiece?
2. How was the ugly chandelier in the drill hall "transformed" into a thing of beauty for the Atlanta fund-raising bazaar?
3. What china hair accessories did Scarlett hand paint for the big fundraising bazaar in Atlanta?
4. What type of receptacle stood just outside Melly and Scarlett's booth at the Atlanta fund-raising bazaar?
5. As the Yankee blockade of Confederate ports tightened during the second year of the war, what type of luxuries became "scarce and dear" to Southerners?
6. What type of "blockaded" sewing supplies and hair accessories did Rhett Butler bring Scarlett from Nassau during the war?
7. What were Scarlett's two 1863 Christmas gifts to Ashley?
8. When Rhett Butler returned to Atlanta from "one of his mysterious trips" in May 1864, what gift did he bring to Aunt Pittypat's house?

9. What possessions of John Wilkes did Uncle Henry Hamilton give to Melanie after her father-in-law's death?
10. What did Scarlett use to fan Melanie during her long and agonizing labor?
11. What was in Ellen O'Hara's rosewood sewing box?
12. Who made the calico-and-bark wallet that Will Benteen carried in his pants pocket?
13. What ornamentals hung from Gerald O'Hara's gold pocketwatch?
14. How did Ashley and Melanie furnish their first house?
15. What type of furniture did Scarlett and Frank Kennedy want to give Melanie and Ashley Wilkes for their first home?
16. What type of presents did Melanie and Ashley receive as housewarming gifts when they invited guests to their new house in Atlanta?
17. What color carpeting was in the Atlanta house that Scarlett had built for her and Rhett after their marriage?
   A. Red
   B. Green
   C. White
   D. Blue
18. What kind of wood furniture did Scarlett have in her bedroom at Tara?
   A. Pine
   B. Oak
   C. Mahogany
   D. Teak

BONUS QUESTION 1. What gifts did Scarlett buy for her family while she and Rhett were on their honeymoon?
BONUS QUESTION 2. What made up the insect collection that Bonnie Butler once wanted to proudly show her father?

QUIZ 29

LETTERS, WRITINGS, SONGS, AND OTHER COMMUNICATORY MATTERS

An odd thought strikes me:—we shall receive no letters in the grave.

—SAMUEL JOHNSON

To write is to write is to write is to write is to write is to write is to write is to write.

—GERTRUDE STEIN

In *Gone with the Wind,* Margaret Mitchell does a magnificent job of conveying just what it was like before the era of instantaneous communication. One scene that truly shows us what it was like to have to depend on letters and the occasional prohibitively expensive telegram to communicate with friends and family is the one in which Scarlett agrees to go to Atlanta after the death of her husband, Charles Hamilton; her mother, Ellen, says, "I'll go write the necessary letters." Letters were the only way to tell someone you were coming to visit. This quiz tests your knowledge of communicatory matters down South before Alexander Bell got around to creating the need for the answering machine.

1. How many of Ellen Robillard's letters to Philippe Robillard were returned to her after Philippe's death?
2. Who wrote the letter that informed Ellen Robillard of Philippe Robillard's death?
3. What English author did Melanie Hamilton feel was "a cynic"?
4. What English author did Melanie Hamilton feel was "a gentleman"?
5. What writer's works did Scarlett have to listen to read aloud while visiting her Aunt Pauline?
6. What instruments were used to perform the rendition of "If You Want to Have a Good Time, Jine the Cavalry" that Scarlett heard from her bedroom window in Aunt Pittypat's house as picnickers passed by the house?

7. What song did Old Levi play when the Home Guard arrived at the Atlanta fund-raising bazaar?

8. What was the name of the song captured from the Yankees in which the Southerners changed the line "In your suit of blue" to "In your suit of gray"?

9. Who wrote Scarlett a letter that began, "I was greatly disturbed to hear of your most recent conduct"?

10. Where did Melanie keep the letters Ashley wrote her while he was away at war?

11. What magazine did Southern ladies often turn to for the latest fashion information?

12. What was usually on the first two pages of the Atlanta *Daily Examiner*?

Just to Dance with You *WIDOW DANCES IN PUBLIC! ATLANTA REELS! In this scene (one of the film's more elaborate production numbers), the supposedly grieving Scarlett shocks the South by actually agreeing to dance the "Ferginny" reel with that Scalawag blockade runner, Rhett Butler.*

13. What was the name of the Atlanta newspaper that published the lists of war dead?

14. What was the only firsthand information Atlanta received about the war in early July 1863?

15. What song did Rhett suggest Scarlett play at Miss Pittypat's dinner party in May 1864?

16. When Scarlett saw Big Sam and the other Negroes marching through Atlanta on their way to dig rifle pits, what song was Sam leading the gang in singing?

17. Who sent a message to Atlanta Confederate headquarters in the summer of 1864 that said, "I have lost the battle and am in full retreat"?

18. During the war, when did mail service out of Atlanta stop?

19. What was the opening line of the letter Uncle Peter brought to Melanie from Ashley after the war?

20. What was the title of the poem Will Benteen once found pasted on the back of a Confederate note?

21. What was in the letter that Scarlett received from Will Benteen while she was in Atlanta waiting for Frank Kennedy to propose, which prompted her to work hard on "convincing" Frank that he should marry her?

22. What book did Ashley Wilkes use to conduct Gerald O'Hara's funeral services?

23. What "engrabin'" did Scarlett suggest putting on the back of Gerald's pocketwatch after she presented it to Pork?

24. What prayer did the mourners at Gerald O'Hara's funeral not know how to recite?

25. Who headed the postbellum Atlanta Saturday Night Musical Circle?

26. How did Atlanta women forced to stay indoors because of the 1866 Klan lynching ask Scarlett for the use of Archie's driving services?

27. What book did Melly read to Aunt Pitty, Scarlett, India, and Archie on the night the Klan raided Shantytown?

28. What did Melly send to Belle Watling after Belle's participation in saving Ashley's life?

29. What song was an ersatz drunken Rhett Butler singing when he arrived at Melly's house on the night the Klan raided Shantytown?

30. In what magazine did Scarlett see a picture of the house she made Rhett build her in Atlanta?

31. What musical blackmail did Rhett promise Scarlett if she refused to marry him?
32. What did the telegram that Rhett sent Scarlett regarding Melanie's illness say?
33. Complete the first line of a song that was popular in 1864: "Into a ward of _____ "?
    A. "Solemn silence."
    B. "Hallowed heroes."
    C. "Doleful regret."
    D. "Whitewashed walls."

BONUS QUESTION. Who wrote Melanie a letter that began, "The Confederacy may need the lifeblood of its men but not yet does it demand the heart's blood of its women"?

SUPER BONUS QUESTION. Why did the newspapers suspend publication after the siege of Atlanta began?

QUIZ 30

MEDICAL PRACTICES AND INJURIES

God and the doctor we alike adore
But only when in danger, not before;
The danger o'er, both are alike requited,
God is forgotten, and the doctor slighted.

—JOHN OWEN, *Epigrams*

The war brought injury beyond imagination to the South, and a blockade-crippled medical community found itself operating without anesthesia, and watching men die from simple, easily curable infections. Answer the following questions about sickness and health in the South before, during, and after the war.

1. What injury did Gerald O'Hara once sustain after jumping his horse?
2. What were the names of the Clayton County father and son doctors?
3. Who doctored Tara's slaves?
4. What "ailment" did Scarlett decide to succumb to in order to win Ashley's heart?
5. What "anti-giddiness" medicinal aid did Scarlett never keep with her?
6. What type of "pacifier" did Mammy give Prissy for Scarlett and Wade's trip to Atlanta?
7. What was the name of the McLure boy who sustained a shoulder wound in Virginia?
8. What were the injuries that sent the Tarleton twins home from the battlefield?
9. Because of the Yankee blockade of Confederate ports in the second year of the war, what medical supplies in particular became very scarce in the South?
10. After a pregnant Melanie fainted in town and had to be brought home by Rhett Butler, what medicinal aids did everyone in Miss Pittypat's household rush to assemble?
11. What did Dr. Meade order Melanie to do during her pregnancy, which Melanie refused to do?
12. By 1864, chloroform was so scarce in Atlanta that it was only used for what?
13. By 1864, opium was so precious in Atlanta that it was only used for what?
14. How did Carey Ashburn die?
15. How did John Wilkes die?
16. What disease killed young Dr. Fontaine at Vicksburg?
17. What drug did the Yankee doctor administer to Carreen and Suellen during the Yankees' occupation of Tara?
18. What medical condition was old Dr. Fontaine afflicted with when he went off to fight in the war?
19. How was Pork injured when attempting to break into a hen coop in Fayetteville in late 1864?
20. What injuries did Scarlett sustain while trying to put out the kitchen fire set by the Yankees on their second "visit" to Tara?
21. What illness was Will Benteen suffering from when he first arrived at Tara?

22. What limb was Will Benteen missing when he first arrived at Tara?
23. What was Ellen O'Hara's "sovereign remedy" for dysentery?
24. What injury did Fanny Elsing's groom sustain during the war?
25. What particular physical war-caused disability did Aunt Pitty feel gave Tommy Wellburn "a very vulgar appearance"?
26. After the war, what disease—"once found only among poor whites"—began appearing in Atlanta's best families?
27. How did Jonas Wilkerson die?
28. What diseases were rampant among the country Negroes who flocked to Atlanta after the war?
29. How did Rhett Butler's grandfather on the Butler side die?
30. What ailment did Uncle Peter conveniently begin to suffer from after Scarlett failed to defend him against insulting postbellum Yankee women, and which forbade him from driving Scarlett around in Aunt Pitty's carriage?
31. What were Archie's two disabilities?
    A. He was deaf and blind
    B. He was missing a leg and an eye
    C. He was missing both feet
    D. He was missing his right thumb and left eye
32. What was the name of the doctor India Wilkes brought back to Melly's house on the night the Klan raided Shantytown?
    A. Dr. Dean
    B. Dr. David Berger
    C. Dr. Edward Stackler
    D. Dr. Charles Gibbs
33. What was the nature of Ashley Wilkes's injuries the night the Klan raided Shantytown?
    A. He was stabbed in the thigh
    B. He was shot in the thigh
    C. He was stabbed in the stomach
    D. He received a flesh wound through the shoulder and fainted from a loss of blood
34. What was the nature of the injury that killed Frank Kennedy?
    A. He was hung by the Ku Klux Klan
    B. He drowned
    C. He was shot through the head during the Klan raid on Shantytown
    D. He was drawn and quartered by Jonas Wilkerson

35. How did Scarlett learn she was pregnant with her second daughter?
   A. She was told by a woman seer
   B. She found out when she was consulting Dr. Meade for a digestive upset
   C. She was told in a dream
   D. She found out during routine surgery for an ingrown toenail
36. What thumb-sucking cure did Mrs. Merriwether suggest to Rhett for Bonnie?
   A. She suggested that Bonnie sleep with gloves on
   B. She suggested that Scarlett spank Bonnie every time she caught her sucking her thumb
   C. She suggested that Rhett put quinine on Bonnie's thumb
   D. She suggested that Scarlett and Rhett put a little brandy in Bonnie's milk

BONUS QUESTION 1. How many doctors were there in Clayton County, Georgia, in the summer of 1864?
BONUS QUESTION 2. What two things did the postbellum returning soldiers visiting Tara have in common?
BONUS QUESTION 3. What scar did Rhett show Wade to prove to the boy that he was as brave as the boy's dead daddy?

QUIZ 31

FOOD AND DRINK

For as in the days that were before the flood they were eating and drinking.

—*Matthew 24:38*

Food was abundant and delicious in the South before the war. After the war, people couldn't even get a decent cup of coffee. Answer the following questions about the victual and potable situation in the Confederate states before and after the Civil War.

1. After Scarlett was born, what "beverage" did Gerald O'Hara serve to every slave at Tara?
2. What was the meal Mammy prepared for Ellen upon Mrs. O'Hara's return from the Slattery farm?
3. Who dominated the conversation at Tara during meals?
4. What beverage did Gerald O'Hara imbibe before he fired Jonas Wilkerson?
5. What meal did Mammy prepare for Scarlett on the morning of the 1861 Twelve Oaks ball?
6. What treat did Scarlett once miss at the Calverts because she had eaten earlier at home?
7. As Scarlett neared Twelve Oaks for the Wilkes's 1861 barbecue and ball, what cooking smells greeted her?
8. At the Wilkes's 1861 barbecue and ball, what did the servants, coachmen, and maids of the guests eat?
9. What type of stew simmered in the giant iron wash-pots at the Wilkes's barbecue?
10. What did Aunt Pittypat keep in her "swoon bottle"?
11. What did Scarlett, Melanie, and Aunt Pittypat have for breakfast the morning after the Atlanta fund-raising bazaar?
12. During the war, what were the only types of meats that were still plentiful in the South?
13. What did the Confederates feed their prisoners of war?
14. What "passed for coffee" in Atlanta during the war?
15. What was used for "long sweetening" in the ersatz "coffee" drunk in the South during the war?
16. After the Yankees' occupation of Tara, what foodstuffs were served at the plantation three times a day?
17. After the Yankees' second "visit" to Tara in November 1864, what did Scarlett and the others eat—but only if Pork was lucky hunting and fishing?
18. In November 1864, what bird did Pork steal so everyone at Tara could eat?
19. Thanks to the generosity of the Fontaines, what did those who were left at Tara have for breakfast in November 1864?
20. What always stood in the passageway by the kitchen door at Tara, and which came in handy when the Yankees set fire to the kitchen?
21. What was the menu Mammy served when Frank Kennedy and a troop from the commissary department visited Tara at Christmas, 1864?

Days of Wine and Roses *The lovely newlyweds, Scarlett and Rhett Butler, enjoying a sumptuous feast on their honeymoon in New Orleans. Scarlett gorged on Creole dishes with such gluttony that Rhett threatened to divorce her if she got as fat as "the Cuban ladies." Scarlett responded by sticking her tongue out at him and continuing to eat.*

22. What did Gerald O'Hara bury in an oak barrel under Tara's scuppernong arbor?
23. What were "ramrod rolls"?
24. On Scarlett's first visit to the Tarletons' plantation after the war, what was served for dinner?
25. What beverage did a Yankee captain give to Scarlett after she fainted upon being told that Rhett could not lend her the money she needed for Tara's tax?
26. When Frank visited Aunt Pitty's house in Atlanta during his "courtship" of Scarlett, what type of hot beverage did Aunt Pitty serve him?
27. How many drinks did it take Scarlett to get to the point where she could tell herself, "I'll think of these things tomorrow when I can stand them better"?

Between the Sheets *Scarlett's breakfast in bed following her passionate night of lovemaking with a drunken (and inhibitionless) Rhett.*

28. What beverage did Scarlett learn the "use" of during the months of her second pregnancy?

29. Scarlett refused to entertain guests in Aunt Pitty's house in postbellum Atlanta until she could offer them what kinds of food and drink?

30. In March 1867, what foodstuffs did Scarlett accuse Johnnie Gallegher of selling behind her back instead of feeding to the leased convicts she had hired to work at her Gallegher-run lumber mill?

BONUS QUESTION. During the war, because of the scarcity of white flour, what type of bread did Southerners resort to eating instead of their usual biscuits, rolls, and waffles?

SUPER BONUS QUESTION. After the Yankees' occupation of Tara, what "savory meals" memories had the power to bring tears to Scarlett's eyes?

QUIZ 32

WHO SAID IT IN <u>GONE WITH THE WIND</u>?

The nice thing about quotes is that they give us a nodding acquaintance with the originator which is often socially impressive.
—KENNETH WILLIAMS, from the preface to *Acid Drops*

A book that furnishes no quotations is, me judice, *no book—it is a plaything.*
—THOMAS LOVE PEACOCK, *Crotchet Castle*

The dialogue in Margaret Mitchell's *Gone with the Wind* is sharp and acerbic. It is also some of the most insightful, emotional, and telling conversation ever to appear in a contemporary American novel. Thus, it is not only just, but necessary, that this quiz be lengthy. Although "Who Said It?" does not attempt to highlight *every* significant quote in the novel, it does focus the spotlight on 156 of the best.

This quiz asks you to identify the speaker of the following quotations, and the person to whom the remark was made. The chapters in which the quotes appear are given in the "Question/Chapter Key" section that follows the quizzes.

1. "Ah has said time an' again, it doan do no good doin' nuthin' fr w'ite trash. Dey is de shifless, mos' ungrateful passel of no-counts livin'. An' Miss Ellen got no bizness weahin' herseff out waitin' on folks dat did dey be wuth shootin' dey'd have niggers ter wait on dem."
2. "Eavesdroppers often hear highly entertaining and instructive things."
3. "God is on the side of the strongest battalion!"
4. "I'll scream out loud if you come near me. I will! I will—at the top of my voice! Get away from me! Don't you dare touch me!"
5. "I'm tired of everlastingly being unnatural and never doing anything I want to do."
6. "Love isn't enough to make a successful marriage when two people are as different as we are."

7. "Most of the misery of the world has been caused by wars. And when the wars were over, no one ever knew what they were all about."

8. "The South and I are even now. The South threw me out to starve once. I haven't starved, and I am making enough money out of the South's death throes to compensate me for my lost birthright."

9. "What most people don't seem to realize is that there is just as much money to be made out of the wreckage of a civilization as from the upbuilding of one."

10. "Why don't you say it, you coward! You're afraid to marry me! You'd rather live with that stupid little fool who can't open her mouth except to say 'Yes' or 'No' and raise a passel of mealy-mouthed brats just like her!"

11. "Why don't you say what you really think? . . . Why don't you say I'm a damned rascal and no gentleman and that I must take myself off or you'll have one of these gallant boys in gray call me out?"

12. "Yes sir, what war does to man's bowels—dysentery and things like that—"

13. "There'll always be wars because men love wars. Women don't, but men do—yea, passing the love of women."

14. "You little fraud. You dance all night with the soldiers and give them roses and ribbons and tell them how you'd die for the Cause, and when it comes to bandaging a few wounds and picking off a few lice, you decamp hastily."

15. "Miss Scarlett, effen we kain git de doctah w'en Miss Melly's time come, doan you bodder. Ah kin manage. Ah knows all 'bout birthin'. Ain' mah ma a midwife? Ain' she raise me ter be a midwife, too? Jes' you leave it ter me."

16. "Never pass up new experiences, Scarlett. They enrich the mind."

17. "Fo' Gawd, Miss Scarlett! We's got ter have a doctah. Ah-Ah-Miss Scarlett, Ah doan know nuthin' 'bout bringin' babies. Maw wouldn' nebber lemme be 'round folkses whut wuz havin' dem."

18. "I should love you, for you are charming and talented at many useless accomplishments."

19. "I will go home! You can't stop me! I will go home! I want my mother! I'll kill you if you try to stop me! I will go home!"

20. "When will you stop looking for compliments in men's lightest utter-ances?"

21. " 'Feeleep! Feeleep!' "

22. "As God is my witness, as God is my witness, the Yankees aren't going to lick me. I'm going to live through this, and when it's over, I'm never going to be hungry again. No, nor any of my folks. If I have to steal or kill—as God is my witness, I'm never going to be hungry again."

23. "For 'tis the only thing in the world that lasts . . . and to anyone with a drop of Irish blood in them the land they live on is like their mother. . . . 'Tis the only thing worth working for, fighting for, dying for."

24. "God intended women to be timid frightened creatures and there's something unnatural about a woman who isn't afraid . . . Scarlett, always save something to fear—even as you save something to love."

25. "We will wait for Mrs. O'Hara. She is late."

26. "White trash, indeed! Well, isn't this generation soft and ladylike!"

27. "Always remember, dear, you are responsible for the moral as well as the physical welfare of the darkies God has intrusted to your care. You must realize that they are like children and must be guarded from themselves like children, and you must always set them a good example."

28. "You look like a nigger."

29. "Dey ain' a soun' set of bowels in de whole Confedrut ahmy. It's mah notion dat 'twarn't de Yankees whut beat our gempmum. 'Twuz dey own innards. Kain no gempmum fight wid his bowels tuhnin' ter water."

30. "Fighting is like champagne. It goes to the heads of cowards as quickly as of heroes. Any fool can be brave on a battle field when it's be brave or else be killed."

31. "In the end what will happen will be what has happened whenever a civilization breaks up. The people who have brains and courage come through and the ones who haven't are winnowed out. At least, it has been interesting, if not comfortable, to witness a Götterdämmerung."

32. "There is nothing left. Nothing left for me. Nothing to love. Nothing to fight for. You are gone and Tara is going."

33. "These are the most beautiful hands I know. They are beautiful because they are strong and every callus is a medal, Scarlett, every blister an award for bravery and unselfishness."

34. "They say Abe Lincoln got his start splitting rails. Just think to what heights I may climb!"

35. "You've been mighty good to me, Miss Scarlett, and me a stranger and nothin' to you at all. I've caused you a heap of trouble and worry and

if it's all the same to you, I'm goin' to stay here and help you all with the work 'till I've paid you back some for your trouble."

36. "Face paint! Well, you ain' so big dat Ah kain whup you! Ah ain' never been so scan'lized! You is los' yo' mine! Miss Ellen be tuhnin' in her grabe dis minute!"

37. "Get off those steps, you trashy wench! Get off this land! Get out!"

38. "I am a monster of selfishness, as you ought to know. I always expect payment for anything I give."

39. "Not outer Miss Ellen's po'teers is you gwine have a new dress, ef dat's whut you figgerin' on. Not w'ile Ah got breaf in mah body."

40. "These are not the hands of a lady."

41. "When you are trying to get something out of a man, don't blurt it out as you did to me. Do try to be more subtle, more seductive. It gets better results."

42. "You look very prosperous and very, very tidy. And almost good enough to eat. If it wasn't for the Yankees outside—but you are quite safe, my dear."

43. "You've remained so faithful to dear Charlie, though you could have married dozens of times. Melly and I have often said how loyal you were to his memory when everyone else said you were just a heartless coquette."

44. "She can get mad quicker and stay mad longer than any woman I ever saw!"

45. "Always tell the truth, Scarlett. You can't lie. The Irish are the poorest liars in the world."

46. "I always felt that women had a hardness and endurance unknown to men, despite the pretty idea taught me in childhood that women are frail, tender, sensitive creatures."

47. "I've found out that money is the most important thing in the world and, as God is my witness, I don't ever intend to be without it again."

48. "The more I see of emancipation the more criminal I think it is. It's just ruined the darkies."

49. "This that's facing all of us is worse than war—worse than prison—worse than death."

50. "Well, of course, you can't expect a silly little woman like me to understand men's affairs."

51. "What a pity they didn't hang you!"

52. "You'll never make a farm hand out of a Wilkes—or anything else that's useful. The breed is purely ornamental."

53. "All you've done is to be different from other women and you've made a little success at it. As I've told you before, that is the one unforgivable sin in any society. Be different and be damned!"

54. "And were ye afther thinkin' an O'Hara of Tara would be follyin' the dirthy thracks of a God-damned Orangeman and a God-damned poor white?"

55. "Death and taxes and childbirth! There's never any convenient time for any of them!"

56. "Dey talked in front of me lak Ah wuz a mule an' couldn' unnerstan' dem—lak Ah wuz a Affikun an' din' know whut dey wuz talkin' 'bout. An' dey call me a nigger an' Ah' ain' never been call a nigger by no w'ite folks, an' dey call me a ole pet an' say dat niggers ain' ter be trus'ed! Me not ter be trus'ed!"

57. "Did you ever hear the Oriental proverb: 'The dogs bark but the caravan passes on?' Let them bark, Scarlett. I fear nothing will stop your caravan."

58. "Ef you wuz jes' half as nice ter w'ite folks as you is ter niggers, Ah spec de worl' would treat you better."

59. "I never liked you much till now, Scarlett. You were always hard as a hickory nut, even as a child, and I don't like hard females, barring myself."

60. "No woman ever really liked me, except Mother. Even my sisters."

61. "It's a poor person and a poor nation that sits down and cries because life isn't precisely what they expected it to be."

62. "Make up your mind to this. If you are different, you are isolated, not only from people of your own age but from those of your parents' generation and from your children's generation too."

63. "Men haven't got much sense, have they, when you get down to rock bottom?"

64. "Miss Suellen, why in hell are you devilin' your poor pa and bringin' up your ma to him? Most of the time he don't realize she's dead and here you are rubbin' it in."

65. "Uncle Peter is one of our family."

66. "We bow to the inevitable. We're not wheat, we're buckwheat! When a storm comes along it flattens ripe wheat because it's dry and can't bend with the wind. But ripe buckwheat's got sap in it and it bends."

67. "Dig up the weeds off Yankee graves? For two cents, I'd dig up all the Yankees and throw them in the city dump!"

68. "I'm not going to be like other women and have a baby every year."
69. "Miss Scarlett, ef you doan quit cahyin' on so, you gwine sour yo' milk an' de baby have colic, sho as gun's iron."
70. "They put me in jail for killin' and they let me out with a gun in my hand and a free pardon to do more killin'."
71. "Ah, Scarlett, how the thought of a dollar does make your eyes sparkle! Are you sure you haven't some Scotch or perhaps Jewish blood as well as Irish?"
72. "Sweet are the uses of motherhood!"
73. "This isn't the first time the world's been upside down and it won't be the last. It's happened before and it'll happen again. And when it does happen, everyone loses everything and everyone is equal."
74. "You can tell your curious friends that when I marry it will be because I couldn't get the woman I wanted in any other way. And I've never yet wanted a woman bad enough to marry her."
75. "You never worked in your life. You're too lazy. All you ever do is finance Carpetbaggers in their thieving and take half the profits and bribe Yankee officials to let you in on schemes to rob us taxpayers."
76. "You'll never get over being the belle of the County, will you? You'll always think you're the cutest little trick in shoe leather and that every man you meet is expiring for love of you."
77. "Dey treat me lak Ah jes' as good as dey wuz, Miss Scarlett, but in dere hearts, dey din' lak me—dey din' lak no niggers. An' dey wuz sceered of me, kase Ah's so big. An' dey wuz allus astin' me 'bout de blood houn's dat chase me an' de beatin's Ah got. An', Lawd, Miss Scarlett, Ah ain' nebber got no beatin's! You know Mist' Gerald ain' gwine let nobody beat a 'spensive nigger lak me!"
78. "I shall be proud to speak to you. Proud to be under obligation to you. I hope—I hope we meet again."
79. "You must not say unkind things about my sister-in-law."
80. "Ah's stood fer all dat but Ah ain' gwine stand fer dis, Miss Scarlett. You kain mahy wid trash. Not w'ile Ah got breaf in mah body."
81. "Beauty doesn't make a lady, nor clothes a great lady!"
82. "I always intended having you, Scarlett, since that first day I saw you at Twelve Oaks when you threw that vase and swore and proved that you weren't a lady. I always intended having you, one way or another."
83. "I want it understood that any of you who do not call on Scarlett need never, never call on me."

84. "I'm riding you with a slack rein, my pet, but don't forget that I'm riding with curb and spurs just the same."
85. "May God damn your cheating little soul to hell for all eternity!"
86. "Melly's a fool and the ladies are right. Scarlett is a slick piece of baggage and I don't see why Charlie ever married her."
87. "My news is this. I still want you more than any woman I've ever seen and now that Frank's gone, I thought you'd be interested to know it."
88. "God help the man who ever really loves you. You'd break his heart, my darling, cruel, destructive little cat who is so careless and confident she doesn't even trouble to sheathe her claws."
89. "Scarlett O'Hara, you're a fool!"
90. "Scarlett, you are a constant joy to me. You unerringly manage to pick the wrong people and the wrong things."
91. "There's nothing after we die, Scarlett. You are having your hell now."
92. "You ain' nuthin' but a mule in hawse harness. You kin polish a mule's feet an' shine his hide an' put brass all over his harness an' hitch him ter a fine cah'ige. But he a mule jes' de same. An' you ain' foolin' nobody, needer. An' dat Butler man, he come of good stock and he all slicked up lak a race hawse, but he a mule in hawse harness, jes' lak you."
93. "You know as well as I do that the man is a rogue. He always has been and now he's unspeakable. He is simply not the kind of man decent people receive."
94. "I married you to keep you for a pet, my dear."
95. "Mist' Rhett, you is bad! Yeah-O, Lawd!"
96. "The happiest days are the days when babies come!"
97. "There are no nice Republicans. And I don't want their help. And I don't intend to make the best of things—if they are Yankee things."
98. "You are boy enough for me, son."
99. "You know I don't want any more children! I never wanted any at all. Every time things are going right with me I have to have a baby."
100. " 'Lusting in your heart.' That's a good phrase, isn't it?"
101. "Cheer up, maybe you'll have a miscarriage."
102. "Dark."
103. "Do you realize that I can divorce you for refusing me my marital right?"
104. "I like these days better."
105. "I never go about the world doing good deeds if I can avoid it."
106. "I shall come home early but drunk as a fiddler's bitch if I please."

107. "I won't think of it now. I'll think of it later when I can stand it."
108. "If something with claws and horns came and sat on your chest, you'd tell it to get the hell off you, wouldn't you? Like hell you would."
109. "Life's under no obligation to give us what we expect. We take what we can get and are thankful it's no worse than it is."
110. "My apologies for my conduct at our last meeting. I was very drunk, as you doubtless know, and quite swept off my feet by your charms —need I enumerate them?"
111. "Observe my hands, my dear."
112. "Sometimes I think she's like the giant Antæus who became stronger each time he touched Mother Earth."
113. "Take it. You are shaking all over. Oh, don't give yourself airs. I know you drink on the quiet and I know how much you drink."
114. "The O'Haras might have been kings of Ireland once but your father was nothing but a smart Mick on the make. And you are no better—"
115. "What a child you are! You have lived with three men and still know nothing of men's natures. You seem to think they are like old ladies past the change of life."
116. "What a white livered, cowardly little bitch you are."
117. "Yo' wais' jes' done got bigger, Miss Scarlett, an' dar ain' nuthin' ter do 'bout it."
118. "You are looking pale, Mrs. Butler. Is there a rouge shortage?"
119. "You grow up and be a brave man like your father, Wade. Try to be just like him, for he was a hero and don't let anyone tell you differently. He married your mother, didn't he? Well, that's proof enough of heroism."
120. "Did it ever occur to you that I loved you as much as a man can love a woman? Loved you for years before I finally got you?"
121. "I can't make money from the enforced labor and misery of others."
122. "I'll think of it all tomorrow, at Tara. I can stand it then. Tomorrow, I'll think of some way to get him back. After all, tomorrow is another day."
123. "Mother, watch me take this one!"
124. "My dear, I don't give a damn."
125. "Now, Miss, no hysterics and no deathbed confessions from you or, before God, I will wring your neck!"
126. "She is the only dream I ever had that lived and breathed and did not die in the face of reality."
127. "She was the only completely kind person I ever knew."

128. "Mah Lawd, it sho is good ter see some of de fambly agin! Huccome you got so mean lak, totin' a gun, Miss Scarlett?"

129. "Cheeks lak ze rose, eyes lak ze emerald! Pretty lak w'en I first see you at ze bazaar. You remembaire?"

130. "I've been trying to think what would be best for Georgia, best for all of us."

131. "Ashley isn't—practical."

132. "You highflying, bogtrotting Irish will find out who's running things around here when you get sold out for taxes."

133. "Ah's sceered of cows, Miss Scarlett. Ah ain' nebber had nuthin' ter do wid cows. Ah ain' no yard nigger. Ah's a house nigger."

134. "Ah ain' figgerin' on havin' happen whut happen at dat las' barbecue w'en Ah wuz too sick frum dem chittlins Ah et ter fetch you no tray befo' you went. You is gwine eat eve'y bite of dis."

135. "People just don't understand you and people can't bear for women to be smart."

136. "Why, Scarlett, what are you doing downtown this time of the day? Why aren't you out at my house helping Melly get ready for the surprise party?"

137. "I won't be havin' no quarrelin' tonight with Mr. O'Hara layin' dead in the parlor."

138. "Scarlett, I will come to Atlanta. . . . I cannot fight you both."

139. "Fo' Gawd, Miss Scarlett. Ah din' spec ter wake up agin 'cept in de Promise Lan'."

140. "It's all yore fault and thar's blood on yore hands."

141. "Ah hope Ah done kill dat black baboon. But Ah din' wait ter fine out. But ef he hahmed you, Miss Scarlett, Ah'll go back an' mek sho of it."

142. "Either you tend to your business and let me tend to mine or I quit tonight."

143. "Ef y'all doan tek me ter Mist' Wynder's, Ah'll lay out in de woods all night an' maybe de patterollers git me, 'cause Ah heap ruther de patterollers git me dan Miss Beetriss when she is in a state."

144. "I knows about convict leasin'. I calls it convict murderin'. Buyin' men like they was mules."

145. "My dear Miss Melly, it is always a privilege and a pleasure to be in your home, for you—and ladies like you—are the hearts of all of us, all that we have left."

146. "It's a foolish war when old fools like me are out toting guns."

147. "I've got to say it and I haven't any right. But I've got to say it. Your—Rhett Butler. Everything he touches he poisons."
148. "Miss Scarlett, 'ness I gits mo' to eat, I kain nuss neither of these chillun."
149. "How the hell—I beg your pardon, Scarlett. But how can a man ask a girl to marry him when his darkies are all freed and his stock gone and he hasn't got a cent in his pockets?"
150. "We must all give grateful thanks to the charming ladies whose indefatigable and patriotic efforts have made this bazaar not only a pecuniary success, but have transformed this rough hall into a bower of loveliness, a fit garden for the charming rosebuds I see about me."
151. "It's an insult to the memory of my blooded darlings to have a mule in their paddock. Mules are misbegotten, unnatural critters and it ought to be illegal to breed them."
152. "Ah, what will the South be like without all our fine boys? What would the South have been if they had lived?"
153. "Such a little beauty! When she grows up she will certainly be a belle. But I suppose you know that any man who courts her will have a tussle with Captain Butler, for I never saw such a devoted father."
154. "I think that if it hadn't been for you, I'd have gone down into oblivion—like poor Cathleen Calvert and so many other people who once had great names, old names."
155. "Lie still, dear. The fire's out."

BONUS QUESTION: "Fear not, fair lady! Your guilty secret is safe with me!"

WHAT MAKES A BOOK A BEST SELLER?*
THE PHENOMENAL SUCCESS OF *GONE WITH THE WIND*
PROMPTS SOME REFLECTIONS
BY EDWARD WEEKS

The success of *Gone with the Wind* is enough to make every editor sit up and take notice. Why should this first novel of Margaret Mitchell's outstrip the sale of any other volume published since the war? There is certainly no Mason-Dixon boundary about the book: I have questioned literally hundreds of its readers, and from their testimony I judge that the average period of consumption is three days, during which interval neither food nor sleep is of the least consequence. I realize, of course, that the Civil War is our Trojan War, and that any story that does justice to the period will move us to tears. *Gone with the Wind* lays hold of our emotions and never lets go till the end. But this is surely not the only secret of its success.

I confess that I began my reading of *Gone with the Wind* with misgivings. It irritated me to see any book so showered with superlatives as this one was. The story is set in the conventional mold of Civil War romances: the novel begins in the leisurely, decorative days before the war; it shows the Southern chivalry and the Southern arrogance which broke into flame against the Abolitionists; it shows the heart-breaking sacrifice which went into this lost cause and it shows the destruction and hate which swept over the land with Sherman's army, the Yankee garrisons and the Carpetbaggers. I have heard the story condemned as being too bitter toward the Yankees. I didn't find it so: it seemed to me that the author was as unsparing of the Southern character as she was of their Northern invaders.

The success of this novel depends largely upon the vitality of the four central characters. These are, first, Ashley Wilkes, a

*From *The New York Times Book Review,* Sunday, December 20, 1936. Copyright © 1936 by The New York Times Company. Reprinted by permission.

musical-comedy Southerner, the incarnation of chivalry, who, when he is not fighting, is sleeping, and who eventually wakes up desolate in a world he doesn't understand. Second is Melanie, Ashley's wife, a thin, steel blade of righteousness who endures all the suffering of Southern women, who bends but never breaks. Ashely and Melanie are intended to wring your heart—and to keep wringing it. Opposed to them are a pair of realists, Scarlett O'Hara, the heroine—a Becky Sharp of Georgia—a vain, selfish belle with Irish temperament, who thinks she knows what she wants but never gets it; and fourth, Scarlett's lover and tor-menter, Rhett Butler, a handsome Charleston outcast, as much of a realist as Sinclair Lewis, who saw the war for the folly it was and who made his fortune out of the Southern ruin.

There are your stage properties and your cast. Now let's estimate the strength and the weakness of the performance. To begin with, the book is over one thousand pages long, which is another way of saying that every dialogue and nearly every description is twice as exuberant as it needs to be. Naturally, a book of such width has to be stuffed with a good many minor characters—"supers," Hollywood would call them—but I could wish that so many of them weren't caricatures. Scarlett's first two husbands are so flat, so unreal, that they might just as well be cut out of cardboard; Scarlett's sisters are the sisters of Cinder-ella; and Scarlett's father—Gerald O'Hara—is an Irishman so improbable that no Bostonian would ever recognize him. (And we know our Irish.)

I would also point out that it is bad writing to pursue a character as openly as Mrs. Mitchell pursues Scarlett. We are told within very brief space that she is vain, that she hasn't a girl friend in the county, and that her brain was not made for analy-sis. Those are the kind of stage directions that don't belong in literature. The reader should be left to draw his own conclusions. Finally, I object to the softening of Rhett's brain and character toward the close. The book had to end some time—but not so weakly as this. This senility which overtakes Rhett at the ad-vanced age of 45 seems to me wholly out of keeping with his character.

On the other hand, the book certainly has its strong points. The story is kept in motion from start to finish: episode follows episode with a power of invention remarkable in a first novel. The big scenes—the Wilkes barbecue, Atlanta waiting for the news of Gettysburg, the shooting of the Yankee, Scarlett's return to Tara, and Gerald's funeral—are superbly drawn. The Negroes in their talk and action are better than any I can remember in current fiction. And although there is romance enough for the lovelorn, I do applaud the salty realism which—thanks to Rhett and Scarlett—saves the novel again and again. This story may not be great literature, but—God's nightgown!—as Scarlett would say—it is uncommonly entertaining. Were I to attempt a chemical analysis of the elements which have made it a success, my formula would be as follows:

Emotional content	25%
Characterization	15%
Invention	10%
Timeliness of the book	45%
Publisher's advertising	5%

In short, I do think that much of the magnetism of the story is due to the fact that it reached us precisely at the moment when we were ready for it.

PART TWO

ALEXANDRA RIPLEY'S SCARLETT

THE SEQUEL TO MARGARET MITCHELL'S

GONE WITH THE WIND

Yes, Margaret Mitchell writes better than I do—but she's dead.
—ALEXANDRA RIPLEY, author of *Scarlett: The Sequel to Margaret Mitchell's "Gone with the Wind"*

PEOPLE

QUIZ 33

SCARLETT

The charming girl has become an elegant, grown-up woman.
— RHETT BUTLER

Scarlett O'Hara changes in *Scarlett*. After battling demons galore along the way, she has finally grown up and this adult Scarlett is somewhat older, definitely wiser, and now manifesting the emotional (and in some cases, physical) scars of the psychologically (and, again, in some cases, physically) battle-tested. Answer the following questions about the new (and improved?) Scarlett.

1. What was the name of the new servant Scarlett took with her to Aunt Pitty's house the first time she was back in Atlanta after Mammy's death?
2. What were Scarlett's assets in late 1873?
3. What was Scarlett's costume for Atlanta's January 1874 masked ball?
4. According to her Aunts Eulalie and Pauline, who had Scarlett grown up to look like?
5. How old had Scarlett been the first time she visited Charleston?
6. In 1874, what beverage did Scarlett move up to from her afternoon drink of sherry?
7. What was Scarlett's sister Carreen's "nun" name?
8. During her visit to Charleston, what did Scarlett tell Mrs. Butler she wanted more than anything else in the world?
9. At what age had Scarlett thoroughly known the Catholic catechism?
10. What order of nuns did Scarlett's sister belong to?
11. What vegetable did Scarlett once send back while she and Rhett were eating at the fanciest restaurant in New Orleans?

12. When Rhett offered Scarlett a bribe to leave Charleston, what was Scarlett's counteroffer?

13. Did Scarlett take milk or lemon in her tea?

14. What did Rhett call Scarlett on New Year's Eve morning when she tried to push him into making breakfast for her quicker than the stove could heat up?

15. What three "unwritten, inviolate rules of the Southern code of behavior" did Scarlett break after being scolded by Aunt Pauline for not writing to Grandfather Robillard?

16. What was the name of the "sleepy-lidded" Charlestonian Scarlett pretended to have an affair with as an attempt to make Rhett jealous?

17. How did Rhett awaken Scarlett when she began to fade into unconsciousness beneath the overturned sailing sloop?

18. How old was Scarlett when she attended the dedication ceremonies at Hodgson Hall?

19. Who escorted Scarlett to the dedication ceremonies at Hodgson Hall?

20. Who taught Scarlett how to dance the Irish reel?

21. What barnyard animal had Scarlett been frightened of her entire life?

22. Who was Scarlett's maid at the O'Hara home in Savannah?

23. What was the last age at which Scarlett had been out of the house without stays?

24. What physical symptoms did Scarlett suffer from during the fifth month of her fourth pregnancy?

25. What "title" was awarded to Scarlett for her strength, trustworthiness, and determination?

26. What unavoidable complication occurred during the cesarean delivery of Cat?

27. TRUE OR FALSE: In the summer of 1876, the last time Scarlett had worn a corset was when Colum and Kathleen had had to cut one off her in Galway.

28. What was the name of the bay gelding Scarlett bought from John Morland?
    A. Knute Lobell
    B. Irish Lass
    C. Full Moon
    D. Half Moon

29. What was the name of the Englishman who fell in love with Scarlett an hour after he met her on the *Golden Fleece*?
   A. David Windsor
   B. Roger Cowperthwaite
   C. Edward Stackler III
   D. Paddy McKillop

30. What did Fenton "expect" from Scarlett when he proposed to her?
   A. "He expected her to be a credit to him. He had observed that she had the ability."
   B. "He demanded obedience, but in lieu of that, he would accept silence."
   C. "He insisted upon carnal knowledge of Scarlett, reminding her that a widow need no longer maintain a facade of innocence."
   D. "He insisted upon taking over control of Scarlett's money, a demand that Scarlett, to her credit, refused to give a moment's consideration."

31. What were the two things Scarlett would not relinquish control over to Charlotte Montague when Charlotte began the transformation of the Big House?
   A. Scarlett would continue to determine the days' menus and she would also personally select the vegetables for Cat's purees.
   B. Scarlett would continue to bathe herself, and no servant girl would be allowed in the bathroom while she was at toilet.
   C. Cat would have a room next to hers, and she would continue to handle her own financial affairs.
   D. Scarlett would oversee production of all the crops, and she would also do all the hiring and firing of the household staff.

BONUS QUESTION. What was the first "real city" Scarlett ever saw?

QUIZ 34

WADE, ELLA, BONNIE, AND CAT: THE CHILDREN OF SCARLETT O'HARA

Frisch weht der Wind der Heizmat zu:
mein irisch Kind, wo weilest du?
Freshly blows the wind to the homeland:
my Irish child, where are you staying?
——RICHARD WAGNER, *Tristan und Isolde,* I, i

This quiz tests your knowledge of Scarlett O'Hara's four children. Even though Wade, Ella, and Bonnie also appear in *Gone with the Wind,* all the answers to these questions are found in *Scarlett.*

1. What was inscribed on Bonnie Butler's grave headstone?
2. What type of hair did Scarlett's daughter Ella have?
3. What type of physique did Scarlett's daughter Ella have?
4. Which of Scarlett's children ate "like a horse"?
5. Who shopped for Wade's clothes?
6. What illness did Wade and Ella contract in late 1873?
7. According to Joseph O'Neill, what type of supernatural being was Cat O'Hara?
8. What color were Cat's eyes when she was born?
9. What color did Cat's eyes change to a week after her birth?
10. What name did the *cailleach* who delivered Cat give to the child, and what did the name mean?
11. What was Cat's full name?
12. What word did Scarlett never use in Cat's presence?
13. Who was Cat's godfather?
14. Who were Cat's two godmothers?
15. How did Ocras die?
16. What did Cat name her pony?
17. What name did Fenton propose for Cat during his discussion of her adoption?
    A. Lady Victoria
    B. Lady Catherine

    C. Lady Diana

    D. Lady Eugenie

18. What was Scarlett's gift to Cat for her second birthday?

    A. A puppy

    B. A big china dollbaby

    C. A mahogany rocking horse

    D. Half-interest in Ballyhara

19. What was the name of Cat's cat?

    A. Grainne

    B. Mr. Butler

    C. Kitty

    D. Ocras

BONUS QUESTION. What were the two names Scarlett considered for her unborn child when she realized there was a possibility she might have the baby on a table that came from a horse's tack room?

QUIZ 35

THE ROBILLARD AND O'HARA FAMILIES

All happy families resemble one another, but each unhappy family is unhappy in its own way.

          —LEO TOLSTOY, *Anna Karenina*

In *Scarlett*, we learn a lot more about the other members of the Robillard and O'Hara families, two tribes that were only mentioned in *Gone with the Wind*. Scarlett was connected to both of these clans, and exhibited characteristics and traits from each side. Answer the following questions about these two Southern-French-Irish families.

1. What religion was Pierre Robillard?
2. What religion was Solange Robillard?

3. What was the name of Grandfather Robillard's "imposing" black manservant?
4. Which of Jamie O'Hara's sons did Scarlett meet first?
5. What color was Jamie O'Hara's hair?
6. What derogatory term did Maureen O'Hara use to describe Pierre Robillard?
7. What was Pierre Robillard's middle name?
8. What was the name of Jamie O'Hara's wife?
9. What were the names of Michael O'Hara's two sisters?
10. Which of Jamie O'Hara's daughters did Scarlett feel looked like a princess?
11. Which of Jamie O'Hara's sons was born in Savannah?
   A. John
   B. Jamie
   C. Sean
   D. Patrick
12. How old was Pierre Robillard when he offered Scarlett his estate?
   A. 62
   B. 93
   C. 77
   D. 89
13. What occupation once practiced by Maureen O'Hara shocked and appalled Scarlett?
   A. Maureen was once a barmaid in an Irish saloon.
   B. Maureen once worked the "red light" district of London.
   C. Maureen once worked on a cargo ship as a cook.
   D. Maureen once worked as a chambermaid in an English mansion.
14. What U.S. President had Pierre Robillard once met?
   A. Quincy Adams
   B. George Washington
   C. Abraham Lincoln
   D. James Monroe
15. TRUE OR FALSE: Patricia O'Hara was married to Billy Carmody.
16. TRUE OR FALSE: Pierre Robillard attended the Independent Presbyterian Church.
17. TRUE OR FALSE: Scarlett O'Hara's paternal grandmother was named Katie Scarlett O'Hara.
18. TRUE OR FALSE: Colum and Kathleen's father's first name was Gerald.

BONUS QUESTION 1. What was the O'Hara dispensation?
BONUS QUESTION 2. To whom did Pierre Robillard leave his estate?

QUIZ 36

RHETT

You can't step twice into the same river.

—HERACLITUS

Rhett's feelings for Scarlett ran the gamut: they had a quintessential love/hate relationship and Rhett used denial to try and convince himself that Scarlett held no sway over him. But we know better, don't we? Answer the following questions about Rhett's activities in the years during which *Scarlett* takes place.

1. Who retired as Rhett's valet immediately prior to Mammy's death?
2. What did Scarlett buy for Rhett for Christmas, 1873?
3. What was Rhett's costume for Atlanta's January 1874 masked ball?
4. What was the only jewelry Rhett approved of for Scarlett?
5. Where did Rhett go "on business" in January 1874?
6. Why did Rhett travel to Philadelphia in November 1874?
7. How old was Rhett when he climbed to the topmost limb of a giant oak tree?
8. What excuse did Rhett make Scarlett offer to his mother to explain why he and Scarlett shared separate bedrooms?
9. What benign aquatic creatures had always been particular favorites of Rhett's?
10. What rumor regarding her divorce from Rhett did Scarlett overhear on the *Golden Fleece* during her return journey to Ireland?
11. Why did Rhett marry Anne Hampton?
12. How long did Rhett's child by Anne Hampton live?
13. Where did Rhett stay during his visit to Galway for the races?
14. TRUE OR FALSE: Rhett Butler hated babies.

15. TRUE OR FALSE: Rhett Butler did not know how to sail.
16. How many acres of garden did Rhett hope to restore at his burned-out plantation?
    A. 1
    B. 100
    C. 10
    D. 500
17. What was Rhett's answer when Scarlett asked him if he missed blockade running?
    A. "Only a fool would miss getting shot at for a shipload of pantalets, my dear."
    B. "Let's just say I'd like to be ten years younger."
    C. "Miss it? No, I don't *miss* it, but let's just say I wouldn't be upset if another war started and I found myself back on the brine again."
    D. "Yes, Scarlett, I do miss it. Those were some of the most thrilling times of my life. I've always needed some kind of blockade to run."
18. What were the two promises Rhett made to Mammy on her deathbed?
    A. That he would see to it that she was buried in her red petticoat.
    B. That he would take care of Scarlett.
    C. That he would see to it that she was buried in Savannah.
    D. That he would adopt Scarlett's children by Charles Hamilton and Frank Kennedy.
19. What are the first words Cat ever said to Rhett?
    A. "Who are you?"
    B. "I love you, Daddy."
    C. "Cat's ears hurt."
    D. "What is your name?"

BONUS QUESTION. What was Rhett's middle name?

QUIZ 37

THE BUTLER FAMILY

One would be in less danger
From the wiles of a stranger
If one's own kin and kith
Were more fun to be with.

—OGDEN NASH, *Family Court*

The following questions concern Rhett's mother, siblings, and other assorted members of the Butler family, as well as facts about the heritage of the clan.

1. What color was Rhett's mother's hair?
2. What improvement had recently been made to the Butler residence when Scarlett visited there in late 1874?
3. What was the first name of Rhett's mother?
4. After Ross Butler lost his plantation, what type of job did Rhett secure for him?
5. How did Mrs. Butler and her lady friends raise money for the Confederate Home for Widows and Orphans?
6. How was Cousin Townsend related to the Butler family?
7. What was the Ellintons' ocular family trait?
8. What was the name of Rhett's brother's wife?
9. What was the name of Rhett's father?
10. What was the name of Rhett's mother's maid?
11. What was the name of Rhett's sister?
12. What was the name of the Butler family manservant?
13. What were the two components of Rhett's mother's "education"?
14. How old was Rhett's sister the first time he ever saw her?
15. What was Rhett's sister's opinion about the intelligence level of the Butler family cousins in Richmond?
16. What was Rosemary Butler's 1874 Christmas gift from Rhett?
17. What was the name of the Butler gentleman who almost married Scarlett's Aunt Eulalie?

18. Who was Rosemary Butler's idol?
    A. Her brother, Rhett
    B. Miss Julia Ashley
    C. Pierre Robillard
    D. Napoléon

19. How did Rhett's great-aunt Alice try to kill herself after Pierre Robil-
    lard wed Scarlett's grandmother, Solange?
    A. She hung herself from the second-story landing.
    B. She tried to drown herself in the wading pond.
    C. She spurred her horse and let go of the reins, hoping the fall would
       break her neck.
    D. She drank a bottle of paregoric, but it didn't work.

20. How many centuries' worth of Butlers were "toes up" in the family
    tomb at the Butler plantation?
    A. Two centuries
    B. One century
    C. A century and a half
    D. Ten centuries

21. What was the official name of the Butler family plantation that was
    burned during the war?
    A. Dunmore Landing
    B. Butler Landing
    C. Butlerdale
    D. Dunmore Heath

22. What year was Rhett's mother born?
    A. 1810
    B. 1811
    C. 1812
    D. 1813

BONUS QUESTION. What was the name of the county in Ireland owned
    by the Butler family?

Q U I Z   3 8

ASHLEY WILKES AND THE WILKES FAMILY

Die Welt des Glücklichen ist eine andere als die des Unglücklichen.
The world of the happy is quite another than the world of the
unhappy.
— LUDWIG WITTGENSTEIN, *Tractatus logico-philosophicus* (1922)

Poor Ashley. Even when he was happy, he seemed sad, didn't he? Winds
of adversity and change haunted him throughout his life, but in *Scarlett,*
he was at least able to find some small measure of peace and happiness.
The following questions concern Ashley and his family.

1. What was Ashley's costume for Atlanta's January 1874 masked ball?
2. What excuse did Joe Colleton give to Ashley regarding Scarlett's
   presence at the building site of her "gimcrack" housing development?
3. What body of Charlestonian water shared Ashley's moniker?
4. According to Scarlett, what did Harriet Kelly and Ashley have in
   common?
5. Who was Ashley's second wife?
6. Who was Beau Wilkes's mammy after Melanie's death?
   A. Dilcey
   B. Prissy
   C. Rebekah
   D. India
7. What school language prize did Ashley proudly tell Scarlett that Beau
   had won?
   A. A French conversation prize
   B. A Latin composition prize
   C. A Spanish composition prize
   D. An Italian conversation prize
8. What did India Wilkes's beau do for a living?
   A. He was a bricklayer.
   B. He was a writer.
   C. He was a farmer.
   D. He was a minister at the Methodist church.

9. TRUE OR FALSE: The first time Scarlett saw Ashley in Atlanta after Melanie's burial, she thought that he looked robust and in the peak of good health.

BONUS QUESTION 1. What promise regarding Beau did Scarlett insist upon from Ashley?

BONUS QUESTION 2. What "title" did Scarlett sarcastically bestow upon India Wilkes when she found out that India was dating a Yankee?

QUIZ 39

HENRY HAMILTON OF ATLANTA AND THE PEOPLE OF CHARLESTON AND ENVIRONS

This is a wide-ranging quiz that covers a lot of ground, both literally and figuratively. There are questions concerning the life and times of Uncle Henry Hamilton of Atlanta, and there are also queries on his Southern neighbors in Charleston and the surrounding areas. To liven things up, the subject of the question (either "Henry Hamilton" or "Charleston") is given for each query, and the formats of the questions are what you might call "mix and match": that is, true or false are mixed with "Q & A"–type questions, multiple choice, and fill-in-the-blanks. (And because these questions are a tad tough, the chapter references are given for *all* the questions in this quiz, even though throughout this book, only the basic "Q & A" questions are given references.)

The "Henry Hamilton" Questions

Somehow a bachelor never quite gets over the idea that he is a thing of beauty and a boy forever.
        —HELEN ROWLAND, *A Guide to Men* (1922)

1. According to Scarlett, what had made Henry Hamilton a misogynist?
2. What role did Henry Hamilton play in Atlanta's January 1874 float parade and carnival?
   A. Grand Marshal
   B. Float Director
   C. Earl Marshal
   D. King of the Carnival
3. What financial responsibilities did Henry Hamilton take over for Scarlett when Scarlett went to Charleston in late 1874?
   A. He took over the financial support of Charles Hamilton's family.
   B. He began day-to-day management of Scarlett's lumber mill.
   C. He took over the financial management of Kennedy's Emporium and the saloon Scarlett leased.
   D. He began managing Rhett's investment portfolio.
4. TRUE OR FALSE: Henry Hamilton told Scarlett that if she divorced Rhett, he would never again handle any of her legal affairs.
5. What fiduciary power did Scarlett, in a letter from Ireland, give Henry Hamilton?
6. Upon her return to Atlanta, what convinced Henry Hamilton that Scarlett had grown up?

The "Charleston" Questions

I denounce war ... for the starvation that stalks after it.
　　　—HARRY EMERSON FOSDICK, sermon in New York
　　　on Armistice Day, 1933

7. In 1874, who was the only Charlestonian who still owned a carriage?
   A. Eleanor Butler
   B. Sally Brewton
   C. Scarlett Butler
   D. Julia Ashley
8. Which of Scarlett's sisters lived in Charleston?
9. After the war, Charlestonians called their newly Spartan dinner parties _____ .

10. How did the Charleston woman behind the counter in the fancy goods draper kill her husband?
    A. She shot him in the head.
    B. She poisoned him.
    C. She hit him in the head with a horseshoe.
    D. She stabbed him through the heart with a sharpened knitting needle.

11. TRUE OR FALSE: Mrs. Butler's Charleston pharmacist once paid a small fortune for a tropical fish because he was convinced it was a small mermaid.

12. TRUE OR FALSE: Josiah Anson was the elderly lawyer who represented the Charleston men, and went to Army headquarters to complain about the alleged Yankee intruder Charlestonian women were finding in their bedrooms.

13. What was the name of the maid who managed Sally Brewton's household?
    A. Lila
    B. Sally
    C. Anna
    D. Elaine

14. What type of house did the Charleston Sisters of Mercy live in?
    A. A wooden gimcrack house
    B. A brick mansion
    C. A converted castle
    D. A former prison

15. As a child, Alicia Savage did not like to wear _____ .

16. TRUE OR FALSE: Lucinda Wragg changed her wedding date in order to deliberately violate a Union curfew.

17. What was Alicia Savage's childhood nickname?
    A. "Pantsy"
    B. "Alice"
    C. "Eagle eye"
    D. "Bunny"

18. TRUE OR FALSE: Tommy Cooper's father died at Gettysburg.

19. Middleton Courtney's wife was named:
    A. Edie
    B. Elena
    C. Eloise
    D. Edith

20. TRUE OR FALSE: The Cracker who once spit tobacco in front of Rhett's boots was Clinch Dawkins.
21. The doctor who examined Scarlett after her ordeal at sea came from Fort _____ .
22. What was the name of the black servant who tended to Scarlett after her ordeal at sea?
23. What was wrong with Henry Wragg's eyes?
    A. He was cross-eyed.
    B. He was walleyed.
    C. He was blind.
    D. He had one blue and one brown eye.
24. Who was president of the Saint Cecilia Society?
    A. Ross Butler
    B. Josiah Anson
    C. Tommy Cooper
    D. Rhett Butler

BONUS QUESTION. Who was the best seamstress in Charleston?

QUIZ 40

COLUM O'HARA

I am one that had rather go out with sir priest than sir knight; I care not who knows so much of my mettle.
                    —SHAKESPEARE, *Twelfth Night*, III, iv

Colum O'Hara believed in a free Ireland, and he believed in it strongly enough to put his life on the line for the cause. During his time in America and Scarlett's time in Ireland, Colum became one of the O'Haras' best friends, and he also served as her confessor, and in more ways than one. Answer the following questions about this dedicated and tenacious Irishman.

1. What color eyes did Colum O'Hara have?
2. What was Colum O'Hara's vocation?
3. How often did Colum travel from Ireland to America?
4. What was the name of the militant Irish revolutionary group that Colum belonged to?
5. Where did Colum lecture to the American Irish volunteer soldiering group?
6. While staying in Savannah, with whom did Colum share a room?
7. What "insulting" behavior of Scarlett's did Colum warn her about?
8. What prayer did Colum whisper after the cesarean birth of Scarlett's daughter?
    A. A Hail Mary
    B. The Lord's Prayer
    C. An Act of Contrition
    D. The Prayer of Exorcism
9. What was Colum's function in the Fenian Brotherhood?
    A. He was the bookkeeper.
    B. He was the treasurer.
    C. He was the armorer.
    D. He was the cook.
10. Why didn't Colum perform the sacraments?
    A. Because he was never officially ordained.
    B. Because his father had been killed while receiving Holy Communion.
    C. Because he was a missionary priest whose work involved easing the suffering of the poor, not administering the sacraments.
    D. Because he didn't believe in them.

BONUS QUESTION 1. How did Colum repair the "Saint Patrick's Day" hole in Scarlett's boot?

BONUS QUESTION 2. What were Colum's last words?

QUIZ 41

THE PEOPLE OF IRELAND AND ENVIRONS

Cast your mind on other days
That we in coming days may be
Still the indomitable Irishry.

—WILLIAM BUTLER YEATS, *Under Ben Bulben*

In *Scarlett,* we get to meet many of Scarlett's Irish relatives and acquaintances, and a more colorful bunch of folks you're not going to find. Answer the following questions about the people of Ireland.

1. What was the name of the Earl's land agent?
2. Who owned the grandest bar in Trim?
3. What names did Mrs. Fitzpatrick and Scarlett agree to call each other in private?
4. What specific physical ailment troubled Scarlett's cook?
5. What was the name of Scarlett's Ballyhara Big House cook?
6. What was the name of Scarlett's parish priest in Ireland?
7. What was the name of the blacksmith who refused to help deliver Scarlett's baby?
8. What was the name of the *cailleach* who delivered Cat?
9. What was the name of the doctor who cared for Scarlett after she gave birth to Cat?
10. What were the names of the three maids hired for Scarlett's Ballyhara Big House?
11. What was the name of the man Kathleen O'Hara married?
12. Who was the youngest of Ballyhara's farmers?
13. What was the name of the woman John Morland was dating at the time Scarlett visited Harrington House?
14. Who was the maid assigned to Scarlett when she visited Harrington House?
15. What was Danny Kelly's crime?
16. What was Harriet Kelly's position in Lord Witley's household?
17. What was Lady Gifford's first name?
18. What was the name of Charlotte Montague's maid?

19. What was the name of Grace Hastings's husband?
20. What was the name of the artist who painted Scarlett's portrait?
21. What was the name of the Italian hairdresser Charlotte commissioned to do Scarlett's hair for her portrait?
22. What was the name of the man Scarlett saw flogged to death as she drove into Trim?
23. What was the name of the "merciless" dressmaker Charlotte Montague commissioned to sew the wardrobe for Scarlett's entrance into Dublin society?

BONUS QUESTION 1. What was the name of the Irish revolutionary group that fought English rule over Ireland?

BONUS QUESTION 2. Who was the Master of the Hounds of the Galway Blazers?

SUPER BONUS QUESTION. What was the composition of Scarlett's Big House staff after Charlotte Montague's "makeover"?

PLACES

QUIZ 42

TARA II

And when Tara rose so high . . .
> —WALTER SAVAGE LANDOR, "The Last Fruit
> off an Old Tree," *Epigrams* LXXXIV

In *Scarlett,* we get to witness the *complete* resurrection of Tara. Thanks to Will Benteen, Tara rose from the ashes to become healthy and strong once again. Granted, it never achieved the heights of glory it once possessed before the war, but it did make enough of a comeback to feed and clothe its residents again. Answer the following questions about Tara in the late 1870s.

1. After Scarlett set up housekeeping in Atlanta with Rhett, who became the "lady of the house" at Tara?
2. In what room in Tara's main house did Mammy live out her final days?
3. What was the name of Big Sam's wife?
4. Who took over as mammy for the Tara children after Mammy got sick?
5. What did Scarlett consider "the best thing that ever happened to Tara"?
6. What was the name of the cook at Tara?
7. Who took over Scarlett's old bedroom at Tara?
8. Who was Mammy buried next to?
9. What childhood illness put Tara under quarantine in late 1873?
10. How much did the Bishop want for Carreen's one-third share of Tara?
    A. $10,000
    B. $100,000
    C. $50,000
    D. $5,000

11. What improvements to Tara did Suellen make with Scarlett's monthly child-support money?
    A. She bought new furniture and furnishings.
    B. She bought Will a new carriage.
    C. She had a new well dug.
    D. She had new headstones carved for Ellen's and Gerald's graves.

12. The name of Suellen and Will's middle daughter was _____ .

13. The name of Suellen and Will's youngest daughter was _____ .

14. What upset Scarlett about Tara's exterior appearance the first time she saw the house upon her return home after Melanie's funeral?
    A. The front porch was gone.
    B. The house had been painted blue.
    C. There were vines hanging down the front of the house, four windows had sagging shutters, and there were no shutters at all on two windows.
    D. The fireplace chimney was gone.

BONUS QUESTION. When Scarlett returned to Tara after Melanie's funeral, what specific "shabbiness" about the interior of the house made her despondent?

QUIZ 43

ATLANTA II

Nor shall this peace sleep with her; but as when
The bird of wonder dies, the maiden phoenix,
Her ashes new—create another heir
As great in admiration as herself.
                    —SHAKESPEARE, *Henry VIII*, V, v

Answer the following questions about a bowed but unbroken Atlanta in the years during Reconstruction.

1. What was the name of the cemetery in Atlanta where Melanie Wilkes was buried?
2. How many "gimcrack" houses did Scarlett initially want to put up on the hundred acres of land she owned on the edge of Atlanta?
3. What was Maybelle Merriwether's costume in Atlanta's January 1874 float parade and carnival?
4. What was Mrs. Merriwether's costume in Atlanta's January 1874 float parade and carnival?
5. What was Mrs. Whiting's costume in Atlanta's January 1874 float parade and carnival?
6. What was the name of Scarlett's Atlanta "friend" whom she believed was "going to be as big as an elephant one of these days"?
7. What was the name of the Atlanta organization formed to oversee the production of the town's 1874 Carnival and Masked Ball?
8. What was the name of the King of Carnival?
9. Where did the 1874 Atlanta Masked Ball take place?
10. Who ordered all business closed in Atlanta on January 6, 1874?
11. Who played "a sneezing representation of The Good Old Days" in Atlanta's January 1874 float parade and carnival?
    A. Scarlett
    B. Mrs. Elsing
    C. Eleanor Butler
    D. Mrs. Meade
12. Who played Betsy Ross in Atlanta's January 1874 float parade and carnival?
    A. Aunt Eulalie
    B. Aunt Pauline
    C. Mrs. Merriwether
    D. Mrs. Elsing
13. What organization bought Scarlett's Peachtree Street Atlanta house?
    A. A girls' school
    B. A church
    C. A convent
    D. A prison
14. TRUE OR FALSE: It was sunny in Atlanta the day of Melanie's funeral.

BONUS QUESTION. What was the area of Atlanta Scarlett loved most?

QUIZ 44

CHARLESTON AND ENVIRONS

Party-spirit, which at best is but the madness of many for the gain of a few.
— ALEXANDER POPE, letter to E. Blount, August 27, 1714

Charleston had the reputation of being the "partyingest" town in the South and it served as a repository for some of the South's grandest—and most notorious—history. (See Question 13, for example.) Answer the following questions about Charleston landmarks and other area locales.

1. What was the most fashionable address in Charleston?
2. What was Charleston's most important "shopping" street?
3. What was Charleston's primary plantation crop?
4. What was "every Charlestonian's timekeeper"?
5. What was the name of the Charleston street where Edward Cooper lived?
6. What was the name of the Charleston street where Ross and Margaret Butler lived?
7. When was Charleston first settled?
8. How many city blocks comprised the Charleston Market?
9. What was the penalty in Charleston for hurting a Union soldier?
10. Where in Charleston was "the place to meet everybody and hear all the news"?
11. In 1874, how many years had it been since it had actually snowed in Charleston?
12. What Ball concluded the Charleston "Season"?
13. What notoriety did Charleston earn regarding the "oldest profession"?
14. What was the record for days of continuous rain in Charleston?
    A. 38
    B. 111
    C. 8
    D. 0
15. What was the "crowning event" of Charleston's social season?
    A. The Mardi Gras
    B. The Carnival

    C. The Saint Cecilia Ball

    D. High Mass at the Cathedral

16. Why did Charlestonians in the Lowcountry leave their plantations every year from the middle of May until after the first frost in October?

    A. Because that was when the plantations were flooded by the first rains of the season.

    B. Because that was the period when malaria rose from the swamps.

    C. Because that was when the "swamp people" held their "fertility rituals."

    D. Because that was the party season in town.

17. The Charleston hall where the Saint Cecilia Ball was held every year was called _____ .

BONUS QUESTION. What was the name of the Charleston street on which "Mulatto Alley" was located?

QUIZ 45

SAVANNAH

Mrs. Ballinger is one of the ladies who pursue Culture in bands, as though it were dangerous to meet it alone.
—EDITH WHARTON, *Xinqu* (1916)

Scarlett and her family all had relatives in Savannah, and the town held an important place in Scarlett's heart because it was where her mother, Ellen, had been born. Answer the following questions about the city of Savannah, Georgia.

1. Which of Eulalie and Pauline's relatives lived in Savannah?

2. How did Cousin Townsend lose his Savannah property?

3. What kind of celebration did Scarlett's grandfather put on in Savannah when Scarlett's mother, Ellen, was born?

4. What religious order had a convent school in Savannah?
5. What color was Grandfather Robillard's house in Savannah?
6. What color was the Savannah Convent of the Sisters of Mercy?
7. What Savannah landmark was located in Chippewa Square?
8. What was "Savannah's place to shop"?
9. Where did the Telfair sisters live?
10. Who were the "recognized cultural guardians of Savannah"?
11. What was the composition of Savannah's sidewalks?
12. What was the name of the Savannah street where the O'Hara family lived?
13. What was Savannah's grocery shopping section called?
14. Where in Savannah was the Independent Presbyterian Church located?
15. What was the name of the Savannah park directly across the street from Hodgson Hall?

QUIZ 46

IRELAND

Now Ireland has her madness and her weather still,
For poetry makes nothing happen.
                    —W. H. AUDEN, "In Memory of W. B. Yeats"

The Emerald Isle called to Scarlett since her childhood, and in *Scarlett*, she fulfilled her dream of seeing the birthplace of the O'Haras. Answer the following questions about the land where leprechauns roam.

1. What was "the center of all Ireland"?
2. Where was Colum O'Hara's father born?
3. What was shopping day in Galway called?
4. What was the name of Danny Murray's hometown in Ireland?
5. What was the name of the hotel where Scarlett spent her first night in Ireland?

6. What was the name of the Irish almost-a-village where the O'Haras lived?
7. According to Colum, what type of supernatural creatures was Ireland "teeming" with?
8. How many buildings were there in Ballyhara?
9. What Irish town had "a bad history," and, thus, no one would live in it?
10. What two rivers acted as the boundaries of Ballyhara?
11. How did Scarlett settle the dispute over the inheritance of Daniel O'Hara's farm?
12. Where was the closest hospital to Ballyhara located?
13. What was the name of the crossroads village near Harrington House?
14. What Galway hotel was a particular favorite of Scarlett's?
15. TRUE OR FALSE: The Giffords' estate was called Kilbawney Abbey.
16. TRUE OR FALSE: John Morland was at a meeting of the Fenian Brotherhood when his tenants burned his stables.
17. THE place to stay in Dublin for the Season was The _____ Hotel.

BONUS QUESTION. Where was the Sutcliffes' estate located?

THINGS

QUIZ 47

CLOTHING, JEWELRY, AND OTHER FINERY II

*She was rich in apparel, but not bedizened with other finery
. . . she well knew the great architectural secret of decorating her
constructions, and never descended to construct a decoration.*
—ANTHONY TROLLOPE, *Barchester Towers*

Answer the following questions about matters of dress, jewelry, and other
finery among the denizens of *Scarlett*.

1. What item of clothing did Mammy tell Rhett she wanted to be buried
   in?
2. What color and style of cap did Scarlett wear at the party where she
   learned about the Dregs's "monument" scam?
3. What color gown did Scarlett wear to the party where she learned
   about the Dregs's "monument" scam?
4. What item of clothing did Scarlett buy for Suellen for Christmas,
   1873?
5. What item of clothing did Scarlett buy for Will Benteen for Christmas,
   1873?
6. What type of gown represented "Night" in the 1874 Atlanta float
   parade?
7. In Charleston's early years, where did Charlestonian women buy their
   pearls?
8. What was Anne Hampton wearing the first time Scarlett saw her?
9. After Rhett's mother explained that Scarlett's wardrobe was somewhat inappropriate for Charleston society, what color buttons did
   Scarlett have sewn onto her green walking-out costume?
10. What color frock was Rosemary Butler wearing the first time Scarlett
    met her?

11. What color and type of gown did Scarlett wear for her first ball of the 1874 Charleston "Season"?
12. What color laces tied the blue velvet slippers that Scarlett wore to her first ball of the 1874 Charleston "Season"?
13. What was the color of the clothing always worn by Miss Julia Ashley?
14. What color parasols did Rhett present to his mother, Scarlett, and his sister as they left for Race Day in January 1875?
15. What did Cousin Townsend Ellington's wife wear to the last ball of the Charleston "Season"?
16. What clothing was Rhett wearing when he arrived back in Charleston after his and Scarlett's ordeal at sea?
17. What color gloves did Scarlett wear when she went to Savannah to visit her grandfather for his birthday?
18. What item of "showy" clothing did Rhett's mother bring Scarlett to wear after Scarlett's ordeal at sea?
19. What did Pierre Robillard wear to the dedication ceremonies at Hodgson Hall?
20. What did Scarlett wear to the dedication ceremonies at Hodgson Hall?
21. What did Scarlett wear to the Saint Patrick's Day festivities at Forsyth Park?
22. What color shawl was Katie Scarlett O'Hara wearing the first time Scarlett met her?
23. What did Cat O'Hara wear for her christening?
24. What did Kathleen O'Hara wear to Cat's christening?
25. What was Mrs. Fitzpatrick wearing during her first interview with Scarlett?
26. What did Scarlett wear to Kathleen O'Hara's wedding?
27. What type of clothing did John Morland tell Scarlett she would need for her visit to Harrington House?
28. TRUE OR FALSE: Charlotte Montague was wearing a gray gown with a plain white linen collar and cuffs when she first visited Scarlett at the Ballyhara Big House.
29. What did Scarlett do with the diamond-and-emerald engagement ring Rhett had given her?
    A. She had it remade into a pendant.
    B. She gave it to Rhett's mother.
    C. She had it remade into earrings.
    D. She donated it to the Association for the Beautification of the Graves of Our Glorious Dead.

30. What was the dominant gemstone in the jewels Fenton sent Scarlett?
    A. Diamonds
    B. Pigeon's blood rubies
    C. Brazilian emeralds
    D. Indian sapphires

QUIZ 48

SOUTHERN AND IRISH DATELINE

Time is the longest distance between two places.
　　　　　—TENNESSEE WILLIAMS, *The Glass Menagerie*

This quiz may seem a bit dry at first (sort of like being tested on history dates in school—remember?), but the questions—and their answers—should provide you with some entertaining information about Scarlett's "post-Tara" life. To make this quiz more fun, all these rather difficult questions are posed in the "easier" formats of multiple choice, fill-in-the-blanks, and true or false, and the chapter reference section for this quiz *does* supply the chapters in *Scarlett* where the answers can be found (even though throughout this book the references have only been for straight "Q & A"-type questions). But as always, you're on your own for the "Bonus" questions! I hope that the format of the questions and the accessibility of the answers will lead you back to the novel and provide you with some enjoyable hunting and gathering. Answer the following questions about dates and times in the South and in Ireland during the years in which *Scarlett* takes place.

1. What was the date Scarlett wrote her first check to Suellen for the care and feeding of Wade and Ella at Tara?
   A. October 11, 1873
   B. July 16, 1853

    C. December 25, 1865

    D. October 31, 1873

2. What was Sally Brewton's "at home" day and time?

    A. The morning of the first Thursday of every month.

    B. The afternoon of the third Sunday of every month.

    C. The afternoon of the first Wednesday of every month.

    D. The morning of the first Wednesday of every month.

3. **TRUE OR FALSE:** The only day of the week that Brewton's sausage was on sale at the Charleston Market was Sunday.

4. How long did the Charleston "Season" last?

    A. One month

    B. One year

    C. Six weeks

    D. Almost eight weeks

5. The 1874 Charleston "Season" began on December _____ , 1874.

6. What year did Solange Robillard wed?

    A. 1800

    B. 1810

    C. 1820

    D. 1830

7. **TRUE OR FALSE:** Scarlett calculated November 14, 1875, as the date for the birth of her fourth child.

8. The date of Rhett and Scarlett's divorce decree was March 26, 18 _____ .

9. What was the date that Patrick O'Hara died?

    A. November 10, 1860

    B. November 11, 1860

    C. December 24, 1861

    D. January 1, 1875

10. **TRUE OR FALSE:** Colum O'Hara's father married Kathleen's mother in 1815.

11. **TRUE OR FALSE:** Scarlett's paternal grandmother was married in the year 1776.

12. What day of the year did the Irish believe that all the spirits from the beginning of the world came out?

    A. All Hallow's Eve

    B. New Year's Day

    C. Saint Patrick's Day

    D. Christmas Day

13. Where did Scarlett and Cat spend Christmas, 1875?

    A. At the Ballyhara Big House

    B. At Tara

    C. In Paris

    D. At Daniel O'Hara's house

BONUS QUESTION. What day of the year did Charlestonians lock up their houses and make sure there were armed men in the house, and why was this a day to be feared?

SUPER BONUS/"FIGURE-IT-OUT" QUESTION. Around what year did Rhett's great-grandfather land in Charleston after leaving Barbados?

QUIZ 49

FURNITURE, SILVERWARE, AND OTHER "PRECIOUS" THINGS II

Dear sensibility! source inexhausted of all that's precious in our joys, or costly in our sorrows!
            —LAURENCE STERNE, *The Bourbonnois*

Answer the following questions about the furnishings, silverware, gifts, and other finery possessed, given, and enjoyed by the people in *Scarlett*.

1. What was Melanie's coffin made of?
2. What were the handles of Tony Fontaine's six-shooters made of?
3. What did Scarlett buy for her daughter, Ella, for Christmas, 1873?
4. What did Scarlett buy for her son, Wade, for Christmas, 1873?
5. What type of furniture did Mrs. Butler have in her dining room?

6. What type of flowers did Rhett give Scarlett for her first ball of the 1874 Charleston "Season"?

7. What was Tommy Cooper's gift for Christmas, 1874?

8. Where in the Butler family mansion was the brass telescope Scarlett used to spy on Rhett and Tommy Cooper?

9. What two items did Scarlett hurl at her bedroom door after Rhett locked her in?

10. What did Scarlett want to offer the Sisters of Mercy in exchange for Carreen's "Tara" dowry?

11. What kind of flowers did Rhett send Scarlett after their ordeal at sea?

12. What was the design "theme" of the silver tureen used to serve the first course of Pierre Robillard's birthday dinner?

13. What type of cane did Pierre Robillard carry?

14. Which of the statuary figures on the fountain in Forsyth Park were Maureen O'Hara's favorites?

15. What did Scarlett give her grandmother for her one-hundredth birthday?

16. What did Seamus O'Hara bring from Trim in honor of the Old One's hundredth birthday?
    A. Three kegs of ale
    B. Six geese and ten pigs
    C. A box of clay pipes and two saddlebags of tobacco
    D. A calf

17. What was Scarlett's personal wedding gift to Kathleen O'Hara?
    A. 100 pounds
    B. 1,000 pounds
    C. Ten acres of land
    D. Ten horses

18. What "title" was bestowed upon Scarlett during the Midsummer Night costume ball at Harrington House?
    A. Queen of the Ball
    B. Titania
    C. Elizabeth
    D. The O'Hara

19. What monetary memento of Cat's second birthday party did the Ballyhara children go home with?
    A. A 1 pound note
    B. A genuine gold nugget

    C. A shilling

    D. A shiny coin

20. The style of furniture that Charlotte Montague chose for Scarlett's private rooms in the Ballyhara Big House was Louis
_____ French design.

BONUS QUESTION 1. What was the "languishing fall"?

BONUS QUESTION 2. What did John Morland do with the paw of the
fox Scarlett was awarded after the hunt at Morland Hall?

QUIZ 50

VEHICLES, TRANSPORTATION, AND MATTERS
OF TRAVEL II

Up, lad: when the journey's over
There'll be time enough to sleep.

—A. E. HOUSMAN, "Reveillé"

Journeys end in lovers meeting,
Every wise man's son doth know.

—SHAKESPEARE, *Twelfth Night,* II, iii

They say you never really know a person until you've either lived with
them . . . or traveled with them. Before the age of mass transit and the
personal (and *private*) automobile, travel was a communal—and time-
consuming—event, and the inhabitants of the *Gone with the Wind* and
Scarlett worlds were not exculpated from such inconveniences. Answer the
following questions about getting about in *Scarlett.*

1. How far was Tara from Jonesboro?
2. What type of horseback riding did Tony Fontaine promise to teach Wade Hampton?
3. How did Tony Fontaine return to Texas?
4. On her trip to Charleston, what train line did Scarlett switch over to in Augusta?
5. What form of transportation in Charleston was only available to the carpetbaggers in late 1874?
6. How did Mrs. Butler and Scarlett return home after their morning of shopping on the first day of Scarlett's visit to Charleston?
7. Why did Sally Brewton have sleigh bells attached to the spokes of her brougham?
8. How long a ride was it by hackney from the Butler residence to the Charleston train station?
9. What was the length of Rhett's sailing sloop?
10. What time did the Charleston morning train to Savannah leave the depot?
11. How far was Adamstown from Mullingar?
12. How long did it take a ship to travel from America to Galway, Ireland?
13. What was the name of the captain of the ship that took Scarlett to Ireland?
14. What was the name of the ship that took Scarlett to Ireland?
15. How did Scarlett travel from Mullingar to Adamstown for her return trip to Daniel's house?
16. What was the name of the ship on which Scarlett originally planned to return to America?
    A. The *Brian Boru*
    B. The *Abraham Lincoln*
    C. The *Golden Fleece*
    D. The *Evening Star*
17. **TRUE OR FALSE:** Scarlett bought a gray horse and a black buggy with a yellow stripe after the birth of Cat.
18. How much was a buggy ride tour of Charleston?
    A. 10 shillings
    B. 50 pence or $2.50 American
    C. $5.00 American
    D. 1 pound

19. What was the name of the excursion boat on which Scarlett took the Charleston Harbor tour while waiting to continue on her return trip to Ireland?
    A. The *Brian Boru*
    B. The *Abraham Lincoln*
    C. The *Golden Fleece*
    D. The *Evening Star*
20. The ship on which Scarlett returned to Ireland in 1876 was _____ .

BONUS QUESTION. What colors were the Charleston horsecars painted?

QUIZ 51

MONEY AND BUSINESS MATTERS

The moral flabbiness born of the bitch-goddess SUCCESS. That—with the squalid cash interpretation put on the word success—is our national disease.
        —WILLIAM JAMES, in a letter to H. G. Wells,
        September 11, 1906

Scarlett became quite wealthy in *Scarlett*, mostly due to a rather notorious "deal" with Rhett. Answer the following questions about money and business doings in *Scarlett*.

1. How much did Scarlett pay Suellen and Will to take care of Ella and Wade at Tara?
2. What did Carreen O'Hara use as her dowry for the convent?
3. How much did Scarlett pay her head clerk at Kennedy's Emporium?
4. How much did a cup of coffee cost at the Market?
5. What type of mine did Rhett invest in in Charleston after the war?
6. What dollar amount did Rhett use as a metaphor for the amount of love he once had in his heart for Scarlett?
7. How much money did Sheba have in an English bank?

8. Who owned the most "lavish and profitable" whorehouse in Charleston?

9. How much did shoes cost in Galway?
   A. 1 shilling
   B. 2 shillings
   C. 3 shillings
   D. 10 pounds

10. How much did skirts cost in Galway?
   A. 1 shilling
   B. 2 shillings
   C. 3 shillings
   D. 10 pounds

11. TRUE OR FALSE: For her trip to Ireland, Scarlett hid the gold coins she wanted to bring by replacing the steel strips of her corset with the coins.

12. What was the amount of Scarlett's final offer for Ballyhara?
   A. 10,000 pounds
   B. $5,000 American
   C. $25,000 American
   D. 15,000 pounds, take it or leave it

13. Scarlett paid _____ pounds for the horse she bought from John Morland.

14. TRUE OR FALSE: The name of the Dublin coffee shop where Scarlett and Cat ate cream buns was Bewley's.

BONUS QUESTION 1. Shortly after her arrival in Ireland, how much money did Scarlett carry in a drawstring bag between her breasts while out for the day with Colum?

BONUS QUESTION 2. How did Charlotte Montague describe her "profession" to Scarlett?

QUIZ 52

LETTERS, WRITINGS, SONGS, AND OTHER COMMUNICATORY MATTERS II

*When men can freely communicate their thoughts and their suf-
ferings, real or imaginary, their passions spend themselves in air,
like gunpowder scattered upon the surface—but pent up by ter-
rors, they work unseen, burst forth in a moment, and destroy
everything in their course.*
> —THOMAS ERSKINE, "Defense of Thomas Paine,"
> December 20, 1792

People say that life is the thing, but I prefer reading.
> —LOGAN PEARSALL SMITH, "Myself," in *Afterthoughts*

The first line of Stephen King's novella "The Body" is "The most important
things are the hardest things to say," and truer words about interpersonal
communication have yet to be writ. This quiz looks at the ways our *Gone
with the Wind* friends communicated with each other. Answer the following questions about letters, books, telegrams, songs, and other forms of
verbal intercourse in *Scarlett*. (The first half or so of this quiz consists of
the more difficult "Q & A"–type questions, and thus, the chapter references
are supplied in the "Question/Chapter Keys" section. The questions for the
second half of the quiz are in easier formats [true or false, multiple choice,
and fill-in-the-blanks] and so references are not supplied.)

1. What particular sections of the Bible did Scarlett read to Mammy as
   Mammy lay on her deathbed?
2. What song was sung at Mammy's funeral that Scarlett felt was totally
   inappropriate?
3. What was the "fashion of the day" in 1873 regarding handwriting for
   personal notes and invitations?
4. What did Scarlett leave at Aunt Pitty's as she left the house at the end
   of her first visit there after Melanie's burial?

5. Who wrote Melanie Wilkes's obituary?

6. How many invitations went out for the 1874 Atlanta Masked Ball?

7. What types of books did Ellen make Scarlett balance on her head in order to teach her how to walk like a lady?

8. What was Scarlett's "visiting book" covered with?

9. What was the makeup of the "Dixie" band that played in Atlanta's January 1874 float parade and carnival?

10. What was the name of the column in the Atlanta paper that Scarlett read faithfully in order to keep up with goings-on in Charleston?

11. In 1874, what were the usual subjects covered in Suellen's letters from Tara to Scarlett?

12. What did Aunt Eulalie do in her personal correspondence in order to save stationery?

13. What did the telegram say that Scarlett sent to her aunts from Augusta on her way to Charleston?

14. What song did Scarlett hear a band playing as she and her aunts walked to the Butler residence during her 1874 visit to Charleston?

15. What type of envelopes did Aunt Eulalie use for her personal correspondence?

16. How did a Charlestonian signify an intent to become acquainted with a person without actually entering their house?

17. What types of communicatory instruments were left at the Butler residence after Scarlett educated Sally Brewton about onions?

18. How did Ross apologize for drunkenly French-kissing Scarlett?

19. What did Rhett's father do to Rhett's name in the family Bible after he disowned him?

20. What novel did Rosemary Butler read the night the Butler residence was searched by Union soldiers?
   A. *Great Expectations*
   B. *Ivanhoe*
   C. *Remembrance of Things Past*
   D. *The Picture of Dorian Gray*

21. TRUE OR FALSE: The magazine *The Nation* published articles by Henry James.

22. What book did Rhett's mother read to Rhett's sister when she was a child as the two of them sat on a bench by the reflecting pool at their plantation?
   A. *Little Women*
   B. *King Solomon's Mines*

    C. *Treasure Island*

    D. *The Ugly Duckling*

23. How did Cousin Townsend notify Eleanor Butler that he and his wife were coming from Philadelphia for a visit?

    A. He didn't notify her before arriving.

    B. He wrote a letter.

    C. He sent a note by messenger.

    D. He sent a telegram.

24. Rhett and Scarlett heard a homesick sailor play the song _____ on a whistle as they walked the docks after the Saint Cecilia Ball.

25. What song did Rhett and Scarlett sing on the streetcar on the way home from the Saint Cecilia Ball?

    A. "Rock of Ages"

    B. "Rock Me on the Water"

    C. "The Rock Island Line"

    D. "Amazing Grace"

26. What songs did Rhett and Scarlett sing while floating beneath the capsized sailing sloop?

    A. They sang a selection of traditional Christmas carols.

    B. They sang the "Yo, ho, ho, and a bottle of rum!" sea chanty from Robert Louis Stevenson's *Treasure Island,* "Little Brown Jug," "The Yellow Rose of Texas," and "Peg in a Low Back'd Car."

    C. They sang a selection of Irish sea chanties.

    D. They sang a selection of popular show tunes.

27. What was the last song played at the Saint Cecilia Ball?

    A. "The Blue Danube Waltz"

    B. "Goodnight, Ladies"

    C. "Dixie"

    D. "The Battle Hymn of the Republic"

28. Who burned the note Scarlett wrote to Rhett's mother before Scarlett left Charleston for Savannah?

    A. Rosemary Butler

    B. Ross Butler

    C. Rhett Butler

    D. Sally Brewton

29. What musical instruments were played by the O'Haras at the feast Scarlett attended in Savannah?

    A. Piano, string bass, and violin
    B. Guitar and accordion
    C. Concertina, squeeze-box, and fiddle
    D. Concertina, tin whistles, fiddle, and bones

30. **TRUE OR FALSE:** Scarlett heard "The Wearing o' the Green" being sung in the Savannah O'Hara house as she walked back to her grandfather Pierre's house.

31. The initials "P.P.C." in the corner of "leave-taking" cards stood for _____ , which meant _____ .

32. What new song did Danny Murray sing for Billy O'Hara in Forsyth Park?
    A. "When Irish Eyes Are Smiling"
    B. "I'll Take You Home"
    C. "The Wearing o' the Green"
    D. "Danny Boy"

33. During their journey to County Meath, what fairy tale did Scarlett mention to Colum?
    A. "Cinderella"
    B. "Rumplestiltskin"
    C. "Goldilocks and the Three Bears"
    D. "Jack and the Beanstalk"

34. To whom did Scarlett send telegrams as soon as she arrived in Savannah from Ireland?
    A. Her Uncle Henry Hamilton and Pansy
    B. Her Aunts Eulalie and Pauline
    C. Will Benteen and Rhett Butler
    D. Her sisters, Suellen and Carreen

35. **TRUE OR FALSE:** John Morland's calling card said, "John Morland, Bart."

36. Harriet Kelly's first letter to Scarlett after her arrival in the United States was _____ pages long.

37. How many people wrote to ask permission to call on Scarlett after she was presented to the Viceroy of Ireland?
    A. Seven gentlemen, including two Knights and a Viscount
    B. None
    C. Ten Knights, six ladies, a Baron, and two Marquesses
    D. Eleven gentlemen (including the Gentleman Usher) and fourteen ladies with their daughters

38. What newspaper did Charlotte Montague want Scarlett to read every day?
    A. The *Times* of London
    B. The *Irish Times*
    C. *The New York Times*
    D. The *Dublin Times*
39. TRUE OR FALSE: Scarlett's marriage to Fenton was announced on the front page of the *Irish Times*.

SUPER BONUS QUESTION. Identify and complete the following biblical quote that Rhett recited to Scarlett, but which she did not recognize: "Though I speak with the tongues of men and angels . . ."

QUIZ 53

FOOD AND DRINK II

Dis-moi ce que tu manges, je te dirai ce que tu es.
Tell me what you eat and I will tell you what you are.
    —ANTHELME BRILLAT-SAVARIN, *Physiologie du goût* (1825),
    "Aphorisms . . . pour servir de prolégomènes . . ."

Der Mensch ist, was er isst.
Man is what he eats.
    —LUDWIG FEUERBACH, Advertisement to Moleschott, *Lehre der Nahrungsmittel: Für das Volk* (1850)

Food meant a lot to the postbellum Southerners and the nineteenth-century Irish. It figures: Anything that took as long to produce and prepare—to *acquire*—as food did in the late 1800s in America and Ireland was bound to be considered supremely important. Answer the following questions about eating and drinking in *Scarlett*.

1. What type of hot soup did Scarlett feed Mammy for breakfast every morning before Mammy died?
2. What was Mamie Bart eating at Scarlett's party when she slobbered butter sauce onto her diamond necklace?
3. By February 1874, what was Scarlett drinking as soon as she got up in the morning?
4. What did Mrs. Butler use moonshine for?
5. What dessert did Scarlett and Rhett's mother have for dinner after Scarlett's first shopping trip to the Market?
6. What did Rhett feed Scarlett for breakfast her first morning at Rhett's burned-out plantation mansion?
7. What type of fish did Rhett's mother feel took to a sauce better than sheepshead?
8. What type of fowl was a particular gustatory favorite of Rhett's mother?
9. What alcoholic beverage did Rhett and Scarlett drink while floating beneath the capsized sailing sloop?
10. What provisions did Rhett bring when he and Scarlett went sailing together?
11. What type of post-Ball stew did the Saint Cecilia Society pride itself on?
12. What was the composition of the Saint Cecilia Society's Ball "punch"?
13. What did Pierre Robillard personally have for dinner the evening that Scarlett visited the Sisters of Mercy Convent?
14. What did Scarlett "order" for dinner in Grandfather Robillard's house after visiting the Sisters of Mercy Convent?
15. What food did Scarlett eat before she fell asleep at the Butler home in Charleston after her ordeal at sea?
16. What food did Scarlett smell cooking when she returned to Grandfather Robillard's house after visiting the Sisters of Mercy Convent?
17. What food was served during Scarlett's first visit to the O'Hara home in Savannah?
18. What was the third course of Pierre Robillard's ninety-third birthday dinner?
19. What type of beverage did Colum O'Hara bring to Jamie O'Hara's house?
20. What did Scarlett have for supper on the evening of the day of the picnic in Forsyth Park?

21. What was Scarlett eating at the Railway Hotel when she interrupted her meal to go outside and dance?

22. What was the very first item of food Scarlett ever ate on the street?
    A. A salmon cutlet in sauce
    B. Boiled tripe
    C. A serving of barm brack
    D. A coconut candy cake

23. According to tradition, what was the first food that could be eaten on New Year's Day?
    A. Liver and onions
    B. A special barm brack
    C. Fruitcake
    D. A salmon cutlet in sauce

24. What baked good was Mrs. Kennedy, the barkeep's wife, renowned for?
    A. Her fruitcake was light and flavorful.
    B. Her cheesecake was redolent of brandy.
    C. The pastry for her meat pies melted in your mouth.
    D. Her peasant bread had a delightfully salty crust.

25. TRUE OR FALSE: Colum once asserted to Scarlett that he would rather eat boiled nettles than eat porridge without salt.

26. TRUE OR FALSE: The cold foods offered to Scarlett for breakfast at the Sutcliffes' on the morning after her tryst with Charles included boiled salt cod and cabbage, hot boiled onions, and porter.

27. Which of the following was *not* served at the outdoor feast to welcome Stephen O'Hara back to Ireland?
    A. Ham, preserved goose, jellied quail eggs, spiced beef, salted fish
    B. Aspics, ices, fruits, cheeses, and breads
    C. Relishes, jams, sauces
    D. Wines, ale, cider, coffee
    E. Cakes, cookies, pastries, candies

28. TRUE OR FALSE: The Ballyhara children tasted fruitcake for the first time at Cat's second birthday party.

DISGUSTING BONUS QUESTION. What type of meats did Rhett tell Scarlett he ate while in California?

SUPER BONUS QUESTION. What was the name of the former slave who became famous for making Brewton's sausage?

QUIZ 54

ITEMS OF IRE

Der Aberglaube ist die Poesie des Lebens.
Superstition is the poetry of life.

—GOETHE, *Sprüche in Prosa* (1819)

This quiz is on items specifically indigenous (with a few exceptions) to Ireland. For instance, it isn't likely you'll find barm brack anywhere but on the Emerald Isle, so answering these questions will take a little Irish detective work. (Unless you're third or fourth generation Irish yourself, that is, which, for this quiz, will be a definite advantage!)

1. What was the tambourine-like drum that Colum played called?
2. What did Kathleen O'Hara leave on her doorstep every evening for the "little people"?
3. What was barm brack?
4. What was the musical instrument that pipers played called?
5. How did the Irish decorate for Christmas?
6. How did the "long-ago O'Haras" get into the tower?
7. What architectural design in Scarlett's Ballyhara Big House did Mrs. Fitzpatrick think was "the most intelligent arrangement" she'd ever seen?
8. What did Scarlett throw at the feet of her workers to show them how to get started clearing her land?
9. How much did the big wooden table in Scarlett's Ballyhara Big House cost?
10. What type of bed was found in the attic of Scarlett's Ballyhara Big House?
11. What was the Irish superstition regarding dark-haired people and New Year's Day?
12. Why did the Irish farmers keep a bucket of water inside the front door of their houses?
13. How did the Irish concur that a deal had been made?
14. What did "ocras" mean in Irish?

15. What does *aroon* mean?
    A. "Darling"
    B. "Witch"
    C. "Sweetheart"
    D. "Master"
16. What was a known protection against witches and spirits?
    A. Rubbing a person's forehead with ashes from a fire burned in a church graveyard
    B. Drinking rum that had been steeped with wintergreen leaves
    C. Turning around three times while saying the Hail Mary
    D. Scrubbing someone with water in which angelica root had steeped all day
17. TRUE OR FALSE: The architectural style in which Scarlett's Ballyhara Big House was built was eighteenth-century Palladian.
18. The Gaelic word for "King" was _____ .
19. What was the original name of John Morland's horse, Dijon?
    A. Diana Joanne
    B. Diana John
    C. Dana Joan
    D. Deanna Joanna
20. TRUE OR FALSE: Comet was the name of Cat's cat.

BONUS QUESTION. Why were ladies' bedrooms supplied with a plate of sandwiches in the more sophisticated Irish society houses?
SUPER BONUS QUESTION. What is a pooka?

QUIZ 55

WHO SAID IT IN <u>SCARLETT</u>?

I hate quotations.
    —RALPH WALDO EMERSON, *Journals*, May 1849

As in the *Gone with the Wind* quotation quiz (Quiz 32), this quiz asks you to identify the speaker of the following quotations, and the person to whom the remark was made. The chapters in *Scarlett* in which the quotes appear are given in the "Question/Chapter Keys" in the back of the book.

1. "Melly . . . Mell—eee! Mell—eee!"
2. "Miss Scarlett, you done what you had to do. Can't nobody do more than that. The good Lord sent you some heavy burdens, and you carried them. No sense asking why they was laid on you or what it took out of you to tote them. What's done is done. Don't fret yourself now."
3. "Now, Missy, ain't I done tole you and tole you not to set foot outside without you wears a bonnet and carries a sunshade . . . Tole you and tole you . . ."
4. "What's going to become of me when I don't have you to love me?"
5. "Men are so bullheaded."
6. "Remember, my pet, I'm a scoundrel, not a gentleman."
7. "That's a whole world gone, an era ended. May she rest in peace."
8. "Do come in, Scarlett. Are you in a hurry to sue somebody?"
9. "Don't show your claws to me, young lady. Settle back in that chair and listen to some hard truths. You've got maybe the best business head I ever met, but otherwise you're about as dimwitted as the village idiot."
10. "I'm a miserable failure, Scarlett. You know it. I know it. The whole world knows it. Why do we all have to act as though it isn't so?"
11. "Maybe you should come out and sit on the steps with me, India. A blind tramp might stumble by and marry you in exchange for room and board."
12. "Dregs! That's what you are. Dregs. Get out of my house, get out of my sight, you make me sick!"
13. "I need work, but not bad enough to work for you."
14. "Rhett, oh Rhett, I need you."
15. "You just can't do nothing with a man who don't have natural human greed, so all the triple-your-money bond deals and certificates for gold mines that I turned loose on them laid a big egg."
16. "Great God Almighty, Scarlett, you've done real well for yourself. I thought some fool had given me directions to a hotel when I saw this big place."
17. "There's not a fence in a hundred miles. That's because there's not much worth fencing in, unless you like dust and dried-up scrub."
18. "Why are there so many damned Yankees in Charleston?"

19. "Check. I overlooked the unpredictable mobility of the queen. But not mate, Scarlett."
20. "It's a fortunate man who receives a greater surprise than he gives."
21. "So this is Scarlett. I might have known Rhett would end up with a fancy piece like her. Come on, Scarlett, give your new brother a friendly kiss. You know how to please a man, I'm sure."
22. "What do you think of the wife? She's not at all what I would have expected. Have you ever seen anything as grotesquely over-decorated as the walking-out costume she was wearing?"
23. "You think you can pass yourself off as a lady, don't you? You couldn't fool a blind deaf-mute."
24. "He doesn't care how old they are. Maybe he's raping your mother right this minute."
25. "I am working harder than I've ever had to work in my life, Scarlett. I burned my bridges in Charleston so thoroughly and so publicly that the stench of the destruction is still in the nostrils of everyone in town."
26. "I should strangle you, Scarlett. The world would be a better place."
27. "These onions were dug up too soon. They look fine enough, but they won't have any flavor. I know, because it's a mistake I made myself."
28. "You're a barbarian, Scarlett."
29. "Rhett said you were feline. I see what he means, with those green eyes. I do hope you'll purr at me and not spit, Scarlett. I'd like for us to be friends."
30. "Who would want to go to Georgia, for pity's sake? I want to go to Rome, the real Rome, the Eternal City. In Italy!"
31. "You were a loathsome little girl. I would have loved you even if you had worn underclothes."
32. "Don't you have anything better to do with your time than bully a household of women?"
33. "Don't lie to me about my mother, Scarlett. I warn you, it's dangerous."
34. "Katie Scarlett, you've got the hands of an angel and the nerve of the devil himself. It's the O'Hara in you, a horse will always recognize an Irishman and give his best for him."
35. "You're miserably ill-groomed as usual, Rosemary, but I'm glad to see you."
36. "Charleston isn't a sink of iniquity, dear. People don't feel any social pressure to be constantly rutting."

37. "He doesn't want you. He told me so."
38. "Pride and loyalty don't weigh much for you when there's money involved, do they, Scarlett?"
39. "They have a saying, the French, that no woman can be truly beautiful who is not also sometimes truly ugly."
40. "Working men don't take kindly to the presence of women."
41. "Come on, my dear, time and tide wait for no man, not even a woman."
42. "Damn you for a quitter, Scarlett O'Hara! I should have let Sherman get you in Atlanta. You weren't worth saving."
43. "I should have killed you the minute you set foot in Charleston."
44. "I've known men with a hunger for opium that was like my hunger for you."
45. "Listen to me. If you let yourself give in to the cold, Scarlett, you'll die. I know you want to sleep but that's the sleep of death. And, by God, if I have to beat you black and blue, I will not allow you to die."
46. "My dear imbecilic child, those are dolphins, not sharks."
47. "Scarlett, what happened out there had nothing to do with love. It was a celebration of survival, that's all. You see it after every battle in wartime. The men who don't get killed fall on the first woman they see and prove they're still alive by using her body. In this case you used mine, too, because you'd narrowly escaped dying. It had nothing to do with love."
48. "When things are at their worst, Scarlett, the only thing to do is find something to laugh about. It keeps you sane . . . and it stops your teeth from chattering from fear."
49. "Discipline is what made the Emperor's armies great; without discipline there is only chaos."
50. *"Et vous, mes filles. Qu'est-ce-que vous voulez cette fois?"*
51. "I haven't lost my memory. But apparently your memory fails you. In this house, young people do not speak until they are spoken to."
52. "I'll wear what I like. I'm over being so eager to please."
53. "Your Pa is the runt of the litter."
54. "Everyone knows that the Irish take certain freedoms with the laws of the Church. You can't really blame them, poor illiterate nation that they are."
55. "Flesh is forbidden during Lent."
56. "He had a glass-sided hearse with four black horses and black plumes on their heads, a blanket of flowers on his coffin and more on the roof, and two hundred mourners following the hearse in their rigs. He's in

a marble tomb, not a grave, and the tomb has a carved angel on top, seven feet high."

57. "I'm not going to stand here and listen to such high and mighty French snobbery. My Pa was never anything but a good man, and his 'influence' was kindness and generosity, something you don't know anything about."

58. "Last time I saw you, you were mourning your husband. Have you found another one yet?"

59. "There's no inviting done here. We're all a family, and you're a part of it. Come anytime you like. My kitchen door has no lock, and there's always a fire on the hearth."

60. "Five roads led to the hill of Tara from every corner of the country, and every third year did all the people come to feast in the banquet hall and hear the poets sing."

61. "Katie Scarlett, darling, you're as dazzling as the Queen of Sheba!"

62. "There's not enough money ever been minted to keep me here. Money can't make living in a tomb bearable."

63. "You are dishevelled and you have ruptured the schedule of my house."

64. "You are not permitted to feel ill."

65. "You don't mind sleeping in the parlor with the pig, I take it."

66. "I never knew that so many interesting things happened to people."

67. "It's a queer sound, and that's the truth of it, but it's English for sure. English the way the English speak it, all up in their noses like they're strangling from it."

68. "The bunting must come down and the headache remedy must be put on the counter where all the sufferers can get to it easy. Celebrating is a fine thing, but the day after can be a fearsome burden."

69. "You cannot imagine what it is to have no food."

70. "By all the saints, he told the truth! You've got eyes green as a cat's. Where did they come from, I'd like to know. I thought Gerald must be drink-taken when he wrote me such a tale. Tell me, young Katie Scarlett, was your dear mother a witch?"

71. "I'm never going to be squeezed into a corset again, never."

72. "It's happy I am you were here for my birthday, Gerald's girl. The only pity is you'll not be at my wake . . . What are you weeping for, girl? Do you not know there's no party for the living half as grand as a wake?"

73. "No one would ever believe it was Rhett's baby. We slept in separate rooms for years. They'd call me a whore and my baby a bastard, and they'd smack their lips in the calling. "

74. "Such a treasure it is, too. A crock of gold, not looking like much, perhaps, to the uneducated eye, but the crock is made with great and deceptive leprechaun cunning, and there's no bottom to it, so you may take out and take out gold to the end of your days, and there'll always be more."

75. "Young Katie Scarlett O'Hara, you honor my house and I bid you welcome. Your father was greatly loved and his absence has been a stone in my breast for all these fifty years and more."

76. "Bury me in O'Hara earth."

77. "Colum, get this butcher out of this house before she kills Mrs. O'Hara and I kill her."

78. "God, my Father, I feel Your presence and Your almighty power. But I cannot see Your face. Why have You turned away from Your people the Irish?"

79. "Here's another one of them. Look at her. These miserable Irish breed like rabbits. Why don't they learn to wear shoes instead?"

80. "I am in Hell! When I see soldiers mocking a mother who must beg to buy food for her children, it is a vision from Hell. When I see old men pushed into the muck of the street so that soldiers will have the sidewalk, I see Hell. When I see eviction, floggings, the groaning carts of grain passing the family with a square meter of potatoes to keep them from death, I say that all Ireland is Hell, and I will gladly suffer death and then torment for all eternity to spare the Irish one hour of Hell on earth."

81. "Do not hope that I can do magic for you."

82. "I promise you on my word of honor, Cat O'Hara. You can grow up to be whatever you are, even if it's as different from me as day from night."

83. "If you're going to have cows, you're going to need hands to milk them."

84. "Ready was I to save the life of The O'Hara when the witch come through the stone wall and throws me with terrible force onto the floor. Then kicks me—and I could feel in my flesh that the foot was no human foot but a cloven hoof. She cast a spell on The O'Hara then and ripped the babe from the womb."

85. "Remember your South, with the boots of the conqueror upon her, and think of Ireland, her beauty and her life's blood in the murdering hands of the enemy. They stole our language from us. Teaching a child to speak Irish is a crime in this land."

86. "Scarlett darling, it's the national character to take the pleasures life has to offer first and worry about duties later. It's what gives the Irish their charm and their happiness."

87. "She started out on time, but her piles bothered her so badly she had to stop overnight every ten miles on the way here. It seems we won't have to worry about her lazing in a rocking chair when she should be on her feet working."

88. "The blessings of all the saints on mother and daughter in the new year to come."

89. "What isn't earned by your own hands is charity."

90. *"Why did you leave us? Ochón! / Ochón! Ochón! Ullagón Ó!"*

91. "Ach, Pa, it's a grand place to be sure, County Meath. You're remembered well, Pa, by all of them. I didn't know, Pa, I'm sorry. I didn't know you should be having a fine wake and all the stories told about when you were a boy."

92. "Cat."

93. "I don't know what your thinking is, Scarlett, and I ain't asking. But I'm telling you this. If anybody comes up the road flapping something legal at me 'bout taking Tara, I plan to meet 'em at the end of the drive with a shotgun in my hand."

94. "May I assume from your cheerful attire that you're no longer mourning my death?"

95. "This is the only plantation the heroic Union forces did not destroy. It was not in the tender heart of their commander to injure the frail spinster woman who lay ill inside."

96. *"Why did you leave me? Ochón! / Ochón! Ochón! Ullagón Ó!"*

97. "You're free from Rhett. Say you'll marry me, Scarlett, and I'll pledge my life to making you happy the way that you deserve to be."

98. "Aren't they entertaining? I do adore the Irish when they go all pagan and primitive like this. If only they weren't so lazy and stupid, I wouldn't mind living in Ireland."

99. "I've been waiting nearly twenty years for someone like you to come along."

100. "You're the exotic bloom in the patch of weeds, Scarlett."

101. "A quiet time is what I dread most, Scarlett *aroon*. Quiet lets the darkness creep into a man's soul."
102. "Beloved."
103. "Damn your eyes, you scared me half to death!"
104. "Easel. Quickly, you cretins. I shall do a portrait that will make me famous."
105. "I hope he falls over his own drunken feet and breaks his neck."
106. "I love you, you abusive wench."
107. "Lonely knows lonely."
108. "Drink yourselves into the floor if you want to—it's a man's right to poison his stomach and addle his head—but don't be blaming your weakness on The O'Hara."
109. "The old ladder is under my quilts, Momma. Grainne told me to save it."
110. "The only thing she didn't measure me for was my shroud."
111. "There are limits to a man's control, my pet, and the one thing I can think of that's more uncomfortable than a wet beach is a stone floor."
112. "Two mares in foal outrank a viceroy every time."
113. "We've got to stop spending so much money."
114. "Why don't you put on an animal's pelt and drag me to your house by my hair?"
115. "You belong with me, Scarlett, haven't you figured that out? And the world is where we belong, all of it. We're not home-and-hearth people. We're the adventurers, the buccaneers, the blockade runners. Without challenge, we're only half alive. We can go anywhere, and as long as we're together, it will belong to us. But, my pet, we'll never belong to it. That's for other people, not us."
116. "Your secret is safe with me, Scarlett."
117. "You will know her at once. She is extremely beautiful, and she carries her head like an empress."
118. "You're a disgrace to your people, Scarlett O'Hara."
119. "You've changed, Scarlett. The charming girl has become an elegant, grown-up woman. I salute you, I really do."
120. "Your Irishness is one of the intriguing things about you. Striped stockings and boiled potatoes one day, partridge and silks the next. You can have it both; it will only add to your legend."

PART THREE

GONE WITH THE WIND

THE FILM

THE SCREEN IN REVIEW*
DAVID SELZNICK'S *GONE WITH THE WIND* HAS ITS LONG-AWAITED PREMIERE AT ASTOR AND CAPITOL, RECALLING CIVIL WAR AND PLANTATION DAYS OF SOUTH—SEEN AS TREATING BOOK WITH GREAT FIDELITY
BY FRANK S. NUGENT

Understatement has its uses too, so this morning's report on the event of last night will begin with the casual notation that it was a great show. It ran, and will continue to run, for about 3 hours and 45 minutes, which still is a few days and hours less than its reading time and is a period the spine may protest sooner than the eye or ear. It is pure narrative, as the novel was, rather than great drama, as the novel was not. By that we would imply you will leave it, not with the feeling you have undergone a profound emotional experience, but with the warm and grateful remembrance of an interesting story beautifully told. Is it the greatest motion picture ever made? Probably not, although it is the greatest motion mural we have seen and the most ambitious film-making venture in Hollywood's spectacular history.

It—as you must be aware—is *Gone With the Wind,* the gargantuan Selznick edition of the Margaret Mitchell novel which swept the country like Charlie McCarthy, the *Music Goes 'Round* and similar inexplicable phenomena; which created the national emergency over the selection of a Scarlett O'Hara and which, ultimately, led to the $4,000,000 production that faced the New York public on two Times Square fronts last night, the Astor and the Capitol. It is the picture for which Mr. Gallup's American Institute of Public Opinion has reported a palpitantly waiting audience of 56,500,000 persons, a few of whom may find encouragement in our opinion that they won't be disappointed in

*From *The New York Times,* Wednesday, December 20, 1939. Copyright ©1939 by The New York Times Company. Reprinted by permission.

Vivien Leigh's Scarlett, Clark Gable's Rhett Butler or, for that matter, Mr. Selznick's Miss Mitchell.

For, by any and all standards, Mr. Selznick's film is a handsome, scrupulous and unstinting version of the 1,037-page novel, matching it almost scene for scene with a literalness that not even Shakespeare or Dickens were accorded in Hollywood, casting it so brilliantly one would have to know the history of the production not to suspect that Miss Mitchell had written her story just to provide a vehicle for the stars already assembled under Mr. Selznick's hospitable roof. To have treated so long a book with such astonishing fidelity required courage—the courage of a producer's convictions and of his pocketbook, and yet, so great a hold has Miss Mitchell on her public, it might have taken more courage still to have changed a line or scene of it.

But if Selznick has made a virtue of necessity, it does not follow, of necessity, that his transcription be expertly made as well. And yet, on the whole, it has been. Through stunning design, costume and peopling, his film has skillfully and absorbingly recreated Miss Mitchell's mural of the South in that bitter decade when secession, civil war and reconstruction ripped wide the graceful fabric of the plantation age and confronted the men and women who had adorned it with the stern alternative of meeting the new era or dying with the old. It was a large panel she painted, with sections devoted to plantation life, to the siege and burning of Atlanta, to carpetbaggers and the Ku Klux Klan and, of course, to the Scarlett O'Hara about whom all this changing world was spinning and to whom nothing was important except as it affected her.

Some parts of this extended account have suffered a little in their screen telling, just as others have profited by it. Mr. Selznick's picture-postcard Tara and Twelve Oaks, with a few-score actors posturing on the premises, is scarcely our notion of doing complete justice to an age that had "a glamour to it, a perfection, a symmetry like Grecian art." The siege of Atlanta was splendid and the fire that followed magnificently pyrotechnic, but we do not endorse the superimposed melodramatics of the crates of explosives scorching in the fugitives' path; and we felt cheated, so ungrateful are we, when the battles outside Atlanta were dismissed in a subtitle and Sherman's march to the sea was summed up in a montage shot. We grin understandingly over Mr. Selznick's romantic omission of Scarlett's first two "birthings," and we regret more comic capital was not made of Rhett's scampish trick on the Old Guard of Atlanta when the army men were rounding up the Klansmen.

But if there are faults, they do not extend to the cast. Miss Leigh's Scarlett has vindicated the absurd talent quest that indirectly turned her up. She is so perfectly designed for the part by art and nature that any other actress in the role would be inconceivable. Technicolor finds her beautiful, but Sidney Howard, who wrote the script, and Victor Fleming, who directed it, have found in her something more: the very embodiment of the selfish, hoydenish, slant-eyed miss who tackled life with both claws and a creamy complexion, asked no odds of any one or anything—least of all her conscience—and faced at last a defeat which by her very unconquerability, neither she nor we can recognize as final.

Miss Leigh's Scarlett is the pivot of the picture, as she was of the novel, and it is a column of strength in a film that is part history, part spectacle and all biography. Yet there are performances around her fully as valid, for all their lesser prominence. Olivia de Havilland's Melanie is a gracious, dignified, tender gem of characterization. Mr. Gable's Rhett Butler (although there is the fine flavor of the smokehouse in a scene or two) is almost as perfect as the grandstand quarterbacks thought he would be. Leslie Howard's Ashley Wilkes is anything but a pallid characterization of a pallid character. Best of all, perhaps, next to Miss Leigh, is Hattie McDaniel's Mammy, who must be personally absolved of responsibility for the most "unfittin' " scene in which she scolds Scarlett from an upstairs window. She played even that one right, however wrong it was.

We haven't time or space for the others, beyond to wave an approving hand at Butterfly McQueen as Prissy, Thomas Mitchell as Gerald, Ona Munson as Belle Watling, Alicia Rhett as India Wilkes, Rand Brooks as Charles Hamilton, Harry Davenport as Doctor Meade, Carroll Nye as Frank Kennedy. And not so approvingly at Laura Hope Crews's Aunt Pitty, Oscar Polk's Pork (bad casting) and Eddie Anderson's Uncle Peter (oversight). Had we space we'd talk about the tragic scene at the Atlanta terminal, where the wounded are lying, about the dramatic use to which Mr. Fleming has placed his Technicolor—although we still feel that color is hard on the eyes for so long a picture—and about pictures of this length in general. Anyway, "it" has arrived at last, and we cannot get over the shock of not being disappointed; we had almost been looking forward to that.

I've Just Seen a Face *"It was an arresting face, pointed of chin, square of jaw. Her eyes were pale green without a touch of hazel, starred with bristly black lashes and slightly tilted at the ends."*

QUIZ 56

WHO PLAYED WHO?

Whence are we, and why are we? Of what scene
The actors or spectators?

—PERCY BYSSHE SHELLEY, *Adonais* (1821)

Match the *Gone With the Wind* film character from Column A with the actor or actress who played the role from Column B.

COLUMN A

_____ 1. Bonnie Blue Butler
_____ 2. A Reminiscent Soldier
_____ 3. Pork
_____ 4. Brent Tarleton
_____ 5. René Picard
_____ 6. Ashley Wilkes
_____ 7. Bonnie's Nurse
_____ 8. A Dying Soldier
_____ 9. Belle Watling
_____ 10. Carreen O'Hara
_____ 11. Aunt "Pittypat" Hamilton
_____ 12. Charles Hamilton
_____ 13. The Corporal
_____ 14. The Yankee Deserter
_____ 15. Scarlett O'Hara
_____ 16. Mrs. Merriwether
_____ 17. Frank Kennedy
_____ 18. Big Sam
_____ 19. A Poker-Playing Captain
_____ 20. A Wounded Soldier
_____ 21. Tom, A Yankee Captain
_____ 22. A Carpetbagger Orator
_____ 23. Prissy
_____ 24. Mammy

COLUMN B

_____ A. Olin Howland
_____ B. William Bakewell
_____ C. Rand Brooks
_____ D. Thomas Mitchell
_____ E. Evelyn Keyes
_____ F. Blue Washington
_____ G. Fred Crane
_____ H. Lillian Kemble Cooper
_____ I. Jackie Moran
_____ J. Tom Tyler
_____ K. Alicia Rhett
_____ L. Cliff Edwards
_____ M. George Reeves
_____ N. Paul Hurst
_____ O. Barbara O'Neil
_____ P. Wallis Clark
_____ Q. Howard Hickman
_____ R. Roscoe Ates
_____ S. Oscar Polk
_____ T. Lee Phelps
_____ U. Vivien Leigh
_____ V. Mickey Kuhn
_____ W. Harry Davenport
_____ X. Robert Elliott

_____ 25. Melanie Hamilton

_____ 26. Maybelle Merriwether

_____ 27. Beau Wilkes

_____ 28. Johnnie Gallegher

_____ 29. A Poker-Playing Captain

_____ 30. The Sergeant

_____ 31. A Hungry Soldier

_____ 32. Cathleen Calvert

_____ 33. John Wilkes

_____ 34. Stuart Tarleton

_____ 35. Phil Meade

_____ 36. A Renegade

_____ 37. Emmy Slattery

_____ 38. A Convalescent Soldier

_____ 39. Ellen O'Hara

_____ 40. Elijah

_____ 41. Gerald O'Hara

_____ 42. Rhett Butler

_____ 43. India Wilkes

_____ 44. Jonas Wilkerson

_____ 45. The Yankee Major

_____ 46. The Carpetbagger's Friend

_____ 47. Doctor Meade

_____ 48. An Amputation Case

_____ 49. Suellen O'Hara

_____ 50. Old Levi

_____ 51. The Renegade's Companion

_____ 52. Mrs. Meade

_____ 53. A Carpetbagger Businessman

_____ 54. Fanny Elsing

_____ 55. The Bartender

_____ 56. Uncle Peter

_____ 57. A Mounted Officer

_____ 58. A Returning Veteran

_____ 59. A Commanding Officer

_____ Y.   Carroll Nye

_____ Z.   Eric Linden

_____ AA. Hattie McDaniel

_____ BB. Irving Bacon

_____ CC. Victor Jory

_____ DD. Ernest Whitman

_____ EE. Zack Williams

_____ FF. Louis Jean Heydt

_____ GG. Albert Morin

_____ HH. Terry Shero

_____ II. Everett Brown

_____ JJ. Isabel Jewell

_____ KK. Cammie King

_____ LL. Ann Rutherford

_____ MM. William Stelling

_____ NN. Clark Gable

_____ OO. Marcella Martin

_____ PP. Ward Bond

_____ QQ. Leona Roberts

_____ RR. Yakima Canutt

_____ SS. Mary Anderson

_____ TT. Adrian Morris

_____ UU. Jane Darwell

_____ VV. J. M. Kerrigan

_____ WW. George Meeker

_____ XX. Laura Hope Crews

_____ YY. William McClain

_____ ZZ. George Hackathorne

_____ AAA. Ona Munson

_____ BBB. Eddie Anderson

_____ CCC. Ed Chandler

_____ DDD. John Arledge

_____ EEE. Butterfly McQueen

_____ FFF. Olivia de Havilland

_____ GGG. Leslie Howard

Q U I Z 5 7

WHO DID WHAT?

And only The Master shall praise us, and only The Master shall
blame;
And no one shall work for money, and no one shall work for fame,
But each for the joy of the working, and each, in his separate star,
Shall draw the Thing as he sees It for the God of Things as They
are!

—RUDYARD KIPLING, "When Earth's Last Picture"

This quiz is somewhat different. It's essentially a matching quiz, except that this quiz asks you to fill in the blanks in the following "Who Did What?" sentences instead of matching up people and their tasks from two columns. The statements are all about the production personnel for the *final* film version of *Gone With the Wind*. The first name and first initial of the person's last name are given to you, as well as the correct number of letters in the person's name. Work off the master list of film personnel that follows the sentences to fill in all 55 blanks. The correctly filled-in sentences appear in the Answers section.

1. The film version of *Gone With the Wind* was directed by VICTOR
   F _ _ _ _ _ _ , from a screenplay by SIDNEY
   H _ _ _ _ _ .
2. The film was produced by DAVID O. S _ _ _ _ _ _ _ _ .
3. The production was designed by WILLIAM CAMERON
   M _ _ _ _ _ _ , with art direction by LYLE
   W _ _ _ _ _ _ and photography by ERNEST
   H _ _ _ _ _ .
4. The musical score was by MAX S _ _ _ _ _ _ _ , with
   contributions from his associate, LOU F _ _ _ _ _ .
5. Special photographic effects were by JACK
   C _ _ _ _ _ _ _ .
6. His associate for fire effects was LEE Z _ _ _ _ _ _ .
7. The costumes were designed by WALTER
   P _ _ _ _ _ _ _ .

8. Scarlett's hats were designed by JOHN
   F _ _ _ _ _ _ _ _ .
9. Interiors were by JOSEPH B. P _ _ _ _ , and interior
   decoration was by EDWARD G. B _ _ _ _ .
10. The supervising film editor was HAL C. K _ _ _ _ , and the
    associate film editor was JAMES E. N _ _ _ _ _ .
11. The scenario assistant was BARBARA K _ _ _ .
12. Makeup and hair styling were by MONTY
    W _ _ _ _ _ _ _ , with assistance from his associates,
    HAZEL R _ _ _ _ _ _ _ and BEN N _ _ .
13. The dance directors were FRANK F _ _ _ _ and EDDIE
    P _ _ _ _ _ .
14. *Gone With the Wind*'s historian was WILBUR G. K _ _ _ _ .
15. *Gone With the Wind*'s technical advisers were SUSAN
    M _ _ _ _ _ and WILL P _ _ _ _ .
16. *Gone With the Wind*'s researcher was LILLIAN K.
    D _ _ _ _ _ _ _ .
17. *Gone With the Wind*'s production manager was RAYMOND A.
    K _ _ _ .
18. The assistant director was ERIC G. S _ _ _ _ _ _ .
19. The second assistant director was RIDGEWAY
    C _ _ _ _ _ _ .
20. Production continuity was supervised by LYDIA
    S _ _ _ _ _ _ _ _ and CONNIE E _ _ _ _ .
21. *Gone With the Wind*'s mechanical engineer was R. D.
    M _ _ _ _ _ _ _ .
22. The construction superintendent was HAROLD
    F _ _ _ _ _ , and the chief grip was FRED
    W _ _ _ _ _ _ _ .
23. The person in charge of wardrobe was EDWARD P.
    L _ _ _ _ _ _ , with assistance from his associates,
    MARIAN D _ _ _ _ _ and ELMER
    E _ _ _ _ _ _ _ _ .
24. The casting managers were CHARLES R _ _ _ _ _ _
    and FRED S _ _ _ _ _ _ _ _ _ _ .
25. The location manager was MASON L _ _ _ _ _ .
26. The scenic department superintendent was HENRY J.
    S _ _ _ _ .

27. The electrical superintendent was WALLY O __ __ __ __ __
and the chief electrician was JAMES P __ __ __ __ __ __ .
28. The properties manager was HAROLD C __ __ __ __ .
29. The person in charge of properties on the set was ARDEN
C __ __ __ __ .
30. The person in charge of greens properties was ROY A.
M __ __ __ __ __ __ __ __ .
31. The person in charge of drapes properties was JAMES
F __ __ __ __ __ .
32. Special properties were made by ROSS B.
J __ __ __ __ __ __ __ .
33. Tara was landscaped by FLORENCE Y __ __ __ .
34. *Gone With the Wind*'s still photographer was FRED
P __ __ __ __ __ __ .
35. The camera operators were ARTHUR A __ __ __ __ __ and
VINCENT F __ __ __ __ __ .
36. The assistant film editors were RICHARD
V __ __ __ __ __ __ __ and ERNEST L __ __ __ __ __ __ .
37. The novel, *Gone with the Wind,* was written by MARGARET
M __ __ __ __ __ __ __ .

GONE WITH THE WIND FILM PERSONNEL

A	D	FLEMING
ARLING	DABNEY	FLOYD
	DEIGHTON	FORBES
		FORNEY
B		FREDERICS
BOYLE	E	
	EARLE	H
C	ELLSWORTH	HALLER
CALLOW		HOWARD
COLES	F	
COSGROVE	FARRAR	J
CRIPE	FENTON	JACKMAN

K

KEON
KERN
KLUNE
KURTZ

L

LAMBERT
LEADLEY
LITSON

M

MCLAUGHLIN
MENZIES
MITCHELL
MUSGRAVE
MYRICK

N

NEWCOM
NYE

O

OETTEL

P

PARRISH
PLATT
PLUNKETT
POTEVIN
PRICE
PRINZE

R

RICHARDS
ROGERS

S

SCHILLER
SCHUESSLER
SELZNICK

STACEY
STAHL
STEINER

V

VAN ENGER

W

WESTMORE
WHEELER
WILLIAMS

Y

YOCH

Z

ZAVITZ

QUIZ 58

WHAT'S THE DIFFERENCE?

One star differeth from another star in glory.
                    —*1 Corinthians,* 15:41

Love that so desires would fain keep her changeless;
Fain would fling the net, and fain have her free.
                    —GEORGE MEREDITH, "Love in the Valley"

As the old 1955 Johnny Mercer song goes, something's gotta give. The makers of the film version of Margaret Mitchell's epic faced a daunting task: translate 1,037 pages of character- and event-rich text into a movie that wouldn't require sleeping arrangements and catering. They did an exemplary job, don't you think? But by necessity things had to be left out and this quiz tests your knowledge of the differences between the original *Gone with the Wind* novel and the final film version.

1. What was the name of the Yankee overseer of the Calvert plantation who was not included in the film?
2. Which of Scarlett's children were eliminated from the film version?
3. The character of the Tarleton twins' body servant was written into the film and his scenes were actually filmed, but he ultimately did not appear in the final film version. What was his name?
4. In the film version, Gerald O'Hara dies after falling from his horse while trying to catch Jonas Wilkerson's carriage. He dies in the same manner (from a broken neck) in the novel, but the *catalyst* for his manic ride was different. Why did he ride off enraged in the novel?
5. In the film version, Charles Hamilton was in love with India Wilkes prior to his "romantic abduction" by Scarlett. He was *not* in love with India, in the novel, however. Who *was* Charles's love interest in the book?
6. What was the name of the cracker not included in the film version who ended up becoming the "man of the house" at Tara after the war?
7. Which of Ellen and Gerald O'Hara's children were not included in the film version?
8. What was the name of Raoul Picard's character in the film version?
9. Which of John Wilkes's daughters is not included in the film version?
10. What was the name of the mulatto woman who lived with Johnnie Gallegher who did not appear in the film version?
11. Gerald O'Hara's mother does not appear in the film version, but is an important character in *Scarlett*. What is her name?
12. Which of Rhett's siblings appeared in both the *Gone with the Wind* and *Scarlett* novels, but did not appear in the film?
13. Pork's wife was not included in the film version. What was her name?
14. What Tara kitchen slave appears in the novel and is mentioned—but not seen—in the film version?
15. What white-haired bachelor lawyer who appears in both the *Gone with the Wind* and *Scarlett* novels is not seen in the film?
16. What is the name of the one-eyed, one-legged ex-convict who becomes Scarlett's protector in the novel but does not appear in the film?

17. Which of the following families appears (or is mentioned) in the novel but does NOT appear in the film?
    A. The Burrs
    B. The Carahans
    C. The Emersons
    D. The McLures
    E. The McRaes
    F. The Deals
    G. The Prudhommes
    H. The Hundons

18. TRUE OR FALSE: Mrs. Elsing's black mammy, Melissy, appears in the film version of *Gone With the Wind*.

19. TRUE OR FALSE: In the film, Tommy Wellborn is one of the men killed during the raid on Shantytown, and his body is brought back to Melanie's house with the wounded Ashley.

20. What is the name of the Atlantan matriarch who appears in the novel and whom Rhett greets on the sidewalk while out wheeling Bonnie, but who is never actually seen?

21. In the film, Rhett fires Bonnie's nurse after she leaves Bonnie alone in her dark bedroom at night and Bonnie wakes up screaming. What are the two major differences in this scene between the film and the novel?

22. Which of the following members of the Fontaine family, all of whom appear in the novel, is the only Fontaine to appear in the film?
    A. Alex Fontaine
    B. Grandma Fontaine
    C. Jane Fontaine
    D. Joe Fontaine
    E. Old Dr. Fontaine
    F. Tony Fontaine
    G. Young Dr. Fontaine

23. What business did Dolly Merriwether start in the novel that is never mentioned in the film?

24. In the novel, Melanie reads aloud from a certain novel by Victor Hugo on the night of the Shantytown raid. In the film, she reads aloud from a novel by Charles Dickens. What are the two books?

25. In the novel, Rhett's last words are "Frankly, my dear, I don't give a damn." What are his last words in the film? (WARNING: TRICK QUESTION!)

QUIZ 59

PRESENTING . . . VIVIEN, CLARK, OLIVIA, LESLIE, BUTTERFLY, AND MORE: QUESTIONS ABOUT THE REAL LIVES AND CAREERS OF THE CAST

The following group of 81 questions concerns 20 of the cast members of *Gone With the Wind*. These questions are about their real lives and careers, *not* their *Gone With the Wind* characters. There are movie trivia questions here, as well as biographical queries, and even TV trivia. The actors and actresses are quizzed in the order in which they appeared in the film, and the questions are divided into two sections, "The Guys" and "The Gals." Answers to these questions can be found in any number of sources, but the books listed in the bibliography section will prove especially helpful since frankly, my dears, most of the questions came from them!

The Guys

1. FRED CRANE *(Brent Tarleton)*
    1-1. What was the film Fred Crane appeared in after *Gone With the Wind*?
    1-2. FOR THE CINEMATIC FANATICS: Fred Crane's second wife acted as what *Gone With the Wind* film actress's double?
    1-3. What two "science fiction" television series did Fred Crane appear in?
2. GEORGE REEVES *(Stuart Tarleton)*
    2-1. What was George Reeves's original name?
    2-2. What Herculean character was George Reeves most famous for playing?
    2-3. How did George Reeves die?
3. THOMAS MITCHELL *(Gerald O'Hara)*
    3-1. What 1939 Academy Award did Thomas Mitchell win?
    3-2. What much-loved Christmas movie did Thomas Mitchell also appear in?
    3-3. FOR THE CINEMATIC FANATICS: Who was Secretary of Labor in the Eisenhower administration, and what does this have to do with Thomas Mitchell?

4. OSCAR POLK *(Pork)*

    4-1. What movie did Oscar Polk appear in that took place in Georgia, told the story of a fiery Southern belle, and had the word "Wind" in the title?

    4-2. What radio program did Oscar Polk appear on?

    4-3. What was the name of the film that Oscar Polk appeared in with Lena Horne, Louis Armstrong, and Duke Ellington?

5. LESLIE HOWARD *(Ashley Wilkes)*

    5-1. Where was Leslie Howard born?

    5-2. What real-life profession did Leslie Howard share with Ashley Wilkes (even though Ashley never got the job)?

    5-3. How did Leslie Howard die?

6. RAND BROOKS *(Charles Hamilton)*

    6-1. FOR THE CINEMATIC FANATICS: What did comedian Stan Laurel of Laurel and Hardy fame have to do with *Gone With the Wind* actor Rand Brooks?

    6-2. What was Rand Brooks's occupation before becoming an actor?

    6-3. What was the last western Rand Brooks made?

7. CARROLL NYE *(Frank Kennedy)*

    7-1. Where was Carroll Nye born?

    7-2. What other member of Carroll Nye's family was involved with the film version of *Gone With the Wind*?

    7-3. What Shirley Temple movie did Carroll Nye appear in immediately before beginning work on *Gone With the Wind*?

8. CLARK GABLE *(Rhett Butler)*

    8-1. FOR THE CLARK CONNOISSEUR: Which of the following was *not* one of Clark Gable's pre-acting occupations? Tire factory worker, oil driller, pharmacy clerk, department store salesman, telephone lineman.

    8-2. How many times was Clark Gable married, and to whom?

    8-3. What did Clark Gable once do in a film that almost ruined the undershirt business?

This Boy *"He was dark of face, swarthy as a pirate, and his eyes were as bold and black as any pirate's appraising a galleon to be scuttled or a maiden to be ravished. There was a cool recklessness in his face and a cynical humor in his mouth . . . but there was undeniably a look of good blood in his dark face. It showed in the thin hawk nose over the full red lips, the high forehead and the wide-set eyes."*

Fools Rush In *Scarlett and Ashley's Mistake: a touching—but damning—scene between two people who should have known better.*

8-4. Which of the following remarks did Clark Gable actually make about the possibility of him being cast as Rhett Butler?
   A. "I've been preparing for this part for the past fifteen years."
   B. "Cast Carole Lombard as Scarlett and I'm all yours."
   C. "I don't want the part for money, chalk, or marbles."
   D. "Who's Rhett Butler?"

8-5. What was the date on which L. B. Mayer signed the contract that allowed Clark Gable to make *Gone With the Wind* for Selznick International, even though Gable was an MGM contract player?

8-6. FOR THE CLARK CONNOISSEUR, PART 2: What was the *original* name of the Gable family and why did they change it to "Gable"?

8-7. TRUE OR FALSE: Samuel Goldwyn once said the following about Clark Gable: "When Clark Gable comes on the screen you can hear his balls clanking together."

8-8. TRUE OR FALSE: Clark Gable never actually worked with the "love of his life," Carole Lombard.

8-9. What was the last film Clark Gable ever made, and with whom did he co-star?

8-10. Name the three films Clark Gable appeared in for which he was nominated for an Academy Award.

9. YAKIMA CANUTT *(A Renegade)*

9-1. FOR THE CINEMATIC FANATICS: What "horse"-related avocation did Yakima Canutt excel in from 1917 to 1924?

9-2. What did Yakima Canutt have to do with the 1959 classic film, *Ben-Hur*?

9-3. What type of Academy Award did Canutt receive in 1966?

10. WARD BOND *(Tom, a Yankee Captain)*

10-1. Prior to *Gone With the Wind,* what film had Ward Bond appeared in with Clark Gable?

10-2. FOR THE CINEMATIC FANATICS: Ward Bond received a Bachelor of Science degree in what discipline?

10-3. Although Ward Bond made almost 200 films (including *Gone With the Wind, The Maltese Falcon,* and *They Were Expendable*), he became most famous for what western TV role?

The Gals

11. VIVIEN LEIGH *(Scarlett O'Hara)*

11-1. Where was Vivien Leigh born?

11-2. What brilliant British actor (considered by many to be the best actor ever) was Vivien Leigh married to from 1940 to 1960?

11-3. FOR THE CINEMATIC FANATICS: While attending the Convent of the Sacred Heart school at Roehampton, England, who was Vivien's favorite classmate, and what does this woman have to do with Woody Allen?

11-4. Vivien Leigh was born Vivian Mary Hartley. She kept her first name (with a different spelling), but where did she come up with "Leigh"?

11-5. THE "EASIER THAN IT SOUNDS" DEPARTMENT: What body part played a coincidental role in Margaret Mitchell's *writing* of Gone With the Wind and Vivien Leigh's *reading* of it?

11-6. Which of the following comments did Vivien Leigh make to Margaret Mitchell in a telegram she sent to the author after clinching the role of Scarlett?

    A. "Dear Margaret: I really wanted to play Melanie but I guess I'll have to make do with Scarlett. Ha-ha. Best wishes."

    B. "Dear Mrs. Marsh: If I can but feel that you are with me on this, the most important and trying task of my life, I pledge with all my heart I shall try to make Scarlett O'Hara live as you described her in your brilliant book. Warmest regards."

    C. "Dear Mrs. Marsh: Words fail me as I try to express the depth of emotion and joy I am feeling at this moment. Thank you for creating Scarlett O'Hara and I hope I can do her justice. With deep affection."

    D. "Dear Mrs. Mitchell: Please pray that I can do justice to your Scarlett, and also that I can lose this bloomin' Limey accent in time. I'm terrified of Selznick. Aren't you? Warmest regards."

11-7. What *physical* illness tormented Vivien Leigh after the making of *Gone With the Wind* and eventually killed her?

11-8. How old was Vivien Leigh when *Gone With the Wind* was released?

11-9. TRUE OR FALSE: Vivien Leigh had a stamp issued in her honor in the country of Umm al-Qaiwain in the 1970s.

11-10. THE "IT *COULDN'T* BE TRUE . . . COULD IT?" DEPARTMENT: TRUE OR FALSE: During a heated argument on the set about how Scarlett should be played, director Victor Fleming once threw the script on the floor and said to Vivien Leigh, "Miss Leigh, you can stick this script up your royal British ass."

12. HATTIE McDANIEL *(Mammy)*

12-1. What movie did Hattie McDaniel appear in that took place in Georgia, told the story of a fiery Southern belle, and had the word "Wind" in the title?

12-2. What was Hattie McDaniel's profession before becoming an actress?

12-3. Where did Hattie McDaniel die?

13. BARBARA O'NEIL *(Ellen O'Hara)*

13-1. What famous *Bus Stop* and *Picnic* director was Barbara O'Neil married to?

13-2. What was the only Academy Award nomination Barbara O'Neil ever received?

13-3. FOR THE CINEMATIC FANATICS: In what other film did Barbara O'Neil *(Ellen O'Hara)* and Thomas Mitchell *(Gerald O'Hara)* play husband and wife?

14. EVELYN KEYES *(Suellen O'Hara)*

14-1. Serendipitously, what was Evelyn Keyes's childhood hometown?

14-2. What famous show business luminaries were Evelyn Keyes's second, third, and fourth husbands, respectively?

14-3. FOR THE CINEMATIC FANATICS: What Stephen King rip-off film did Evelyn Keyes appear in in 1987?

15. ANN RUTHERFORD *(Carreen O'Hara)*

15-1. What family connection was there between Ann Rutherford and Olivia de Havilland?

15-2. Before *Gone With the Wind,* Ann Rutherford was best known for her role as Mickey Rooney's girlfriend, Polly Benedict, in what popular film series of the 1930s?

15-3. FOR BOOB-TUBE BUFFS: What bizarre all-women panel talk show did Ann Rutherford appear on in the early 1950s?

16. BUTTERFLY McQUEEN *(Prissy)*

16-1. What was Butterfly McQueen's original name?

16-2. FOR CINEMATIC FANATICS: Butterfly McQueen appeared in what 1986 adventure film that also starred Harrison Ford?

16-3. FOR BOOB-TUBE BUFFS: Butterfly McQueen appeared in what 1980s TV sitcom set in Atlanta?

17. OLIVIA DE HAVILLAND *(Melanie Hamilton)*

17-1. Where was Olivia de Havilland born?

17-2. FOR BOOB-TUBE BUFFS: Olivia de Havilland appeared in what famous 1979 TV miniseries about slavery and the Old South?

17-3. ANOTHER ONE FOR BOOB-TUBE BUFFS: Olivia de Havilland guest-starred in what popular "cruise ship" TV series?

17-4. Which of the following comments did Olivia de Havilland make when told about the plans for a sequel to *Gone With the Wind*?

    A. "Oh dear, do you realize that poor Melanie will not be in it?"

    B. "Frankly, my dear, it cannot be done."

    C. "A *Gone With the Wind* sequel without Margaret Mitchell would be like *The Wizard of Oz* without the Wizard."

    D. "Oh, do let's find a way of having Melanie appear, even if only in a dream!"

17-5. What was the name of the 1948 film about mental illness in which Olivia de Havilland appeared and for which she was nominated for a Best Actress Academy Award and for which she won a New York Film Critics' Award?

17-6. For what picture did Olivia de Havilland win her first Best Actress Academy Award?

17-7. What famous woman writer did Olivia de Havilland play in the 1946 film, *Devotion*?

17-8. How many children does Olivia de Havilland have and what are their names?

17-9. TRUE OR FALSE: Olivia de Havilland has lived in France since the 1950s.

17-10. THE "WINDS OF CHANGE" DEPARTMENT: On February 3, 1945, a California statute went into effect called The Olivia de Havilland Decision. What was the subject of the Decision?

18. LAURA HOPE CREWS *(Aunt "Pittypat" Hamilton)*

18-1. What other show business professions did Laura Hope Crews excel in?

18-2. Who did Laura Hope Crews beat out for the plum role of Aunt Pitty?

18-3. What Broadway role was Laura Hope Crews unable to play because of illness?

19. ONA MUNSON *(Belle Watling)*

19-1. What radio program did Ona Munson appear on?

19-2. TRUE OR FALSE: Mae West was actually considered for the role of Belle Watling, but Ona Munson's audition was so good that she got the part instead.

19-3. How did Ona Munson die?

20. CAMMIE KING *(Bonnie Blue Butler)*

20-1. What was the only other film Cammie King ever made?

20-2. What *Gone With the Wind* crew member was Cammie King's stepfather?

20-3. How old was Cammie King when *Gone With the Wind* was released?

"RHETT" BY CLARK GABLE

My reaction to playing Rhett Butler is both frank and simple. "The condemned man ate a hearty meal." Now don't get me wrong. As an actor, I loved it. As a character, he was terrific. As material for the screen, he was that "once in a lifetime" opportunity. But as Clark Gable, who likes to pick his spots and found himself trapped by a series of circumstances over which he had no control, I was scared stiff.

This is no alibi. I cannot but honestly admit that the actual making of the picture was one of the most thoroughly pleasant and satisfying experiences I have ever known. During the filming, I was on familiar ground. Once in the atmosphere of the settings, facing a camera in costume, playing scenes that were dramatically realistic, I felt for the first time that I had an understanding of Rhett. The long months I had studied him and tried to know him as I know myself made me believe I was Rhett. These were things I could get my hands on. They were part of my job as an actor. It was those things I couldn't get my hands on that had me worried.

In way of explanation, let me go back to the beginning. I never asked to play Rhett. I was one of the last to read the book. I know, because out of curiosity I have inquired, that I definitely was not Miss Margaret Mitchell's inspiration for creating Rhett. When she was writing her book, Hollywood never had heard of me, and I am certain Miss Mitchell was not interested in an obscure Oklahoma oil field worker, which I was at the time. The first few times I heard the name, Rhett Butler, it was with growing irritation. Nobody likes to appear stupid. It was annoying to have people say breathlessly, "But, of course, you've read *Gone with the Wind,*" and then look painfully surprised when I said I hadn't. It got to the point where anyone who hadn't read the book was considered illiterate, if not actually a social outcast. Besides, everything in Hollywood out of the ordinary is "colossal." You get used to it. The greatest book ever written that will make the greatest picture of all time appears regularly every week. It is usually forgotten just as quickly. That's what got me about *"The Wind."* It kept right on blowing.

As I have said before, every minute of the five months the picture was in production was enjoyable. It was the preceding twenty-four months of conversation that had me on my ear. When it got to the point where Spencer Tracy was greeting me with "Hello, Rhett," I read the book. Before that, I had held out even when my best friends told me, "It's made to order for you." I had heard that one before.

In the interest of truth, I became a fan of Miss Mitchell's with the rest of America after going halfway through the book. It was good, too good in fact. Rhett was everything a character should be, and rarely is, clear, concise and very real. He breathed in the pages of the book. He was flawless as a character study. He stood up under the most careful analysis without exhibiting a weakness. That was the trouble.

I realized that whoever played Rhett would be up against a stumbling block in this respect. Miss Mitchell had etched Rhett into the minds of millions of people, each of whom knew exactly how Rhett would look and act. It would be impossible to satisfy them all. An actor would be lucky to please even the majority. It wasn't that I didn't want to play Rhett. I did. No actor could entirely resist such a challenge. But the more popular Rhett became, the more I agreed with the gentleman who wrote, "Discretion is the better part of valour."

My reading of the book enabled me to see clearly what I was in for if I played the part. I decided to say nothing. It became more apparent, anyhow, that it was out of my hands. The public interest in my doing Rhett puzzled me. Long before anyone had been cast for the picture, I was asked for interviews. When I refused comment, the columnists did it for me. My mail doubled and then trebled. I saw myself pictured as Rhett, with sideburns. I don't like sideburns. They itch. I was the only one, apparently, who didn't take it for granted that I was going to play Rhett. It was a funny feeling. I think I know now how a fly must react after being caught in a spider web. It wasn't that I didn't appreciate the compliment the public was paying me. It was simply that Rhett was too big an order. I didn't want any part of him.

To make sure that I hadn't erred in my first impression, I read *"Gone"* again. It convinced me more than ever that Rhett was too much for any actor to tackle in his right mind. But I couldn't escape him. I looked for every out. I even considered writing Miss Mitchell at one time. I thought it would be great if she would simply issue a statement saying, "I think Clark Gable would be the worst possible selection for Rhett Butler." Perhaps after Miss Mitchell sees my Rhett, or rather what I've done to her Rhett, she'll wish she had. It may be of interest as a sidelight that my own sincere choice for Rhett was Ronald Colman. I still think he would have done a fine job of it.

I found upon investigation that Miss Mitchell, and it was most intelligent of her, didn't care a hang what Hollywood was going to do with her book. All she wanted was peace and quiet. She wrote a book because it was the thing she liked to do, and having innocently caused more excitement than any author in memory, asked only to be left alone. On learning this bit of information, I immediately felt a sympathetic fellowship with Miss Mitchell, whom I never have had the pleasure of meeting. I am sure we would understand one another, for after all, Rhett has caused more than a little confusion in both our lives.

During the months when the casting of *"Gone"* reached the proportion of a national election, and acrimonious debate was being conducted on every street corner, Rhett became more of a mental hazard than ever. I was still the only one who didn't have anything to say about him. I never did have. For when the time came to get down to business, I was still out on a limb.

I knew what was coming the day David O. Selznick telephoned me. His purchase of the book for a mere $50,000 had started the riot. Our talk was amicable. I did the sparring and he landed the hard punches. David's idea was to make a separate deal, providing my studio would release me to make the picture. I thought my contract was an ace in the hole. It specified that my services belonged exclusively to Metro-Goldwyn-Mayer. I told David that, adding on my own that I was not interested in playing Rhett.

That didn't stop David. Being a friend of long standing and knowing him, I knew that it wouldn't. He pointed out that no actor ever had been offered such a chance. There had never been a more talked-of role than Rhett. That was exactly my reason for turning him down. He put his cards on the table. He was going to try to get me from M-G-M if he could. We shook hands on it.

I could have put up a fight. I didn't. I am glad now that I didn't. Hollywood always has treated me fairly. I have had no reason to complain about my roles and if the studio thought I should play Rhett, it was not up to me to duck out. I had nothing to do with the negotiations. I learned that I was to play Rhett in the newspapers. As a part of the deal, Metro-Goldwyn-Mayer was to release the picture.

I was pleased with the choice of Miss Vivien Leigh as Scarlett. She made Scarlett so vividly lifelike that it made my playing of Rhett much simpler than I had expected. I was equally pleased that Victor Fleming was to direct. He had directed me in *Test Pilot*. I had complete confidence in him. One thing stands out in those months of preparation for the picture. There was never any divergence of opinion. No single individual, with the exception of Miss Mitchell, deserves credit more than another. It was teamwork that counted.

There was only one way to make *"Gone."* That was as Miss Mitchell wrote it. There was only one problem, but it was not an easy one to solve. Miss Leigh and I discussed it a hundred times. We reached the conclusion that Scarlett and Rhett, while definite and powerful characters and individualists, depended on one another for characterization. In this respect, I would like to pay tribute to Miss Leigh. She was Scarlett every minute and I am greatly indebted to her for her contributions to my performance.

"Gone" was different from any picture I have ever made. I often have smiled in the past at actors who "live" their roles. My attitude to making pictures is realistic. But I must admit that all of us, and I am speaking for everyone who had any connection with the picture, had a definite feeling of living it. Miss Mitchell wrote of a period that is typically American, that is inspirational, that is real. When electricians, grips, make-up men and carpenters, who are blasé to making movies, stood around and watched scenes being rehearsed, and even broke into spontaneous applause after Miss Leigh had played some of her highlight dramatic scenes, you know you have something. They are the world's severest film critics.

QUIZ 60
(PART 1)

REEL INTEREST: PART 1

Questions from the 1988
Video Documentary
The Making of a Legend:
Gone With the Wind

The truth is, Gone With the Wind *came out of chaos and confusion, blind faith and great good luck.*
   —From the opening narration for the documentary *The Making of a Legend: Gone With the Wind*

These questions are all drawn from the 1988 documentary, *The Making of a Legend: Gone With the Wind* (TNT and TBS), written by David Thomson, directed by David Hinton, and narrated by Christopher Plummer. It runs two hours and is available on video in most video stores. It also appears frequently on cable and broadcast TV and is must-viewing for *Gone With the Wind* fans. It contains an incredible treasure trove of *Gone With the Wind* information, trivia, and behind-the-scenes looks at the making of the film, as well as details on the lives and times of the people behind and in front of the cameras. The best way to take this quiz is to either rent or tape the documentary and try to answer the questions while watching it, or watch it and see how many questions you can answer when you take the quiz later.

1. What did the "O" in David O. Selznick stand for?
   A. Otto
   B. Nothing. He added it himself for "flourish, rhythm, and production value."
   C. Oscar
   D. Oswald

2. How old was David O. Selznick in 1936 when he began producing *Gone With the Wind*?

3. How old was David O. Selznick when he began working in the movies?

4. What was the name of the powerful MGM tycoon who became David O. Selznick's father-in-law?

5. What was the name of David O. Selznick's executive assistant during the making of *Gone With the Wind*?

6. Who first brought the *Gone with the Wind* novel to David O. Selznick's attention?

7. Where did David O. Selznick first read *Gone with the Wind*?

8. The following actresses were the winners in a "Vote for Scarlett" radio contest put on by radio announcer Jimmie Fidler. Put the actresses in the proper order (with number 1 being the first choice to play the role).

   _____ Joan Crawford

   _____ Barbara Stanwyck

   _____ Miriam Hopkins

   _____ Bette Davis

   _____ Katharine Hepburn

   _____ Margaret Sullivan

9. David Selznick received hundreds of letters recommending actresses for the role of Scarlett. How many actresses were eventually suggested to Selznick for the part?

10. Who was the very first actress to do a screen test for the part of Scarlett O'Hara?

11. How long would *Gone With the Wind* had to have been if Sidney Howard's original script adaptation had been filmed?

12. What was the 1938 Warner Bros. *Gone With the Wind*–like film that starred Bette Davis and Henry Fonda?

13. What was the backlot called where *Gone With the Wind*'s sets were built?

14. What was the date of the very first scene shot for *Gone With the Wind*, and what was filmed?

15. Who first introduced David O. Selznick to Vivien Leigh?

16. Who were the four absolutely final contenders for the role of Scarlett O'Hara?

17. On what holiday did Vivien Leigh learn that she had won the role of Scarlett?

18. How old was Leslie Howard when *Gone With the Wind* began filming?

19. What did David O. Selznick have to promise to Leslie Howard in order to get Howard to agree to appear in *Gone With the Wind*?

20. What was the first actual "actors" scene filmed for *Gone With the Wind*?
    A. The Atlanta Bazaar scene
    B. The "Melanie childbirth" scene
    C. The Tara bedroom "lacing scene" with Scarlett and Mammy
    D. The "evening prayers" scene

21. How many times was the film's opening "Scarlett/Tarleton twins" porch scene shot?
    A. Five times
    B. Twice
    C. Once
    D. Ten times

22. What was the first scene Clark Gable shot for the film?
    A. The "Wilkes barbecue/war" scene
    B. The Atlanta "jailhouse" scene
    C. The "I could crush your head" scene
    D. The Atlanta Bazaar scene

23. What were the two things that Butterfly McQueen absolutely refused to do in the film?
    A. Kiss Clark Gable and slap Leslie Howard
    B. Be slapped and eat watermelon
    C. Use a "Negro" accent and wear a turban
    D. Eat watermelon and sing "Dixie"

24. TRUE OR FALSE: *Gone With the Wind*'s *first* director was Victor Fleming.

25. Who did David O. Selznick bring in to rewrite *Gone With the Wind*'s script after George Cukor's departure?

26. What stimulant did David O. Selznick heavily rely upon during the making of *Gone With the Wind*?
    A. Benzedrine
    B. Caffeine
    C. Dexedrine
    D. Cocaine

27. Who was the director brought in to resume filming after the departure of George Cukor?

28. Who was the director brought in to resume filming after the collapse of Victor Fleming?

29. How long did preparations take for the "crane/wounded soldiers" shot?
    A. Six months
    B. Two weeks
    C. Two years
    D. One year

30. Why did Victor Fleming have to be particularly careful with the composition of, and pullback from, the "crane/wounded soldiers" shot?

31. **TRUE OR FALSE:** Margaret Mitchell's husband John Marsh, after first seeing the "crane/wounded soldiers" scene, remarked, "Why, if we'd had that many soldiers, we'd have won the war."

32. What was unique about all the interior ceilings seen in the film?

The Horror, The Horror . . . *Scarlett, the reluctant nurse in a makeshift hospital, surrounded by wounded and dying Confederate soldiers.*

33. How did Sidney Howard die?
34. What was the first theater to show a sneak preview of the still-unfinished *Gone With the Wind*?
35. What was the name of the Hollywood censor who fought David O. Selznick about Clark Gable's use of the word "damn" in the film's final scene?

BONUS QUESTION 1. What was the production control number of Tallulah Bankhead's "Scarlett" screen test?

BONUS QUESTION 2. What was the date of the press announcement confirming that Vivien Leigh, Olivia de Havilland, and Leslie Howard had signed on to do *Gone With the Wind*?

BONUS QUESTION 3. On what date was Melanie's childbirth scene shot?

BONUS QUESTION 4. Who were the two composers hired to help Max Steiner with the score to *Gone With the Wind*?

BONUS QUESTION 5. What was the headline in the *Atlanta Constitution* that heralded the arrival of the cast for the world premiere of the film?

QUIZ 60
(PART 2)

REEL INTEREST: PART 2

Film Facts: Questions About the Film Version of
Gone With the Wind

Oh, all right. Go ahead and have a vulgar commercial success.
—Moss Hart, in a December 19, 1939, telegram to David O.
Selznick following the successful Atlanta premiere of the
film version of *Gone With the Wind*

Walk This Way *Scarlett and Gerald O'Hara strolling the grounds of Tara.*

No movie has a right to be that long!
    —PRESIDENT FRANKLIN DELANO ROOSEVELT, upon awakening
    after falling asleep during a screening of *Gone With the
    Wind* at the White House

This quiz tests your visual acuity, your attention span, and your ability to notice details. In other words, to answer these questions, many of you may have to watch the movie to find the correct answers! This quiz focuses on the film version of *Gone With the Wind* and all questions are drawn from the boxed two-tape videotape edition of *Gone With the Wind* and from sources listed in the Bibliography.

1. What scene is shown while the "Overture" plays?
2. What is the first actual "live action" scene in the film?
3. Who is listed first in the film's opening cast credits?
4. What character has the first line of dialogue in the film?
5. What is Mammy doing the first time we see her?
6. What are Mammy's first words?
7. What is the first word Ashley says in the film?
8. What was the inscription on the Twelve Oaks sundial?
9. What is Rhett Butler's first line of dialogue?
10. What is the first word we hear Melanie Wilkes say?
11. What did Scarlett see from a window at Twelve Oaks that convinced her to marry Charles Hamilton?
12. What neck jewelry did Scarlett wear for her marriage to Charles Hamilton?
13. PAUSE-BUTTON QUESTION: In the Christmas furlough train station scene, what did the sign that began "Women of Georgia!" ask for?
14. What was the name of the bank on which Scarlett drew her Kennedy "Tara tax" check?
15. What sign did Scarlett post in the Wilkes & Kennedy store?
16. PAUSE-BUTTON QUESTION: According to the clock on the wall in Melly's living room, what time did Rhett bring Ashley and Dr. Meade home the night Ashley was wounded in the Shantytown raid?
17. Whose voices does Scarlett hear in her mind after Rhett tells her he doesn't give a damn, and what do they say to her?
18. What is the last line of dialogue spoken in the film version of *Gone With the Wind* and how does it differ from the last line of dialogue in the novel?

Every Breath You Take *Mammy lacing up Scarlett's corset. Southern belles often wore their corsets so tight that they would occasionally faint from lack of oxygen. Rampant sexism, obsession with female appearance, and of course slavery were some of the more regrettable customs of the antebellum South. (By the way, notice the ring on Scarlett's "wedding" finger. Wishful thinking, perhaps, or a costume gaffe?)*

19. What year was *Gone With the Wind* re-released in a 70-millimeter wide-screen version?
20. How many Academy Award nominations did *Gone With the Wind* receive, and what were they?
21. What was the date of the Atlanta World Premiere of the film version of *Gone With the Wind*?
22. What television network bought the rights to produce the miniseries of the *Gone With the Wind* sequel, *Scarlett*?

Rescue Me *Scarlett in Atlanta during the war. Almost anything that moved was commandeered for use as an ambulance. Often the soldiers died before they got to the "hospital."*

The "Oops!" Section

Answer the following questions about mistakes and errors of continuity in *Gone With the Wind*.

BLOOPER #1. What is wrong with the shadows that the carriages drive through in the scene where the guests arrive at the Wilkes's 1861 Twelve Oaks barbecue?

BLOOPER #2. What "jewelry blooper" occurs in the scenes where Scarlett is dressing for the Wilkes's barbecue and then later in the "nap" scene at Twelve Oaks?

BLOOPER #3. In the scene in the church hospital where Melly and Scarlett kneel over a dying soldier, what specifically is wrong with their shadows on the wall behind them?

BLOOPER #4. When did Thomas Edison invent the electric light bulb, and what has this got to do with the film version of *Gone With the Wind*?

BLOOPER #5. What specifically is amiss about Scarlett's wardrobe during the sequence where she and Rhett flee Atlanta for their return to Tara? (Hint: We're talking about her wardrobe from *the neck up* for this question.)

BONUS QUESTION 1. What was the name of Frank Kennedy's Atlanta store?

BONUS QUESTION 2. What is the only material from Ben Hecht's contribution to the *Gone With the Wind* script that remained in the final version of the film?

BONUS QUESTION 3. Vivien Leigh refused to make the retching sounds needed for the scene at the conclusion of Part 1 of the film in which Scarlett eats a radish and then vomits it up. Who graciously obliged to make the necessary retching noises for the sound track?

"SCARLETT" BY VIVIEN LEIGH

A year has gone by since the night we stood watching the first scenes being made for *Gone With the Wind*. It was an awesome spectacle—whole blocks of sets being consumed by flames as Atlanta buildings burned, and I was a little confused by the grandeur of it and what seemed to be a frightening confusion.

That was the night I met Mr. David O. Selznick, the man who was producing *Gone With the Wind,* and who had yet to select a Scarlett O'Hara for the film.

In retrospect, it seems to me that the fantastic quality of that tremendous fire, the confusion I felt and the feeling of loneliness in the midst of hundreds of people was indicative of what was to come. I could not know then, of course, what lay ahead—and if someone had ventured to predict it, I probably would have passed it off as nonsense.

The unexpected happened: it made me, for these months at least, and whether I wished it so or not, into the character known as Scarlett O'Hara. Now the difficulty is to view that character objectively. That it was a great role for any actress was obvious, yet I can truthfully say that I looked on Mr. Selznick's request that I take a test for Scarlett as something of a joke. There were dozens of girls testing, and I did not seriously consider that I might actually play the part. Yet once it was decided upon I discovered that there was no joking about playing Scarlett. From then on, I was swept along as though by a powerful wave—it was Scarlett, Scarlett, Scarlett, night and day, month after month.

At once, I was asked two questions, and they persisted. First, everyone wanted to know if I was afraid of the part. And second, what did I think of Scarlett, anyway?

Perhaps if I had struggled, wished and worried about getting the role, I might have been fearful. As it was I had no time to let worry get the upper hand. That, and the sympathetic understanding of Mr. Selznick, eliminated fear before it got started.

As for Scarlett herself—my own views on that headstrong young lady are so bound up with my own experience in playing her that I find it difficult, now, to analyze just how I do feel about her. I lived Scarlett for close to six months, from early morning to late at night. I tried to make every move, every gesture true to Scarlett, and I had to feel that even the despicable things Scarlett did were of my doing.

From the moment I first began to read *Gone with the Wind* three years ago, Scarlett fascinated me, as she has fascinated so many others. She needed a good, healthy old-fashioned spanking on a number of occasions—and I should have been delighted to give it to her. Conceited, spoiled, arrogant—all those things, of course, are true of the character.

But she had courage and determination, and that, I think, is why women must secretly admire her—even though we can't feel too happy about her many shortcomings.

Try as I might to bring these characteristics from Margaret Mitchell's work into reality, there were bound to be times when I felt depressed. With so much painstaking effort going into the filming, every detail worked out to the finest point, days spent in recreating an exact situation, it was inevitable that I should feel sometimes that my work might not measure up to the standards which Mr. Selznick demanded, and which Victor Fleming, the director, strove so hard to reach. Yet Mr. Selznick seemed to sense these moments and was there to lend his encouragement, a help I am deeply grateful for. Mr. Fleming, faced with the task of keeping these thousand and one details coordinated, seemed to have an inexhaustible supply of patience and good humor. I think we all felt that here, above all times, it was imperative that we be good troupers, submerging ourselves to the task at hand.

There were months when I went to the studio directly from my home at 6:30 o'clock in the morning; breakfasted while making-up and having my hair done, then reported to the stage for the first "shot" at 8:45 A.M. And it was the rule, rather than the exception, to leave the studio at 9 or 10 o'clock that night. Needless to say, I saw none of Hollywood's night life!

I do not mean that all the grueling work was without its compensations and amusements. After so many weeks together, the company had its own jokes, its own forms of fun to lessen the tension. Mr. Fleming could always prepare me for some difficult work with an elaborate bow and a "Now, Fiddle-dee-dee—" which was the name bequeathed me, and Clark Gable's natural humor was always there to comfort us at the moments when tempers were shortest. Leslie Howard, as you can well imagine, is the soul of good humor; rarely upset and apt to come out with a bit of dry wit at the most unexpected moments.

You will recall that Rhett Butler, on a certain night, carries Scarlett up a long flight of stairs. We were ready to shoot this scene late in the afternoon, after a particularly difficult day. As so often happens, a number of things went wrong—and poor Clark had to carry me up the stairs about a dozen times before the shot was satisfactory. Even the stalwart Mr. Gable was beginning to feel it, I'm afraid—the set designer certainly made that stairway long enough.

"Let's try it once more, Clark," said the director. Clark winced, but picked me up and made the long climb.

"Thanks, Clark," said Fleming. "I really didn't need that shot—I just had a little bet on that you couldn't make it."

Even Clark saw the joke, although I'm not so sure I should have if I'd been in his place.

Perhaps the hardest days I spent, hard that is from the point of actual physical exertion, were during the time we made the scene where Scarlett struggles through the populace as it evacuates Atlanta.

Naturally this could not be done all in one continuous "take," and so for what seemed an eternity I dodged through the maze of traffic on Peachtree Street, timing myself to avoid galloping horses and thundering wagons.

And between each shot, the makeup man—he seemed to be everywhere at once—came running to wash my face, then dirty it up again to just the right shade of Georgia clay dust. I think he washed my face about 20 times in one day—and dusted me over with red dust after each washing.

Here, of course, was where the tremendous task of organizing was at its most spectacular. Horses and riders had to cross certain places at just the right time—and so did I. I can assure you that it is not a pleasant experience to see a gun caisson charging down on you—even when you know the riders are experts and the whole thing planned. In fact, I was so intent on being in the right place at the right time all day that I did not realize until I got to bed that night that Scarlett O'Hara Leigh was a badly bruised person.

Oddly enough, the scenes of physical strain were not so wearing as the emotional ones. One night we worked at the Selznick Studios until about 11 o'clock, then went out to the country for a shot against the sunrise, when Scarlett falls to her knees in the rundown fields of Tara and vows she'll never be hungry again. The sun rose shortly after 2 A.M. and I could not sleep, although I had a dressing room in a trailer. We made the shot and I arrived at home about 4:30 A.M., yet I do not recall that I was so terribly tired.

Instead, I think of the day that Scarlett shoots the deserter, and I recall that after that nerve-wracking episode, both Olivia de Havilland, the wonderful Melanie of the film, and myself were on the verge of hysterics—not alone from the tenseness of the scene, but from the too realistic fall as the "dead" man went down the stairs before us.

Yet when the day came that meant the film was completed, I could not help feeling some little regret that our parts were done and that the cast and the crew—who were all so thoughtful and kind throughout—were breaking up. Clark Gable, Leslie Howard, Olivia de Havilland, Tom Mitchell, Barbara O'Neil—fine players all. We should see each other again, of course—but never again would we have the experience of playing in *Gone With the Wind*!

PART FOUR

MISCELLANEOUS
GONE WITH THE WIND
QUIZZES

QUIZ 61

WHEN DID IT HAPPEN?

All of the following events took place in either *Gone with the Wind* or its sequel, *Scarlett*. Your mission is to identify the correct book for each event.

1. Pierre Robillard dies.
2. Scarlett's water breaks . . . "and it's red."
3. Boys throw rocks at Cat.
4. Union soldiers ransack Charleston homes looking for Ross Butler.
5. The Tarleton twins die.
6. Phil Meade dies.
7. Charles Hamilton dies.
8. Pierre Robillard laughs.
9. Tommy Cooper gets laid.
10. Fenton squeezes Scarlett's breast.
11. Archie kills his wife for layin' with his brother.
12. Scarlett gives birth to Ella Lorena.
13. Fenton sucks Scarlett's tongue into his mouth.
14. Mrs. Sims asks Scarlett to call her Daisy.
15. Scarlett's skirt catches fire. Twice.
16. Scarlett O'Hara takes Cat O'Hara to Tara.
17. Scarlett meets Miss Julia Ashley.
18. Clinch Dawkins calls Rhett Butler a nigger lover.
19. Rhett Butler cuts off the end of Clinch Dawkins's nose.
20. Poor whites break into Dunmore Landing and drink Rhett's whiskey.
21. Frank Kennedy proposes to Suellen O'Hara.
22. Rhett and Scarlett make love on a beach.
23. Fairhill burns to the ground.
24. Dilcey breast-feeds Melanie's baby.
25. Ellen O'Hara dies.
26. Scarlett enters a bar and brewery for the first time in her life.
27. Scarlett O'Hara eats on the street.
28. Cathleen Calvert marries Mr. Hilton, the Yankee overseer.
29. Scarlett vomits into a magnolia tree.
30. Ashley Wilkes admits to Scarlett that he is a coward.

31. Scarlett washes Ash Wednesday ashes off her forehead.
32. Pierre Robillard asks Scarlett to be the chatelaine of his house.
33. Will Benteen arrives at Tara.
34. Rhett Butler is jailed in Atlanta for allegedly killing a Negro.
35. Scarlett O'Hara goes to Atlanta in her mother's velvet curtains and the tail feathers of a rooster.
36. Ashley Wilkes reads prayers at Gerald O'Hara's funeral.
37. Cat burns her hand on a pan.
38. Scarlett gives Pork Gerald O'Hara's gold pocketwatch.
39. Carreen O'Hara enters the convent.
40. Will Benteen and Suellen O'Hara are married.
41. Ashley Wilkes proposes to Scarlett.
42. Scarlett's breasts are bared by a Negro thief who rips open her basque looking for money.
43. Rhett Butler proposes marriage to Scarlett Kennedy after Frank Kennedy's funeral.
44. Melanie covets Scarlett's daughter.
45. Pork retires.
46. A drunken Rhett carries Scarlett upstairs and makes love to her all night.
47. A drunken Rhett cries with his head in Melanie's lap.
48. A monster sits on Bonnie Butler's chest.
49. India Wilkes, Archie, and Mrs. Elsing catch Scarlett and Ashley in an embrace.
50. Mammy dies.
51. Melanie sees a man cry for the first time in her life.
52. Rhett Butler approves a $2,000 bank loan to Mrs. Merriwether.
53. Tony Fontaine returns to Clayton County.
54. Scarlett quits drinking.
55. Rhett reveals to Scarlett that he knew she pretended he was Ashley when they were making love.
56. Scarlett falls backwards down a flight of stairs.
57. Scarlett sells a lumber mill to Ashley Wilkes.
58. Bonnie Butler dies.
59. Rhett Butler shoots and kills Mr. Butler.
60. Ashley Wilkes attempts to hurl himself into his dead wife's grave.
61. Scarlett opens a secret charge account at Kennedy's Emporium for Ashley, India, and Aunt Pitty.
62. Melanie convinces Rhett to allow Bonnie's funeral and burial.

63. Ross Butler sticks his tongue in Scarlett's mouth.
64. Scarlett meets Sally Brewton.
65. Melanie Wilkes has a miscarriage.
66. Scarlett gets indigestion for the first time in her life.
67. Melanie Hamilton marries Ashley Wilkes.
68. Pansy vomits over the side of Rhett's boat.
69. Scarlett and Rhett are capsized at sea.
70. Scarlett O'Hara marries Charles Hamilton.
71. Jonas Wilkerson "sires" Emma Slattery's baby.
72. Charles Hamilton proposes to Scarlett O'Hara.
73. Aunt Pittypat tries to invest $500 in a nonexistent gold mine, but is stopped by Henry Hamilton.
74. Rhett Butler "bids" $150 in gold to dance with Scarlett O'Hara Hamilton.
75. Big Sam digs ditches "fer de wite gempmums ter hide in w'en de Yankees come."
76. Prissy drops Melanie's newborn son.
77. Rhett Butler asks Scarlett O'Hara to be his mistress.
78. Rhett Butler joins the Confederate army.
79. Rhett Butler marries Anne Hampton.
80. Scarlett—for the first time in her life—strikes a slave.

QUIZ 62

FAMILY TREES

Fables and endless genealogies.

— 1 Timothy 1:4

Hail wedded love, mysterious law, true source
Of human offspring, sole propriety,
In Paradise of all things common else.

—MILTON, *Paradise Lost*

This quiz asks you to fill in the parents, the children and, in one case, the grandchildren, for four families of the *Gone with the Wind* and *Scarlett* worlds. The organization of these "Family Trees" is random (other than the standard genealogical ordering of parent-child-grandchild), covers the pro-creative happenings in both books, and when a daughter has a child, the father's name is given parenthetically. The A level = the parents of the family; the B.1, B.2, etc., levels = the children; and the B.1.1, B.1.2, etc., levels = the children's children (the parents' grandchildren).

1.
The O'Haras
(Tara)

1-a1. _____ , father
1-a2. _____ , mother,
  1-b1. _____ , daughter
    1-b1.1. _____ , daughter (by Will Benteen)
    1-b1.2. _____ , daughter (by Will Benteen)
    1-b1.3. _____ , daughter (by Will Benteen)
  1-b2. _____ , daughter
  1-b3. _____ , daughter
    1-b3.1. _____ , son (by Charles Hamilton)
    1-b3.2 _____ , daughter (by Frank Kennedy)
    1-b3.3. _____ , daughter (by Rhett Butler)
    1-b3.4. _____ , daughter (by Rhett Butler)
  1-b4. _____ , deceased son
  1-b5. _____ , deceased son
  1-b6. _____ , deceased son

2.
The O'Haras
(Savannah)

2-a1. _____ , father
2-a2. _____ , mother
  2-b1. _____ , son
  2-b2. _____ , daughter

2-b3. _____ , daughter
2-b4. _____ , son
2-b5. _____ , daughter

3.
The Tarletons

3-a1. _____ , father
3-a2. _____ , mother
   3-b1. _____ , daughter
   3-b2. _____ , daughter
   3-b3. _____ , son
   3-b4. _____ , son
   3-b5. _____ , daughter
   3-b6. _____ , daughter
   3-b7. _____ , son
   3-b8. _____ , son

4.
The Butlers

4-a1. _____ , father
4-a2. _____ , mother
   4-b1. _____ , son
   4-b2. _____ , son
   4-b3. _____ , daughter

QUIZ 63

SOUTHERN COOKING
A 3-PART QUIZ FROM THE "GONE WITH THE WIND" COOK BOOK

Cookery is become an art, a noble science: cooks are gentlemen.
        —ROBERT BURTON, *Democritus to the Reader*

Il faut n'appeler Science: *que* l'ensemble des recettes qui réussissent toujours.—*Tout les rest est* Littérature.
The term *Science* should not be given to anything but *the aggregate of the recipes that are always successful.* All the rest is *Literature.*
        —PAUL VALÉRY, *Moralités* (1932)

Kissing don't last: cookery do!
        —GEORGE MEREDITH, *The Ordeal of Richard Feverel* (1859)

The "Gone with the Wind" Cook Book, first published in 1940, collected Southern recipes "thinking you would like to keep their deliciousness alive by serving them at dinner, luncheon, or bridge parties." [From the foreword.] The book was rereleased in an inexpensive ($6.95) facsimile edition in 1991 by Abbeville Press, and the three sections of questions in this quiz are all drawn from this delightful *Gone with the Wind* collectible.

Part 1

The "Gone with the Wind" Cook Book offered suggestions for three "Gone with the Wind" parties: a Dinner Party, a Luncheon Party, and a Sunday Night Supper. For this quiz, identify the menu items by the meal. Use "DP" for a Dinner Party item, "LP" for a Luncheon Party item, and "SS" for a Sunday Night Supper item.

_____ 1. Brunswick Stew
_____ 2. Gerald O'Hara Ham Steak
_____ 3. Broiled Oysters on the Half Shell
_____ 4. Eggnog Ice Cream
_____ 5. Tidewater Country Fried Soft-shelled Crabs
_____ 6. Cracklin Bread
_____ 7. Watermelon Slices
_____ 8. Aunt Pittypat's Coconut Pudding
_____ 9. Sally Lunn
_____ 10. Vegetable Salad Bowl
_____ 11. Chicken Pilau
_____ 12. Pralines
_____ 13. Lady Baltimore Cake
_____ 14. Southern Vegetable Soup
_____ 15. Green Salad Bowl

Part 2

For this group of queries, your culinary quest is to answer the following questions about ten of the recipes in The *"Gone with the Wind" Cook Book*.

1. What are the three spices used in "Mammy's Shrimp Cakes"?
2. How many oysters were needed for the "Tarleton Twins' Broiled Oysters on the Half Shell"?
3. How did the recipe for "Fried Frogs' Legs" recommend removing the skin from the frogs' legs?
4. What vegetables were used in "Mammy's Creole Rice"?
5. At what temperature was "Melanie's Shirred Eggs with Ham" to be cooked?
6. How much flour was used in the recipe for "Melanie's Popovers"?
7. What three shapes were suggested for "Aunt Pittypat's Cream Scones"?
8. What fruits were used in the recipe for "Tara Fruit Cake"?
9. How long did the mixture for "Twelve Oaks Plum Pudding" have to be steamed before serving?
10. What size unbaked pie shell was needed for "Melanie's Sweet Potato Pie"?

Part 3

This final group of questions asks you to match the alcoholic beverage from the left column with the specific Southern *"Gone with the Wind" Cook Book* drink recipe from the right column. (Hint—as if you couldn't tell!—two of the recipes allow for several different spirits to be used.)

1. Bourbon
2. Rye
3. Cognac brandy
4. Jamaica rum
5. Claret
6. Sherry
7. Brandy

A. "Claret Punch"
B. "Eggnog Beverage"
C. "Eggnog"

PART FIVE

GENESIS

AN INTERVIEW WITH
MARGARET MITCHELL'S
HUSBAND,
JOHN R. MARSH

GONE WITH THE WIND WON ITS FIRST READER*
HE, AUTHOR'S HUSBAND, PERSUADED HER TO SUBMIT IT
ONLY AFTER LONG URGING

The first man to read the best-selling novel, *Gone with the Wind*, finds himself in an enviable position. He can say "I told you so," and his wife has no defense.

He is John R. Marsh, the "J.R.M." to whom his wife, Margaret Mitchell, dedicated her book.

It was ten years ago he began telling his wife her book was good.

He insisted she should have it published, but she would never agree it was good enough. Now, with 850,000 copies already published and new editions coming out steadily in this country, England and Canada, he no longer tells his wife "I told you so." He merely looks at her and she registers embarrassment.

During the years the book lay around their apartment in the form of stacked, dog-eared manuscript he was the only person, except the author herself, who read any part of the book.

He never read the book through from front to back until less than a year ago, but had read it in fragments as his wife wrote it.

"Imagine reading right up to one of the most exciting points in the book, and then having to wait a year or maybe three years to read the next chapter, because it had never been written," he said.

"Of course, I never dreamed it would be a record-breaking success," he added. "Both of us would have been proud if a few thousand copies had been sold. That is the best a first novel can hope for.

"But I knew it was better than the ordinary run of novels. I could see there was great dramatic power in the story. I urged her to offer it to a publisher, but she could not be persuaded until about a year ago.

"I am tremendously proud of her success, but I was as much surprised as she when the sales began to mount into the hundreds of thousands."

Mr. Marsh never has written or attempted to write a book, but he has been in the writing business all of his life, first as a newspaperman and for the last several years as advertising manager of an electric power company. He is 41.

His wife attracted attention in this area some years ago as a newspaper feature writer. They were married in 1925, have no children and live quietly in the same apartment they have occupied for years.

QUIZ 64

MARGARET MITCHELL: HER LIFE AND TIMES

As to where I "fit in" in the book, I do not know. I tried to write as completely an objective book with nothing of myself in it. I am sure I am not Scarlett, and I could not hope to be Melanie! However, I know that the personality of an author will creep into a book no matter how hard the author struggles, but I do not know what part of me is in it. All I know is that a number of years of my life and a lot of sweat went into that book.
　　　　　　　—MARGARET MITCHELL, letter to Mr. A. W. Wootton,
　　　　　　　October 15, 1936

God bless our little Peggy Marsh.
—JULIAN BOEHM, at the conclusion of the world premiere of
the film *Gone With the Wind* in Atlanta on December 15,
1939, as quoted in an article by Harold Martin in the
Atlanta *Georgian* of December 16, 1939

Margaret Mitchell was an intelligent, free-thinking woman gifted with almost-legendary social grace and charisma. She was also a brilliant writer who became an unwilling participant in the furor and tumult caused by the publication of her first and *only* novel. The following questions concern the life and times of Margaret Mitchell and the answers can be found in Darden Asbury Pyron's masterful biography, *Southern Daughter,* Anne Edwards's Mitchell bio, *Road to Tara,* and also in several of the other volumes listed in the Bibliography.

1. In what year was Margaret Mitchell born?
2. What was Margaret Mitchell's middle name?
3. What was Margaret Mitchell's occupation?
4. What was the name of the lieutenant Margaret Mitchell was engaged to prior to his World War I battlefield death?
5. What was the name of Margaret Mitchell's first husband?
6. What was the name of Margaret Mitchell's second husband?
7. Where did Margaret Mitchell attend college?
8. How much was the advance Margaret Mitchell received from Macmillan for the book *Gone with the Wind*?
9. To whom is *Gone with the Wind* dedicated?
10. What year did Margaret Mitchell win the Pulitzer Prize for *Gone with the Wind*?
11. What childhood fire accident did Margaret Mitchell recreate in *Gone with the Wind*?
12. How much did Margaret Mitchell receive for the film rights to *Gone with the Wind*?
13. What was the name of Margaret Mitchell's secretary?
14. What role did Margaret Mitchell want Charles Boyer to play in the film version of *Gone With the Wind*?
15. Which of the Marx Brothers did Margaret Mitchell suggest to play Rhett in the film version of *Gone With the Wind*?
16. What date did Margaret Mitchell die?
17. How did Margaret Mitchell die?

18. What year was Margaret Mitchell immortalized on a U.S. postage stamp, and what denomination was the stamp?

19. What was the title of the 60-page (now destroyed) novella by Margaret Mitchell that was submitted to Macmillan with the *Gone with the Wind* manuscript?

20. TRUE OR FALSE: In 1936, U.S. Under Secretary of the Interior Harry Slattery publicly stated that he was thrilled that his family name had been used for one of the characters (Emmie Slattery) in *Gone with the Wind*.

21. TRUE OR FALSE: Not only did Margaret Mitchell instruct that all her papers be destroyed after her death, she also left instructions that her house on Peachtree Street similarly be destroyed after her brother, Stephens, was through with it.

22. TRUE OR FALSE: Margaret Mitchell willed all rights to *Gone with the Wind* to her servant and companion, Bessie Jordan.

23. TRUE OR FALSE: David O. Selznick once proposed to Margaret Mitchell that she write a sequel to *Gone with the Wind* called *The Daughter of Scarlett O'Hara*, and that Vivien Leigh play Scarlett's daughter in the movie version of the story.

BONUS QUESTION. What was the name of Margaret Mitchell's childhood cat?

SUPER BONUS QUESTION. What is the title of the *other* authorized sequel to *Gone with the Wind*, who is its author, and why wasn't it ever published?

AN INTERVIEW WITH
MARGARET MITCHELL

SUCCESS AMAZES PEGGY MITCHELL; SHE HAD SUBMITTED BOOK ON "DARE"*

AUTHOR OF GONE WITH THE WIND HAD HOPED FOR A SALE OF 5,000 COPIES, BUT 476,000 HAVE BEEN BOUGHT—SHE BEGAN WRITING IT TEN YEARS AGO

Once the train was out of Atlanta and well on the way to the Coast, he had the porter bring his new suitcase to him.

He smiled as he pulled the stiff new straps out of the buckle and pressed open the bag. There before him was the huge mass of manuscript he had received a few hours before.

It would be curious if it—

It was very much like a story plot itself, this manuscript.

He had come South on a scouting trip. The Macmillan Company had sent him, H. S. Latham, on a hunt for new authors. Two friends had urged him to ring up friends in Atlanta. They were sure to know any new writers there.

And so it came about that he had had lunch that very day with Margaret Mitchell and Mrs. Medora Perkerson, both of whom had done newspaper work on the same staff. They had talked of the South and of the writers produced by the South, the old ones and the new. Peggy Mitchell and Mrs. Perkerson had suggested this person and that person as possibilities.

Finally, near the end of the luncheon, Mrs. Perkerson had said: "Peggy has written a book."

*From *The New York Times,* Sunday, October 4, 1936. Copyright © 1936 by The New York Times Company. Reprinted by permission.

235

Scribbled on Old Papers

Mr. Latham recalled how Miss Mitchell had blushed and waved aside the suggestion. Something had prompted him to ask questions. But she said it was nothing. So they had gone riding into the hills to see the dogwood, which was in bloom. And there the matter of the novel had rested.

Later, at home, she had thought—there it was in a closet, stacks of it. She had worked at it at periods over ten years. It was not complete. Some of the chapters had three versions. Chapters were missing. Some of it was typed. Some of it was scribbled on laundry slips and old newspaper copy sheets. It didn't even have a first chapter.

Ten years before she had thought of the book. The story had grown in her mind. And for that many years she had done odd jobs of work on the novel.

So, why not let him have a look at it? It was something of a dare. So, on the impulse, she gathered it from the closet, dusted it off, tied it up, drove to the hotel, called Mr. Latham.

He tried to get the manuscript into his bag but saw it was hopeless. A few minutes later a clerk in a nearby luggage shop had sold a new suitcase. Mr. Latham left for New York.

One day a telegram came to Miss Mitchell. It said that the Macmillan Company had accepted the book, and Mr. Latham would bring the contract.

Locks Herself In Room to Work

The book was to be titled *Gone with the Wind*. In long years of reading she had discovered Ernest Dowson. And that poem of his which is written to a lost love has in its third stanza this line:

*"I have forgot much Cynara,
gone with the wind—"*

In the story which was in her mind a great many things and a great many people had gone with the wind of the war between the States, and with the wind that followed it. And some things, and some people, had not. That was her story.

There were conferences. And finally the writing of the book

itself from that great pile of manuscript. For six months she worked.

Locked in her room, she pounded away and turned out the chapters. They were written and rewritten. It was six months of toil, in which she learned to hate the work.

Finally, it was ready. She hoped it would sell 5,000 copies. That would be tremendous. It was very exciting, waiting. Even if she was worn out and tired of the book.

Then one morning at breakfast the maid brought the mail. There was a letter there from Macmillan. It said that the Book-of-the-Month Club had accepted her book as its choice for the month of its publication. When she handed the letter to her husband her hand shook and she could not talk.

It was in June that the book appeared, just about a year after Mr. Latham had come to Atlanta and she and Medora Perkerson had tried to think of some authors for him to scout. And now her novel was out—1,036 [*sic*] pages.

Orders Come In a Flood

Two sets of presses couldn't print the books fast enough to keep up with orders. *Gone with the Wind*—100,000 copies gone—another 100,000 and the book hardly on the shelves and tables of the book shops and stores—another 100,000 copies and still more orders.

In Atlanta, Peggy Mitchell was unable to understand it. She had written a book. She knew those six months of nerve-wracking toil. But whose book was this that was sweeping the country? It didn't really seem hers. But it was.

Peggy Mitchell left Atlanta to rest. That six months of constant work had weakened her eyes. The day the book's sales passed the 476,000 mark the doctor put her to bed in a darkened room for two weeks to rest those eyes. She plans no new writing just now. She wants to regain the old, quiet life again.

This book has its theme, if you must have one, on pages 430 and 431. It is the story of carrying one's burdens. Peggy Mitchell, although she is just 30 years old, grew up in the war between the States, figuratively, and the effect was almost literal. She heard stories of the bombardment of Atlanta; she heard stories from people who were there during all the hysteria of Sherman's coming; she felt all the horror and tragedy of the great mass of refugees streaming toward Macon to escape the war. So she wrote a story of the tragic era of reconstruction and one central figure—Scarlett O'Hara.

Lifelong Resident of Atlanta

Miss Mitchell was born and has lived all her life in Atlanta. Her father, Eugene Mitchell, was a lawyer and an authority on Georgia and the South in general. Since she was old enough to spell out letters, she has been a voracious reader, with her preferences running largely to books about the Civil War and the reconstruction period.

As a child, books of fiction-history gave her rich accounts of Southern heroism and Southern victory, and it was not until she was 10 years old that she learned that Robert E. Lee had been defeated.

It was her ambition to study medicine, but she was seriously injured in an accident and had to walk with the aid of crutches for three years. Those were years of intense reading—mystery stories, history, biography, anything she could find. She worked on *The Atlanta Journal* for six years, doing reportorial work and writing signed feature stories.

In 1926 she began her *Gone with the Wind,* which was published last June.

In private life she is Mrs. John R. Marsh. Her husband is advertising manager of the Georgia Power Company.

THE <u>GONE WITH THE WIND</u>
CROSSWORD PUZZLE

This is a puzzling world.
> —GEORGE ELIOT, *The Mill on the Floss*

You didn't heave a sigh of relief when you answered the last question in the last quiz in the last section of this book, now did you!?

Because if you did, suck it back in and go sharpen your pencil, ladies and gentlemen, for here is one more quiz. The *Gone with the Wind* Crossword Puzzle is the lexical equivalent of a pleasure our Hobbit friends, Frodo and Bilbo Baggins, called "filling up the corners," only what they were referring to was the post-prandial picking and snacking that goes on after a big and satisfying meal is over, but before everyone has left the table.

This puzzle allows you to use all your brand-spanking-new *Gone with the Wind* knowledge in a puzzle format known and loved by all.

The clues and answers in this puzzle are drawn from *Gone with the Wind,* the novel, *Gone With the Wind,* the film, and *Scarlett,* the sequel to *Gone with the Wind.*

Some of these clues are easy; many are not, but the majority of the answers are readily accessible either in the three works mentioned, or somewhere in *The Official "Gone with the Wind" Companion.* (There is one question that's really hard [specifically 7 Down], so don't feel bad if you can't pull the correct answer out of your *Gone with the Wind* mental file cabinet. I deliberately included it to drive you crazy, and I hope you'll think well of me anyway.)

The correctly filled-in puzzle is in the Answers section.

Happy Puzzling!

ACROSS

1 Suellen's father
4 Rhett
6 ____ Wilkerson
8 Carroll ____
9 Rhett's mother
10 Ellen O'Hara's maiden name
14 ____ Blue Butler
15 The priest in the family
16 Melanie's ex-con
19 Scarlett's Atlanta aunt
20 Scarlett was an outright ____ when she went to see Rhett in jail
23 ____ Lorena
24 Mrs. Meade's cook
25 "Do Not Squander ____"
26 Big ____
30 Uncle Peter's great-niece
31 "As ____ is my witness . . ."
33 Pauline's sister
34 Scarlett shot the Yankee deserter in the ____
35 Sir ____ Morland
37 Honey's sister
39 "There was a land of Cavaliers and ____ Fields . . ."
41 Tony ____
43 The Brian ____
44 Scarlett's first husband
45 Uncle Tom's ____

DOWN

1 ____ With the Wind
2 Scarlett definitely did not look ____ at the Twelve Oaks barbecue
3 "Scarlett O'Hara, you're a ____!"
4 The location of South Carolina's first recorded whorehouse
5 Scarlett's third husband
7 ____ Carter (played the unseen Jeems)
10 One of Scarlett's goals in life was to be this
11 One of the most important things in the world to Gerald O'Hara
12 What killed the Old South
13 ____ Levi
14 ____ Watling
15 ____ County
16 ____ Wilkes
17 Scarlett's fourth child
18 Scarlett's "other mother"
19 Dilcey's wench
21 Carreen's sister
22 Mammy
27 The Confederate color
28 The ____ Brotherhood
29 The Director
31 Irish wise woman
32 Philip was Tara's ____ man
36 Randa's sister
38 Scarlett's firstborn
40 Home
41 "The languishing ____"
42 ____ Seidel (played Tony Fontaine)

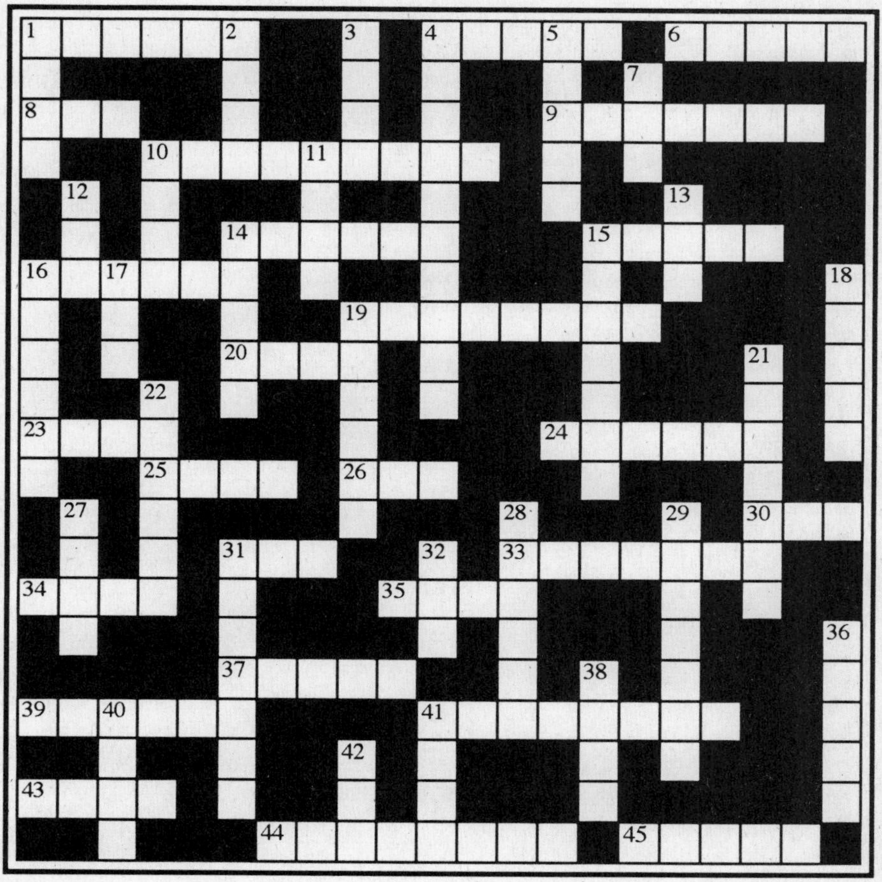

THE CONCORDANCES

These "Chapter/Page Concordances" are to be used in conjunction with the "Question/Chapter Key." After using the "Question/Chapter Key" to determine which chapter of *Gone with the Wind* or *Scarlett* a particular quiz question relates to, use these "Chapter/Page Concordances" to find the relevant pages in either *Gone with the Wind* (Avon paperback) or *Scarlett* (Warner hardcover). These page-number references can save you from flipping through the novels to find the needed chapter.

A GONE WITH THE WIND CHAPTER/PAGE CONCORDANCE

A SCARLETT CHAPTER/PAGE CONCORDANCE

THE QUESTION/CHAPTER KEYS

CHAPTER REFERENCES FOR ALL THE BASIC "Q & A"–TYPE QUESTIONS IN THE OFFICIAL "GONE WITH THE WIND" COMPANION

You will find it a very good practice always to verify your references, sir!
—DR. ROUTH, quoted in *Lives of Twelve Good Men* (1888 ed.), Volume I, page 73

This section serves as a reference to the "Q & A"–type questions asked in *The Official "Gone with the Wind" Companion*. If you can't answer a question immediately, don't give up. Instead turn to this section, pinpoint the chapter in either *Gone with the Wind* (quizzes 1–32) or *Scarlett* (33–55) in which the answer can be found, and then GO FIND IT! This should add to the fun and also give you the pleasure of rereading the two books. Note: These references are *only* for the "Q & A"–type questions. The true or false, multiple-choice, fill-in-the-blank, and Bonus questions are not similarly clued. For those, you'll have to ferret out the info unassisted! (But don't fret if you can't figure out one of the "hintless" questions. Remember: Every single "text" answer given in the Answers section also provides the correct page number in both *Gone with the Wind* and *Scarlett* where the answer information can be found.)

247

QUIZ 1: 1-I; 2-I; 3-I; 4-III; 5-I; 6-I; 7-III; 8-VI; 9-IX; 10-XI; 11-XV; 12-XVIII; 13-XXIX; 14-XXIX; 15-XXXIII; 16-XXXVI; 17-XL; 18-XLI; 19-XLII; 20-XLII; 21-XLII; 22-XLVIII; 23-XLVII; 24-XLVII; 25-XLVII; 26-L.

QUIZ 2: 1-VI; 2-VI; 3-VI; 4-IX; 5-IX; 6-IX; 7-IX; 8-IX; 9-XII; 10-XII; 11-XIII; 12-XIII; 13-XXII; 14-XXXIV; 15-XXXIV; 16-XXXIV; 17-XXXIII; 18-XXXVI; 19-XXXVI; 20-XXXVIII; 21-XLIII; 22-XLIII; 23-XLIII; 24-XLIII; 25-XLV; 26-XLVIII; 27-XLVII; 28-LII; 29-LII.

QUIZ 3: 1-II; 2-I; 3-I; 4-XV; 5-XV; 6-XV; 7-XV; 8-XVI; 9-XVI; 10-XXX; 11-XXXI; 12-XL; 13-XXXIX; 14-XLII; 15-LVII.

QUIZ 4: 1-II; 2-VI; 3-VIII; 4-XVI; 5-XXII; 6-XXIII; 7-XXI; 8-XXV; 9-XXVI; 10-XXVI; 11-XXVII; 12-XXXV; 13-L; 14-LVI; 15-LXI; 16-XLI; 17-XLI.

QUIZ 5: 1-II; 2-II; 3-XXV; 4-XXIV; 5-XXIV; 6-XXVI; 7-XXX; 8-XXXIII; 9-XXII; 10-XLII; 11-XLVII; 12-XLIX; 13-L; 14-LIX; 15-LIX.

QUIZ 6: 1-III; 2-III; 3-II; 4-II, III; 5-III; 6-II; 7-III; 8-III; 9-II; 10-V; 11-XXVI; 12-XXXVIII; 13-XXXIX; 14-XXXVIII; 15-XL; 16-LII; 17-II; 18-XXXIX.

QUIZ 7: 1-III; 2-II; 3-III; 4-I; 5-II; 6-III; 7-III; 8-VI; 9-XIII; 10-XXIV; 11-XXIV; 12-XXVII; 13-XLIV.

QUIZ 8: 1-I; 2-IV; 3-VI; 4-VI; 5-VI; 6-XV; 7-XVIII; 8-XX; 9-XLI; 10-XLI; 11-XLI; 12-XLI; 13-XLI; 14-XLVIII; 15-LV.

QUIZ 9: 1-I; 2-VI; 3-XXVII; 4-VI; 5-VI; 6-VII; 7-VII.

QUIZ 10: 1-IV; 2-VI; 3-VI; 4-XXVII, XXIX; 5-VI; 6-XXXV; 7-XXXV; 8-XXXVI; 9-XXXVI; 10-XXXVI; 11-XXXVII; 12-XXXVI; 13-XXXVIII.

QUIZ 11: 1-VIII; 2-VIII; 3-VIII; 4-IX; 5-XII; 6-XII; 7-XVIII; 8-XXVIII; 9-XXVIII; 10-XXXIII; 11-XXXV; 12-XXXIII; 13-XXXVI; 14-XXXVI; 15-XXXVIII; 16-LV; 17-LV; 18-LIX.

QUIZ 12: 1-I; 2-I; 3-I; 4-I; 5-I; 6-V; 7-V; 8-V; 9-VI; 10-XXIX; 11-XL; 12-LVII; 13-LVII.

QUIZ 13: 1-V; 2-II; 3-II; 4-II; 5-II; 6-II; 7-IV; 8-III; 9-XIX; 10-XXV; 11-XXVIII; 12-XXIX; 13-XXX; 14-XXXV; 15-XXXIX; 16-XXXIX; 17-XL; 18-LVII.

QUIZ 14: 1-III; 2-II; 3-II; 4-II; 5-II; 6-III; 7-III; 8-I; 9-IV; 10-IV; 11-III; 12-III; 13-XVII; 14-XXIV; 15-XXVI; 16-XLI; 17-XLIV; 18-XLIV; 19-XLIV; 20-III.

QUIZ 15: 1-II; 2-IV; 3-IX; 4-XV; 5-XIV; 6-XVI; 7-XVI; 8-XVI; 9-XVII; 10-XVII; 11-XIX; 12-XXVI; 13-XXIV; 14-XXVI; 15-XXIV; 16-XXVII; 17-XXXVII; 18-XXXVII; 19-XXXVIII; 20-XXXVIII; 21-XXXVIII; 22-XLV; 23-XLV.

QUIZ 16: 1-II; 2-II; 3-III; 4-IV; 5-XVIII; 6-XXIV; 7-IV.

QUIZ 17: 1-XXV; 2-XXVIII; 3-XXXI; 4-XXX; 5-XXXI; 6-XXX; 7-XXIX; 8-XXXI; 9-XXXVII; 10-XXXVII; 11-XLI; 12-XLII; 13-XLII; 14-XLV; 15-XLV; 16-XXXVII; 17-LVII.

QUIZ 18: 1-I; 2-I; 3-III; 4-III; 5-V; 6-XXIV; 7-XXIX; 8-XL.

QUIZ 19: 1-VIII; 2-VIII; 3-VIII; 4-VIII; 5-VIII; 6-VIII; 7-VIII; 8-VIII; 9-XII; 10-XII; 11-XIV; 12-XVI; 13-XXVIII; 14-XXVIII; 15-XXXIV; 16-XXXV; 17-XXXIII; 18-XXXVII; 19-XLI; 20-XLVII; 21-XLVII; 22-XLVIII.

QUIZ 20: 1-I; 2-II; 3-IV; 4-XII; 5-XIV; 6-XXII; 7-XXX; 8-XXXIV; 9-XXXIII; 10-XXXIII; 11-XXXVI; 12-XL; 13-XL; 14-XXXVIII; 15-XXXVIII; 16-XL; 17-XLI; 18-XLVII.

QUIZ 21: 1-III; 2-VI; 3-IX; 4-IX; 5-IX; 6-XI; 7-XIV; 8-XV; 9-XV; 10-XV; 11-XVII; 12-XVII; 13-XVIII; 14-XVIII; 15-XXI; 16-XXIII; 17-XLII; 18-XLIV.

QUIZ 22: 1-I; 2-II; 3-II; 4-IV; 5-IV; 6-IV; 7-IV; 8-V; 9-V; 10-V; 11-V; 12-VI; 13-VI; 14-VI; 15-VI; 16-VII; 17-VII; 18-VIII; 19-IX; 20-IX; 21-IX; 22-X; 23-IX; 24-XII; 25-XIII; 26-XVI; 27-XXIII; 28-XXIV; 29-XXXI; 30-XXIX; 31-XXIX; 32-XXXV; 33-XXXII; 34-XXXV; 35-XXXV; 36-XXXIV; 37-XXXIV; 38-XXXIV; 39-XXXVIII; 40-XXXIX; 41-XLIII; 42-XLVII; 43-XLVII; 44-LIII; 45-LIII; 46-LIII; 47-LIX; 48-LIX.

QUIZ 23: 1-III; 2-V; 3-VII; 4-VII; 5-VII; 6-VII; 7-VIII; 8-XV; 9-XIV; 10-XIV; 11-XVI; 12-XVII; 13-XXI; 14-XXVII; 15-XXIX; 16-XXIX; 17-XXXI; 18-XXIX; 19-XXX; 20-XXXVIII; 21-XLII; 22-XLII; 23-LVI.

QUIZ 24: 1-II; 2-VII; 3-VIII; 4-IX; 5-XIII; 6-XVII; 7-XXVI; 8-XXVIII; 9-XXVII; 10-XXXI; 11-XXXI; 12-XXXIII; 13-XXXIV; 14-XXXIV; 15-XLIII; 16-XLIV.

QUIZ 25: 1-VIII; 2-VIII; 3-XIII; 4-XVIII; 5-XX; 6-XXV; 7-XXXVII; 8-XXXVI; 9-XXXVI; 10-XXXIX; 11-XLII; 12-XLV.

QUIZ 26: 1-III; 2-VI; 3-XII; 4-XIII; 5-XIII; 6-XXXVI; 7-XXXVII; 8-XXXVI; 9-XXXIX; 10-XLI; 11-XLI; 12-XLII; 13-XLII; 14-XLIX.

QUIZ 27: 1-V; 2-V; 3-V; 4-V; 5-V; 6-VI; 7-VI; 8-XVIII; 9-XXIII; 10-XXIV; 11-XXIV; 12-XXV; 13-XXVIII; 14-XXVII; 15-XXXV; 16-XXXVIII; 17-L; 18-LIX.

QUIZ 28: 1-VI; 2-IX; 3-IX; 4-IX; 5-XII; 6-XII; 7-XV; 8-XVII; 9-XIX; 10-XXII; 11-XXVI; 12-XXX; 13-XLI; 14-XLI; 15-XLI; 16-XLI.

QUIZ 29: 1-III; 2-III; 3-VI; 4-VI; 5-VII; 6-IX; 7-IX; 8-IX; 9-X; 10-XI; 11-XII; 12-XIII; 13-XIV; 14-XIV; 15-XVII; 16-XVII; 17-XXI; 18-XXVIII; 19-XXX; 20-XXX; 21-XXXVI; 22-XL; 23-XLI; 24-XL; 25-XLI; 26-XLII; 27-XLV; 28-XLVI; 29-XLV; 30-XLVIII; 31-XLVII; 32-LXI.

QUIZ 30: 1-II; 2-III; 3-II; 4-V; 5-VI; 6-VIII; 7-IX; 8-X; 9-XII; 10-XVI; 11-XVI; 12-XVII; 13-XVII; 14-XVIII; 15-XIX; 16-XXVI; 17-XXIV; 18-XXVI; 19-XXVIII; 20-XXVII; 21-XXX; 22-XXX; 23-XXX; 24-XXXV; 25-XXXIII; 26-XXXVII; 27-XXXVII; 28-XXXVII; 29-XXXVII; 30-XXXVIII.

QUIZ 31: 1-III; 2-IV; 3-IV; 4-V; 5-V; 6-V; 7-VI; 8-VI; 9-VI; 10-X; 11-X; 12-XII; 13-XVI; 14-XVII; 15-XXI; 16-XXV; 17-XXVIII; 18-XXVIII; 19-XXVI; 20-XXVII; 21-XXVIII; 22-XXIV; 23-XXVIII; 24-XXIX; 25-XXXIV; 26-XXXVI; 27-XXXVIII; 28-XXXVIII; 29-XLI; 30-XLIV.

QUIZ 32: 1-IV; 2-VI; 3-VI; 4-VII; 5-V; 6-VI; 7-VI; 8-XIII; 9-IX; 10-VI; 11-IX; 12-VI; 13-XIV; 14-XVII; 15-XIX; 16-XVII; 17-XXI; 18-XIX; 19-XXIII; 20-XIX; 21-XXIV; 22-XXV; 23-XXV; 24-XXVI; 25-XXV; 26-XXVI; 27-XXVIII; 28-XXVII; 29-XXX; 30-XXXI; 31-XXXI; 32-XXXI; 33-XXXI; 34-XXXI; 35-XXX; 36-XXXV; 37-XXXII; 38-XXXIV; 39-XXXII; 40-XXXIV; 41-XXXIV; 42-XXXIV; 43-XXXIII; 44-XXXVI; 45-XXXVI; 46-XXXVI; 47-XXXVI; 48-XXXVI; 49-XXXVII, XXXI; 50-XXXVI; 51-XXXVI; 52-XXXVI; 53-XXXVIII; 54-XXXIX; 55-XXXVIII; 56-XXXVIII; 57-XXXVIII; 58-XLI; 59-XL; 60-XXXVIII; 61-XXXVIII; 62-XXXVIII; 63-XXXVIII; 64-XXXIX; 65-XXXVIII; 66-XL; 67-XLI; 68-XLI; 69-XLII; 70-XLII; 71-XLIII; 72-XLIII; 73-XLIII; 74-XLIII; 75-XLIII; 76-XLIII; 77-XLIV; 78-XLVI; 79-XLVI; 80-XLVII; 81-XLVIII; 82-XLVII; 83-XLIX; 84-XLVIII; 85-XLVIII; 86-XLIX; 87-XLVII; 88-XLVII; 89-XLVII; 90-XLVIII; 91-XLVII; 92-XLVII; 93-XLVII; 94-L; 95-L; 96-L; 97-XLIX; 98-L; 99-L; 100-LIV; 101-LVI; 102-LII; 103-LI; 104-LIII; 105-LVII; 106-LII; 107-LIII; 108-LII; 109-LIII; 110-LIV; 111-LIV; 112-LVII; 113-LIV; 114-LII; 115-LI; 116-LIII; 117-LI; 118-LVI; 119-LII; 120-LXIII; 121-LVII; 122-LXIII; 123-LIX; 124-LXIII; 125-LXI; 126-LXI; 127-LXIII; 128-XLIV; 129-XXXV; 130-XLII; 131-LXI; 132-XXXII; 133-XXIV; 134-V; 135-LV; 136-LIII; 137-XXXIX; 138-XLI; 139-XXIV; 140-XLV; 141-XLIV; 142-XLIV; 143-I; 144-XLII; 145-XLI; 146-XIX; 147-LI; 148-XXV; 149-XXIX; 150-IX; 151-XXIX; 152-XXIX; 153-LVI; 154-LIII; 155-XXVII.

QUIZ 33: 1-5; 2-3, 5, 6; 3-8; 4-10; 5-1; 6-9; 7-9; 8-11; 9-15; 10-16; 11-15; 12-18; 13-22; 14-24; 15-27; 16-25; 17-31; 18-41; 19-41; 20-39; 21-46; 22-43; 23-51; 24-59; 25-61; 26-65; 27-68; 28-73; 29-70; 30-86; 31-75.

QUIZ 34: 1-1; 2-2; 3-2; 4-3; 5-2; 6-8; 7-63; 8-63; 9-63; 10-65; 11-63; 12-65; 13-63; 14-63; 15-80; 16-79; 17-86; 18-75; 19-75.

QUIZ 35: 1-27; 2-27; 3-33; 4-34; 5-35; 6-36; 7-37; 8-35; 9-37; 10-35; 11-35; 12-42; 13-40; 14-40; 15-42; 16-40; 17-46; 18-49.

QUIZ 36: 1-3; 2-8; 3-8; 4-8; 5-8; 6-10; 7-16; 8-18; 9-31; 10-70; 11-73; 12-89; 13-89.

QUIZ 37: 1-10; 2-10; 3-9; 4-13; 5-11; 6-13; 7-13; 8-11; 9-13; 10-11; 11-11; 12-11; 13-16; 14-20; 15-19; 16-21; 17-22.

QUIZ 38: 1-8; 2-9; 3-18; 4-81; 5-83.

QUIZ 39: 1-5; 2-8; 3-10; 4-38; 5-57; 6-68; 7-10; 8-9; 9-14; 10-11; 11-11; 12-16; 13-15; 14-16; 15-18; 16-18; 17-18; 18-18; 19-25; 20-23; 21-32; 22-32; 23-29; 24-30.

QUIZ 40: 1-41; 2-41; 3-47; 4-46; 5-43; 6-43; 7-61.

QUIZ 41: 1-51; 2-51; 3-65; 4-65; 5-65; 6-61; 7-62; 8-65; 9-65; 10-62; 11-71; 12-71; 13-74; 14-74; 15-80; 16-80; 17-81; 18-76; 19-75; 20-77; 21-77; 22-79; 23-75.

QUIZ 42: 1-1; 2-1; 3-1; 4-1; 5-3; 6-2; 7-3; 8-3; 9-8.

QUIZ 43: 1-1; 2-6; 3-8; 4-8; 5-8; 6-7; 7-8; 8-8; 9-8; 10-8.

QUIZ 44: 1-1; 2-11; 3-14; 4-11; 5-12; 6-12; 7-14; 8-14; 9-16; 10-15; 11-18; 12-18; 13-18.

QUIZ 45: 1-10; 2-13; 3-13; 4-28; 5-33; 6-33; 7-34; 8-34; 9-33; 10-33; 11-37; 12-35; 13-40; 14-40; 15-44.

QUIZ 46: 1-42; 2-42; 3-47; 4-44; 5-47; 6-48; 7-49; 8-58; 9-52; 10-58; 11-66; 12-60; 13-74; 14-89.

QUIZ 47: 1-2; 2-7; 3-7; 4-8; 5-8; 6-8; 7-14; 8-11; 9-15; 10-19; 11-21; 12-21; 13-21; 14-26; 15-29; 16-32; 17-33; 18-32; 19-41; 20-41; 21-46; 22-50; 23-63; 24-63; 25-61; 26-71; 27-74.

QUIZ 48: 1-3; 2-15; 3-15; 4-18; 5-21; 6-27; 7-58; 8-54; 9-49; 10-49; 11-49; 12-61; 13-65.

QUIZ 49: 1-1; 2-4; 3-8; 4-8; 5-11; 6-21; 7-25; 8-25; 9-28; 10-33; 11-32; 12-37; 13-40; 14-44; 15-54.

QUIZ 50: 1-1; 2-4; 3-9; 4-10; 5-10; 6-11; 7-11; 8-19; 9-31; 10-32; 11-48; 12-45; 13-46; 14-46; 15-58.

QUIZ 51: 1-3; 2-3; 3-6; 4-15; 5-17; 6-24; 7-29; 8-29.

QUIZ 52: 1-2; 2-3; 3-3; 4-5; 5-6; 6-8; 7-7; 8-7; 9-8; 10-8; 11-9; 12-9; 13-10; 14-10; 15-9; 16-16; 17-16; 18-19; 19-20.

QUIZ 53: 1-2; 2-7; 3-9; 4-11; 5-15; 6-17; 7-15; 8-16; 9-31; 10-31; 11-30; 12-30; 13-34; 14-34; 15-32; 16-34; 17-35; 18-37; 19-41; 20-44; 21-48.

QUIZ 54: 1-43; 2-52; 3-48; 4-54; 5-65; 6-59; 7-61; 8-60; 9-62; 10-62; 11-65; 12-61; 13-72; 14-75.

QUIZ 55: 1-1; 2-1; 3-1; 4-1; 5-3; 6-2; 7-2; 8-5; 9-5; 10-6; 11-6; 12-7; 13-7; 14-7; 15-7; 16-9; 17-9; 18-10; 19-12; 20-11; 21-13; 22-12; 23-12; 24-17; 25-17; 26-17; 27-15; 28-17; 29-19; 30-19; 31-18; 32-19; 33-21; 34-22; 35-22; 36-27; 37-23; 38-26; 39-27; 40-25; 41-31; 42-31; 43-28; 44-32; 45-31;

46-31; 47-32; 48-31; 49-34; 50-33; 51-33; 52-32; 53-34; 54-36; 55-37; 56-35; 57-36; 58-35; 59-35; 60-9; 61-41; 62-42; 63-40; 64-41; 65-38; 66-43; 67-47; 68-46; 69-43; 70-50; 71-57; 72-55; 73-57; 74-49; 75-50; 76-66; 77-62; 78-67; 79-60; 80-67; 81-65; 82-64; 83-65; 84-63; 85-67; 86-59; 87-65; 88-65; 89-60; 90-66; 91-69; 92-71; 93-69; 94-72; 95-69; 96-69; 97-68; 98-74; 99-74; 100-74; 101-86; 102-81; 103-82; 104-77; 105-89; 106-89; 107-87; 108-84; 109-89; 110-75; 111-89; 112-81; 113-82; 114-85; 115-89; 116-78; 117-78; 118-88; 119-78; 120-75.

ANSWERS

(NOTE: The Answer sections for the *Gone with the Wind* and *Scarlett* quizzes also provide the page numbers where the answer can be found in the original texts. The page numbers are given parenthetically following the correct answer and refer to the Avon paperback edition of *Gone with the Wind* and the Warner Books hardcover edition of *Scarlett: The Sequel to Margaret Mitchell's "Gone with the Wind."*)

QUIZ 1

1. Sixteen. (5). 2. "Pale green without a touch of hazel." (5). 3. The Fayetteville Female Academy. (7). 4. Katie Scarlett O'Hara. (57). 5. Seventeen inches. (5). 6. Mammy Jincy. (11). 7. Mathematics. (63). 8. "Fiddle-dee-dee." (104). 9. She waved at men as they passed by her bedroom window. (161). 10. Fourteen. (213). 11. Second sight, "especially where death premonitions were concerned." (271). 12. Death. "It was tempting Providence to mention death." (310). 13. Latin. (487). 14. Every morning he had to go out with a basket and pick up twigs and chips to start the fires with. (480). 15. Poverty. (546). 16. She could add a long column of figures in her head, and fractions were no problem to her at all. (607). 17. Ostensibly, it was because he was worried about her miscarrying, but Grandma Fontaine said it was because he didn't want Scarlett to "hear the clods dropping on [Gerald's] coffin." (705). 18. Ashley and Melanie's flat-roofed postbel-

lum Ivy Street Atlanta home. (722).   19. Ella Lorena. (737).   20. She was named Ella Lorena: Ella, for her grandmother, Ellen. Lorena, because it was the most fashionable name of the time. (737).   21. Three weeks. (738).   22. "Execrable." (849).   23. "We're hungry." (819).   24. New Orleans. (837).   25. In her bottom bureau drawer beneath her underwear. (814).   26. Her actual name was Eugenie Victoria Butler, but she was known as Bonnie Blue Butler. (881).   27. D. Whist. (856).   28. B. 100 brush strokes every night. (921).   29. C. 20 inches. (881).   30. A. 28. (1019). BONUS QUESTION 1. "Lady Bountiful" was a self-assumed title that Scarlett fantasized being called after she got her money back during Reconstruction and imagined herself then devoting her time to philanthropic and humanitarian concerns and interests. (668). (Margaret Mitchell may have gotten the name "Lady Bountiful" from the poem "The Beaux' Stratagem" by George Farquhar [1678–1707] which contains the line, "My Lady Bountiful."). BONUS QUESTION 2. Trying to win Ashley's love (while keeping a dozen other beaux dangling); concealing breaches of conduct from her elders; dealing with jealous girlfriends; and hair and clothing concerns. (466).

QUIZ 2

1. West Point. (101).   2. Charleston, South Carolina. (101).   3. Frank Kennedy. (101).   4. Jet-black. (179).   5. A gold cigar case. (185).   6. The Southern system of mourning, "of immuring women in crêpe for the rest of their lives." (182).   7. The Hindu system of mourning which dictates that when a husband dies, his body is burned on a pyre instead of being buried, and that his wife must climb on the flaming pyre and burn with him. When told about it by Rhett, Scarlett remarked that she thought this was a "dreadful" custom. (182).   8. He was a blockade runner for the South. (164).   9. Twenty. (223).   10. Guns. (223).   11. Rice. (238).   12. "R.K.B." (248).   13. At the Atlanta Hotel. (366).   14. Franklin. (563).   15. France and England. (566).   16. "Nihil desperandum." (This phrase, of which the traditional usage is "Nil desperandum," translates literally as "Never say die" or "Never despair," but Rhett told Scarlett it meant, "Maybe." He gave this "motto" as his reply when Scarlett asked him if he thought he had any chance of getting out of the Yankee jail in Atlanta.) (567).   17. They offered him a long horse trough in which the entire Yankee regiment had already bathed. Rhett declined the offer. (555).   18. He blackmailed a highly placed federal government official from whom he bought goods for the Confederacy during the war. (614).   19. A lie. (620).   20. Either gambling in the Girl of the Period Saloon, or hobnobbing with Yankees and Carpetbaggers in Belle Watling's bar. (669).   21. He gave him the training to be "a Charleston gentleman, a good pistol shot and an excellent poker player." (758).   22. Rosemary. (760).   23. In New Orleans. (757).   24. On the Battery in Charleston. (760).   25. He went in through a private back entrance for which he had a key. (802).   26. He told Scarlett he spent his early youth as a gambler on a riverboat. (840).   27. Rufus Bullock. (833).   28. Her fear of the dark. (900).   29. "I'll contribute to their damned charities and I'll go to their damned churches. I'll admit and brag about my services to the Confederacy and, if worst comes to worst, I'll join their damned Klan—though a merciful God could hardly lay so heavy a penance on my shoulders as that. And I shall not hesitate to remind the fools whose necks I saved that they owe me a debt." (892).   30. C. At Belle Watling's house. (932).   31. B. At the Atlanta bank. (898).   32. D.

45. (1021). BONUS QUESTION 1. Fifty yards. (221). BONUS QUESTION 2. He would whisper to her that God probably didn't approve of such amusements. (844).

QUIZ 3

1. Three years. (27).   2. Gray. (28).   3. Because "he was the best rider in the County" and because of his "cool head." (20).   4. He was Major Ashley Wilkes, C.S.A. (261).   5. He made her promise that she would look after Melanie. (270).   6. Christmas. (260).   7. Mose. (264).   8. Mose.   (280).   9. Rock   Island.   (282).   10. George.   (498).   11. Bull   Run. (519).   12. The Episcopal burial service. (701).   13. Because he felt as though he wasn't earning his keep on the plantation and it bothered him that he was a man living on a woman's (Scarlett's) charity. (686).   14. There were sick friends he had to sit with; and he was part of an organization of Democrats who gathered every Wednesday to try and find a way of getting back on the ballot. (744).   15. They told him that the money was sent to him by someone he nursed through a case of smallpox at Rock Island during the war. (963).   16. TRUE. (38).   17. TRUE. (519).   18. FALSE. It was at Bull Run. (520).   19. TRUE. (998).   20. FALSE. (999). BONUS QUESTION 1. She described Ashley as "bred to read books and nothing else." (711). BONUS QUESTION 2. If he liked a person, he sold them lumber on credit—without checking to see if they had any money or other collateral. (736).

QUIZ 4

1. Gerald O'Hara. (35).   2. Brown. (104).   3. She vomited. (158).   4. She was "quite narrow." (279).   5. Two long towels that Scarlett had knotted together and tied to the foot of the bed. (361).   6. Her dead brother Charles's sword and a daguerrotype of Charles. (375).   7. "It wasn't very bad, really." (349).   8. "Auntee." (425).   9. Melanie's modesty. (Scarlett made Melanie give up her shimmy to cover the dead Yankee, and Melanie was completely naked underneath.) (437).   10. She picked cotton for an hour, "fainted quietly," and then had to stay in bed for a week. (448).   11. Beau. (454).   12. "Jesus." (595).   13. After the baby's birth, Melly said that her eyes were going to be blue—"as blue as the bonnie blue flag"—and the name Bonnie Blue stuck from that point on. (881).   14. "Brats." (945).   15. That Scarlett would take care of Beau and Ashley. (997).   16. She had "a respectful deference to her elders that was very soothing to dowagers . . ." (725).   17. The house was directly behind Aunt Pittypat's house and the two backyards ran together. Melanie wanted to be near her family. (722).   18. B. "Captain Butler—be kind to him. He—loves you so." (999).   19. FALSE. She invited her in when Belle came by the house in her carriage. (809).   20. TRUE. (941).   21. FALSE. It was Honey Wilkes. (126).   22. TRUE. ("Folks'll talk sumpin' scan'lous.") (233).   23. FALSE. It was a surprise birthday party for *Ashley* Wilkes. (907).   24. FALSE. Prissy bathed him first. (364).   25. TRUE. (34). BONUS QUESTION. She became secretary of the Association for the Beautification of the Graves of Our Glorious Dead and the Sewing Circle for the Widows and Orphans of the Confederacy. (727).

QUIZ 5

1. In the bedroom of Ellen O'Hara's mother. (25).   2. It was a contradiction because, even though Mammy was a slave *owned* by the O'Haras, Mammy "felt that *she owned* the O'Haras, body and soul." [Emphasis added.] (24).   3. Worms. (424).   4. She told Scarlett she wished she was "jes' daid alongside Miss Ellen!" (409).   5. She put it in the well. (404-5).   6. That she had "never ever" been a "yard nigger." (It didn't work: Scarlett made her work picking cotton anyway, but Mammy's lamentations convinced Scarlett to send her back to the kitchen to cook.) (448).   7. "No lice-ridden soldier should come into Tara." (494).   8. Twenty years earlier when she was in Savannah with Miss Ellen. (547).   9. Two hundred pounds. (536).   10. She insisted she could smell a Republican. (741).   11. A $10 gold piece. (837).   12. "Cap'n Butler," never, "Mist' Rhett." (859).   13. Rheumatism. (880).   14. She told her there was "ghos'es an' buggerboos in de dahk." (984).   15. Lil Miss. (982).   16. FALSE. She was pure African through and through. (25).   17. FALSE. She "had been born in the Robillard great house, not in the quarters. . . ." (448).   18. FALSE. (836).   19. FALSE. (26).   20. FALSE. (979).

QUIZ 6

1. Twenty-eight. (44).   2. Twenty-one. (44).   3. He was sixty. (32).   4. "[L]ittle more than five feet tall." (32). Five feet, four and a half inches tall. (45).   5. Poker. (47).   6. Land. (39).   7. "Remember who ye are and don't be taking nothing off no man." (45).   8. Each was named Gerald O'Hara, Jr. (59).   9. County Meath, Ireland. (31).   10. Beatrice Tarleton. (87).   11. "Puss." (429).   12. June 1866. (678).   13. She wanted him to sign the Iron Clad Oath, which stated that he was a loyal Union sympathizer. (692).   14. He always described it as being "in the family way." (674).   15. Pork. (696).   16. She had his "short sturdy" legs, his wide blue eyes, and his small square jaw. She also had Gerald's "sudden temper." (900).   17. Blue. (32).   18. "Look, Ellen! Watch me take this one!" (695).   19. FALSE. (695).   20. FALSE. (695). BONUS QUESTION. Three years' crops. (276).

QUIZ 7

1. Thirty-two. (42).   2. Fifteen. (36).   3. Each of the three boys died before they learned how to walk. (59).   4. French. (5).   5. Solange Robillard. (25).   6. Savannah, Georgia. (44).   7. Her cousin Philippe Robillard. (44).   8. She taught them to say, "[Insert name of gentleman], I am not unaware of the honor you have bestowed on me in wanting me to become your wife, but this is all so sudden that I do not know what to say." (110).   9. Candy, flowers, a book of poetry, an album, or a small bottle of Florida water. (242).   10. That she was a little girl back in Savannah. (411).   11. A narrow French Empire bed with curling head and foot. (407).   12. Garnet earrings. (457).   13. A week. (773).   14. FALSE. She had black hair. (42).   15. TRUE. (43).   16. FALSE. She grew up in Savannah. (44).   17. C. She superintended the cooking. She actually performed the other three duties. (43).   18. C. Typhoid. (411).   19. A. (59).   20. B. (63). BONUS QUESTION. Pauline and Eulalie. (138).

QUIZ 8

1. Stuart. (16).   2. Prissy. (66).   3. "Plain." (97).   4. Because she "indiscriminately addressed everyone from her father to the field hands by that endearment." (97).   5. Three days. (106).   6. In Atlanta, to see Ashley. (261).   7. Macon, to stay with the Burrs. (310).   8. She made Scarlett promise to take her baby if she died during childbirth. As she put it, "Honey and India are sweet but—" (344).   9. She thought anyone who was not from the eastern seaboard was "a boor and a barbarian." (723).   10. She felt him coarse, and disapproved   of   the   marriage.   (723).   11. Twenty-five.   (723).   12. Mississippi. (723).   13. She moved in with Ashley and Melanie into their Ivy Street house. (723).   14. According to Rhett, she was there to "keep the bogyman away." (848).   15. Because Scarlett was involved with Stuart Tarleton. (938). BONUS QUESTION. She described India as a "dried-up old maid," and she described Honey as a "man-crazy fool with no more sense than a guinea hen." (710).

QUIZ 9

1. Honey   Wilkes.   (11).   2. Brown.   (99).   3. William.   (459).   4. Wade   Hampton. (108).   5. Twenty. (109).   6. He slept in an armchair in the corner of the room because Scarlett wouldn't let him near her. (133).   7. He died of pneumonia, following measles, while serving in the Confederate Army under Colonel Wade Hampton. (135).   8. C. Wade Hampton Hamilton. (135).   9. A. In Atlanta's Oakland Cemetery. (173).   10. B. A large sapphire solitaire ring. (457).

QUIZ 10

1. Suellen O'Hara. (75).   2. Forty. (98).   3. It was "ginger-colored." (98).   4. "Old fussbudget Frank," and "Ginger Whiskers." (468, 489).   5. Land. (98).   6. A red bandanna. (587).   7. He caught a minié ball through the shoulder. (581).   8. Two weeks. (602).   9. The gizzard. (608).   10. "What will the neighbors say?" (632).   11. "Sugar." (641).   12. "Strangers." (604).   13. He embarrassedly called it "your condition." (674).   14. C. March 1867. (803).   15. TRUE. (813). BONUS QUESTION. She determined that he was "no beauty," he had very bad teeth, his breath smelled, he was old enough to be her father, and he was nervous, timid, and well meaning, attributes she considered "damning qualities" in a man. (585).

QUIZ 11

1. Sarah Jane Hamilton. (155).   2. Uncle Peter. (142).   3. Miss Merriwether and Miss Elsing. (148).   4. René Picard. (168).   5. She felt they should be hanged. (231).   6. After the wedding ceremony. (216).   7. Her personal carriage and horse. (321).   8. Brick. (473).   9. Because it was made of brick and had a slate roof that kept the sparks from

setting it afire. Also, it was on the north end of town and the fire wasn't too bad there. (473). 10. Because she had not been able to pay the taxes on her estate and they were confiscated for back taxes. (548). 11. New Orleans. (594). 12. The LaGrange Female Institute. (551). 13. She gave music lessons. (628). 14. She was a schoolteacher. (628). 15. "Nigger." (664). 16. Because Scarlett was more popular than her daughter, Fanny. (937). 17. She agreed to accept money from her brother, Henry Hamilton (even though it humiliated her to do so). (942). 18. Wash. (978). 19. D. (155). 20. FALSE. (942). BONUS QUESTION. Size three. (198).

QUIZ 12

1. He was given to them on their tenth birthday. (13). 2. Eight. (9). 3. One hundred. (9). 4. Money, horses, and slaves. (6). 5. Tom and Boyd. (7). 6. Strawberry blonde. (89). 7. "Curb them but don't break their spirits." (87). 8. Betsy. (89). 9. In the overseer's house. (463). 10. "They were lovely and pleasant in their lives, and in their death they were not divided." (487). 11. Macon. (487). 12. She lost her first baby when she saw a bull gore one of her darkies on her plantation. (706). 13. He was fat and had one arm. (961). 14. B. (6). 15. TRUE. (961). BONUS QUESTION 1. The University of Georgia. (7). BONUS QUESTION 2. The Universities of Virginia, Alabama, and South Carolina. (7).

QUIZ 13

1. Twenty inches. (81). 2. Caroline Irene. (33). 3. Susan Elinor. (33). 4. Suellen. (33). 5. Carreen. (33). 6. Suellen. (31). 7. Fourteen. (69). 8. One year old. (59). 9. Typhoid. (329). 10. "Baby." (427). 11. Because her beau, Frank Kennedy, was visiting. (468). 12. "Oh, if only Mother was here!" (483). 13. Going over to Jonesboro or Fayetteville with Will Benteen. (506). 14. Scarlett told Frank that Sue was marrying Tony Fontaine because she got tired of waiting for Frank. (588). 15. She entered a convent in Charleston. (684). 16. Will Benteen. (684). 17. His daughter, Suellen O'Hara. (697). 18. Susie. (961). 19. FALSE. The feud started when Suellen wanted to use Tara's only *horse* to go visiting and Scarlett felt that the horse should only be used for plowing and other work and not for travel. (483). BONUS QUESTION. Carreen contributed her slippers, and Suellen contributed her Irish-lace collar. (539).

QUIZ 14

1. He won him in an all-night poker game with a planter from St. Simons Island. (47). 2. Prissy. (34). 3. Dilcey. (26). 4. Rosa. (26). 5. Toby. (41). 6. To remove basting threads and carry Ellen's rosewood sewing box from room to room. (43). 7. Pork. (48). 8. Pork. (10). 9. Dilcey. (65). 10. Twelve. (65). 11. Sitting on the front steps with a towel and waving it at geese and turkeys that wanted to eat the front lawn. (60). 12. Field hand. (61). 13. Nearly six and a half feet tall. (300). 14. A hundred.

(401).   15. Cotton picking.   (448).   16. Pork.   (714).   17. She called him "Mister." (772).   18. A Yankee colonel "retained" him to do body servant work, even though Sam was only a field hand. (772).   19. Because he had killed a white Yankee soldier and the Union Army was after him. He thought they wouldn't find him at Tara. (774). 20-1-B. (60). 20-2-G. (60). 20-3-C. (60). 20-4-E. (69). 20-5-D. (60). 20-6-A. (68). 20-7-H. (71). 20-8-F. (74).

QUIZ 15

1. Hugh Calvert. (38).   2. Because he was a Yankee and an overseer. (68).   3. New York. (188).   4. They bought soldiers from Europe by the thousands. (272).   5. Grant. (250).   6. To fight the Indians for two years, with a promise of release after that. (283).   7. Grant. (275).   8. Sheridan. (275).   9. Tea. He brought it to Miss Pittypat's house in May. (287).   10. General Sherman. (284).   11. "The Yankees raped women and ran bayonets through children's stomachs and burned houses over the heads of old people." (332).   12. Silk dresses and gold earbobs. (442).   13. Yams. (401).   14. In a shallow pit under the scuppernong arbor. (438).   15. The cellar. (402).   16. Eight miles. (456).   17. He said that "niggers had a right to . . . white women." (637).   18. Tony Fontaine. (636).   19. *Uncle Tom's Cabin.* (662).   20. Slave concubinage. (662).   21. Because the Yankees knew that they had harbored Tony Fontaine just before Tony fled to Texas after murdering Jonas Wilkerson. (651).   22. He was playing poker with two drunk Yankee captains and they let it out. (788).   23. Captain Tom Jaffery. (791).   24. FALSE. The Yankees intended to stamp out the Klan—even if it meant burning down Atlanta again and hanging every Southern male over ten. (676). BONUS QUESTION. "They'd be most charming if they weren't always telling you that they can take care of themselves, thank you." (304).

QUIZ 16

1. Run Tara and Twelve Oaks together and build Scarlett a fine house. (36).   2. Ellen O'Hara's. (32).   3. White-blossomed magnolias. (60).   4. Jonas Wilkerson. (67).   5. Five miles. (318).   6. Five hundred years. (397).   7. Ellen's little office. (67). BONUS QUESTION. The hand of Fate and a hand of poker. (48).

QUIZ 17

1. Three bales. (417).   2. "[N]o one should ever talk of the fine meals they had eaten in the past or what they would eat now, if they had the opportunity." (466).   3. Jonas Wilkerson. (512).   4. Confederate soldiers walking home. (492).   5. The Freedmen's Bureau. (511).   6. In the parlor. (494).   7. The Fontaine boys. (480).   8. Southerners who had turned Republican ("very profitably") after the war. (511).   9. Atlanta. (649).   10. The "surest way for a white person to get himself into trouble was to bring a complaint of any kind against a negro." (645).   11. The daughters of some of the city's most prominent

families who had no qualms about associating with Yankee officers. (726).   12. "Abraham Lincoln" and "Emancipation." (738).   13. They refused to ratify it. (750).   14. In the biggest chimney of the old Sullivan plantation. (799).   15. In the cellar of the half-burned Sullivan plantation out the Decatur road near Shantytown. (788).   16. Outrages against Southern women by free darkies. (647).   17. Tara. (But it was definitely a *farm*—a two-mule farm—and no longer a plantation.) (962). BONUS QUESTION 1. Mint (the Yankees fed it to their horses) and sugar (it wasn't available because of the blockade). BONUS QUESTION 2. "Word had been spread among the negroes that there were only two political parties mentioned in the Bible, the Publicans and the Sinners. No negro wanted to join a party made up entirely of sinners, so they hastened to join the Republicans." (893). SUPER BONUS QUESTION. There were usually nine: "If England had recognized us—"; "If Jeff Davis had commandeered all the cotton and gotten it to England before the blockade tightened—"; "If Longstreet had obeyed orders at Gettysburg—"; "If Jeb Stuart hadn't been away on that raid when Marse Bob needed him—"; "If we hadn't lost Stonewall Jackson—"; "If Vicksburg hadn't fallen—"; "If we could have held on another year—"; "If they hadn't replaced Johnston with Hood—"; "If they'd put Hood in command at Dalton instead of Johnston—." (732).

QUIZ 18

1. Cotton. (9).   2. Cotton. (9).   3. The Slatterys. (51).   4. The MacIntosh plantation. (51).   5. Fairhill. (88).   6. The Mallory place. (387).   7. Pine Bloom. (484).   8. The seedling pine and the blackberry brambles. (696).   9. TRUE. (464).   10. FALSE. Tom Slattery and his two oldest boys worked their cotton fields alone. (52). BONUS QUESTION. Their "murderous rages." (638). SUPER BONUS QUESTION. "She looked Cracker, even worse. She looked poor white, shiftless, slovenly, trifling." Scarlett believed that if Cathleen wasn't dipping snuff already, she soon would be. (699).

QUIZ 19

1. Marthasville. (140).   2. Mrs. Merriwether, Mrs. Elsing, and Mrs. Whiting. (148).   3. Terminus. (140).   4. Peachtree Trail. (142).   5. Ten thousand. (141).   6. The Atlanta Hotel. (153).   7. Dr. Meade. (150).   8. "[F]or fear they would see sights unfit for virgin eyes." (159).   9. Rhett Butler. (222).   10. Peachtree Street. (233).   11. Whitehall Street. (255).   12. Twenty thousand, up from ten thousand before the war started. (277).   13. They looted it. They broke open vaults and dug up graves looking for jewelry and the silver handles and trimmings on the coffins. They left the corpses amid the splintered caskets. (472). 14. The Atlanta depot. (369). 15. City Hall. (559).   16. "[L]onesome blackened chimneys" that were the only evidence left of Atlanta's beautiful homes after the burning of the city. (579).   17. They lived with the Elsings because their own house had been burned to the ground during the siege of Atlanta. (549).   18. Belle Watling. (649).   19. Six. (723).   20. The fact that he had saved the lives of some of Atlanta's most prominent men. (831).   21. Rhett and Scarlett. (831).   22. The

bridal suite of the National Hotel. (848). 23. J. (941). BONUS QUESTION. Melanie and Ashley's son, Beau. (945). SUPER BONUS QUESTION. Because its railroads were "arteries throbbing with the never-ending flow of men, munitions and supplies." (277).

QUIZ 20

1. Jonesboro. (22). 2. Fairhill. (29). 3. Charleston, South Carolina. (69). 4. Three times (216). 5. They dyed them all black. (259). 6. Putting a knife under Miss Melly's bed. (363). 7. That any traveler, "great or humble," could not go on his way without "a night's lodging, food for himself and his horse and the utmost courtesy the house could give." (500). 8. They couldn't resist one. (564). 9. A hot brick wrapped in flannel. (556). 10. "[N]o chaste woman ever rode in a hired conveyance—especially a closed carriage—without the escort of some male member of her family. Even the presence of a negro maid would not satisfy the conventions." (543). 11. They were raised to believe that "men were omniscient and women none too bright." (611). 12. Purgatory. He knew that at least half of the people present had never heard of the place. (700). 13. Quarrels and shootings were often caused by the County custom of saying a few words over the coffins of departed neighbors. (698). 14. Southern chivalry said that "A Southern lady could lie about a gentleman but a Southern gentleman could not lie about a lady or, worse still, call the lady a liar." This allowed Scarlett to lie about her lumber competitors' quality and prices and get away with it. (654). 15. They called it being "in a fix." (674). 16. "To them she had done worse than murder her father. She had tried to betray him into disloyalty to the South. And to that grim and close-knit community it was as if she had tried to betray the honor of them all. She had broken the solid front the County presented to the world." (697). 17. Families always made room gladly in their homes for these women. (723). 18. "Reverence for the Confederacy, honor to the veterans, loyalty to old forms, pride in poverty, open hands to friends and undying hatred to Yankees." (832). 19. B. (233). 20. A. (278). BONUS QUESTION 1. Statesmen, soldiers, planters, doctors, lawyers, and poets. (145). BONUS QUESTION 2. Being "ignorant, thick-headed, intolerant and incapable of thinking along any lines except what other gentlemen of the old school thought." (759).

QUIZ 21

1. The discovery of a "small arsenal of rifles under the O'Hara pigsty" in Ireland. (45). 2. Stuart Tarleton. (124). 3. Twenty-five. (177). 4. Blue and white striped pants, cream gaiters, and a red jacket. (168). 5. The Home Guard. (169). 6. It was returned to his sister, Melanie, who hung it beneath a Confederate flag in her bedroom. (208). 7. The Battle of Gettysburg. (252). 8. Pieces of captured Yankee uniforms. (264). 9. He had the good fortune to shoot a Yankee scout. (264). 10. The mother of a Charleston boy Melanie had nursed until his death. (265). 11. In Georgia. (284). 12. "Plow furloughs": Men would go home to plow their crops, returning to the ranks when they could. (289). 13. Two Mexican War pistols. (308). 14. Long thick poles with iron-pointed tips. (308). 15. They

threw them open to the citizens of Atlanta and allowed them to salvage whatever food they could carry before the city was invaded. (354).   16. Two ivory-handled, long-barreled dueling pistols. (371).   17. A pistol and a bowie knife. (741).   18. She kept Frank Kennedy's pistol tucked in the upholstery of her buggy. (769).   19. FALSE. There were none. (113). BONUS QUESTION. "To Colonel William R. Hamilton, From His Staff. For Gallantry. Buena Vista. 1847." (459).

QUIZ 22

1. Flat-heeled green morocco slippers. (5).   2. A gray broadcloth with a wide black cravat, and a wide Panama hat. (27).   3. The head of a Medusa in cameo. (27).   4. Pink. (70).   5. Plaid. (67).   6. Ellen's garnet necklace. (70).   7. Calico. (65).   8. Apple-green. (77).   9. She wore her rose organdie with the long pink sash. (77).   10. A new gray broadcloth. (84).   11. Her black bombazine with the puffed sleeves and princess lace collar. (77).   12. Her shimmy. (101).   13. Mustard-colored trousers and black coat, a pleated shirt, and black cravat. (99).   14. A gray organdie dress with a cherry-colored satin sash, a yellow hat with long cherry streamers, and earbobs with a long gold fringe. (104).   15. Linen. (114).   16. "Hideous black dresses" and no jewelry except for "onyx mourning brooches or necklaces made from the deceased's hair." (136).   17. Her mother Ellen's. (132).   18. Paisley. (149).   19. An apple-green tarlatan with cream-colored (and blockade-acquired) Chantilly lace. (174).   20. A black broadcloth suit with a ruffled shirt. (179).   21. Her gold seed-pearl hair ornament. (185).   22. Her gold chain. (198).   23. Her wedding band. (185).   24. Rhett Butler. (225).   25. "Cats, Rats and Mice." (245).   26. $200 to $800 a pair, depending on whether they were cardboard or real leather. (276).   27. A white linen coat and trousers, an embroidered gray watered-silk waistcoat, a ruffled shirt, and a wide Panama hat. (371).   28. A lace-trimmed petticoat that she had made with linen and lace Rhett had brought her through the blockade. (394).   29. Pieces of carpet. (509).   30. A piece of twine. (490).   31. A blue organdie with sash, and black velvet slippers. (490).   32. A pot of rouge. (591).   33. A red plaid gown with a black velvet paletot and a flat red velvet hat with ribbons that tied in the back. (527).   34. A jar of quince-seed jelly. (591).   35. Cologne water. (591).   36. Her diamond earrings. (558).   37. She wore Aunt Pitty's seal muff. (558).   38. She wore Aunt Pitty's black broadcloth cloak. (557).   39. A green mantalet (that hid her blooming figure) and a green pancake hat. (653).   40. Mrs. Meade. (679).   41. A new green challis dress trimmed with yards of black rickrack braid, and a new lace house cap. (754).   42. The center stone was a four-carat diamond, and surrounding it were a number of emeralds. (831).   43. In England. (831).   44. A jade-green watered-silk dress that was cut low in the bosom. The skirt had an enormous bustle on which was a huge bunch of pink velvet roses. (919).   45. She wanted to cut bangs and frizzle them on her forehead. (907).   46. A dull-green changeable taffeta frock (it looked lilac in some lights) and a new pale-green bonnet that was circled about with dark-green plumes. (907).   47. He let her wear blue taffeta dresses with lace collars, while Mammy wanted to dress her in dimity frocks and pinafores. (975–6).   48. A blue velvet habit and a black hat with a red plume. (977).   49. D. (5). 50. A. (101). BONUS QUESTION. In convents. (841).

QUIZ 23

1. 1844. (57).   2. April 1861. (76).   3. Three years. Then she could shorten it to shoulder length. (136).   4. Two months. (130).   5. May 1, 1861. (131).   6. April 30, 1861. (131).   7. 1836. (140).   8. December 21, 1863. (262).   9. May 1863. (249).   10. July 5, 1863. (252).   11. "Cold rains and wild winds." (274).   12. "[S]ixteen hundred and something." (303).   13. September 1864. (353).   14. November 1864. (450).   15. Twenty years. (485).   16. Two weeks later. (479).   17. January 1866. (509).   18. April 1865. (479).   19. June 1865. (495).   20. June 1866. (652).   21. "[N]igh on forty years." (746).   22. The Milledgeville jail. (747).   23. Three months. (943).   24. B. (100). BONUS QUESTION. January 19, 1861. (It's a trick question because the actual date is not given in the text of *Gone with the Wind,* but it *is* said that the Troop was organized "the very day that Georgia seceded from the Union." You needed to look up the date of Georgia's secession in order to learn the correct answer to the question. [Without cheating and looking back here, that is!]) (20).

QUIZ 24

1. $3,000. (34).   2. $100 in Confederate bills. (139).   3. Henry Hamilton. (155).   4. $150 in gold. (191).   5. $50 in gold. (247).   6. $1.00. (301).   7. He had a stack of Confederate bonds and $3,000 in Confederate bills. (430).   8. He put it all in Confederate bonds. (477).   9. Inside Melanie's son Beau's diaper. (455).   10. Forty acres and a mule. (512).   11. $300. (513).   12. She rented her house to a Yankee officer and his family. (550).   13. She hoped to pay him back out of the following year's cotton. (571).   14. Her diamond earrings, and a mortgage on Tara. (571).   15. They said they bought it with a large insurance policy that Rhett's father had beggared himself to pay, when in actuality, the house had been bought for them by Rhett. (760).   16. $30. (776). 17-1-C. (276). 17-2-D. (276). 17-3-B. (276). 17-4-A. (276). BONUS QUESTION 1. "The world was crying out for cotton." (59). BONUS QUESTION 2. Twenty bales. (565). BONUS QUESTION 3. 1 cent a pound and 50 cents a pound, respectively. (865).

QUIZ 25

1. At least a month, usually a lot longer. (152).   2. Twenty-five miles. (141).   3. One. (234).   4. Farm wagons, ox carts, and even private carriages were used as ambulances. (314).   5. They would make bonfires of the crossties, lay the torn up rails in the fire until they were red hot, and then twist the rails around telegraph poles "until they looked like giant corkscrews." (339). 6. None, except walking. (422). 7. Sunday afternoons. (649).   8. Two wagons, two mules, and a horse and buggy for her own use. (620).   9. Uncle Peter. (628).   10. Will Benteen patched it up and kept it in use at Tara. (683).   11. Because she leased convicts to work in her mills, and Archie had told her that if she ever did that, he'd never drive her again. (Archie had been in prison for forty years and didn't believe in convict leasing.) (752).   12. After hearing how Sam had saved Scarlett

from being robbed, Frank Kennedy had Uncle Peter drive Sam to Rough and Ready in their buggy, and then Sam took a train to Jonesboro the following morning. It is assumed he walked to Tara from the Jonesboro station. (782). 13. A. (223). 14. FALSE. Either Saratoga or White Sulphur would have been their honeymoon location. (134). BONUS QUESTION. Nothing. They rode free. (894).

QUIZ 26

1. Ellen O'Hara. (42). 2. He told them that the South was lacking in iron foundries, woolen mills, cotton factories, and tanneries. (113). 3. Wilmington or Charleston. (222). 4. He bought up several thousand bales of cotton at "dirt-cheap prices" and stashed them in England. (239). 5. Rue de la Paix. (241). 6. A saloon. (629). 7. Saloons, gambling houses, and houses of prostitution. (649). 8. On Peachtree Road just outside of Atlanta. (621). 9. Ashley Wilkes. (687). 10. The state "leased" convicts to those needing large labor forces to rebuild railroads and to work in turpentine forests and lumber camps. (735). 11. They insisted on getting paid every day, they would get drunk on their wages, and often not show up for work the next day. (734). 12. Ten. Five for each mill. (752). 13. Johnnie Gallegher. (753). 14. "Caveat Emptorium." (859). 15. B. (898). BONUS QUESTION. She would tell them that her competitors' lumber was "far too high in price, rotten, full of knot holes and in general of deplorably poor quality." (654).

QUIZ 27

1. "Lak a bird." (79). 2. "Lak a hawg." (79). 3. Snakes and mouses. (81). 4. A rabbit. (79). 5. Beatrice Tarleton. (87). 6. A rabbit. (97). 7. He broke his leg and Gerald had to shoot him. (118). 8. He rode Mrs. Tarleton's favorite mare, Nellie. (309). 9. The horse was emaciated, its back was raw with sores and harness galls, and "he breathed as no sound horse should." (376). 10. A cow. (393). 11. They turned the animals loose in Tara's garden. (401). 12. An old sow and her litter. (416). 13. They were all left homeless and hungry, and the stronger ones began attacking the weaker. (472). 14. The Yankees shot it. (458). 15. A "timid old brown field rabbit." (602). 16. Bloodhounds. (662). 17. Tom. (876). 18. Mr. Butler. (977). 19. TRUE. (6). BONUS QUESTION. Because he drank so much of the "precious" milk. (464).

QUIZ 28

1. A tiny china rose-bowl that had two smirking china cherubs on it. (121). 2. Ivy and wild grapevines were twined around its rusty chains. (166). 3. She painted china hair receivers and mustache cups. (160). 4. A spittoon. (181). 5. Tea, coffee, silks, whalebone stays, colognes, fashion magazines, and books. (215). 6. Papers of pins and needles, buttons, spools of silk thread, and hairpins. (219). 7. A small "housewife" made of flannel that contained needles, three linen handkerchiefs, two spools of thread, and a pair of

scissors, and a long yellow sash made of China silk. (266, 269).   8. A large box of bonbons packed in paper lace. (286).   9. John's gold watch with the dangling seals, and a pair of cuff buttons. (328).   10. A wide palmetto leaf. (360).   11. A gold thimble, a gold-handled scissors, and a tiny gold-topped acorn of emery. (433).   12. Carreen O'Hara. (506).   13. A chain with many fobs and seals. (713).   14. They bought the cheapest pine and oak furniture in Frank Kennedy's store on credit. (723).   15. The finest mahogany and carved rosewood in their store, but Melanie and Ashley refused because they were buying on credit and wouldn't take anything but the barest necessities. (724).   16. They received "bric-a-brac, pictures, a silver spoon or two, linen pillow cases, napkins, rag rugs, [and] small articles . . . saved from Sherman. . . ." (725).   17. A. (857).   18. C. (76). BONUS QUESTION 1. She bought Wade a St. Bernard puppy; Beau, a Persian kitten; Ella, a coral bracelet; Aunt Pitty, a moonstone necklace; Melanie and Ashley, a complete set of Shakespeare; Uncle Peter, an elaborate livery; and Dilcey and Cookie, dress lengths. (841). BONUS QUESTION 2. Mangled beetles and roaches. (902).

QUIZ 29

1. Four. (57).   2. A New Orleans priest. (57).   3. William Makepeace Thackeray. (110).   4. Charles Dickens. (110).   5. Bulwer-Lytton. (138).   6. Banjo and harmonica. (160).   7. "Bonnie Blue Flag." (169).   8. "When This Cruel War Is Over." (194).   9. Her mother, Ellen, after hearing about Scarlett's conduct dancing with Rhett Butler at the Atlanta fund-raising bazaar. (198).   10. In a square rosewood writing box in her bedroom. (208).   11. *Godey's Lady's Book*. (225).   12. Advertisements of slaves, mules, plows, coffins, cures for private diseases, abortifacients, and restoratives of lost manhood; and announcements of houses for sale or rent. (233).   13. *The Daily Examiner*. (253).   14. A "hasty" note from Darcy Meade to his father, Dr. Meade. (251).   15. "My Old Kentucky Home." (She had been playing maudlin battle songs that were depressing everyone.) (291).   16. "Go Down, Moses." (300).   17. General Hardee. (353).   18. August 1864. (470).   19. "Beloved, I am coming home to you—" (498).   20. "Lines on the Back of a Confederate Note." (507).   21. Will wrote her that Jonas Wilkerson had returned to Tara to harass Ashley and the others for the tax money and this "hammered into her mind" that time was getting short and that she had to somehow come up with the tax money. (602).   22. He used Carreen O'Hara's Book of Devotions. (698).   23. She suggested, "To Pork from the O'Haras—Well done good and faithful servant." Pork declined to have the watch "engrabed," fearing that Scarlett might sell it if the watch left his possession. (714).   24. The Hail Mary. (701).   25. Melanie Wilkes. (726).   26. They would send a child or a negro servant to Aunt Pitty's the morning of the day they wanted to use Archie. Some of the notes said, "If you aren't using Archie this afternoon, do let me have him. I want to drive to the cemetery with flowers." Or, "I must go to the milliners." Or, "I should like Archie to drive Aunt Nelly for an airing." Or, "I must go calling on Peters Street and Grandpa is not feeling well enough to take me." (744).   27. *Les Misérables*. (792).   28. She sent her a thank-you note that Belle scolded her for sending. It could have gotten into the hands of the Yankees. (809).   29. "Marching through Georgia." (793).   30. *Harper's Weekly*. (848).   31. He swore he would play a guitar under her window every night and

compromise her reputation. (825). 32. "Mrs. Wilkes ill. Come home immediately." (993). 33. D. (290). BONUS QUESTION. Rhett Butler, to accompany the return of Melanie's redeemed wedding band. (198). SUPER BONUS QUESTION. "Short of paper, short of ink, short of men." (337).

QUIZ 30

1. He broke his knee. (31).   2. Dr. Fontaine and young Dr. Fontaine. (43).   3. Ellen O'Hara. (40).   4. "If fainting, or pretending to faint would do the trick, then she would faint." (83).   5. Smelling salts. (123).   6. A "sugar-tit." (144).   7. Dallas. (163).   8. Stuart got shot in the knee, and a minie ball went through Brent's shoulder. (201).   9. Quinine, calomel, opium, chloroform, iodine, and linen and cotton bandages. (215).   10. Hot bricks, blankets, and whisky. (281).   11. Stay in bed. (281).   12. The worst amputations. (296).   13. "To ease the dying out of life, not the living out of pain." (296).   14. He was shot in the head in battle. (315).   15. A shell hit him and Nellie. (328).   16. Dysentery. (440).   17. Opium. (404).   18. Rheumatism. (440).   19. He was shot in the leg with small shot. (465).   20. She was burned on her hands, face, and shoulders. (462).   21. Pneumonia. (501).   22. One of his legs was gone at the knee. (501).   23. A brewed, bitter concoction of blackberry roots. (493).   24. A shoulder wound. (593).   25. A bursting shell wounded him "low down" and did something to his legs which made them "spraddle." Aunt Pitty felt that the way he walked did not look very pretty. (551).   26. Pellagra. (651).   27. Tony Fontaine "cut him to ribbons." (636).   28. Smallpox, typhoid, and tuberculosis. (646).   29. He was killed in a saloon brawl before Rhett was born. (673).   30. He got a "mizry" in his back. (667).   31. B. He was missing a leg and an eye. (741).   32. A. Dr. Dean. (798).   33. D. He received a flesh wound through the shoulder and fainted from a loss of blood. (798).   34. C. He was shot through the head during the Klan raid on Shantytown. (803).   35. B. She found out when she was consulting Dr. Meade for a digestive upset. (871).   36. C. She suggested that Rhett put quinine on Bonnie's thumb. (899). BONUS QUESTION 1. After old Dr. Fontaine joined the army, there were none. (320). BONUS QUESTION 2. Lice and dysentery. (493). BONUS QUESTION 3. He showed him a long raised scar that ran down his chest into his abdomen. It was actually the souvenir of a knife fight in the California gold fields, not the scar from a battle wound. (890).

QUIZ 31

1. Rum. (57).   2. Biscuits, a fried chicken breast, and a yam with melted butter. (70).   3. Gerald O'Hara. (64).   4. Brandy. (83).   5. Two large yams with butter, buckwheat cakes and syrup, and a large slice of ham in gravy. (78).   6. Ice cream made out of ice and brought in from Savannah. (79).   7. The smell of roasting pork and mutton. (95). 8. Hoecakes, yams, chitterlings, and watermelons. (96). 9. Brunswick stew. (95).   10. Brandy. (207).   11. Waffles. (195).   12. Hog meat and chicken. (215).   13. Pork fat and dried peas. (282).   14. A "bitter brew of parched corn and dried sweet potatoes." (295).   15. Sorghum. (345).   16. Apples, yams, peanuts, and milk. (423).   17. Rabbit, pos-

sum, and catfish. (464). 18. A rooster. (464). 19. Fried eggs. (446). 20. A bucket of drinking water. (461). 21. Parched corn, side meat, dried peas, stewed dried apples, and peanuts. (469). 22. Corn whisky. (402). 23. A mixture of corn meal and water (and salt when available) which was wrapped around ramrods and roasted over a camp fire by the Confederate soldiers. The rolls were "as hard as rock candy and as tasteless as sawdust." (469). 24. Side meat and dried peas. (486). 25. Brandy. (575). 26. Coffee laced with brandy. (604). 27. Three. (678). 28. Brandy. (677). 29. Good wine, juleps, baked ham, and cold haunches of venison. (730). 30. Five sacks of white flour, a sack each of sugar and coffee, five hams, ten pounds of side meat, and "God knows how many bushels of yams and Irish potatoes." (777). BONUS QUESTION. Corn bread. (215). SUPER BONUS QUESTION. Rolls, corn muffins, biscuits, waffles, ham, fried chicken, collards, snap beans, fried squash, stewed okra, carrots in cream sauce, chocolate layer cake, vanilla blanc mange, and pound cake topped with sweet whipped cream. (423).

QUIZ 32

1. Mammy (to everyone, and to no one in particular). (68). 2. Rhett Butler (to Scarlett). (122). 3. Napoleon (to his troops). (114). 4. Scarlett O'Hara (to Charles Hamilton on her wedding night). (133). 5. Scarlett O'Hara (to Mammy). (81). 6. Ashley Wilkes (to Scarlett). (119). 7. Ashley Wilkes (to the male guests at the Wilkes's 1861 barbecue and ball). (111). 8. Rhett Butler (to Scarlett). (238). 9. Rhett Butler (to Scarlett). (193). 10. Scarlett O'Hara (to Ashley Wilkes). (120). 11. Rhett Butler (to Scarlett). (187). 12. Mr. McRae (to the young male guests at the Wilkes's 1861 barbecue and ball). (112). 13. Rhett Butler (to Scarlett). (258). 14. Rhett Butler (to Scarlett). (298). 15. Prissy (to Scarlett). (322). 16. Rhett Butler (to Scarlett). (303). 17. Prissy (to Scarlett). (359). 18. Rhett Butler (to Scarlett). (334–5). 19. Scarlett O'Hara Hamilton (to Rhett Butler). (373). 20. Rhett Butler (to Scarlett). (331). 21. Dilcey (relating Ellen O'Hara's last words to Scarlett). (411). 22. Scarlett O'Hara (to herself). (421). 23. Gerald O'Hara (to Scarlett). (428). 24. Grandma Fontaine (to Scarlett). (446). 25. Gerald O'Hara (to Scarlett). (415). 26. Grandma Fontaine (to Scarlett). (441). 27. Ellen O'Hara (to Scarlett). (465). 28. Scarlett O'Hara Hamilton (to Melanie Wilkes). (462). 29. Mammy (to everyone, and to no one in particular). (493). 30. Ashley Wilkes (to Scarlett). (518). 31. Ashley Wilkes (to Scarlett). (517). 32. Scarlett O'Hara Hamilton (to Ashley Wilkes). (525). 33. Ashley Wilkes (to Scarlett). (517). 34. Ashley Wilkes (to Scarlett). (516). 35. Will Benteen (to Scarlett). (504). 36. Mammy (to Scarlett). (591). 37. Scarlett O'Hara Hamilton (to Emmie Slattery Wilkerson). (528). 38. Rhett Butler (to Scarlett). (564). 39. Mammy (to Scarlett). (536). 40. Rhett Butler (to Scarlett). (569). 41. Rhett Butler (to Scarlett). (577). 42. Rhett Butler (to Scarlett). (564). 43. Aunt Pittypat Hamilton (to Scarlett). (551). 44. Frank Kennedy (to himself, about Scarlett). (632). 45. Rhett Butler (to Scarlett Kennedy). (616). 46. Rhett Butler (to Scarlett Kennedy). (613). 47. Scarlett Kennedy (to Rhett Butler). (621). 48. Scarlett Kennedy (to Frank Kennedy). (630). 49. Ashley Wilkes (to Scarlett, as *remembered* by Scarlett. [635] Ashley's actual words were, "And this which is facing all of us now is worse than war and worse than prison—and, to me, worse than death . . ." [520]). 50. Scarlett (to Frank Kennedy). (604). 51. Scarlett Kennedy (to Rhett Butler). (612). 52. Rhett Butler (to Scarlett

Kennedy). (619).   53. Rhett Butler (to Scarlett). (670).   54. Gerald O'Hara (to Suellen O'Hara). (694).   55. Scarlett Kennedy (to herself). (659).   56. Uncle Peter (to Scarlett). (665).   57. Rhett Butler (to Scarlett). (671).   58. Pork (to Scarlett). (714).   59. Grandma Fontaine (to Scarlett). (708).   60. Scarlett (to Rhett Butler). (672).   61. Tommy Wellburn (to Scarlett). (656).   62. Rhett Butler (to Scarlett). (672).   63. Scarlett Kennedy (to Tommy Wellburn). (656).   64. Will Benteen (to Suellen O'Hara). (691).   65. Scarlett Kennedy (to a Yankee woman from Maine). (664).   66. Grandma Fontaine (to Scarlett). (710).   67. Mrs. Meade (to the Association for the Beautification of the Graves of Our Glorious Dead and the Sewing Circle for the Widows and Orphans of the Confederacy). (727).   68. Scarlett Kennedy (to herself). (737).   69. Mammy (to Scarlett). (739).   70. Archie (to Scarlett). (747).   71. Rhett (to Scarlett). (759).   72. Rhett (to Scarlett). (766).   73. Rhett (to Scarlett). (765).   74. Rhett (to Scarlett). (757).   75. Scarlett (to Rhett). (756).   76. Rhett (to Scarlett). (762).   77. Big Sam (to Scarlett). (773).   78. Melanie Wilkes (to Belle Watling). (811).   79. Melanie Wilkes (to Belle Watling). (811).   80. Mammy (to Scarlett). (836).   81. Rhett (to Scarlett). (840).   82. Rhett Butler (to Scarlett Kennedy). (823).   83. Melanie Wilkes (to Mrs. Elsing, Mrs. Bonnell, Mrs. Merriwether, India Wilkes, and several other members of the Ladies' Sewing Circle for the Widows and Orphans of the Confederacy). (854).   84. Rhett (to Scarlett). (850).   85. Rhett (to Scarlett). (845).   86. Uncle Henry Hamilton (to Grandpa Merriwether). (855).   87. Rhett Butler (to Scarlett Kennedy). (822).   88. Rhett Butler (to Scarlett Kennedy). (829).   89. Rhett Butler (to Scarlett Kennedy). (826).   90. Rhett (to Scarlett). (840).   91. Rhett Butler (to Scarlett Kennedy). (818).   92. Mammy (to Scarlett). (836).   93. Mrs. Merriwether (to Scarlett). (834).   94. Rhett (to Scarlett). (871).   95. Mammy (to Rhett). (879).   96. Melly (to Mammy). (875).   97. Melanie (to Scarlett). (863).   98. Rhett (to Wade). (877).   99. Scarlett (to Rhett). (872).   100. Rhett (to Scarlett). (925).   101. Rhett (to Scarlett). (950).   102. Bonnie Butler (to Rhett). (902).   103. Rhett (to Scarlett). (884).   104. Ashley (to Scarlett). (912).   105. Rhett (to Scarlett). (965).   106. Rhett (to Scarlett). (903).   107. Scarlett (to herself). (917).   108. Rhett (to Scarlett). (903).   109. Ashley (to Scarlett). (915).   110. Rhett (to Scarlett). (932).   111. Rhett (to Scarlett). (926).   112. Rhett (to Melanie). (957).   113. Rhett (to Scarlett). (923).   114. Rhett (to Scarlett). (891).   115. Rhett (to Scarlett). (886).   116. Rhett (to Scarlett). (918).   117. Lou (to Scarlett). (882).   118. Rhett (to Scarlett). (949).   119. Rhett (to Wade Hampton). (891).   120. Rhett (to Scarlett). (1016).   121. Ashley (to Scarlett). (967).   122. Scarlett (to herself). (1024).   123. Bonnie Butler (to Scarlett). (979).   124. Rhett (to Scarlett). (1023).   125. Dr. Meade (to Scarlett). (996).   126. Ashley (to Scarlett). (1002).   127. Rhett (to Scarlett). (1011).   128. Big Sam (to Scarlett). (771).   129. René Picard (to Scarlett). (594).   130. Ashley Wilkes (to Scarlett). (751).   131. Melanie (to Scarlett). (999).   132. Jonas Wilkerson (to Scarlett). (528).   133. Prissy (to Scarlett). (394).   134. Mammy (to Scarlett). (79).   135. Melanie (to Scarlett). (937).   136. Ashley (to Scarlett). (908).   137. Will Benteen (to Scarlett). (688).   138. Ashley Wilkes (to Scarlett and Melanie). (722).   139. Prissy (to Scarlett). (388).   140. Archie (to Scarlett). (790).   141. Big Sam (to Scarlett). (781).   142. Johnnie Gallegher (to Scarlett). (778).   143. Jeems (to the Tarleton twins). (23).   144. Archie (to Scarlett). (746).   145. Dr. Meade (to Melanie Wilkes). (731).   146. Uncle Henry Hamilton (to Melanie and Scarlett). (326).   147. Ashley (to Scarlett). (883).   148. Dilcey (to Scarlett). (423).   149. Alex Fontaine (to Scarlett). (481).   150. Dr. Meade (to the guests at the Atlanta fund-raising bazaar). (184).   151. Beatrice Tarleton (to Scarlett, Melanie, Carreen, and Suellen). (486). 152. Melanie Hamilton Wilkes (to Scarlett). (489). 153. Aunt Pauline (to Scarlett). (947). 154. Ashley (to Scarlett). (911). 155. Melanie Wilkes (to Scarlett). (462). BONUS. Rhett Butler (to Scarlett). (183).

QUIZ 33

1. Rebecca. (51). 2. Kennedy's Emporium, the building, and the trade; the saloon on her lot near the depot; $25,000 in gold; one-half of Aunt Pittypat's house on Peachtree Street in Atlanta; and one-third of Tara. (35, 54, 67). 3. The Queen of Hearts. (88). 4. Her mother, Ellen. (113). 5. Seventeen. (10). 6. Whiskey. (100). 7. Sister Mary Joseph. (102). 8. Another baby. (124). 9. Twelve. (163). 10. Carreen belonged to the Sisters of Mercy. (165). 11. Carrots. (161). 12. "You stop acting so hateful to me, you act nice and help me have a good time. We go through the Season like a devoted, happy husband and wife. Then, come spring, I'll go home and start over." (188). 13. Milk. (230). 14. Miss Greedy. (245). 15. She said the word "money"; "[she] reminded her dependents of the charity she'd given, and [she] kicked a downed foe." (266). 16. Middleton Courtney. (255). 17. He slapped her. Hard. (310). 18. Thirty. (395). 19. Her grandfather, Pierre Robillard. (394). 20. Her seven-year-old cousin, Peggy O'Hara. (381). 21. Cows. (432). 22. Kathleen. (408). 23. Eleven. (485). 24. She had an ache in her lower back that never went away, and she spotted blood on her underwear and sheets. (540). 25. She was given the title of "The O'Hara." (556). 26. Grainne "lifted [Scarlett's] womb with the baby" and didn't have the skills to restore it. (591). 27. TRUE. (623). 28. D. Half Moon. (659). 29. B. Roger Cowperthwaite. (641). 30. A. "He expected her to be a credit to him. He had observed that she had the ability." (779). 31. C. Cat would have a room next to hers, and she would continue to handle her own financial affairs. (681). BONUS QUESTION. Dublin. (704).

QUIZ 34

1. It said, "Eugenie Victoria Butler," and beneath that, "Bonnie." (5). 2. She had the "ginger-colored curly hair of her father, Frank Kennedy." (21). 3. Skinny and angular. (21). 4. Wade Hampton. (33). 5. Rhett. (20). 6. Chicken pox. (80). 7. A changeling. (579). 8. Blue. (580). 9. Green. (580). 10. She gave her the name of Dara, which meant oak tree. (592). 11. Katie Colum O'Hara. (578). 12. "Father." (597). 13. Colum O'Hara. (578). 14. Kathleen O'Hara and Mrs. Fitzpatrick. (578). 15. He was strangled, disemboweled, and left on the doorstep of the Big House. (731). 16. Ree. It was Gaelic for "King." (717). 17. B. Lady Catherine. (780). 18. B. A big china dollbaby. (679). 19. D. Ocras. (680). BONUS QUESTION. "Foal" or "Jumper." (568).

QUIZ 35

1. Protestant. (270). 2. Catholic. (270). 3. Jerome. (328). 4. Daniel. (342). 5. Flaming red. (343). 6. She called him an "old loo-la." (356). 7. Auguste. (364). 8. Maureen. (345). 9. Clare and Peg. (368). 10. Helen. (345). 11. C. Sean. (346). 12. B. 93.

(404).   13. A. Maureen was once a barmaid in an Irish saloon. (388).   14. D. James Monroe. (385).   15. TRUE. (400).   16. TRUE. (385).   17. TRUE. (434).   18. FALSE. It was Patrick. (468). BONUS QUESTION 1. This was a Church dispensation from Lenten fasting granted to people who survived the Irish potato famine. (411). BONUS QUESTION 2. His daughters Pauline and Eulalie. (733).

QUIZ 36

1. Pork. (31).   2. A gold cigar-cutter. (80).   3. Appropriately, he went as Edward Teach, commonly known as Blackbeard the Pirate. (91).   4. Pearls. (84).   5. South America. (93).   6. To buy back the Butler family silver. (114).   7. Three. (166).   8. He made Scarlett tell Eleanor that he snored. (189).   9. Dolphins. (305).   10. She heard that the rumor was that *she* had left Rhett for another man, rather than Rhett leaving her. (639).   11. Because he stayed out with her past dark looking for a lost child, which meant that she was compromised and that he had to marry her. (666).   12. Four days. (805).   13. The Jury's Hotel. (804).   14. FALSE. He loved babies. (815).   15. FALSE. He was a very good sailor. (301).   16. B. 100. (182).   17. B. "Let's just say I'd like to be ten years younger." 18. A and B. (25).   19. D. "What is your name?" (814). BONUS QUESTION. Kinnicutt. (509).

QUIZ 37

1. "[S]hining white." (118).   2. The house had recently been painted. (118).   3. Eleanor. (102).   4. He got him a job as a bank teller. (148).   5. They held cake sales and bazaars of handcrafts. (124).   6. He wasn't really a cousin, but a third cousin twice removed. (143).   7. They were all cross-eyed. (143).   8. Margaret. (124).   9. Steven. (149).   10. Celie. (119).   11. Rosemary.   (124).   12. Manigo.   (119).   13. Governesses and travel. (168).   14. Thirteen. (205).   15. She felt that the whole lot of them were "hopeless dolts." (198).   16. The Grand Tour of Europe. (212).   17. Kemper Butler. (225).   18. B. Miss Julia Ashley. (220).   19. D. She drank a bottle of paregoric, but it didn't work. (269).   20. C. A century and a half. (252).   21. A. Dunmore Landing. (238).   22. A. 1810. (269). BONUS QUESTION. Kilkenny. (664).

QUIZ 38

1. A Harlequin. (89).   2. Joe told Ashley that Scarlett was thinking of building another store on the site. (99).   3. The Ashley River. (188).   4. They both lived out of books and were "hopeless in the real world." (741).   5. Harriet Stewart Kelly. (761).   6. A. Dilcey. (31).   7. B. He won a Latin composition prize. (619).   8. D. He was a minister at the Methodist church. (761).   9. FALSE. She thought "[h]e looked desperately ill." (52) BONUS QUESTION 1. She made him promise that he would let her send Beau and Wade to the University and then on a European Grand Tour. (620). BONUS QUESTION 2. "Miss Confederacy Noble Cause." (761).

QUIZ 39

1. Growing up in the same house with Aunt Pittypat. (54).   2. C. Earl Marshal. (85).   3. C. He took over the financial management of Kennedy's Emporium and the saloon Scarlett leased. (109).   4. TRUE. He told her she'd have to give all her legal business to the lawyer who handled her divorce. He wouldn't do anything for her anymore. (371).   5. Total control over all her money. (522).   6. She didn't call him "Uncle Henry." (618).   7. B. Sally Brewton. (116).   8. Carreen. She lived in a convent. (102).   9. "Starvation parties." (153).   10. D. She stabbed him through the heart with a sharpened knitting needle. (122).   11. TRUE. (122).   12. TRUE. (171).   13. A. Lila. (160).   14. B. A brick mansion. (165).   15. Undergarments. (192).   16. TRUE. (203).   17. C. "Eagle eye." (192).   18. FALSE. He died at Bull Run. (193).   19. D. Edith. (256).   20. TRUE. (236).   21. Fort Moultrie. (319).   22. Rebekah. (319).   23. B. He was walleyed. (286).   24. B. Josiah Anson. (293). BONUS QUESTION. Sheba. (290).

QUIZ 40

1. Blue. (396).   2. He was a Roman Catholic priest. (399).   3. At least twice a year. (444).   4. The Fenian Brotherhood. (437).   5. The Jasper Greens. (410).   6. Stephen O'Hara. (411).   7. He told her not to make fun of the Irish people's superstitions and beliefs. (561).   8. A. The Hail Mary. (574).   9. C. He was the armorer. (612).   10. C. Because he was a missionary priest whose work involved easing the suffering of the poor, not administering the sacraments. (562). BONUS QUESTION 1. He put a discarded ice cream paper in her boot. (429). BONUS QUESTION 2. "Follow me, you English butchers, and we'll die together for the freedom of Ireland." (811).

QUIZ 41

1. Mr. Alderson. (482).   2. The Mahoneys. (485).   3. Scarlett would call Mrs. Fitzpatrick "Mrs. Fitz," and Mrs. Fitzpatrick would call Scarlett "Mrs. O." (588). 4. Piles. (587).   5. Mrs. Keane.   (588).   6. Father Flynn.   (561). 7. Joseph O'Neill. (572).   8. Grainne. (590).   9. Dr. Devlin. (589).   10. Annie Doyle, Mary Moran, and Peggy Quinn. (565).   11. Kevin O'Connor. (646).   12. Tommy Doyle. (648).   13. Honourable Louisa Ferncliff. (669).   14. Sarah. (670).   15. He attacked an English officer in a bar. (724).   16. Assistant governess.   (724).   17. Florence.   (736).   18. Evans.   (693). 19. Julian. (682).   20. Monsieur François Hervé. (703).   21. Serafina. (702).   22. Daniel Kelly. (722).   23. Mrs. Sims. (683). BONUS QUESTION 1. The Fenian Brotherhood. (437). BONUS QUESTION 2. John Graham. (748). SUPER BONUS QUESTION. In addition to Mrs. Fitzpatrick, the staff consisted of a cook, four kitchen maids, two parlor maids, four upstairs maids, three dairymaids, a head laundress, three laundry maids, a butler, eight footmen, two boys, a stableman, six grooms, and five gardeners. (687).

QUIZ 42

1. Her sister Suellen. (10).   2. The small room off the kitchen where they used to hang the hams. (13). 3. Delilah. (12). 4. Lutie. (12). 5. Will Benteen. (36). 6. Delilah. (19). 7. Susie, Suellen's oldest child. (32). 8. Miss Ellen. (29). 9. Chicken pox. (80). 10. D. $5,000. (506). 11. A. She bought new furniture and furnishings. (628). 12. Martha. (626). 13. Jane. (626). 14. C. There were vines hanging down the front of the house, four windows had sagging shutters, and there were no shutters at all on two windows. (11). BONUS QUESTION. All the furniture needed reupholstering, the house needed new curtains, and all the carpeting was worn out. (35).

QUIZ 43

1. The Oakland Cemetery. (4). 2. One or two hundred. (68). 3. Pocahontas. (86). 4. Queen Victoria. (86). 5. Florence Nightingale. (86). 6. Mamie Bart. (73). 7. The Twelfth Night Revelers. (82). 8. Rex. (85). 9. The DeGives Opera House. (83). 10. The mayor's office. (85). 11. D. Mrs. Meade. (86). 12. D. Mrs. Elsing. (86). 13. A. A girls' school. (623). 14. FALSE. It was raining. (3). BONUS QUESTION. Five Points. (9).

QUIZ 44

1. The Battery. (113).   2. King Street. (120).   3. Rice. (151).   4. The bells in St. Michael's steeple. (123). 5. Church Street. (137). 6. Water Street. (137). 7. 1682. (151). 8. Five. (155). 9. Execution. (171). 10. The Market. (155). 11. Thirty. (191). 12. The Saint Cecilia Ball. (189). 13. Charleston had "the first recorded whorehouse 'for gentlemen only.' " (195). 14. A. One year it rained thirty-eight days in a row. (191). 15. C. The Saint Cecilia Ball. (257). 16. B. Because that was the period when malaria rose from the swamps. (252). 17. The Hibernian Hall. (289). BONUS QUESTION. Chalmers Street. (291).

QUIZ 45

1. Their father. (112).   2. It was confiscated by Sherman. (143).   3. He hired an Italian from New York to put on a fireworks display. (144). 4. The Sisters of Mercy. (285). 5. Pink. (327). 6. White. (333). 7. A fountain. (338). 8. Broughton Street. (340). 9. In a house on Saint James' Square in Savannah. (332). 10. The Telfair sisters, Mary and Margaret. (332). 11. Packed sand-and-shell. (363). 12. South Broad Street. (345). 13. City Market. (386). 14. Chippewa Square. (385). 15. Forsyth Park. (415).

QUIZ 46

1. Tara. (401).   2. County Meath, Ireland. (402).   3. Market Day. (450).   4. Connemara. (418).   5. The Railway Hotel. (449).   6. Adamstown. (456).   7. Fairies. (462).   8. Forty-six, plus two churches. (529).   9. Ballyhara. (493).   10. The Boyne and the Knightsbrook. (529).   11. She gave it to Seamus O'Hara. (607).   12. At the Work House in Dunshauglin, fourteen miles away. (549).   13. Pike Corner. (668).   14. The Railway. (801).   15. TRUE. (736).   16. FALSE. He was at a race at Balbriggan. (802).   17. The Shelbourne Hotel. (707). BONUS QUESTION. Kilbride. (747).

QUIZ 47

1. The red silk petticoat he had bought for her. (25).   2. She wore a white ruffled Mary Stuart style cap. (72).   3. She wore a black beaded gown. (72).   4. A beaded silk reticule with a $20 gold piece in the pocket. (80).   5. A sheepskin jacket. (It was the third she had given him.) (80).   6. A deep blue velvet ballgown with embroidered silver stars. (84).   7. India. (151).   8. A "brown dress with white linen collar and cuffs and an old-fashioned bonnet covered in brown silk." (129).   9. Plain black. (154).   10. A dull browny-green. (198).   11. Blue watered silk. (217).   12. Black. (217).   13. Black. (220).   14. He gave them green-and-white-striped parasols. (258).   15. A pearl-sewn ruby brocade ball gown and diamond dog-collar. (287).   16. He was wearing a Yankee soldier's uniform. He had borrowed a sergeant's clothes because his were wet. (321).   17. She wore apple-green kid gloves. (328).   18. Scarlett's fur cape. (321).   19. An "old-fashioned" dress suit with satin knee breeches, a velvet tailcoat, and a red sash. (394).   20. A gold brocaded silk gown that was trimmed with gold lace and that had a four foot long gold brocaded train, a strand of pearls, and diamond earbobs. (394).   21. A green watered silk gown and green morocco leather slippers. (431).   22. Bright blue. (474).   23. An embroidered linen gown. (578).   24. Her best blue frock with a lace collar. (578).   25. A gray gown with a plain white linen collar and cuffs. (555).   26. A dark green skirt with blue and red petticoats underneath, and yellow and green striped stockings. (647).   27. "[L]ight frocks in the daytime and something rather naked for dinner at night." (671).   28. FALSE. She was wearing a gray linen jacket and skirt with a lace jabot and gray kid gloves. (674).   29. A. She had it remade into a pendant. (695).   30. B. Pigeon's blood rubies. (795).

QUIZ 48

1. A. October 11, 1873. (36).   2. C. The afternoon of the first Wednesday of every month. (161).   3. FALSE. It was only available on Saturdays. (159).   4. D. Almost eight weeks. (189).   5. December 26. (215).   6. C. 1820. (269).   7. TRUE. (534).   8. March 26, 1875. (509).   9. B. November 11, 1860. (468).   10. TRUE. (469).   11. FALSE. It was 1789. (469).   12. A. All Hallow's Eve. (562).   13. D. At Daniel O'Hara's house. (594). BONUS QUESTION. New Year's Day. Because Lincoln issued the Emancipation Proclamation on

January 1, all former slaves got drunk and celebrated and Charlestonians feared for their safety. (226). SUPER BONUS/"FIGURE-IT-OUT" QUESTION. Approximately 1725 (1875 minus "around a hundred and fifty years.") (239).

QUIZ 49

1. It was a plain pine box. (4).   2. Carved ivory. (42).   3. A lady doll with a leather trunk full of clothes. (80).   4. A pair of six-shooters, with his initials engraved in the ivory-inlaid handles. (80).   5. Hepplewhite. (125).   6. White camellias. (216).   7. A small sailboat. (254).   8. In the card room on the second floor. (254).   9. A mantel clock and a fireplace poker. (279).   10. A stained glass window for the new Cathedral. (334).   11. Hothouse roses. (322).   12. The tureen was decorated with ornamentation depicting a forest, complete with trees and wildlife. (365).   13. He used a malacca cane. (385).   14. The figures she called the "serpent-men." They were actually bronze mermen. (416).   15. A lace collar. (502).   16. C. A box of clay pipes and two saddlebags of tobacco. (503).   17. A. 100 pounds. (647).   18. B. Titania. (671).   19. D. A shiny coin. (678).   20. Louis Sixteenth French design. (685) BONUS QUESTION 1. A particularly slow unfurling of a lady's fan. (255). BONUS QUESTION 2. He mounted it on a silver base. (662).

QUIZ 50

1. Five miles. (10).   2. Western. (45).   3. By train. (98).   4. The South Carolina line. (110).   5. Carriages. (116).   6. They took the horsecar. (122).   7. She was such a terrible driver that her husband insisted she use the bells to warn unsuspecting pedestrians and other drivers. (128).   8. Five minutes. (196).   9. Sixteen feet. (302).   10. Ten of twelve. (323).   11. Twenty miles. (457).   12. Two weeks and a day. (430).   13. Seamus O'Brien. (435).   14. The *Brian Boru*. (435).   15. She bought a pony and trap in Mullingar. (528).   16. D. The *Evening Star*. (513).   17. TRUE. (593).   18. B. 50 pence or $2.50 American. (632).   19. B. The *Abraham Lincoln*. (632).   20. *The Golden Fleece*. (629). BONUS QUESTION. Bright green and yellow. (122).

QUIZ 51

1. $100 a month. (33). 2. Her one-third share of Tara. (35). 3. $4.25 a week. (59). 4. $2.00. (157). 5. A phosphate mine. (184). 6. $1,000 in gold. (246). 7. More than $1 million in gold. (291). 8. Sheba the seamstress. (291). 9. A. 1 shilling. (452). 10. B. 2 shillings. (452). 11. TRUE. (446). 12. D. 15,000 pounds, take it or leave it. (530). 13. 140 pounds. (657). 14. TRUE. (756). BONUS QUESTION 1. She carried $200 in gold. (485). BONUS QUESTION 2. She told Scarlett she was "a professional houseguest and friend." (675).

QUIZ 52

1. Scarlett read her the Psalms. (24).   2. "Climbing Jacob's Ladder." (31).   3. It was the fashion to add complicated loops to every capital and add a "parabola of swirls" beneath the signature. (36).   4. A calling card. (She left it because she said Aunt Pitty was afraid to see her in person.) (53).   5. Scarlett. (60).   6. Almost 300. (83).   7. Waverley novels. (76).   8. Velvet. (70).   9. Two drummers, two pennywhistles, and a cornet. (86).   10. "Our Charleston Letter." (82).   11. Ella's naughtiness and money. (101).   12. She "crossed" the letter, which involved writing on the page and then turning the sheet at a right angle and writing on top of the previously-written lines. This made her letters a tad difficult to read. (102).   13. "ARRIVING FOUR PM TRAIN FOR VISIT STOP ONLY ONE SERVANT STOP LOVE SCARLETT" (110).   14. "Oh, Susanna." (117).   15. Onionskin. (101).   16. They left their calling card with one corner bent. (166).   17. "A blizzard of calling cards." (166).   18. He wrote a "florid letter of apology." (196).   19. He inked it over. (205).   20. B. *Ivanhoe*. (202).   21. TRUE. (199).   22. D. *The Ugly Duckling*. (251).   23. D. He sent a telegram. (286).   24. "Across the Wide Missouri." (298).   25. C. "The Rock Island Line." (296).   26. B. They sang the "Yo-ho-ho, and a bottle of rum!" sea chanty from Robert Louis Stevenson's *Treasure Island,* "Little Brown Jug," "The Yellow Rose of Texas," and "Peg in a Low Back'd Car." (312).   27. A. "The Blue Danube Waltz." (293).   28. A. Rosemary Butler. (324).   29. D. Concertina, tin whistles, fiddle, and bones. (353).   30. TRUE. (355).   31. The initials stood for *"Pour prendre congé,"* which meant "to take leave." Coastal Georgians and South Carolinans left the cards at the homes of friends whenever they left town after visiting. (374).   32. B. "I'll Take You Home." (418).   33. C. "Goldilocks and the Three Bears." (462).   34. A. Her Uncle Henry Hamilton and Pansy. (617).   35. FALSE. It said, *"Sir* John Morland, Bart." (664).   36. Eight pages. (761).   37. D. Eleven gentlemen (including the Gentleman Usher) and fourteen ladies with their daughters. (709).   38. B. The *Irish Times*. (696).   39. TRUE. (801) SUPER BONUS QUESTION. The passage was 1 Corinthians, Chapter 13, Verse 1, and read, "Though I speak with the tongues of men and angels, and have not charity, I am become as sounding brass, or a tinkling cymbal." (282, and any favorite edition of the Good Book).

QUIZ 53

1. Beef broth. (19).   2. An oyster patty. (73).   3. A glass of brandy. (100).   4. Soaking fruitcakes. (122).   5. A Huguenot Torte. (162).   6. Biscuits, hominy, butter, ham, and eggs. (179).   7. Flounder. (158).   8. Roast duck. (172).   9. Rum. (311).   10. Hardtack and rum. (303).   11. Oyster stew. (293).   12. It was made largely of champagne and brandy. (294).   13. Mashed potatoes and soggy carrot pieces. (336).   14. A chicken thigh, a breast, potatoes with plenty of gravy, and rolls with butter. (337-8).   15. Hot bean soup and corn muffins. (322).   16. Fried chicken. (336).   17. Meat pies, roast beef, ham with cloves, turkey, potatoes, creamed carrots, roast onions, whipped sweet potatoes, relishes, cake, and whiskey. (349).   18. Potted doves with gravy, pureéd potatoes, and turnips. (366).   19. He brought a keg of real Irish ale. (397).   20. Cheese toast and potato soup. (419).   21. A salmon cutlet in sauce. (453).   22. D. A coconut candy cake. (428).   23. B. A special barm

brack. (595).   24. C. The pastry for her meat pies melted in your mouth. (559).   25. TRUE. (545).   26. FALSE. She was offered boiled salt *beef* and cabbage, hot boiled *potatoes,* and porter. (732).   27. E. Cakes, cookies, pastries, and candies were not mentioned as being part of the feast. The menu consisted of ham, preserved goose, jellied quail eggs, spiced beef, salted fish, aspics, ices, fruits, cheeses, breads, relishes, jams, sauces, wines, ale, cider, and coffee. (753).   28. FALSE. The treat they all tasted for the first time was ice cream. (678). DISGUSTING BONUS QUESTION. Buffalo, goat, mule, and dead human. (246). SUPER BONUS QUESTION. Lucullus. (160).

QUIZ 54

1. A *bodhran.* (409).   2. A saucer of milk and a plate of crumbled bread. (489).   3. Fruit-filled light bread. (457).   4. *Pibs willeann.* (504).   5. They put up holly branches on the mantels and over the doors and windows, and they put a big red candle in one window to light the Christ Child's way. (594).   6. They used a ladder to climb to the door (which was twelve feet off the ground) and then they pulled the ladder in behind them. (541).   7. A balustraded gallery one level above the kitchen that allowed one to secretly observe goings-on in the kitchen. (558).   8. A handful of nettles. (545).   9. A few bars of soap. (567).   10. A State Bed. (566).   11. It was good luck for the whole year if a dark-haired person visited someone's house on New Year's Day. (596).   12. They worked in bare feet and they would rinse the dirt off their feet before entering the house. (559).   13. The seller and buyer spit into their hands and slapped them together. (657).   14. "Hungry." (680).   15. A. "Darling." (692).   16. D. Scrubbing someone with water in which angelica root had steeped all day. (679).   17. TRUE. (680).   18. The Gaelic word for "King" was "Ree." (717).   19. B. Diana John. (791).   20. FALSE. Comet was one of Scarlett's Ballyhara hunting horses. (690). BONUS QUESTION. So that female guests could invite a man into their room without coming right out and asking. If the tray was left outside the door, it was an invitation. (695). SUPER BONUS QUESTION. "[A] fearful creature, malicious and sly. He'll curdle your cream in an instant or tangle your hair with your own brush." (560).

QUIZ 55

1. Ashley Wilkes (to Melanie Wilkes). (7).   2. Mammy (to Scarlett). (15).   3. Mammy (to Scarlett). (13).   4. Scarlett (to Mammy). (18).   5. Scarlett (to Suellen). (33).   6. Rhett (to Scarlett). (26).   7. Rhett (to Scarlett). (25).   8. Uncle Henry Hamilton (to Scarlett). (54).   9. Uncle Henry Hamilton (to Scarlett). (54).   10. Ashley (to Scarlett). (66).   11. Scarlett (to India). (62).   12. Scarlett (to Bill Weller, Mamie and Amos Bart, the Conningtons, and the rest of her party guests). (76).   13. Joe Colleton (to Scarlett). (69).   14. Scarlett (to Rhett). (78).   15. Bill Weller (to Amos Bart and one other man). (74).   16. Tony Fontaine (to Scarlett). (96).   17. Tony Fontaine (to Scarlett). (97).   18. Scarlett (to Aunt Eulalie and Aunt Pauline). (117). 19. Rhett (to Scarlett). (134).   20. Rhett (to Scarlett). (132).   21. Ross Butler (to Scarlett). (146).   22. Emma Anson (to Sally Brewton). (138).   23. Rhett (to Scarlett). (135).   24. Scarlett (to Rhett). (178).   25. Rhett (to Scarlett).

(185).   26. Rhett (to Scarlett). (178).   27. Scarlett (to Sally Brewton). (160).   28. Rhett (to Scarlett). (182).   29. Rosemary Butler (to Scarlett). (198).   30. Rosemary Butler (to Scarlett). (199).   31. Rhett (to Alicia Savage). (192).   32. Rosemary Butler (to a Union captain). (200).   33. Rhett (to Scarlett). (211).   34. Gerald O'Hara (to Scarlett). (227).   35. Julia Ashley (to Rosemary Butler). (229).   36. Sally Brewton (to Scarlett). (274).   37. Rosemary Butler (to Scarlett). (240).   38. Rhett (to Scarlett). (259).   39. Eleanor Butler (to Scarlett). (270).   40. Rhett (to Scarlett and Rosemary). (250).   41. Rhett (to Scarlett). (301).   42. Rhett (to Scarlett). (312).   43. Rhett (to Scarlett). (277).   44. Rhett (to Scarlett). (318).   45. Rhett (to Scarlett). (311).   46. Rhett (to Scarlett) (304).   47. Rhett (to Scarlett). (317).   48. Rhett (to Scarlett). (309).   49. Pierre Robillard (to Scarlett). (336).   50. Pierre Robillard (to Eulalie and Pauline). (329).   51. Pierre Robillard (to Scarlett). (329).   52. Scarlett (to Pansy). (323).   53. Gerald O'Hara (to Scarlett). (342).   54. Aunt Pauline (to Scarlett). (358).   55. Aunt Pauline (to Scarlett). (364).   56. Scarlett (to Uncle James O'Hara). (347).   57. Scarlett (to Aunts Eulalie and Pauline). (358).   58. Uncle James O'Hara (to Scarlett). (346).   59. Maureen O'Hara (to Scarlett). (355).   60. Colum O'Hara (to Scarlett). (102).   61. Jamie O'Hara (to Scarlett). (395).   62. Scarlett (to Pierre Robillard). (406).   63. Pierre Robillard (to Scarlett). (388).   64. Pierre Robillard (to Scarlett). (396).   65. Pierre Robillard (to Scarlett). (373).   66. Scarlett (to Maureen O'Hara). (409).   67. Colum O'Hara (to Scarlett). (448).   68. Jamie O'Hara (to Maureen, Kathleen, and Scarlett O'Hara). (433).   69. Maureen O'Hara (to Scarlett). (412).   70. Katie Scarlett O'Hara (to Katie Scarlett O'Hara). (474).   71. Scarlett (to Colum). (526).   72. Grandmother Katie Scarlett O'Hara (to Katie Scarlett O'Hara). (513).   73. Scarlett (to Colum). (524).   74. Colum O'Hara (to Scarlett). (467).   75. Daniel O'Hara (to Scarlett). (478).   76. Daniel O'Hara (to Scarlett). (603).   77. Mrs. Fitzpatrick (to Colum). (571).   78. Colum (to God). (614).   79. An English soldier (to Scarlett). (552).   80. Colum (to Scarlett). (614).   81. Grainne (to Scarlett). (590).   82. Scarlett (to Cat). (586).   83. Mrs. Fitzpatrick (to Scarlett). (599).   84. Joseph O'Neill (to anyone who would listen). (579).   85. Colum (to Scarlett). (611).   86. Colum (to Scarlett). (539).   87. Mrs. Fitzpatrick (to Scarlett). (587).   88. Mrs. Fitzpatrick (to Scarlett). (595).   89. Daniel O'Hara (to Scarlett). (553).   90. Peggy O'Hara (to the dead Daniel O'Hara). (605).   91. Scarlett (to the dead Gerald O'Hara). (628).   92. Cat (to her reflection). (647).   93. Will Benteen (to Scarlett). (627).   94. Rhett (to Scarlett). (655).   95. The Charleston Harbor excursion boat commander (to the passengers). (633).   96. Scarlett O'Hara (to the dead Gerald O'Hara). (628).   97. Ashley (to Scarlett). (620).   98. The Honourable Louisa Ferncliff (to her party companions). (673).   99. Charlotte Montague (to Scarlett). (675).   100. John Morland (to Scarlett). (672).   101. Colum (to Scarlett). (778).   102. Charles Ragland (to Scarlett). (738).   103. Scarlett (to members of the Royal Irish Constabulary). (746).   104. Monsieur François Hervé (to his assistants). (703).   105. Scarlett (to John Morland). (805).   106. Rhett (to Scarlett). (819).   107. Grainne (to Scarlett). (788).   108. Colum (to the patrons at Kennedy's bar). (767).   109. Cat (to Scarlett). (823).   110. Scarlett (to Charlotte Montague). (684).   111. Rhett (to Scarlett). (819).   112. John Morland (to Scarlett). (737).   113. Scarlett (to Mrs. Fitzpatrick). (743).   114. Scarlett (to Fenton). (772).   115. Rhett (to Scarlett). (822).   116. Rhett (to Scarlett). (713).   117. Charlotte Montague (to the Shelbourne Hotel doorman). (707).   118. Colum (to Scarlett). (794).   119. Rhett (to Scarlett). (713).   120. Charlotte Montague (to Scarlett). (677).

QUIZ 56

1-KK.   2-L.   3-S.   4-G.   5-GG.   6-GGG.   7-H.   8-DDD.   9-AAA.   10-LL.   11-XX.
12-C.   13-BB.   14-N.   15-U.   16-UU.   17-Y.   18-II.   19-WW.   20-ZZ.   21-PP.
22-TT.   23-EEE.   24-AA.   25-FFF.   26-SS.   27-V.   28-VV.   29-P.   30-CCC.   31-FF.
32-OO.   33-Q.   34-M.   35-I.   36-RR.   37-JJ.   38-R.   39-O.   40-EE.   41-D.   42-NN.
43-K.   44-CC.   45-X.   46-DD.   47-W.   48-Z.   49-E.   50-YY.   51-F.   52-QQ.   53-A.
54-HH.   55-T.   56-BBB.   57-B.   58-MM.   59-J.

QUIZ 57

1. The film version of *Gone With the Wind* was directed by VICTOR **FLEMING,** from a screenplay by SIDNEY **HOWARD.**
2. The film was produced by DAVID O. **SELZNICK.**
3. The production was designed by WILLIAM CAMERON **MENZIES,** with art direction by LYLE **WHEELER,** and photography by ERNEST **HALLER.**
4. The musical score was by MAX **STEINER,** with contributions from his associate, LOU **FORBES.**
5. Special photographic effects were by JACK **COSGROVE.**
6. His associate for fire effects was LEE **ZAVITZ.**
7. The costumes were designed by WALTER **PLUNKETT.**
8. Scarlett's hats were designed by JOHN **FREDERICS.**
9. Interiors were by JOSEPH B. **PLATT,** and interior decoration was by EDWARD G. **BOYLE.**
10. The supervising film editor was HAL C. **KERN,** and the associate film editor was JAMES E. **NEWCOM.**
11. The scenario assistant was BARBARA **KEON.**
12. Makeup and hair styling were by MONTY **WESTMORE,** with assistance from his associates, HAZEL **ROGERS** and BEN **NYE.**
13. The dance directors were FRANK **FLOYD** and EDDIE **PRINZE.**
14. The film's historian was WILBUR G. **KURTZ.**
15. The film's technical advisers were SUSAN **MYRICK** and WILL **PRICE.**
16. The film's researcher was LILLIAN K. **DEIGHTON.**
17. The film's production manager was RAYMOND A. **KLUNE.**
18. The assistant director was ERIC G. **STACEY.**
19. The second assistant director was RIDGEWAY **CALLOW.**
20. Production continuity was supervised by LYDIA **SCHILLER** and CONNIE **EARLE.**
21. The film's mechanical engineer was R. D. **MUSGRAVE.**
22. The construction superintendent was HAROLD **FENTON,** and the chief grip was FRED **WILLIAMS.**
23. The person in charge of wardrobe was EDWARD P. **LAMBERT,** with assistance from his associates, MARIAN **DABNEY** and ELMER **ELLSWORTH.**
24. The casting managers were CHARLES **RICHARDS** and FRED **SCHUESSLER.**

25. The location manager was MASON **LITSON.**
26. The scenic department superintendent was HENRY J. **STAHL.**
27. The electrical superintendent was WALLY **OETTEL** and the chief electrician was JAMES **POTEVIN.**
28. The properties manager was HAROLD **COLES.**
29. The person in charge of properties on the set was ARDEN **CRIPE.**
30. The person in charge of greens properties was ROY A. **McLAUGHLIN.**
31. The person in charge of drapes properties was JAMES **FORNEY.**
32. Special properties were made by ROSS B. **JACKMAN.**
33. Tara was landscaped by FLORENCE **YOCH.**
34. The film's still photographer was FRED **PARRISH.**
35. The camera operators were ARTHUR **ARLING** and VINCENT **FARRAR.**
36. The assistant film editors were RICHARD **VAN ENGER** and ERNEST **LEADLEY.**
37. The novel, *Gone with the Wind,* was written by MARGARET **MITCHELL.**

QUIZ 58

1. Hilton.   2. Wade Hampton and Ella Lorena.   3. Jeems.   4. After his daughter Suellen tries to get him to sign a Union loyalty oath, he gallops away in anger and dies after a failed jump.   5. Honey Wilkes.   6. Will Benteen.   7. Their three dead sons, Gerald, Jr., Gerald, Jr., and Gerald, Jr.   8. Napoleon Picard. He is only mentioned.   9. Honey Wilkes.   10. Rebecca.   11. Katie Scarlett O'Hara.   12. His sister, Rosemary Butler.   13. Dilcey.   14. Cookie the cook.   15. Henry Hamilton.   16. Archie.   17. None of the families listed appear in the film.   18. FALSE.   19. FALSE. Tommy Wellburn does not appear in the film, but he *is* killed in the Shantytown raid in the novel.   20. Mrs. Whiting.   21. In the novel, this scene takes place in Atlanta, and in the film, in London; and in the novel, it was the servant girl, Lou (Uncle Peter's great-niece), who apparently left Bonnie without a light, while in the film, it was an unnamed nurse who left Bonnie in the dark and who then suggested that Rhett simply let his daughter cry.   22. F. Tony Fontaine.   23. In the novel, she started a bakery after the war.   24. In the novel she reads from Hugo's *Les Misérables;* in the film, Dickens's *David Copperfield.*   25. Rhett's last onscreen words are "Frankly, my dear, I don't give a damn." But after he leaves, Scarlett hears his voice in her mind (along with the voices of Gerald and Ashley) and the last thing we actually hear Rhett say is "Tara!"

QUIZ 59

1-1. *The Cisco Kid* (1945).   1-2. Ruth Ceder was one of Vivien Leigh's doubles.   1-3. *Lost in Space,* and *Voyage to the Bottom of the Sea.*   2-1. George Bessolo.   2-2. He played Superman in the television series of the same name.   2-3. He committed suicide by shooting himself.   3-1. He won Best Supporting Actor for his performance in *Stagecoach.*   3-2. *It's a Wonderful Life.*   3-3. The Secretary of Labor was Thomas Mitchell's nephew, James Mitchell.   4-1. The 1942 Cecil B. DeMille epic, *Reap the Wild Wind.*   4-2. "Big Sister."   4-3. The 1943 film, *Cabin in the Sky.*   5-1. London, England.   5-2. Leslie Howard was a bank clerk.   5-3. His plane was shot down in June 1943 over the Bay of Biscay. He was fifty years old.   6-1. Stan Laurel was once Rand Brooks's father-in-law. (Rand was married to Stan Laurel's daughter, Lois.)   6-2. He owned an ambulance company.   6-3. The 1962 film, *Stagecoach to Danger's Rock.*   7-1. Canton, Ohio, October 4, 1901.   7-2. His brother, Ben Nye, was a makeup artist for *Gone With the Wind.*   7-3. The 1938 film, *Rebecca of Sunnybrook Farm.*   8-1. Clark Gable was never a pharmacy clerk.   8-2. Five. He was married to Josephine Dillon, Maria ("Ria") Lucas Langham, Carole Lombard, Lady Sylvia Ashley, and Katherine Williams Spreckles.   8-3. In *It Happened One Night,* Gable unbuttoned his dress shirt and revealed that he was not wearing an undershirt. American men, thinking it was more masculine to go bare-chested beneath their shirts, immediately emulated Clark by not wearing undershirts, and within one year, sales of undershirts plunged by 75 percent.   8-4. C. He made this remark to David Selznick.   8-5. August 24, 1938.   8-6. The original family name was "Goebel," which they changed because of its similarity to the name of Hitler's chief of propaganda, Joseph Goebbels.   8-7. TRUE. He made this remark to Hedda Hopper.   8-8. FALSE. They starred together in the 1932 comedy-drama, *No Man of Her Own.*   8-9. The last film Gable ever made was *The Misfits* with Marilyn Monroe and Montgomery Clift.   8-10. He was nominated—and won—Best Actor for the 1934 film, *It Happened One Night;* he was nominated—and lost to Victor McLaglen—Best Actor for the 1935 film, *Mutiny on the Bounty;* and he was nominated—and lost to Robert Donat—Best Actor for *Gone With the Wind.*   9-1. He was a World Champion Rodeo Rider from 1917 to 1924.   9-2. He was a second unit director on the film.   9-3. He was awarded an Honorary Academy Award for his achievements as a stunt man and for developing safety devices to protect stunt men.   10-1. The 1934 film, *It Happened One Night.*   10-2. Bond graduated from the University of Southern California in 1931 with a degree in engineering.   10-3. Ward Bond played Major Seth Adams from 1957–1961 on TV's long-running western series, *Wagon Train.*   11-1. Darjeeling, India, November 5, 1913.   11-2. Laurence Olivier.   11-3. Her favorite classmate was Maureen O'Sullivan, the woman who would grow up to give birth to Mia Farrow, who would later become Woody Allen's paramour and the mother of his son.   11-4. From the middle name of her then-husband, Herbert *Leigh* Holman.   11-5. Margaret Mitchell began writing *Gone with the Wind* while recuperating from a sprained ankle and Vivien Leigh began reading *Gone with the Wind* while recuperating from a broken ankle.   11-6. B.   11-7. Tuberculosis.   11-8. She was 26.   11-9. TRUE, as did Clark Gable.   11-10. TRUE. (I wouldn't have made that up, I swear.)   12-1. The 1942 Cecil B. DeMille epic, *Reap the Wild Wind.*   12-2. She was a singer.   12-3. At the Motion Picture County Home in Woodland Hills, California, on October 26, 1952.   13-1. Joshua Logan.   13-2. She was nominated as Best Supporting Actress for her role in the 1940 film, *All This and Heaven, Too.*   13-3. They played husband and wife in the 1938 Warner Bros. film, *Love, Honor and Behave.*   14-1. She grew up in Atlanta, Georgia.   14-2. Her second husband was director Charles Vidor; her third husband was director John Huston; her fourth husband was musician Artie Shaw.   14-3. *Return to 'Salem's Lot.* (King had nothing to do with the film, and other than the title, *Return to 'Salem's Lot* had nothing to do with King's novel, *'Salem's Lot.*)   15-1. In the 1950s, Ann Rutherford married William Dozier (Joan Fontaine's ex-husband—Fontaine and de Havilland were sisters), which made her stepmother to de Havilland's niece.   15-2. The "Andy Hardy" films.   15-3. *Leave It to the Girls.*   16-1. Thelma McQueen. (The "Butterfly" came from her first stage appearance when she danced the "Butterfly Ballet" in the ballet *A Midsummer Night's Dream* in 1935.) 16-2. *The Mosquito Coast.* 16-3. *Designing Women.* 17-1. Tokyo, Japan. 17-2. *Roots: The Next Generation.* 17-3. *The Love Boat.* 17-4. A. 17-5. *The Snake Pit.* 17-6. The 1946 film, *To Each His Own.* 17-7. Charlotte Brontë. 17-8. She has a son named Benjamin Goodrich and a daughter named Gisele Galante. 17-9. TRUE. 17-10. Enforced labor. 18-1. She was a voice coach and a play director as well as an actress. 18-2. "Too-thin" actress, Billie Burke. 18-3. She had accepted a role in *Arsenic and Old Lace* on Broadway when she fell ill with kidney disease in October 1942. She died one month later. 19-1. "Big Town." 19-2. TRUE. David Selznick had actually considered casting Mae West "as a stunt." 19-3. She committed suicide with an overdose of barbiturates in February 1955. 20-1. The 1942 animated film, *Bambi.* 20-2. Technicolor company president Herbert T. Kalmus. 20-3. She was five years old. (She was born in 1934.)

QUIZ 60 (PART 1)

1. B. Nothing. He added it himself for "flourish, rhythm, and production value." 2. He was 34. 3. He was 12. 4. Louis B. Mayer. Selznick married Mayer's daughter, Irene. 5. Marcella Rabwin. 6. His Eastern story editor, Katherine "Kay" Brown. 7. He first read the book in Hawaii. 8. 1st: Katharine Hepburn; 2nd: Miriam Hopkins; 3rd: Margaret Sullivan; 4th: Joan Crawford; 5th: Barbara Stanwyck. 9. He received suggestions for 121 actresses, including one vote for Vivien Leigh from a guy in New Zealand. 10. Tallulah Bankhead. 11. 5½ hours. 12. *Jezebel.* 13. Forty Acres. 14. The date was December 10, 1938, and the burning of Atlanta was filmed by George Cukor. 15. Myron Selznick. 16. Joan Bennett, Jean Arthur, Paulette Goddard, and Vivien Leigh. 17. She found out on Christmas Day, 1938. 18. He was 46. 19. He had to agree to let Howard be associate producer (and star) in the film, *Intermezzo.* 20. C. The Tara bedroom "lacing scene" with Scarlett and Mammy. 21. A. Five times. 22. D. The Atlanta Bazaar scene. 23. B. Be slapped and eat watermelon. 24. FALSE. It was George Cukor. 25. Ben Hecht. 26. A. Benzedrine. 27. Victor Fleming. 28. Sam Wood. 29. D. One year. 30. Because just outside the top line of the shot was the real Culver City, and they couldn't let that show. 31. TRUE. 32. They were all painted into the shot. None of them were real. 33. He died in a tractor accident at his Massachusetts farm in 1939. 34. The Fox Theater in Riverside, California. 35. Wilbur Hayes. BONUS QUESTION 1. 46–106. BONUS QUESTION 2. January 13, 1939. BONUS QUESTION 3. February 7, 1939. BONUS QUESTION 4. Franz Waxman and Herbert Stockard. BONUS QUESTION 5. "Cheers Greet Flashing-Eyed Scarlett."

QUIZ 60 (PART 2)

1. Scarlett and Gerald O'Hara standing on a hill overlooking Tara. 2. Under the credits, slaves are seen working in the fields of Tara. 3. "Clark Gable as Rhett Butler." And then, Vivien Leigh, Leslie Howard, and Olivia de Havilland. 4. Brent Tarleton. (He says, "What do we care if we *were* expelled from college, Scarlett? The *war's* going to start any day now,

so we'd have left college anyhow!")   5. Hanging out an upstairs window and scolding Scarlett.   6. "Miss Scarlett!"   7. "Scarlett."   8. "Do Not Squander Time—That Is The Stuff Life Is Made Of."   9. "I think it's hard winning a war with words, gentlemen."   10. "Scarlett."   11. She saw Ashley kissing Melanie from atop his horse.   12. A three-strand pearl choker.   13. It said, "Our brave defenders need clothing. You cannot fight! But you can sew!"   14. The Atlanta National Bank.   15. "THE WAR IS OVER Don't Ask For Credit."   16. 12:25 A.M.   17. She hears the voices of Gerald O'Hara, Ashley Wilkes, and Rhett Butler. Gerald's voice says, "Do you mean to tell me, Katie Scarlett O'Hara, that Tara doesn't mean anything to you? Why, land's the *only* thing that matters —it's the only thing that lasts." Ashley's voice says, "Something you love better than me, though you may not know it—Tara!" And Rhett's voice says, "It's this from which you get your strength—the red earth of Tara."   18. "After all, tomorrow is another day." It was said by Scarlett. There is no difference between the film and the novel. The novel also ends with Scarlett saying, "After all, tomorrow is another day."   19. 1967.   20. The film garnered thirteen nominations: Picture, Actor (Clark Gable), Actress (Vivien Leigh), Supporting Actress (two nominations: Olivia de Havilland and Hattie McDaniel), Director (Victor Fleming), Screenplay (Sidney Howard), Cinematography (Ernest Haller and Ray Rennahan), Interior Decoration (Lyle Wheeler), Sound Recording (Thomas T. Moulton), Original Score (Max Steiner), Film Editing (Hal C. Kern and James E. Newcom), and Special Effects (John R. Cosgrove [Photographic] and Fred Albin and Arthur Johns [Sound]).   21. Friday, December 15, 1939.   22. CBS. BLOOPER #1. The shadows do not fall on the carriages as they move through them because the background was a matte painting and there wasn't time in post-production to make sure that the shadows fell on the carriages. BLOOPER #2. While hurriedly dressing for the barbecue, we don't see Scarlett put any jewelry on around her neck, and yet later, at Twelve Oaks, she is seen wearing a coral necklace. BLOOPER #3. The shadows are in the wrong place based on where they're kneeling and the supposed source of light. BLOOPER #4. Edison developed a prototype light bulb in 1879. In the film version of *Gone With the Wind,* in the scene where Scarlett flees the Atlanta hospital in disgust (numbered 176 in the screenplay), the camera pans past a lamppost in which an electric light bulb is clearly visible. This scene takes place in 1864, *fifteen years* prior to Edison's invention. BLOOPER #5. Scarlett flees Atlanta hatless, and then suddenly and mysteriously a black bonnet appears on her head at the depot, and it stays there until just before Rhett leaves her to join the army, when it just as mysteriously disappears. BONUS QUESTION 1. The "Frank Kennedy Company." BONUS QUESTION 2. A slightly edited version of the onscreen "There was a land of Cavaliers and Cotton Fields . . ." text scroll from the beginning of the film. Everything else he wrote was eliminated. (The final version of this "Foreword" substituted "pretty" for "patrician" and "Gallantry" for "Age of Chivalry." It also capitalized "Cotton Fields.") BONUS QUESTION 3. Olivia de Havilland is the one heard vomiting on the soundtrack.

QUIZ 61

1. *Scarlett.* (733).   2. *Scarlett.* (567).   3. *Scarlett.* (698).   4. *Scarlett.* (202).   5. *Gone with the Wind.* (257).   6. *Gone with the Wind.* (363).   7. *Gone with the Wind.* (134).   8. *Scarlett.*

(337).   9. *Scarlett.* (195).   10. *Scarlett.* (771).   11. *Gone with the Wind.* (746).   12. *Gone with the Wind.* (737).   13. *Scarlett.* (771).   14. *Scarlett.* (797).   15. *Gone with the Wind.* (461).   16. *Scarlett.*   (663).   17. *Scarlett.*   (229).   18. *Scarlett.*   (242).   19. *Scarlett.* (242).   20. *Scarlett.* (242).   21. *Gone with the Wind.* (479).   22. *Scarlett.* (314).   23. *Gone with the Wind.* (463).   24. *Gone with the Wind.* (407).   25. *Gone with the Wind.* (399).   26. *Scarlett.* (457).   27. *Scarlett.* (428).   28. *Gone with the Wind.* (490).   29. *Scarlett.*   (432).   30. *Gone   with   the   Wind.*   (518).   31. *Scarlett.*   (357).   32. *Scarlett.* (405).   33. *Gone with the Wind.* (501).   34. *Gone with the Wind.* (552).   35. *Gone with the Wind.* (541).   36. *Gone with the Wind.* (700).   37. *Scarlett.* (729).   38. *Gone with the Wind.* (713).   39. *Gone with the Wind.* (722).   40. *Gone with the Wind.* (722).   41. *Scarlett.* (620).   42. *Gone with the Wind.* (780).   43. *Gone with the Wind.* (823).   44. *Gone with the Wind.* (874).   45. *Scarlett.* (31).   46. *Gone with the Wind.* (929).   47. *Gone with the Wind.* (952).   48. *Gone with the Wind.* (902).   49. *Gone with the Wind.* (915).   50. *Scarlett.* (25).   51. *Gone with the Wind.* (953).   52. *Gone with the Wind.* (898).   53. *Scarlett.* (40).   54. *Scarlett.* (104).   55. *Gone with the Wind.* (927).   56. *Gone with the Wind.* (950).   57. *Gone with the Wind.* (965).   58. *Gone with the Wind.* (979).   59. *Gone with the Wind.*   (981).   60. *Scarlett.*   (7).   61. *Scarlett.*   (63).   62. *Gone   with   the   Wind.* (986).   63. *Scarlett.* (146).   64. *Scarlett.* (127).   65. *Gone with the Wind.* (993).   66. *Scarlett.*   (162).   67. *Gone   with   the   Wind.*   (133).   68. *Scarlett.*   (191).   69. *Scarlett.* (306).   70. *Gone with the Wind.* (130).   71. *Gone with the Wind.* (74).   72. *Gone with the Wind.* (109).   73. *Gone with the Wind.* (153).   74. *Gone with the Wind.* (191).   75. *Gone with the Wind.* (301).   76. *Gone with the Wind.* (365).   77. *Gone with the Wind.* (335).   78. *Gone with the Wind.* (385).   79. *Scarlett.* (515).   80. *Gone with the Wind.* (359).

QUIZ 62

THE O'HARAS (TARA)

1-a1. Gerald.
1-a2. Ellen.
    1-b1. Suellen.
        1-b1.1. Susie.
        1-b1.2. Martha.
        1-b1.3. Jane.
    1-b2. Carreen.
    1-b3. Katie Scarlett.
        1-b3.1. Wade Hampton.
        1-b3.2. Ella Lorena.
        1-b3.3. Eugenie Victoria ("Bonnie Blue").
        1-b3.4. Katie Colum ("Cat").
    1-b4. Gerald, Jr.
    1-b5. Gerald, Jr.
    1-b6. Gerald, Jr.

THE O'HARAS (SAVANNAH)

2-a1. Jamie.
2-a2. Maureen.
    2-b1. Daniel.
    2-b2. Patricia.
    2-b3. Helen.
    2-b4. Brian.
    2-b5. Mary Kate.

THE TARLETONS

3-a1. James.
3-a2. Beatrice.
    3-b1. Randa.
    3-b2. Camilla.
    3-b3. Brent.
    3-b4. Stuart.
    3-b5. Betsy.
    3-b6. Hetty.
    3-b7. Tom.
    3-b8. Boyd.

THE BUTLERS

4-a1. Steven.
4-a2. Eleanor.
    4-b1. Rhett.
    4-b2. Ross.
    4-b3. Rosemary.

QUIZ 63

Part 1: ("DP" = a Dinner Party item, "LP" = a Luncheon Party item, and "SS" = a Sunday Night Supper item.)

1-SS.   2-DP.   3-LP.   4-LP.   5-DP.   6-SS.   7-SS.   8-DP.   9-LP.   10-LP.   11-LP. 12-DP.   13-LP.   14-DP.   15-SS.

Part 2: 1. Salt, mace, and black pepper. 2. The recipe called for 18 oysters in shell. 3. "Wash legs, and remove skin by turning it down and pulling it off like a glove." 4. Onion, celery, tomatoes, and peas. 5. 350°F. 6. The recipe called for 1 cup of sifted flour. 7. Squares, diamonds, or triangles. 8. White raisins, citron, candied pineapple, candied cherries, and mixed orange and lemon peel. 9. The mixture had to be steamed for 2 hours. 10. The recipe called for a 9-inch unbaked pie shell.

Part 3: 1. B, C; 2. B, C; 3. B, C; 4. B, C; 5. A; 6. A; 7. A.

QUIZ 64

1. 1900. 2. Munnerlyn. 3. She was a reporter. 4. Lieutenant Clifford Henry. 5. Berrien Kinnard Upshaw. 6. John R. Marsh. 7. Smith College in Northampton, Massachusetts. 8. $500. 9. Margaret Mitchell's second husband, John R. Marsh. (The dedication reads simply, "To J.R.M.") 10. 1937. 11. When Mitchell was almost three, her skirt caught fire when she sat too close to a fireplace grate. In *Gone with the Wind,* Scarlett's skirt catches fire as she tries to put out the fire in Tara's kitchen started by the Yankees. 12. She was initially paid $50,000, and then another $50,000 was sent to her as a "bonus" after the film opened. 13. Margaret Baugh. 14. Rhett Butler. 15. Groucho. 16. August 16, 1949. 17. She was struck by a taxi on August 11, 1949, while fleeing from the path of a drunk driver. 18. 1986, the fiftieth anniversary of the novel. It was a one-cent stamp. 19. " 'Ropa Carmagin." According to Darden Asbury Pyron in his biography of Margaret Mitchell, *Southern Daughter,* Mitchell's secretary Margaret Baugh is quoted as saying, "All I remember [about the novella] was its Faulkneresque quality and its decayed aristocratic girl in a crumbling big old house and a hint of miscegenation." Pyron's research, however, reveals that the novella was actually a reworking of a Southern gothic ghost story by an Atlanta friend of the Mitchells' named Harvey Smith. (See *Southern Daughter* for a synopsis of the plot of Smith's original story.) 20. FALSE. He was mortally offended and threatened to sue Margaret Mitchell for slander. He changed his mind after a series of correspondences with the author made him realize that not only had Margaret Mitchell not intended to insult him, she had, in fact, never even heard of him! 21. TRUE. 1401 Peachtree Street was torn down in the 1950s. 22. FALSE. She willed all rights to the book to her husband, John Marsh. Upon his death, the rights went to Margaret Mitchell's brother, Stephens Mitchell. 23. TRUE. Margaret Mitchell rejected this idea. BONUS QUESTION. Piedy. SUPER BONUS QUESTION. The only other authorized sequel to *Gone with the Wind* is a 600-page (according to Cynthia Marylee Molt) unpublished novel called "Tara: The Continuation of Gone with the Wind," and it was written by Margaret Mitchell's first biographer, Anne Edwards, author of *Road to Tara: The Life of Margaret Mitchell.* The project began life as a movie sequel authorized by Margaret Mitchell's brother, Stephens Mitchell, and purchased by Richard Zanuck and David Brown for production by a partnership consisting of MGM and Universal Pictures. According to author Anne Edwards (writing in the preface to *Road to Tara*), *"Tara: The Continuation of Gone with the Wind* was completed and was approved by Richard Zanuck and David Brown in the fall of 1978. James Goldman was assigned to write the screenplay. Unfortunately, at this writing [1983], the film has not yet come to fruition." According to author Pauline Bartel, writing in *The Complete "Gone with the Wind" Trivia Book,* the book that Edwards submitted was 775 pages long, "supposedly was set in 1872–82 and showed a divorce for Scarlett and Rhett, a subsequent remarriage for Scarlett,

and more intrigue between the former Mrs. Butler and her ex." According to Bartel, MGM was not pleased with either the book or James Goldman's (apparently completed) screenplay and the "book was shelved, and the deal collapsed." There is no mention of "Tara: The Continuation of Gone with the Wind" in Pyron's biography nor is any other information available as to whether or not Edwards's sequel was reconsidered when *Scarlett* was being negotiated.

ANSWERS TO THE <u>GONE WITH THE WIND</u> CROSSWORD PUZZLE

BIBLIOGRAPHY, FILMOGRAPHY, AND SOURCES FOR ADDITIONAL INFORMATION

A GONE WITH THE WIND BIBLIOGRAPHY AND FILMOGRAPHY

<hr>

This Bibliography is by no means a complete listing of books about the *Gone with the Wind* phenomenon. Cynthia Molt's annotated bibliography in her superb *Gone with the Wind* reference book lists more than 600 books and articles about the novel and the film. Rather, this listing compiles the books and other materials I referred to and used for research while writing *The Official "Gone with the Wind" Companion,* and aside from things like the film script and the Keyes autobiography, most should still be in print and readily available. (The script *is* available in a trade paperback edition which is out of print but should still be around in remainder bookstores and libraries.) The books listed here comprise an excellent starting library for the *Gone with the Wind* fan. Following the Bibliography is a brief Filmography that lists films of interest to *Gone With the Wind* fans that are available on video, as well as films and TV shows currently unavailable on video, but worth noting for videotaping consideration.

Bibliography

The Art of "Gone with the Wind" by JUDY CAMERON and PAUL J. CHRISTMAN (New York: Prentice Hall Press, 1989).

This is an oversized trade paperback loaded with hundreds of photos, many of which are rare stills from the making of the film. The book is indexed and focuses primarily on the film.

The Book of Sequels by HENRY BEARD, CHRISTOPHER CERF, SARAH DURKEE, and SEAN KELLY (New York: Random House, 1990).

This is an oversized trade paperback comprised of phony sequels to some of the world's best-loved and most respected books. Of interest to *Gone with the Wind* fans is the chapter "Back with the Wind," which presents what four sequels to *Gone with the Wind* would read like IF they were written by Erica Jong, Tama Janowitz, Joyce Carol Oates, and Alice Walker. Jong's contribution, the authors/editors theorize, would be titled *The Scarlett Fanny;* Janowitz's, *Slaves of Atlanta;* Oates's, *Southern Bellefleur;* and Walker's, *The Color Scarlett.* This is very funny stuff and the creators of this hilarious volume have got the respective writers' styles down pat. (Well, *parodies* of their styles, I should say.) These four parodies offer an interesting spin on the *Gone with the Wind* story and they are important because of the acknowledgment of the story's huge impact on popular culture. (There are a lot of other very funny parodies here as well: Have you read the sequel to L. Ron Hubbard's *Dianetics, Diuretics?* Or how about the sequel to Whitley Streiber's *Communion, First Communion?* I particularly liked *The Lighter Side of Sylvia Plath, T. S. Eliot's Wasteland Theme Park, The Satanic Reverses,* and *The Word-a-Day in the Life of Ivan Denisovich Calendar.* Like I said, funny stuff.)

Civil War Photographs 1861–1865, Compiled by HIRST D. MILHOLLGEN and DONALD H. MUGRIDGE (Washington, D.C.: The Library of Congress, 1977).

This paperback is subtitled "A Catalog of Copy Negatives Made from Originals Selected from the Mathew B. Brady Collection in the Prints and Photographs Division of the Library of Congress" and offers reprints of 1,047 Civil War–era public domain photographs. The book is broken into five parts ("The Main Eastern Theater of War," "The Federal Navy and Seaborne Expeditions against the Atlantic Coast of the Confederacy," "The War in the West," "Washington, 1862–1865," and "Portraits"), and each main section is broken into even more specific categories of photographs. There is a complete description of each photograph listed, and there are also indexes organized by Photographers, General Subjects, and Specific Subjects and Persons. The Library of Congress charges a reprint fee for each print you order (at this writing an 8" × 10" glossy was $12.00), and photographs can be used in books and magazines free of charge as long as a credit is given to the Library of Congress. Of course, photos can also be ordered for personal use, such as framing and as gifts for Civil War buffs. *Civil War Photographs 1861–1865* can be ordered from the Library of Congress by sending $4.50 to The Library of Congress, Photoduplication Service, Department C, Washington, D.C. 20540. Checks should be made payable to the Library of Congress, Photoduplication Service.

The Civil War Sourcebook: A Traveler's Guide by CHUCK LAWLISS (New York: Harmony Books, 1991).

This volume could be considered a Civil War "Companion." It is comprehensive and contains a variety of entertaining and historically accurate information. It actually can be used as a traveler's guide, or just read for enlightenment and pleasure. The book contains numerous photos, illustrations, sidebars, maps, lists, and a superb index. Recommended.

The Complete "Gone with the Wind" Trivia Book by PAULINE BARTEL (Dallas, TX: Taylor Publishing Company, 1989).

This is a fun book that collects scads of *Gone with the Wind* information into a very accessible and entertaining volume. It's got some nice photos and unlike other "trivia" books, *The Complete "Gone with the Wind" Trivia Book* also offers a very complete and helpful index. This is an excellent introductory volume to the *Gone with the Wind* experience.

Gone with the Wind by MARGARET MITCHELL (New York: Macmillan, 1936; New York: Avon Books, 1973).

The genesis. Go reread it.

"Gone With the Wind" As Book and Film, edited by RICHARD HARWELL (New York: Paragon House Publishers, 1987).

This is a superb collection of scholarly articles, reviews, essays and reprints that intelligently covers the *Gone with the Wind* phenomenon. Richard Harwell also edited *Margaret Mitchell's "Gone with the Wind" Letters: 1936–1949* and is an acknowledged expert on the entire *Gone with the Wind* world. Sure, there is present here the occasional stodgy academic interpretive piece, but overall, the volume is a must-read for *Gone with the Wind* enthusiasts.

The "Gone with the Wind" Cook Book (New York: Abbeville Press, 1991).

This was a tie-in to the film which was originally published in 1940 and contained *Gone with the Wind*–related recipes. A facsimile edition was published in 1991 by Abbeville Press.

Gone With the Wind: The Definitive Illustrated History of the Book, the Movie, and the Legend by HERB BRIDGES and TERRYL C. BOODMAN (New York: Simon & Schuster, 1989).

This is an oversized, picture-packed volume that contains reproductions of the film's original Call Sheets, rare promotional material, and other exotic memorabilia. The book was written by one of the world's bona fide *Gone with the Wind* authorities (Herb Bridges was an usher at the Loew's Grand Theater the day of the film's premiere) and thus contains unpublished photos, anecdotes, and other insider info. Recommended.

"Gone With the Wind" on Film: A Complete Reference by CYNTHIA MARYLEE MOLT (Jefferson, NC: McFarland & Company, 1990).

This book is incredible. It is exactly what the title says it is: a complete reference to the entire *Gone with the Wind* phenomenon. Author Molt packs so much information into this volume one wonders how she ever found the time to do anything else. The book has eleven chapters and covers everything from the characters in the novel and the people who auditioned for the film to an unbelievably complete annotated *Gone with the Wind* bibliography that covers such exotica as jewelry, sheet music, and other collectibles. The book also contains a magnanimously titled "Foreword" by Butterfly McQueen, which consists of exactly two sentences and thirty-eight words, sixteen of which are the title of the book, and the names of Molt, Mitchell, and Selznick. Nonetheless, this book is the definitive reference to the *Gone with the Wind* experience and even though the title emphasizes the film focus, there is so much information in here about everything to do with *Gone with the Wind* that it is fair to consider this a genuine *Gone with the Wind* encyclopedia. Kudos to Molt for her magnificent achievement with this book.

Gone With the Wind Final Shooting Script, January 24, 1939; Screenplay by SIDNEY HOWARD (Selznick International).

The version of the script that is closest to what finally appeared on screen.

Gone With the Wind: The Screenplay by SIDNEY HOWARD; edited and with an Introduction by Herb Bridges and Terryl C. Boodman (New York: Dell Publishing, 1989).

The published version of the final shooting script. This volume contains a nice photo section and an informative introduction by Bridges and Boodman. It's fun to watch the movie and read along with the script and see where the actors made minor changes in the dialogue. There are also scenes and dialogue in this screenplay that did not make it into the final version of the film. For completists, then, this volume is a must.

Margaret Mitchell's "Gone with the Wind" Letters: 1936–1949; edited by RICHARD B. HARWELL (New York: Macmillan, 1976).

Margaret Mitchell was an avid letter writer and this is a collection of her letters having to do with *Gone with the Wind.* I suppose history demanded the publication of this volume, but one wonders what Mrs. Mitchell might have had to say about her letters being collected and published in a book. This is the woman, you must remember, who insisted that her personal papers and manuscripts be destroyed after her death. (They were—except for some *Gone with the Wind* manuscript pages sealed in a bank to prove Mitchell's authorship of the novel, if sometime in the future it was ever necessary to do so.) These considerations aside, though, it *is* good to have these letters accessible and preserved for their historical significance.

A Pictorial History of "Gone With the Wind" by GERALD GARDNER and HARRIET MODELL GARDNER (New York: Bonanza Books, 1980, 1983).

This is a general interest oversized hardcover that looks at the *Gone With the Wind* phenomenon, as well as ancillary events and people. For instance, there are photos from Leslie Howard's films, and a side-by-side listing of a chronology of the making of the film and the events of World War II. It is a moderately interesting volume that might not have enormous appeal to serious *Gone With the Wind* fans because of the non-*Wind* material included. There is an interesting feature called "By the Numbers," which details the numerical facts surrounding the phenomenon, a decent bibliography, and an index. A section of the many and varied Display Cards used to promote the film over thirty years is also quite entertaining.

Road to Tara: The Life of Margaret Mitchell by ANNE EDWARDS (New York: Bantam Books, 1986).

This first biography of Margaret Mitchell is by the author of what Cynthia Molt calls a "psychological biography" of Vivien Leigh. Anne Edwards also wrote the first authorized sequel to *Gone with the Wind* (which is still unpublished). *Road to Tara* is very well done and almost reads like a thrillingly real novel. This biography should not be passed over in favor of the more recent Pyron biography. Do yourself a favor: Read both.

Scarlett: The Sequel to Margaret Mitchell's "Gone with the Wind" by ALEXANDRA RIPLEY (New York: Warner Books, 1991).

This is the authorized sequel to Margaret Mitchell's epic, written by a Southern writer known for her historical romances. The research is impeccable, and the writing, accomplished but occasionally clichéd. The narrative—when one seriously ponders what might have happened to Scarlett after the end of *Gone with the Wind*—is a reasonable, valid, and quite plausible offering that unfortunately sometimes meanders and ends up not quite coming together. *Scarlett* may not be what Margaret Mitchell might have come up with, but the book evinces a meticulous attention to the characters and their lives as depicted in *Gone with the Wind*. Overall, *Scarlett* must be considered either a qualified success or a semi-failure. You'll have to judge for yourself.

Scarlett O'Hara's Younger Sister: My Lively Life In and Out of Hollywood by EVELYN KEYES (Secaucus, NJ: Lyle Stuart, 1977).

Evelyn Keyes's autobiography will only be of marginal interest to *Gone with the Wind* fans because of the paucity of coverage about the film in the book. If you want to know about Evelyn Keyes, then this is the book. If you want to know about the making of the film and the behind-the-scenes goings-on, then this is *not* the book. It is worth a look though, if only for the scene where Keyes describes an in-heat, Benzedrine-cranked David Selznick chasing her around his office.

Southern Daughter: The Life of Margaret Mitchell by DARDEN ASBURY PYRON (New York: Oxford University Press, 1991).

The definitive Margaret Mitchell biography. This is the place to look for the final word on the life and times of the creator of *Gone with the Wind*. *Southern Daughter* is authoritative and thorough and contains detailed notes for each chapter, as well as a *very* complete index. It is also a wonderfully entertaining read. Recommended.

Vivien Leigh: A Biography by ANNE EDWARDS (New York: Simon & Schuster, 1977).

A comprehensive and interesting highly-acclaimed biography of the tormented "Scarlett" by the author of *Road to Tara*.

Vivien: The Life of Vivien Leigh by ALEXANDER WALKER (New York: Weidenfeld & Nicolson, 1987).

An excellent biography of Vivien Leigh that has photos, a superb chronology, a lengthy bibliography and index, and a very complete notes section. Walker's research is fastidious and thorough, and this biography had the approval and participation of Vivien Leigh's daughter, Suzanne Farrington, as well as the participation of Vivien's secretary, Rosemary Geddes. Recommended.

Filmography
(Available on Video)

Carol Burnett: My Personal Best. 1987.
   This tape contains highlights from Carol Burnett's long-running CBS series, *The Carol Burnett Show,* and it includes her hilarious and brilliant *Gone With the Wind* "drapes" parody.

Gone With the Wind. MGM/UA Home Video; VHS HI-FI, Digitally Enhanced for Stereo, 2-videotape boxed set; approx. 3 hours, 51 minutes.
   The remixed and enhanced version of the masterpiece. If you can't afford to buy it (around $90 or so), then at least rent it once or twice. If the only copy of *Gone With the Wind* you have (and/or have seen) is one made off broadcast or cable TV, you'll be pleasantly surprised by the difference in quality.

Intermezzo. MGM/UA Home Video, 1939.
   This is the film that Selznick had to promise to Leslie Howard in order to persuade him to play Ashley. Howard insisted on an associate producer credit—and he got it.

The Making of a Legend: Gone With the Wind. TNT and TBS; 1988, 2 hours.
   A superb documentary on the making of the film. This wonderful chronicle contains countless rare *Gone With the Wind* scenes and film clips, including screen tests, reshootings, and behind-the-scenes footage. Rent it, watch it, and then take the quiz on it in this volume.

MGM's Greatest Moments. MGM/UA Home Video. 1988.
   A compilation that includes coverage of *Gone With the Wind.*

That's Entertainment!, Parts 1 & 2. MGM/UA Home Video. 1974, 1976.
   Comprehensive and gala look at the movies with appropriate coverage and adulation given to MGM's jewel, *Gone With the Wind.*

The Wizard of Oz. 1939.
   The *other* movie Victor Fleming directed in 1939.

(The following are unavailable on video but worth noting for videotaping consideration)

Bewitched. The episode, "Samantha Goes South for a Spell," 1969. ABC-TV.
   An envious witch thinks Samantha is Serena and sends her back to New Orleans in 1868.

Charleston. Made-for-TV, 1979. NBC-TV.

A *Gone With the Wind*-clone that starred Delta Burke and was set in the postbellum South.

Dear Mr. Gable. MGM, 1968.

Documentary on the life and times of Rhett Butler's alter ego.

Gable and Lombard. 1976.

Theatrical release about the love affair between Clark and Carole starring James Brolin and Jill Clayburgh as Gable and Lombard.

The Laurence Olivier Interviews. PBS, 1985.

These programs consisted of interviews with Sir Larry, Vivien Leigh's longtime love, and if your local PBS station ever reruns them, they would be worth taping for your "Vivien Leigh" collection.

The Scarlett O'Hara War. Made-for-TV, 1980. NBC-TV.

Melodrama about David Selznick's search for the right actress to play Scarlett O'Hara in the film version of *Gone With the Wind.* This 3-star film starred Tony Curtis, Sharon Gless, Harold Gould, and Bill Macy.

Also, the following TV shows either referred to or parodied *Gone With the Wind* in one or more episodes:

Fantasy Island.
Fresno. (1986).
Hart to Hart. (1981).
Here's Lucy. (1971).
Our World. (1987).

SOURCES FOR ADDITIONAL INFORMATION

The Gone With the Wind Society
Cynthia Marylee Molt
364 North May Avenue
Monrovia, CA 91016
　　This society is headed by Cynthia Molt, the author of *"Gone with the Wind" On Film: A Complete Reference,* and it publishes a bimonthly periodical called *The Wind.*

The Gone With the Wind Society
P.O. Box 192
Sharpsburg, GA 30277
　　This Georgia-based society is not affiliated with Cynthia Molt's California-based society of the same name, so you'll have to join both if you're a *Wind* completist.

The Gone With the Wind Collector's Club
Marlene Fisch
RD 5 Box 5095, Myers Road
Spring Grove, PA 17362
　　Marlene Fisch told me in spring 1992 that the Collector's Club was not active at the time, but that she still had back issues of Issues 1 through 29 of the club newsletter available for $4.00 each.

297

The Tara Collectors Club
P.O. Box 1200
Jonesboro, GA 30236

It isn't clear if this organization is still active. Correspondence sent to this address in early 1992 was not returned, but it was not answered either.

The Gone with the Wind Newsletter
c/o LASER
420 4th Avenue
Bethlehem, PA 18018
(215) 758-9934

This newsletter is available by subscription for $9.95 a year.

The Gone With the Wind Museum
152 Nassau Street, N.W.
Atlanta, GA 30303
(404) 522-1526

This museum, which is open to the public (call first for admission prices), houses an enormous collection of *Gone with the Wind* memorabilia. A must-see if you're going to be in Atlanta.

The University of Georgia
Special Collections Library
Athens, GA 30602
(404) 542-2716

The University's Special Collections Library contains many films, books, photographs, scripts, and periodicals about *Gone with the Wind* and Margaret Mitchell. Call first to inquire about usage and visitation privileges.

The Bradford Exchange
9333 Milwaukee Avenue
Niles, IL 60648
(800) 541-8811

This is the company that offers *Gone with the Wind* collectors' plates and other limited edition memorabilia. Call for information.

Bits & Pieces
1 Puzzle Place
Stevens Point, WI 54481-7199
(800) JIGSAWS
FAX: (715) 341-5959

This company offers an 800-piece *Gone With the Wind* jigsaw puzzle. Call for information.

ABOUT THE AUTHOR

STEPHEN SPIGNESI (called "the world's leading expert on Stephen King" by *Entertainment Weekly* magazine) is a full-time writer of books about popular culture subjects.

In addition to *The Official "Gone with the Wind" Companion*, Steve is also the author of the *Andy Griffith Show* encyclopedia, *Mayberry, My Hometown* (Ann Arbor, MI: Popular Culture, Ink.), the 750,000 word *Complete Stephen King Encyclopedia* (Chicago: Contemporary Books), *The Stephen King Quiz Book* (New York: NAL/Signet), *The Woody Allen Companion* (Kansas City, MO: Andrews and McMeel), and *The Second Stephen King Quiz Book* (New York: NAL/Signet).

Steve's work has appeared in *Harper's, Cinefantastique, Midnight Graffiti,* and *Gauntlet* magazines.

Steve lives in New Haven, Connecticut, with his wife, Pam, and their extraordinary cat, Ben, and he agrees with Woody Allen that money is better than poverty, if only for financial reasons.